Winners and Losers

.

Stefan Szymanski and Tim Kuypers

VIKING

For Hayley, Edward, William and Kitty s.s.

For Jennifer and my parents T.K.

VIKING

Published by the Penguin Group
Penguin Books Ltd, 27 Wrights Lane, London W8 5TZ, England
Penguin Putnam Inc., 375 Hudson Street, New York, New York 10014, USA
Penguin Books Australia Ltd, Ringwood, Victoria, Australia
Penguin Books Canada Ltd, 10 Alcorn Avenue, Toronto, Ontario, Canada M4V 3B2
Penguin Books (NZ) Ltd, Private Bag 102902, NSMC, Auckland, New Zealand

Penguin Books Ltd, Registered Offices: Harmondsworth, Middlesex, England

First published 1999
10 9 8 7 6 5 4 3 2 1

Copyright © Stefan Szymanski and Tim Kuypers, 1999

The moral right of the authors has been asserted

Set in 11/14½pt Linotype Sabon
Typeset by Rowland Phototypesetting Ltd, Bury St Edmunds, Suffolk
Printed in Great Britain by Clays Ltd, St Ives plc

A CIP catalogue record for this book is available from the British Library

ISBN 0–670–88486–3

Contents

Acknowledgements

Many people helped us when we were writing this book. Credit should go to Professor Steve Davies of UEA, who suggested writing a book on the football business to us several years ago. Various people helped with data sources including Delroy Johnson, Professor Wray Vamplew, David Murtagh, Michael Crick, David Barber, the excellent librarian of the Football Association, Tim James from Soccer Analyst, Brian Sturgess, Vi Bellamy from Companies House and Jim Hawes. A big thank you is due to Gerry Boon's football team at Deloitte & Touche, who kindly gave us a sneak preview of 1998's Annual Review of Football Finance, the best financial data source for football clubs currently available. Several people gave us helpful comments on earlier drafts including Rob Beasley, Geoffrey Myers, Professor Alan Manning, Val Brophy, Professor Steve Ross, Geoffrey Dicks, Tom Hoehn and Tim Walton. We would also like to thank Professors John Kay, Ron Smith and David Norburn for their support. Yuri Gabriel has our special gratitude. We thank Tony Lacey, Liz Halsall and the staff at Penguin for their faith in this project and Bela Cunha for editing the manuscript intelligently and promptly.

'Football is a big business'

William McGregor, 'Father' and founder of the Football League,
The Book of Football, 1905

'The subject of strategy analyses the firm's relationships with its environment, and a business strategy is a scheme for handling these relationships'

John Kay, *Foundations of Corporate Success*, 1993

'Strategy is about winning'

Rob Grant, *Contemporary Strategy Analysis*, 1995

Why football is a business

Football is a game, but it is also a business. The worldwide football business is said to be worth in the region of £150bn.[1] In mid-1998 Manchester United was valued at over £400m, making it one of the 350 largest companies quoted on the London Stock Exchange. In September 1998 BSkyB, the broadcaster of Premier League football, bid £623.4m for the company. Before the bid there were twenty UK clubs quoted on the stock market, with a combined value of over £1bn. The valuation of football clubs on the stock market has increased significantly amid rumours that leading media and branded goods companies (such as Time Warner, Sony, Canal Plus, NTL, Granada and Carlton) were about to buy a club.

Behind this frenzy of speculation lie business interests generating substantial incomes. In 1998 the income of English football clubs was around £700m. English football clubs directly employ about 10,000 people and many more jobs depend on football in the sports and leisure industries, media and construction. Since 1990 £600m has been invested by clubs in upgrading football grounds alone, while the net asset value of the ninety-two professional English clubs is around £200m in total. If the players in whose contracts the clubs invest were valued as assets, the net asset value of the clubs would be in excess of £1bn. The current contract for Premier League television coverage alone is worth £670m over five years. Football clubs are limited companies, with boards of directors, bankers, financial advisers and accountants. They are able to make profits and pay dividends like any other business. Ultimately, like any other business, they can go bankrupt.

Furthermore, while the organization of football varies country by country, a similar story could be told about the business of football in Italy, Spain, Brazil, Argentina, Germany and elsewhere.

This book is about the business of football. Many books have been written about football: its history, its heroes and its villains. Some salacious books have been written about the personalities involved in the football business. But this is the first book to try to analyse the business of football in a systematic, dispassionate fashion. To many football fans, talk of business and finance is tantamount to heresy. The business side of the game is viewed as either a necessary evil or the source of all that is wrong with the modern game – or both. However, the relationships between football clubs depend critically on the structure of the business environment, and the performance of each individual club depends on its position within that structure. Thus the analysis has implications both for predicting the performance of individual clubs and for understanding developments in the structure of the football leagues. Just as in any other business, football is a contest in which the size of the resources available to each side and the effectiveness with which they are deployed significantly affect the outcome. Even if the element of chance makes the game interesting, there is enough about the game of football which is systematic to make outcomes, to a degree, predictable. Business strategy is about trying to understand what is systematic about the success of businesses, and because business strategy is also about winning, this book should interest the fan just as much as the businessman.

Football did not start out as a business but as a game to be played for its character-forming qualities: self-discipline and team spirit. The origins of Association Football lie in the English public school system. Early Victorian schoolmasters encouraged the development of team games as exercises for the future leaders of empire.[2] Each school developed its own version of the game of football. On leaving school and meeting with football players from other schools they found that their rules differed. It was former public schoolboys who laid down a unifying set of rules and established the Football Association in 1863, and their primary motivation was to enable alumni from different schools to come together to play football. The principles of these men were firmly rooted in the cult of 'amateurism'. To be an amateur was to be a gentleman: to play the game for its own sake rather than for personal gain, and to stand above any commercial dealings. The notion of football as a business was anathema to the founding fathers of the game,[3] an attitude that has been echoed by football fanatics in England ever since. So how did football turn into a big business?

In a word, competition. Competition, the FA Cup in particular, encouraged the development of football clubs.[4] Clubs were originally no more than associations of players, vehicles for playing the game. The main function of the club was to co-ordinate fixtures, an innovation essential for those wanting to play regularly. Some football clubs were formed by public schoolboys returning to their home towns (for example, Blackburn Rovers was formed by local graduates of Shrewsbury public school), others were set up by cricketers keen to maintain contacts during the winter season (e.g. Sheffield Wednesday and Sheffield United) and yet others were formed by young clergymen and churchgoers eager to promote healthy exercise among parishioners (Queen's Park Rangers and Everton). The early football clubs soon started to attract supporters since for most people watching skilled players performing on the field proved more of an entertainment than playing the game themselves. For many, playing and supporting have always gone hand in hand. Watching good teams play is a way of seeing others do what one cannot do oneself. But most football supporters do not play the game, just as most visitors to art galleries are not painters and most theatregoers are not actors.

As soon as football became an entertainment, facilities

were required to cater for supporters. Facilities demanded expenditure, which had to be covered by entrance charges. In this way, football became a business. Despite the fact that many supporters are the most vigorous opponents of the commercialization of football, they are in fact its cause. Fans, by definition, want their team to win. Moreover, teams that win more often tend to attract more support.[5] Although there is an element of chance in the outcome of a football game, to win consistently demands the employment of a consistently better team of players. To satisfy the demands of supporters, football clubs tried to find the best players. Initially players were entirely amateur. As winning, rather than merely playing, became more important, the bigger clubs offered inducements to the best players: lavish expenses, employment support, payment for lost time and so on. Paid professionals are known to have played since at least 1876[6] and were formally recognized in 1885, just three years before the establishment of the English Football League. Gate money paid for the players, the best players attracted the biggest crowds and were paid the highest wages. Commercialization and professionalization were two sides of the same coin.

These developments affected only the élite. Of the 10,000 football clubs[7] affiliated to the FA by 1905 few could reasonably be considered businesses. They were football clubs in the sense which the founders of the FA would have recognized: associations of like-minded individuals coming together to play the game, usually paying a small subscription for the privilege and seldom watched by anybody, apart perhaps from occasional friends and family. The clubs that became businesses were the professional clubs, those that were admitted to the Football League before the First World War (the old First and Second Divisions) and those which created the lower two divisions just after the First World War. By 1921 the League consisted of eighty-six teams. Since 1888 only 126 clubs have appeared in the Football League, mostly on a fully professional basis, while few clubs outside the League have generated enough income to maintain a salaried squad. Since the 1920s matches have attracted between 16 and 41 million paying spectators each season, and with the advent of television the potential audience has been expanded further still. Professional football clubs are large organizations, and they are run as businesses.[8]

There is little evidence that the early football clubs were founded with a view to making money. Football clubs were founded by enthusiasts for the sake of promoting the playing of the game. In English law a 'club' is a legal entity which belongs to all its members, who elect a committee to carry out the business of the club. Such a structure is suitable for a small-scale organization whose function is primarily social and whose financial requirements are limited. However, once football clubs became employers with wage bills and invest-ment programmes the possibility arose that money would need to be paid out for services which would only produce an income at a later date. The burden of providing the bridging finance fell to committee members, who were obliged either to lend their own money or to provide security for bank borrowing.[9] In 1888 Small Heath (now Birmingham City) was the first club to incorporate itself as a limited company, three years after having turned professional (i.e. fielding pro-fessional players exclusively). Limited companies are owned by their shareholders and run by their directors, and limited liability enabled the directors to arrange borrowings from the bank without having to assume personal liability for the borrowing. Soon most other clubs followed suit. For example, Aston Villa turned professional in 1885 and became a limited company in 1896 in order to raise £10,000 to fund the construction of its new stadium at Villa Park. Two thousand shares of £5 each were sold to just under 700 individuals,[10] who became the owners of the football club. Arsenal turned professional in 1891 and was incorporated in 1893, Everton in 1885 and 1892 and Newcastle in 1889 and 1890. In most football clubs the original investors represented a wide cross-section of society, from local gentry and businessmen down to ordinary working men. In general the new shareholders were the same people who had been involved with the running of the old club.[11] However, from the earliest days the Football Association prohibited the payment of club directors for their services, thus ensuring that 'the right class of men who love football for its own sake'[12] controlled the clubs. As football clubs grew, so did the scale of the necessary financial backing. Increasingly, wealthy local businessmen became involved as both owners and directors.[13]

By the First World War almost all the professional clubs had become limited liability companies. As the game grew in popularity the directors had to deal with the kinds of problems which arise in any business. Most clubs invested heavily in building a stadium of sizeable capacity, many of which incorporated athletic and cycling facilities for generating other sources of income. Maximizing income became critical to maintaining the club financially and improving the performance on the pitch. In the early days football had been careless when it came to money. While clubs built small stands for their wealthier patrons, most spectators watched from a mound or grass bank, to which admission was generally administered in haphazard fashion by gatekeepers. When Aston Villa introduced turnstiles for spectators in 1892, reported (as opposed to actual) attendance figures immediately trebled. As more business-like directors came to dominate the

Table 1.1 The commercialization and professionalization of English football

1863	Foundation of the Football Association with eleven member clubs
1871	Establishment of the FA Cup (Association now has fifty members)
1876	First recorded professional players (Sheffield Heeley Club)
1885	Professionalism accepted by the FA
1888	Foundation of the Football League
	Transfer of players between Football League clubs requires its consent
	Small Heath first club to become a limited company
1891	Signing-on fees limited to £10
1892	Creation of the Football League Second Division
1894	FA Amateur Cup established
1896	FA imposes maximum dividend of 5 per cent on member companies
1900	FA imposes maximum wage of £4 per week
1908	FA imposes a £350 maximum transfer fee, which is withdrawn three months later

boardroom, established business methods were introduced to the operations of football clubs. Some of the new breed of directors may also have entertained motives which went beyond the playing success of the club and into the generation of profit, for the shareholders in general or for themselves in particular.

Whether the motivation of owners and directors is profit, playing success or some other end, they are more likely to achieve their objective if the club's business is well run. All the problems surrounding the running of a football club appear in one form or another in the business world. Like any business, clubs must generate revenues by selling their product to the paying customers: they must engage in advertising, marketing and promotion. They have to invest in the facilities which enable them to sell their product in the right environment. Above all they have to pay wages to players and invest in the development of talent in order to achieve winning perform-ances, perhaps for their own sake, but also to keep the public interested in the club and willing to pay for its product. In all this the club must compete in a hostile environment against large numbers of highly motivated rivals. But it must also co-operate with these rivals to some degree in organizing the structure of competitions, agreeing basic rules by which every-one must abide and developing new initiatives which benefit the industry as a whole. These, then, are the basic elements of the football business, and they have been since the earliest days of the professional game: a product (the entertainment of a game of football) supplied by workers (players and coaching staff) using land (grounds), buildings (stadiums) and equipment (balls, boots, kit) for a wage and sold to customers (supporters and other spectators) in competition and through co-operation with rivals.

Competition and co-operation
Competition and co-operation are the two fundamental modes of human interaction; most human activities involve both,

operating simultaneously. Assembly-line workers in the Ford Motor Company co-operate to produce cars which can then be sold to customers. Ford's cars compete for customers in the marketplace with the products of Nissan, Renault, Fiat and other rival producers. Civil servants in the Treasury co-operate to control the government's expenditure while competing with spending departments over the direction of resources and competing among themselves for promotion to better jobs. Research scientists co-operate to find a cure for cancer while competing to obtain the Nobel prize in recognition of the discovery. Nation states sign treaties to create alliances of co-operation while competing with other countries politically, economically or militarily. Even parents, who co-operate in raising their children, have been known to compete for their affection.

War is perhaps the best example of how competition and co-operation co-exist. The outcome of twentieth-century wars has to a large extent depended on the economic resources available to the belligerents and their ability to concentrate these on fighting the war. The United States, the Soviet Union and Great Britain were able to defeat Germany and Japan in the Second World War by virtue of their greater resources in manpower and hardware and their ability to motivate their entire populations to the war effort. By contrast the United States was unable to defeat the Vietcong guerrillas in Vietnam because, while the latter were totally focused on the single goal of driving out the Americans, the United States was unable to concentrate its vast resources on the one objective of defeating the Vietcong (largely because that objective did not command the assent of a significant proportion of the American people). Success in warfare is about achieving maximum co-operation to focus internal resources on the defeat of the enemy.

Military analogies are frequently employed in relation to economic competition between firms. However, this can be quite misleading. The foundation of economic activity is exchange. Trade developed long before mass production as a means for individuals to improve their economic well-being. An individual can profitably trade a good that he owns in relative abundance for another good in which his endowment is relatively small. Trade emerges because natural endowments differ. Specialization in production enhances these relative differences and so enhances the scope for profitable trade. Thus, in Adam Smith's famous example, Britain has long traded its woollen textiles for Portuguese wine, but this trade became even more profitable as investment and specialization in each form of production improved the productivity of British textile producers and Portuguese vineyards. Both sides gain from trade, and the gain increases with specialization. Britain could conceivably produce all its own wine and Portugal all its own textiles, but in both cases each good would be more expensive and available in smaller quantities than is possible through the mechanism of trade. Recognition of the benefits which derive from economic exchange has led to the development of agreements between the majority of world nations to uphold the principles of free trade. Free trade is desirable because it is not like war: both sides can be winners.

Football lies somewhere between war and economics. Football competition is driven by the motivation to win: this is the dominant consideration both for the players and for the supporters. In this sense football is like war, and like war it has winners and losers. One of the most important functions of a team coach is to motivate the players so that they are not merely capable of defeating the opposition, but that they want to. This represents the difference between the capacities of the individual players and their ability to realize these capacities as a team faced by the opposition. Partly this depends on the preparation and motivation of the individuals, but in part it depends on team cohesion. Among the methods used to achieve this end are denigration of the opposition or the suggestion that the opposition have in some way belittled the team.[14] In *Football Against the Enemy* Simon Kuper explains how the Dutch came to see their football rivalry with Germany in both moral and military terms in the late 1980s: 'Holland vs. Germany, Good vs. Evil'. The psychology of winning at football involves many of the same ideas that are used to motivate soldiers in a battle. For example: make the contestants believe that the enemy are bad people who deserve to be defeated while your own side consists of good people who have been unfairly treated and deserve to win. Football is not war, but there are some similarities.

Yet co-operation and exchange are also central to the organization of football competition. The need for co-operation appears in every facet of football. When we speak about co-operation we often talk about working towards a common 'goal'. The sense that team games are based on co-operation is the very reason that football was first encouraged in the public schools. Coaches devote an enormous amount of time to developing team cohesion, an attitude of co-operativeness among the players. It is received wisdom in any sport that a less talented group of players acting as a team can defeat a highly talented collection of individualists. Co-operation within the side has many dimensions: passing the ball to a player with a clear chance at goal rather than selfishly trying to take a difficult shot, covering for a defender who is out of position, running off the ball to create space for the player in possession, mutual encouragement and support. All of these are aspects of co-operation which increase team productivity.

Co-operation also takes place between the players and all the other participants in the activities of the club: the manager, the owners and critically the fans. All of these must work together if the club is to succeed, and must also trust each other to participate equally. If everyone is not perceived to be working towards the same end, problems emerge. Players become demoralized; the fans' support is only half-hearted. If some players are perceived as less than committed to the team, then the fans may stop supporting the club altogether. Selfish (often profit-oriented) owners, disloyal supporters and uninterested players are the commonly identified faults of most failing clubs.

A football match cannot take place without a competitor, but even when competing a football team co-operates in a variety of ways with the 'other side'. Above all, to stage a football match the teams must co-operate in abiding by the rules. Generally this means not only the letter of the law, without which a game of football descends into unplayable anarchy, but also in accepted ways laid down by tradition. For example, frequently a player will kick the ball into touch if an opponent appears seriously injured. The game stops, the player is attended to, and the game restarts with a throw-in which freely returns possession to the side which put the ball into touch. None of this is required by the rules, but this form of co-operation almost never breaks down. Since each team can expect its players to be injured in either current or future games, there is no point in making life difficult in the future by undermining accepted standards of behaviour.

Football teams co-operate with each other in order to create competition. Team sports are often described as an exceptional business activity because without co-operation there would be no competition, and no business at all. League organization systematizes the competition among members and fulfils a number of co-ordinating roles. The first commercial sports league of any significance was the National League of Professional Baseball Clubs created in 1876.[15] England's Football League was therefore a relative latecomer when founded in 1888 at the initiative of William McGregor, but it was the first of its type for the Association game. The establishment of the Football Leagues, as in other team sports, was motivated primarily by the need to maintain a standardized fixture list, without which clubs found it difficult to organize regular games. But from their foundation sporting leagues have usually set out to regulate the game in other ways that they consider best for their members. Leagues enforce rules which limit the behaviour of individual members because of potential damage to other members. They also provide a mechanism through which the clubs can harness their power collectively in negotiations with outsiders. In the past it was not uncommon for league executives to argue that their function is to ensure that members engage in the 'right' kind of competition (on the playing field) while limiting other forms of (business) competition. In other words 'professional team sports leagues are classic, even textbook examples of business cartels'.[16] From its foundation the Football League set out to control competition between clubs in a number of ways: competition for fans (by fixing minimum admission prices), competition for players (through the transfer system) and competition for profits (by fixing a maximum dividend). For around sixty years the Football League provided a major benefit to all clubs by fixing a maximum wage. More recently the Football League and now the Premier League have negotiated football television rights on behalf of all clubs. By bargaining as a single unit the clubs expected to gain more than they could on the basis of individual settlements.

However, while co-operation yields benefits, it can be difficult to maintain. The decision of the big clubs to break away from the Football League and establish the Premier League was in part due to their belief that they could obtain a better deal for themselves on their own rather than as part of the larger group. Co-operation can only be sustained when members of the group see it to be in their interests to continue as members. The ultimate threat of any association or assembly is expulsion from it; when some members no longer fear expulsion, the association breaks down.

Business strategy
Business strategy is a branch of learning aimed primarily at managers, taught mostly in business schools to students studying for a Masters degree in Business Administration (MBA)

or in expensive, private seminars to businesses. Many MBAs become consultants, using ideas from business strategy to advise companies on the problems of the day such as brand management, cost and quality control, mergers and acquisitions, corporate finance and globalization. The advice of business strategists is sought on activities such as corporate restructuring, developing new markets, new systems of management control and employee motivation.

As a discipline in its own right business strategy has a difficult relationship both with business and with the academic world in which it operates. Businessmen looking for solutions to problems are interested in prescriptions: how do I boost sales, how can I cut costs? To answer these questions a proper knowledge of the business concerned is essential, just as offering advice on dress depends on the person's appearance, diagnosis of symptoms necessitates acquaintance with the patient's medical history and investment advice requires knowledge of the client's financial position. Thus the *application* of business strategy to business problems (*strategy implementation*) demands specific knowledge. One way, therefore, to display a knowledge of business strategy is to describe the process of strategy in a specific case: a case study, which has been the traditional mode of discourse of business schools. But professors from other academic disciplines traditionally find it difficult to assess the extent to which case studies reflect academic achievement. Case studies represent knowledge of the *specific*, whereas the goal of research is usually described as the development of *general* principles. Newton's case study was the apple falling from the tree, but he would not be remembered as a scientist had he not progressed from this to a formal statement of the general principle of gravity.

Is it possible to describe strategy and the process of formulating a strategy independently of the details of a particular business? Are there principles in business which rise above the specific and become general? Not obviously so, since many human activities fail to have general principles as to how they should be conducted. Strategy often involves making deliberately unexpected choices in order to wrong-foot an adversary. As an example consider the children's game of rock, scissors, paper, in which two players must simultaneously choose one of these three options: scissors, rock or paper. According to the rules scissors beats paper, paper beats rock and rock beats scissors. No systematic strategy can help a player to win this game; the only way to play it is to choose randomly. That is because any systematic strategy is predictable and therefore can be defeated by the appropriate response. Some business strategists have argued that business strategy is like that: always contingent, never systematic. However, this seems too pessimistic. There are facts about the world that can help guide decision-making. Water does not freely flow up hills, the sun does rise every morning, businesses need customers and every resource devoted to one activity is necessarily denied to alternative activities. These may not be profound insights, but it may be that a deeper analysis can provide some general foundations for the conduct of business activity. In this book we will develop the analysis of football as a business, not because we believe that everything about football can be understood in this way, but because we think that it is possible to acquire more insightful understanding of football by applying to it some basic principles from business strategy.

Business, profits and performance

Two issues which are central to the effective running of a football club are the identification of its objectives and the trade-off between financial success and success on the field.

Football club objectives

'Is professional football a sport or an industry? Is it an enterprise whose only profit to itself is the pleasure it gives to millions or . . . is it a business which is fired by dreams of financial gain?'

Alan Hardaker, former secretary of the Football League[17]

'Any club management which allows the club to make a profit is behaving foolishly'
Anonymous club chairman[18]

'Alan Sugar is no sugar-daddy and he was determined that the subject of his investment would be profitable'
Fynn, A. and Guest, L.[19]

Behaviour depends on objectives. The environment in which an organization operates determines the constraints which it faces in pursuing its objectives, but the performance of any organization (its success) must be measured against its objectives. Behaviour can usually be interpreted very differently depending on the objectives that are believed to underlie it. Unfortunately, identifying objectives is no simple matter. One approach is to consider the legal obligations of a club laid down by its officially constituted rules. Another is to examine past behaviour and try to work out the underlying objectives from the specific choices made.

Football clubs in England are limited companies. Legally, their objectives are defined in the memorandum and articles of association of the companies, which are in turn laid down by the founder shareholders. These rules, once written, are quite difficult to change, since they usually require a considerable degree of consensus among shareholders – and the more numerous the shareholders, the more difficult it becomes. However, the objectives of a company are generally quite anodyne. Thus for a football club they would specify that the company's business is to run a football club, arrange fixtures, sell tickets and so on. That all this is done for a profit is usually tacit rather than explicit, since the directors who run the company and are therefore responsible for profits are answerable to and can be fired by the shareholders. In the case of many football clubs the directors have themselves often been the major shareholders, limiting conflicts of interest. The most important issue that a commercial football club must resolve is the appropriate balance and consistency between the pursuit of profit and the pursuit of competitive success, most notably playing success.

An historical, or (as psychologists might call it) behavioural approach, looks at what football clubs, through the shareholders and directors, actually do. Unfortunately this is not as simple as asking individuals what their motives are, because the incentive to reveal objectives truthfully may be limited. Thus, even if it is true that their objective is profit, most businessmen will tell you that their primary aim is to serve the customer. Indeed, the two objectives may amount to the same thing in many circumstances, but in cases where they do not, no entrepreneur could admit to putting profit before customers without expecting to lose some goodwill, which is costly for any business. If telling the truth is not profitable, historians and psychologists must attempt to infer objectives from evidence about the persons involved, both their backgrounds and their actions.

Most researchers have traditionally rejected the idea that football clubs are pure profit maximizers,[20] arguing instead that they maximize a composite objective function based on playing performance, attendances, prestige in the local community and profits.[21] Profits themselves are often deemed to be relatively unimportant, not least because of restrictions imposed by the Football Association. In 1896 the FA placed a limit of 5 per cent of the paid-up share capital as the maximum dividend that a member club could pay out. This was raised to 7.5 per cent in 1920, to 10 per cent in 1974 and 15 per cent in 1983. Certainly, for the last fifty years this has implied an extremely low return even if dividends were paid in full.[22] In practice, most clubs stopped paying dividends in the 1950s.

Before the 1990s professional investors interested primarily in financial performance, such as pension funds or City institutions, had seldom viewed football clubs as attractive investments. Financially, football clubs were too small, too unprofitable and too risky to warrant serious interest. While stockbrokers were willing to facilitate trades in football club shares they did not actively seek to promote the trade, and a large proportion of football club shares were held in small blocks by club supporters. Owners of football club shares have traditionally been fans, whose most likely motive for owning football club shares was to obtain a discount on a season ticket rather than to realize a substantial capital gain. Where large blocks of shares have been created or traded, this has either been due to a financial crisis as a result of which a local businessman has stepped in to rescue the club, or simply a decision on the part of a rich supporter to invest in raising the club's profile. Jack Walker, who sank in excess of £55m into Blackburn Rovers, is the most famous example from a list of wealthy football club benefactors. Walker, a lifelong Rovers fan, is a steel millionaire who sold his company to British Steel for £330m in 1990. In January 1991 he acquired 62 per cent of Blackburn Rovers Ltd and started an investment programme which included a £17m redevelopment of the ground and a total personal investment of £55m in his club. Most of this involved buying new players at a net cost of £28m in the seven-year period 1990–91 to 1996–7, as well as hiring Kenny Dalglish, one of the most successful managers in the history of English football. The result of this massive investment was that the club won the league title in the 1994–5 season but registered a cumulative pre-tax loss of £27m over the seven years. No dividends were paid by the club during this period. Subsequent playing performance has not matched up to the achievements of 1995, and despite selling Alan Shearer for £15m in 1996 (at that date the world record), the club is still not profitable. Other examples of financial generosity from wealthy fans in recent times include the late Matthew Harding at Chelsea (an estimated investment of £26.5m, partly in interest-free loans), Steve Gibson at Middlesbrough, who has invested around £5om in players and a new stadium, and Sir Jack Hayward at Wolverhampton Wanderers, who spent about £15m on players over three years and possibly double this amount on a new stadium. These are substantial sums of money which have shown, at least thus far, a negligible financial return measured by accounting profits, dividends or interest.

However, in 1996 the stock market demonstrated that it had come to believe that football clubs could be profitable investment vehicles by providing several hundred million pounds of capital for investment in football club shares. Suddenly there was a demand from institutional and professional investors for football club shares, not as a hobby, nor as a way of participating in the running of the sport, but simply because the market value of these businesses was expected to increase. Since 1996 Chelsea, Newcastle, QPR (indirectly as Loftus Road PLC) and Aston Villa have floated on the stock market. Birmingham, Bolton, Charlton, Derby, Everton, Leeds, Leicester City, Manchester City, Nottingham Forest, Preston North End, Sheffield Wednesday, Southampton, Sunderland, Swansea, West Bromwich Albion, West Ham and Wimbledon have all been involved in take-overs or capital-raising exercises. In most cases the existing owners have enjoyed substantial paper gains and in many cases have enhanced their personal wealth by selling shares. Even owners such as Sir John Hall of Newcastle United and Jack Walker have recovered, at least on paper, more than they invested, thanks to the appetite of investors.

The trend towards the stock market listing of football clubs can be traced back to the flotation of Tottenham Hotspur under the management of Irving Scholar back in 1983. He accumulated a significant stake in the company in the early 1980s by tracing as many as possible of the 500 shareholders from the official register. Many of them had inherited their stake from a football fan but had no interest in the game themselves. Scholar offered a few hundred pounds for what may have seemed like worthless pieces of paper and found plenty of willing sellers. Having bought their shares and gained a controlling interest he organized a stock market flotation. Tottenham became the first major UK club to be traded on the Stock Exchange and followed by professional investors: traders interested in owning the shares purely for financial gain. The experiment was not a huge success. The club diversified into making sportswear, women's fashions and computerized ticketing systems, none of which generated great profits but formed a distraction from the performance of the football team. The company fell into debt and in 1991 a controlling interest passed to Alan Sugar, although the club is still quoted on the stock market.

Manchester United was the second big club to come to the stock market, eight years after Tottenham, and it is the most striking example in recent years of a football club treating itself as a business. When Manchester United raised £7m in a stock market flotation in 1991 it decided to transfer its fixed assets and non-footballing businesses to a company so that the company, not the club, would receive a 'substantial part' of future advertising, sponsorship and promotional income as well as the rental income from the use of the ground. Furthermore, while the Football Association must approve the appointment of directors of member clubs, these rules would not apply to the new company. Most importantly, the company (the PLC) is not affiliated to the FA and so is not bound by the FA's restrictions on the payment of dividends (the company owns the club, Manchester United Limited, which is affiliated to the FA and does not pay a dividend). On the face of it, one might have thought at the time that the dividend restriction would not be all that important. The club had registered a pre-tax loss in four out of the five years prior to 1991 and had averaged an annual pre-tax loss of £130,000 over the seventeen years from 1974 to 1990. Manchester United PLC's cumulative profit from 1991 to 1997 has been £81.8m (an average of £13.6m per year), while the total dividend payout has been around £20m. An investor who paid 385p for a share in 1991 has seen its value rise to the equivalent of £24.75 by mid-1998, an annualized return of over 30 per cent. Thus an investor who sank £100 in Manchester United PLC in 1991 could have realized a profit of over £500 by selling out in mid-1998, in addition to having eight years of dividends. Few stock market investments could have offered a similar profit over this period. Better still, when BSkyB decided to bid for the entire company in September 1998, it offered a price for the shares that was more than 50 per cent greater than the market price had been earlier in the summer. Despite all its accumulated growth, and the apparently generous price offered for the shares, many City analysts have argued that BSkyB would still be getting a bargain at such a price. At the same time the club (Manchester United Ltd) has continued to make a pre-tax loss.

Shareholders and stakeholders

An important question which arises when a football club becomes an investment vehicle concerns the balance which needs to be established between the pursuit of financial gain and performance on the field. This problem forms part of a wider debate which has developed over the years in management science. The classical view of the firm has been that it is a profit-maximizing organization, operated by directors on behalf of shareholders whose sole interest is financial gain. In this view the objective of the owners is enforced by incentives. Three incentive mechanisms exist which help to focus directors and managers on the pursuit of profits. Bankruptcy awaits any director who fails to pay any attention at all to profit. More subtly, take-overs (and redundancy for the directors) are likely to occur when an investor believes the existing managers are missing profitable opportunities and can therefore offer a price for the shares that is greater than their current value but less than the value the company will come to possess. Finally, directors and senior managers are provided with direct incentives such as profit-related bonuses and share options schemes which bring their own self-interest into line with the interests of the shareholders.

More recently, however, this view has been challenged by those who believe that a firm is something more than simply a financial vehicle and has more constituents than shareholders alone.[23] A firm is an organization that combines the interests of customers, employees and suppliers, all of whom voluntarily participate in its activities and all of whom contribute to its success. Each of these groups has a legitimate interest in the running of the firm. Some of them, such as bank creditors, may have legal rights in relation to the operation of the firm that limit the ownership rights of the shareholders. Others, such as employees, may have no legal right to control of the firm but none the less possess a legitimate interest in the running of the firm. Successful businesses are often those which give some weight to these interests. Similarly, the customers of the business have few if any rights to dictate to the company how it should be run, but they have a legitimate interest in the quality of the products it produces. The theory that managers should consider themselves accountable to a wider constituency than simply the shareholders is often called the 'stakeholder' approach.

In many circumstances what is good for the shareholder is also good for the other stakeholders. Satisfied customers buy more goods, confident creditors lend on better terms and a happy workforce tends to work more efficiently than a disaffected one. Keeping these stakeholders happy is likely to bring in greater profits for the shareholders. However, conflicts of interest are also possible. Quality and service typically involve higher costs, prompt payment of creditors reduces cash balances and there are few methods of pleasing the workforce that do not involve some expense for the business. The shareholder/stakeholder issue concerns the appropriate balance to strike between conflicting claims when they arise. What is moot is whether a stakeholder approach implies a different framework for evaluating decisions and a different kind of corporate behaviour from that which would be observed in a company run by profit-maximizing managers. This issue is central to the development of football clubs as businesses. Historically clubs have seemed far more like stakeholder enterprises, supporting the community, investing in the playing success but yielding tiny financial gains for the owners. Now that clubs such as Manchester United are to a large degree owned by professional city investors and pension funds whose primary requirement is to show an adequate financial return, will it be possible to reconcile profits with performance on the pitch? Is it possible for a club whose objective is profit to keep the fans and the players happy? Can a football club which puts the interests of supporters first make enough profit to keep investors happy?

Playing success and financial success

If the relationship between playing success and financial success is pivotal to interpreting the performance of football clubs as businesses, the first place to begin a consideration of this relationship is the historical record. There are three possibilities. First, higher profits might automatically lead to better team performance and greater playing success might lead to greater profit, so that there would be no conflict between trying to satisfy the fans' desire for success and the shareholders' desire for profit. Second, playing success might be unrelated to profitability and then at least the pursuit of profit would not interfere with the pursuit of playing success (and vice versa). Third, playing success might automatically lead to lower profits, in which case football club owners and managers would have to decide upon the appropriate trade-off between profit and playing performance.

From accounting data and sport statistics it is possible to examine the historic relationship between profit and team performance. An important fact about football, and about sports business in general, is that there is a lot more data available than there is for other business activities. Like most businesses, football clubs in England must publish annual accounts which are available for inspection by the public at

Companies House. The added advantage of studying football clubs is that data on their performance, productivity and achievements are both measurable and readily available. This makes it possible to interpret the financial data in relation to the performance of clubs. Throughout this book we will draw heavily on accounting data in order to understand the forces at work in football. In the Data Appendix on page 345 we list the database of financial accounts on which our research is based. Football club accounts are available from the beginning of this century, but in most of our analysis we draw on a sample of around forty clubs for whom we have a complete accounting record over the last quarter of a century. This sample of clubs is representative of the entire Football League (and the Premier League). It includes the major clubs such as Manchester United and Liverpool, and a fair sample of the minor clubs such as Scunthorpe United and Rochdale.[24] It also provides sufficient historical perspective to understand some of the changes which have taken place in recent years.

Profits are easily measured from company accounts, particularly since football clubs (unlike most limited companies of any size) have only one significant financial activity, which is the operation of the football club itself. Playing success can be measured in many ways, but the most reliable guide is performance in the league. League competition involves around forty games over a season, with each club playing the other members of their division, once at home and once away. To win the league a club must sustain a high performance level against all the teams in their division under all possible conditions. Another way to measure success would be to look at performance in cup competitions. However, cup competitions are more a matter of chance: the luck of the draw.

Occasionally a team may win the FA Cup by beating all the best teams, but as often as not the winning club has avoided encounters with several of the top clubs, as well as benefiting from home advantage along the way.

A simple way to examine the relationship between profits

and performance, using league position and the reported pre-tax profits of football clubs, is simply to graph profits against league position. Figure 1.1 plots position against pre-tax profits for forty clubs over twenty years (1978–97). There are 800 separate observations in the sample and each dot represents the combination of profit and league position for a particular club in a particular year. The most notable feature of the graph is that all the dots are clustered around 0 on the profits axis, whether clubs achieve a high position or a low one. There are a few outliers, and the range of profit outcomes grows much larger for higher position. There is a small number of cases where clubs at the top end of the league made larger profits, but there is also a significant number of cases combining a high league position and financial losses. For example, there are only fourteen instances of clubs achieving a profit in excess of £3m, and all of these cases concerned clubs in the Premier League/First Division. There are twenty-four cases of pre-tax losses in excess of £3m, of which twenty concerned clubs in the Premier League/First Division. Taken on its own, the graph does not suggest a very strong link between profits and performance.

Fig 1.1 Profits and league positions for forty football Clubs, 1978–97

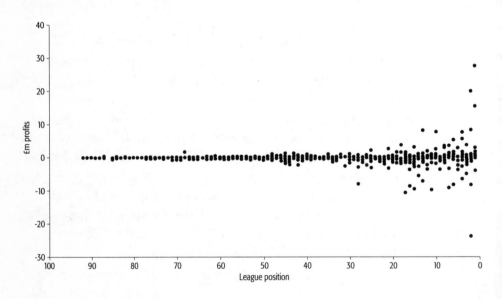

The average levels of profit and league position for each club in the data set are shown in Table 1.2. Only seven clubs out of the forty averaged a profit over the entire period, but both average profits and average losses were relatively small for most of the clubs. Thus only five clubs averaged losses of over £1m per year (Leeds, Coventry, Newcastle, Blackburn and Everton), while only Manchester United had annual profits over £1m on average. Five of the six highest ranked clubs did manage to record positive profits on average, but then the next eleven clubs all averaged a loss. Comparing individual clubs, the most consistently successful, Liverpool, achieved a lower average profit than less successful rivals such as Arsenal, Tottenham and Aston Villa. Since the profits of an individual club may change considerably from year to year, these averages may be concealing an underlying pattern of relationships between changes in position and changes in profits. A more precise way to examine the relationship is to look at annual co-movements in the two variables.

From the data we can calculate 760 separate cases of changing position and profits (from one year to the next). In any one year the change in a club's league position can be 'up' or 'down'. 'No change' is so unusual that the few cases have been lumped together with 'up'. The same is true for pre-tax profits, and so there are four possible outcomes. If league position and profits were positively correlated,[25] we would expect to see the combination 'up, up' and 'down, down' more frequently than the other two possibilities. If profits bore no relation to league position, then we would expect to see clubs fall into each of the four possible categories roughly one quarter of the time (only 'roughly' for the same reason that any repeated sequence of coin tossing will result in 'heads' only roughly 50 per cent of the time). The other possibility would be negative correlation, so we should see profits going down when position rises and vice versa, more frequently than movements of profits and position in the same direction.

As can be seen from Table 1.3, the distribution of

Table 1.2 Profits
and league
position for forty
football clubs
1978–97

Club	Average position	Average pre-tax profits (£000)
Liverpool	3	280
Manchester United	5	3,304
Arsenal	5	657
Everton	9	–1,168
Tottenham	9	742
Aston Villa	10	444
Southampton	12	–335
Coventry	14	–1,336
West Ham	17	–517
Leeds	17	–1,597
Newcastle	20	–1,493
Sheffield Wednesday	21	–259
Blackburn	25	–1,498
Leicester	25	–335
Luton	25	–118
Derby	26	–702
West Brom	27	–62
Oldham	31	38
Birmingham	32	–186
Sheffield United	36	–790
Barnsley	37	2
Bolton	43	–738
Swindon	48	–170
Bristol Rovers	49	–146
Shrewsbury	49	–82
Huddersfield	51	–59
Plymouth	52	–69
Hull	54	–179
Reading	54	–133
Brentford	55	–17
Cambridge	56	–16
Southend	57	–147
Rotherham	58	–289
Preston	60	–11
Burnley	60	–15
Wrexham	65	–69
Bury	66	–188
Peterborough	68	–52
Mansfield	71	–39
Scunthorpe	78	–89

Note: Annual profit figures converted into real 1997 prices adjusting figures for inflation

Table 1.3
Co-movements
in profits and
league position
in a given year

		Change in current year league position	
		Up	Down
Change in current year profits	Up	27%	22%
	Down	25%	27%

Note: Figures may not sum to 100% due to rounding errors

Winners and Losers / 26

outcomes is little different from what one might find if there were no underlying relationship between profits and position. It is slightly more likely that changes in position and profit go in the same direction (in 53 per cent of cases), but in 47 per cent of cases they moved in the opposite direction to league position. Put another way, a strategy which guaranteed a higher league position would be expected to generate an increase in profits only 52 per cent of the time (27 ÷ (27+25)). Similarly, a strategy guaranteeing higher profits would be expected to produce a higher league position 55 per cent of the time (27 ÷ (22+27)). In either case, the outcome is little more predictable than tossing a coin.

The failure to find a significant relationship might be due to timing. It could be argued that a higher position in the current year will lead to greater profits in the following year, perhaps because success generates greater support in the following season. However, Table 1.4 shows that there is no basis for believing that better positions lead to higher future profits. In 48 per cent of cases profits and position moved in the same direction, while in 52 per cent of cases they moved in the opposite direction, suggesting almost no correlation at all.

Finally, one might imagine that the effect could run in the opposite direction: higher profits today might lead to higher positions in the future, perhaps because higher profits mean greater resources available for investment in the team. However, this notion is also not supported by the data, which show (Table 1.5) that in only 49 per cent of cases did current profits and future position move in the same direction.

Table 1.4 Co-movements of league position in a given year with profits in the following year

		Change in current year league position	
		Up	Down
Change in following year profits	Up	25%	25%
	Down	27%	24%

Note: Figures may not sum to 100% due to rounding errors

The Business of Football: Profits and Performance / 27

Table 1.5 Co-movements of profits in a given year with league position in the following year

		Change in following year league position	
		Up	Down
Change in current year profits	Up	25%	24%
	Down	27%	24%

Note: Figures may not sum to 100% due to rounding errors

A simple way of summarizing the relationship between changes in profits and changes in league position is through the correlation coefficient. This is a statistical measure which must lie between −1 and +1. A correlation coefficient of +1 between two variables implies that they always move together in the same direction, while a coefficient of −1 implies that they always move in exactly the opposite direction to each other. A coefficient of zero means there is no co-movement at all. The correlation coefficient for changes in football clubs' profits and league position is −0.0037: approximately zero.

The absence of any strong relationship between profits and position is highlighted by examining those cases where clubs are either promoted or relegated from one division to another (Table 1.6). Promotion means playing matches against more successful and attractive clubs, increasing the interest for fans and raising attendances. In the data set there are 165 cases of divisional movement. In 47 per cent of these cases profits moved in the opposite direction to the change in division, while in just over half of all cases promotion was associated with an increase in profits. Promoted clubs experienced an increase in profits only 50 per cent of the time ($26 \div (26+26)$),

Table 1.6 Co-movements in profits and league position in a given year for clubs promoted or relegated

		Change in division	
		Up	Down
Change in profits	Up	26%	21%
	Down	26%	27%

Note: Figures may not sum to 100% due to rounding errors

Winners and Losers / 28

while demoted clubs experienced a drop in profits 56 per cent of the time $(27 \div (21+27))$.

Even winning the Premier League/First Division Championship, the greatest domestic prize of all, does not appear to affect profits significantly. Each of the championship winners in the data set had in the previous season been near the top: the biggest jump being six places in the cases of Aston Villa (1981) and Everton (1985). In five cases the same team (Liverpool on three occasions and Manchester United on two) had won the league in the previous year. Out of the nineteen championship victories contained in the data, the profits of the winning club rose that year in eleven cases and fell in eight. The story is not much different in the year following winning the league, when position cannot rise and usually falls. In nine cases profits fell and in nine cases profits rose.

The absence of a powerful relationship between changes in position and changes in profits is one of the most important regularities in the business of football. It implies that there is no simple formula that relates financial success to success on the pitch. In the past, when the club directors did not place great emphasis on financial success as a rationale for club policies, this did not matter. However, in recent years directors have become more and more concerned with the creation of financial profits from football.

Nineteen ninety-six represents a watershed in the management of football clubs. In that year there was an explosion of interest in football clubs as financial investments. By the end of it around half of the Premier League clubs were quoted on the stock market, and many were owned by professional investors interested primarily in making a profit. The absence of any direct relationship between profit and performance creates the potential for continuing tension between profit-oriented managers (installed by the shareholders) and the results-oriented fans. In 1996 the Nomura Index of football club stock market prices rose from 250 to 900, a 360 per cent increase. Clearly, the stock market took the view that there is money to be made in football. To a large extent this opinion was based on the experience of just one club: Manchester United.

The Manchester United business

Set in the context of football club profitability in general, Manchester United has bucked the trend. By deciding to turn itself into a profit-making enterprise the club embarked on a fundamental restructuring of the way a football club is operated. At the same time the club emphasized in its flotation document that its 'success is based upon the commitment and loyalty of its supporters and staff. The Directors intend to encourage this by providing attractive and entertaining football.' Thus to make money for the shareholders the football on the pitch would have to be good. So far this enterprise has been a resounding success. However, at the start it was by no means apparent that it would be.

Manchester United Ltd was controlled by the Edwards family from the early 1960s. Louis Edwards, a Manchester meat trader, was an acquaintance of Matt Busby, who was looking for supportive businessmen to steer the club in a way sympathetic to his own philosophy. Edwards was elected to the board in 1958 and became chairman in 1962, owning seventeen of 4,132 shares in the company. He then pioneered the acquisition technique that was later perfected by Irving Scholar at Tottenham: he went through the shareholders' register and approached the shareholders one by one with an offer to buy their shares, until by 1964 he held a controlling interest in Manchester United Limited. His son Martin became chief executive of the club in 1981. Over the years he searched for ways to realize the value of some of his father's investment, almost selling the club to Michael Knighton in 1989. But finally, in 1991, the Edwards family managed to sell part of their shareholding through a stock market flotation.

In selling part of the club to professional investors

Manchester United has attempted to balance the interests of shareholders and fans, as the quotation above suggests. However, prior to flotation the club was seldom able to generate a profit and in the previous twenty years had achieved only modest success on the field, given its almost unrivalled expenditure on players.

Under the management of Sir Matt Busby Manchester United became a legend of English football and achieved world renown. Busby was manager from 1945 to 1971, during which time the club won the league championship five times and the FA Cup twice. The club's fame spread wider in the aftermath of the 1958 Munich air disaster in which eight young squad members died. After rebuilding the team Busby achieved his greatest triumph by winning the European Cup in 1968, the first English side to do so. Busby created teams with a reputation for exciting play, and during this period some of the most famous names in football – George Best, Denis Law and Bobby Charlton – played for the club. However, after his retirement the club's performance on the pitch declined, notwithstanding a very high level of investment in the team. The continued expenditure was only feasible because Manchester United was the best supported club in the country, regularly enjoying attendances far higher than teams which achieved better results on the pitch.

In 1986 the club sacked Ron Atkinson as manager and appointed Alex Ferguson. Ferguson had been one of the most successful managers in the history of Scottish football, turning Aberdeen into a serious rival to the long-dominant duo of Celtic and Rangers. In his first full season at Manchester United the club came second in the league, better than anything it had achieved under Atkinson. However, in the years that followed things did not go so well. It is possible to understand what happened at United by looking at the accounting data for the first two full financial years of Ferguson's tenure.

Table 1.7 presents the key financial statistics of Manchester United in the financial years 1987–8 and 1988–9.

	87–8	88–9	Change year on year
League position	2	11	–9
Revenue (£000)	7,577	9,441	+25%
Football	4,775	5,222	+9%
Commercial activities	2,092	3,445	+65%
Catering	730	774	+6%
Expenditure (£000)			
Wages	2,448	2,909	+19%
Transfer spending	2,496	19	–99%
Other (mostly operating charges)	3,563	4,434	+24%
Pre-tax profit (£000)	–930	2,079	3,009

Table 1.7 Manchester United: League position and profits 1987–9

Income at the time was rising, there being a particularly healthy increase in revenue from commercial activities such as conferences held at the club's facilities. The major difference in financial terms between the two years is the substantial drop in transfer spending, from £2.5m to a mere £19,000. Combined with the rise in income, this led to a £3m change in profits, from a £930,000 loss to a healthy-looking profit of £2,079,000. But this also meant that total spending on players fell from £4.9m to £2.9m. At the time the club needed to rebuild its squad following the departure of Atkinson. In fact, the main transfer expenditure of 1987–8 had been £1.6m for Mark Hughes, who was returning to United after two years at Barcelona. Given that Alex Ferguson sold most of the players bought by Atkinson in the previous five years,[26] United were clearly in need of some new blood.[27] However, at the time the profit-conscious board of directors, led by Martin Edwards, were unwilling to sanction the level of spending that Ferguson had expected when he came to the club. Interviews from the time illustrate his frustration: 'I came here thinking I would have the luxury of buying players. I have done a lot of hard work at youth levels but to win the league we need to buy. I'm disappointed I haven't had that kind of money. Liverpool have bought the best and what sticks in my gullet is the difference between them and us ... He [Martin Edwards] is now facing two very tough choices between having a very good team and balancing the books.'[28] An illustration of the financial straitjacket Ferguson found himself in came in the summer of 1988 when he tried to sign Paul Gascoigne but was refused permission by Edwards.[29]

Things changed in the summer of 1989. Between July and September Ferguson was allowed to go on a spending spree. He bought five players – Gary Pallister, Neil Webb, Paul Ince, Mike Phelan and Danny Wallace – for somewhere in the region of £8m, an astronomical outlay for the time. That season the club spent £5.2m net on transfer fees. Why the change of heart? The simplest explanation is that, having already found a buyer and struck a deal, Edwards was no longer concerned about balancing the books. Thus in May Edwards felt obliged to deny that he was interested in selling the club, so strong were the rumours that he was trying to do so. On 18 August it was announced that Michael Knighton would buy the club for £20m. Ironically, the bid fell through in October because Knighton could not raise the money, but not before Ferguson had been able to complete his purchases.

Despite having signed a new three-year contract in September, Ferguson was clearly under pressure to prove that he could achieve something after all this expenditure. The season did not start particularly well. A 5-1 defeat by Manchester City was followed by a string of draws in the league, and it was widely said that Ferguson would have been fired had they lost a third-round FA Cup tie against Nottingham Forest in January 1990. By February the club was falling into the relegation zone and only continuing participation in the FA Cup stopped the pressures mounting further. In the end the club managed to finish only thirteenth in the league that season. However, none of that mattered because Ferguson finally brought Manchester United a trophy, if only just. Drawn away from home in every round, the club won the 1990 FA Cup against Crystal Palace in a replay after a 3-3 draw.[30] From this point onward Manchester United returned to winning habits, and Ferguson's position was secure. Each year brought additional trophies. The club won the European Cup Winners' Cup in 1991, the League Cup in 1992 and, most important of all, the inaugural Premier League Championship in 1993. The club then won four of the first five Premier League Championships as well as two more FA Cups. It was the transfer spending in the summer of 1989 that marked the watershed for the club, in particular the acquisitions of Pallister and Ince, who formed the backbone of the team over the coming years. While Ferguson had wanted to buy in the market for some time, it seems that it was only the miscalculations of the Knighton take-over bid that freed him from the financial constraints.

Bryan Robson was a key player at Manchester United between 1981 and 1994, an international footballer of world class, who had been involved in the management of the England national team and is now a club manager. He once made the following comment: 'When I first played for England, I used to ask the Liverpool players what they did, what was their secret? They'd say, "Five-a-sides". They wouldn't work on set pieces and that sort of thing. Liverpool never did much in training but they all knitted together well in a certain formation. When I was at United we would work on a lot of things but we always fell short of what Liverpool did. Then all of a sudden when we were successful at United, from 1990, I saw why. It was simply because in seven or eight places you could probably say we had the best players in those positions in the country ... the secret of success is good players.'[31]

In many ways this is a surprising statement from one of the best players of his generation. When he moved to Manchester United for £1.5m, his transfer fee broke the British record at the time. Throughout the 1980s Manchester United spent heavily in the transfer market in order to buy the best possible players for their team. In fact, between 1987–8, Alex Ferguson's first full season as manager, and 1992–3, when the club won its first League Championship since 1967, the club spent just over £15m (net) on transfers, presumably trying to obtain the best players. Over this period only four teams spent more than £10m, the others being Liverpool, who won two championships during this time (1988 and 1990), Leeds (who won in 1992) and Blackburn (who won in 1994). The only other team to win then was Arsenal (1989 and 1991), who spent a mere £3.5m net on transfers, which still made them eighth in the list of biggest spenders for this period.

Of course, buying an expensive player means paying high wages as well. Between 1988 and 1993 the highest wage spender was Liverpool, who paid nearly £32m in salaries. Manchester United was third in the list (£26m), Arsenal fourth (£25m) and Leeds sixth (£20m). If we add these two types of expenditure on players together, five of the six biggest aggregate spenders over this period were (in order) Liverpool, Manchester United, Leeds, Arsenal and Blackburn. All won at least one league title as a reward for this outlay.

The story of Manchester United illustrates just how vital spending is to playing success. From Alex Ferguson's own words it appears that what was critical in turning Manchester United around was not the playing system, the personalities or skills of the players but managing to persuade the club chairman to spend more money. Teams that invest in players do better on the pitch. The examples of Manchester United and other big clubs illustrate the point (and a much more detailed analysis of the data is provided in Chapter 5). Sometimes clubs can spend a lot of money and achieve very little in terms of league position; just occasionally teams on which very little money has been spent achieve remarkably high league positions. But these cases are exceptions and, in general, higher expenditure leads to higher league position.

However, as was shown in the previous section, higher positions do not necessarily lead to higher profits; sometimes they do and sometimes they do not. Furthermore, it is impossible to predict whether an increase in expenditure will trigger a rise or fall in profits. Since the flotation of Manchester United in 1991, an increase in player expenditure has always led to an increase in profits. The evidence that Manchester

United has created this virtuous circle has led professional investors to believe that the same connection can be created at other clubs. Whether or not this has been the case is the principal theme of this book.

Football and its environment

Football in the 1990s is seen as a great money-spinner, but for most of the postwar era English football clubs have struggled financially. As standards of living rose, football declined in popularity faced with competition from newer leisure activities. Like much of British industry, football club management was mired in tradition and unreceptive to change. Almost the only response of the clubs to their deteriorating revenue base was to increase prices for their diminishing audience. Clubs were too busy competing with each other to focus on competing with rival leisure businesses. Only when football became fashionable once again did clubs start to develop a strategy for the exploitation of their revenue-raising potential. This chapter documents the fall and rise of English football and examines the changing structure of football club income.

Since the late 1970s there has been a significant shift in the relative importance of football clubs' revenue sources. The importance of gate receipts has declined significantly as developments in other industries such as sportswear and broadcasting have created new opportunities. These changes, particularly over the last ten years, have had a significant impact not only on football's revenue potential but also on the distribution of revenue between clubs. Many of the changes in football have been driven not by decisions made by clubs and league officials but by changing technologies, particularly in broadcasting.

Figure 2.1 shows the change in the real revenue of football clubs since 1946 ('real' in this context means after adjusting the figures for inflation[1]). Between 1946 and 1988 there was a

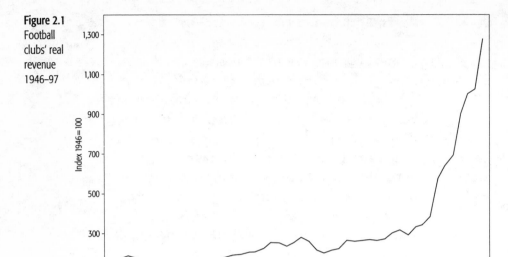

Figure 2.1
Football
clubs' real
revenue
1946–97

small trend increase in club revenue of 3 per cent a year on average. However, since 1988 there has been an extraordinary explosion in revenue generation and the average growth rate has risen to over 18 per cent per year. This is due not only to the increased interest in football and increasing prices but also to the development of significant new revenue sources.

Figure 2.2 illustrates the main revenue sources of football clubs in England. Traditionally the most important source of revenue is gate receipts from supporters attending matches. In addition to gate receipts on match days, catering operations often provide significant revenue. The services offered range from bars and simple snacks such as the traditional meat pies to corporate hospitality comprising silver service. On non-match days most clubs offer facilities for functions and conferences. Recently clubs have become more sophisticated in the provision of catering services, sometimes teaming up with established operators (e.g. Liverpool have a McDonald's franchise in the Kop) and sometimes developing club-branded products (e.g. Manchester United cola is available at Old Trafford).

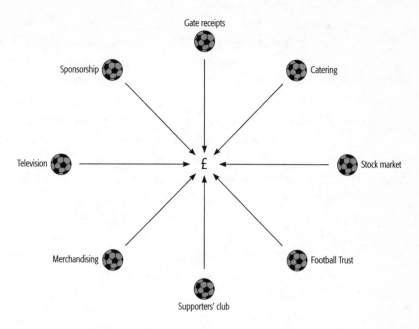

Figure 2.2
Football
clubs' revenue
sources

Gate receipts

Sponsorship

Catering

Television

£

Stock market

Merchandising

Football Trust

Supporters' club

Clubs are also able to exploit their popularity via merchandising. As well as the traditional souvenirs (e.g. books, badges, scarves, etc.) clubs are capitalizing on the strong video retail market and the current boom in leisurewear goods. In addition to replica kits the current Reebok Liverpool range includes over forty different items of clothing. The clubs are attractive to advertisers and sell advertising space on perimeter boards, programmes, tickets, etc. Sponsorship of the club, the stadium and the kit is also common. For example, at Arsenal the club sponsors are JVC and the kit sponsors/providers are Nike. Club sponsors usually have their name on club kits as well as a significant profile inside the ground. Some club sponsorship has also included the stadium, for example Middlesbrough's stadium is known as the Cellnet Riverside Stadium and Bolton Wanderers' new ground is known officially as the Reebok Stadium.

As well as earning income directly clubs also receive money from their league/association. The two major sources of revenue for the league/association are sponsorship (currently the

Premier League is sponsored by Carling, the FA Cup by AXA) and television revenue. The Premier League sells the television rights to the competition as a package and distributes the majority of the income between clubs. This is also true for the FA Cup, League Cup and UEFA Champions' League.

Other less significant revenue sources include the Football Trust, the stock market and supporters' clubs. Clubs receive grants from the Football Trust, a body set up to collect money from the Pools companies and to distribute this to clubs for ground improvements, safety projects and policing. In the 1990s several clubs have issued bonds or equities on the stock market as a means of raising finance. Revenue contributed by supporters' clubs, while not so important to the modern game, was a significant source of income in the 1960s.

By far the most important source of revenue is gate receipts. Figure 2.3 shows gate receipts as a share of total revenues for Arsenal, West Bromwich Albion and Shrewsbury for twenty years beginning in 1974. The three clubs have vastly different playing strengths, with Arsenal having an

Figure 2.3 Gate receipts share of total income

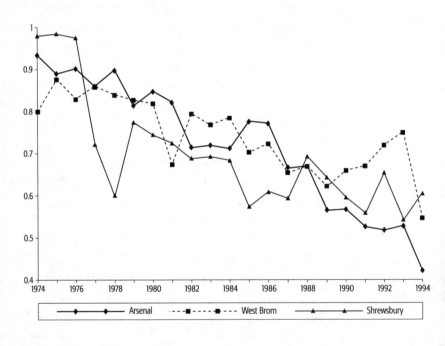

average league position over the period of seven, WBA twenty-five and Shrewsbury fifty. In 1974 gate receipts were by far the biggest source of income, making up 80–95 per cent of each club's income. However, since then there has been a distinct downward trend in its importance. This decline seems more marked for the top clubs, as evidenced by Arsenal, whose gate receipts made up only just over 40 per of the income in 1994.

Gate receipts: football's bread and butter

The Football League was founded with twelve clubs in 1888 and grew rapidly so that by 1924–5 there were eighty-eight. Figure 2.4 shows attendance from the formation of the League to the start of the Second World War. In the first season attendances totalled 612,000. The best supported clubs were Everton, who averaged 7,260 per home game, and Preston, with 6,280. By the 1898–9 season the League had expanded to two divisions with eighteen clubs in each. Total attendances grew over the decade on average by over 20 per cent per year and reached 4.4 million in the 1898–9 season. The League expanded further in 1905–6, when two teams were added to each division. Attendances more than doubled over the decade to 1908–9 and continued growing rapidly until the First

Figure 2.4 Pre-Second World War total league attendance

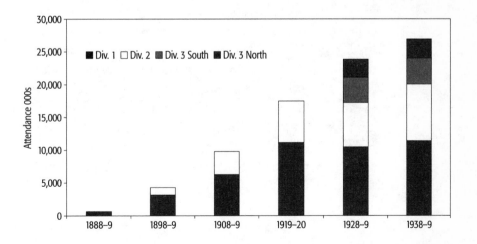

World War. Average attendances were then close to modern-day figures, with Newcastle and Chelsea being the best-supported teams, averaging crowds of over 29,000 each.

The end of the First World War precipitated another football boom. In 1919 league attendances matched the pre-war figure but the addition of a third division in 1920–21 and a fourth division in 1921–2 (known as the Third Division North) attracted more fans, and by 1928–9 there were almost 24 million football spectators. During this period the attendance was more evenly divided than at any other period in football's history. The average attendances in the top division had not increased by much over the previous twenty years. In 1928–9 the top First Division clubs, Manchester City and Newcastle, were attracting crowds of around 31,000 – not a significant increase on the average of 29,000 that Newcastle achieved in 1908–9. Strong growth was occurring in the Second Division, which closed the attendance gap between the top two divisions. In 1898–9 First Division attendances were 2.3 times bigger than Second Division, but this had fallen to 1.5 times by 1928–9. During the depression years of the 1930s attendances continued to rise, although at a much slower rate, and by the beginning of the Second World War over 27 million people attended English league games.

Football continued to be played between 1939 and 1945 but the usual league competition was replaced by regional competitions and no trophies were awarded.[3] The ending of the Second World War led to another football boom. With the resumption of league competition in 1946–7 attendances reached 36 million, 33 per cent up on 1939, and by 1949 the total had reached 41 million. Figure 2.5 shows league attendance in the four divisions in the postwar era[4] and Figure 2.6 shows real (i.e. adjusted for inflation) admission prices. Four distinct postwar periods can be identified and these are shown in Table 2.1.

Figure 2.5
Post war
league
attendance
(millions)

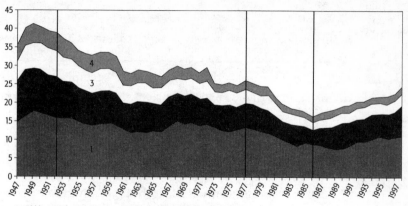

1 = Division 3 North; 1958–9 to 1991–2: Division 4; 1992–3 and after: Division 3.
2 = Division 3 South; 1958–9 to 1991–2: Division 3; 1992–3 and after: Division 2.
3 = Division 2; 1992–3 and after: Division 1. 4 = Division 1; 1992–3 and after: Premier League.

Figure 2.6 Real
admission prices
1946–95[5]

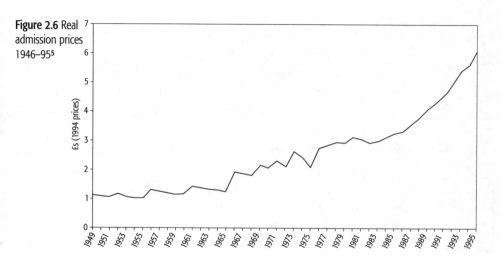

Postwar boom (1947–52)

After the end of the war the country was economically
exhausted from the war effort and rationing was still in force.
In 1946 Entertainment Duty, first levied in 1916, was reduced
for live theatre and spectator sports including football. In two
years the duty fell from 7½d per spectator to 1d, and at the
Chancellor's specific request football clubs reduced their minimum admission price from 1s 6d to 1s 3d. In the climate of
postwar austerity it was easy for football, a readily available

Revenue / 43

Table 2.1		Average annual growth in attendance	Average annual change in real admission prices	Average annual growth in real consumers' expenditure
Attendances, price and consumers' expenditure since 1947[6]	1947–52	+1.8%	+1.6%*	+2.0%
	1953–77	−1.4%	+4.2%	+2.4%
	1978–86	−5.0%	+1.8%	+2.8%
	1987–96	+2.8%	+6.9%**	+2.1%

* 1949–52
** 1987–94

cheap mass entertainment, to flourish. But football was not alone. In 1946 45 million people attended dog racing, speedway was drawing crowds of over 300,000 a week, and during the summer of 1947 3 million spectators went to cricket grounds. Nor was the rush for entertainment confined to sport. Thirty million people went to the seaside in 1946,[7] and cinema attendances topped a billion.[8]

It was during this period that many attendance records were set. In 1948–9 41,271,414 people attended league football, a total that has not been matched since. Average attendances were large with two clubs (Newcastle and Arsenal) averaging over 50,000 and a further nine (Manchester United, Spurs, Aston Villa, Chelsea, Sunderland, Everton, Liverpool, Wolves and Charlton) averaging over 40,000. Big matches could attract much larger crowds. For example, Liverpool had 61,905 people crammed into Anfield for a game against Wolverhampton Wanderers in 1952 and Everton had 78,299 people to watch a Merseyside derby in 1948. Over these six seasons on average more than 38.5 million people passed through clubs' turnstiles each year. During this period the First Division accounted on average for 42 per cent of all attendances, with the Second taking 29 per cent, the Third 17 per cent and the Fourth 12 per cent.

Football clubs were not doing anything particularly new to attract these record crowds. The entertainment offered and the facilities provided were much the same as before the Second World War, perhaps worse in some cases due to bomb damage. Football's boom was not of the clubs' making; they were merely benefiting from the social and economic conditions of the time. Increasing attendances resulted in increased revenues for clubs. Indeed between 1947 and 1952 clubs' revenue increased on average by over 20 per cent a year.

Steady decline (1953–77)

Football failed to maintain its immediate postwar popularity, and between 1953 and 1977 attendances fell by an average of 1.4 per cent each season. But at the same time real admission prices rose on average by 4.2 per cent a season. Although increasing prices may have contributed to the fall in attendance, because prices were rising faster the total income of the clubs actually grew. In other words, the clubs were able to exploit the loyalty of the remaining fans. In the jargon of economics the demand for football is said to be 'price inelastic': it does not respond strongly to changes in prices.[9] Over the years there have been a number of studies by economists attempting to estimate the price elasticity of the demand for football,[10] all of which confirm that demand is insensitive to changes in price, taking into account all the other factors that might influence demand.

This decline in attendances contrasts sharply with a general increase in the wealth of the population; over the period consumers' expenditure grew by over 2.4 per cent per year. As disposable income increased from the mid-1950s onwards so did the opportunities for spending it. It was during this period that consumer goods in homes became commonplace with televisions, vacuum cleaners, fridges and washing machines all vying for the consumer pound. For example, in 1950 there were only 344,000 television sets in the UK but ten years later this had increased to 10.5 million and by 1968 to 15 million.[11]

The relative attractiveness of visiting a decrepit football ground declined as new forms of entertainment, most notably television, became available. Television was a competitor not only for consumers' money but also for their time. People started to take more holidays, particularly abroad; home ownership and home improvement absorbed both money and time. Thus, while increasing consumer income enabled football clubs to charge higher prices, it also created competition from alternative pastimes.

Changes in the structure of society brought further problems for football. The working week was gradually shortened to five days, which meant that large numbers of men were no longer finishing work at midday on Saturday in the inner city areas in which football clubs were based. Football became more distant from its traditional customers, and few clubs seized the opportunity to relocate their grounds. Furthermore, higher living standards meant that public tolerance for poor facilities at the grounds was diminishing. Football started to become the province of the die-hard fan rather than the recreation of the average working man.

Many traditional supporters voted with their feet. Football was not alone, and most of the leisure activities popular in the pre-war era started to decline during this period. In fact, football clubs fared better than many of the old seaside resorts and cinemas. As Table 2.2 shows, between the late 1940s and early 1980s football lost over half its spectators. But this was not as bad as cricket, which lost two-thirds of its audiences, and cinema attendance, which fell to less than one-tenth of its 1948 level.

If competition from new leisure activities was responsible for the decline of football attendances, this decline was not inevitable. It reflects the failure of football clubs to respond to these new competitive threats and to the changing social patterns. Attempts to attract new fans through imaginative

Table 2.2 Entertainment attendances 1947–8 to 1995–6	000s	1947–8	1971–2	1981–2	1988–9	1995–6
	Football	40,259	28,704	20,006	18,464	21,844
	Cricket	3,000	984	994	751	958
	Cinema	1,396,000	176,000	96,000	82,900	112,100

Source: Social Trends, Walvin, J. (1994), Social Trends 20 (1990) and English Cricket Board

pricing, marketing and advertising were non-existent. Clubs retained inflexible pricing structures, seldom discounting the less attractive fixtures even when attendances fell well below capacity. Often the only discounts available were for juniors, and few efforts were made to tailor what was offered to the differing capacity to pay of the fans. Significant investment in the facilities was lacking and it seemed as if the clubs were making no attempt to make the experience of going to a football match enjoyable other than through what was on offer on the pitch.

Football's failure is put into sharp perspective by comparing attendance in English football and in US sports. In 1953 the English league matches enjoyed attendances of 37 million while Major League Baseball in the US attracted only 14.5 million. By 1997 league attendances dropped to only 22 million while baseball rose to 63 million. Figure 2.7 compares changes in attendance between 1953 and 1997 for English football with the National Football League (NFL), the National Basketball Association (NBA) and Major League Baseball (MLB) in the United States. While it should be pointed out that the NFL and NBA were starting from a significantly lower base (2.2 and 1.2 million compared to the

Figure 2.7
Attendance growth in US sports and English football

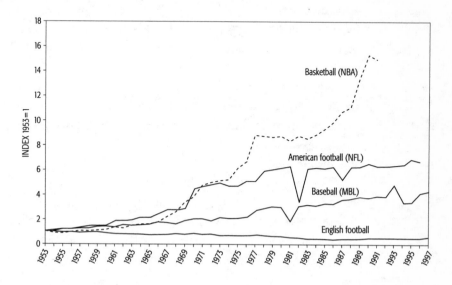

Football League's 37 million annual spectators) and there is a huge difference in the countries' population, the difference in growth rates is stark. Between 1953 and 1991 the NFL attendances grew by over six times (interrupted by two strikes in 1982 and 1987), the NBA's by over fifteen times, while the English League's fell by a half. Thus in 1991 the gap in total attendances had closed significantly with the NFL having 13 million spectators, the NBA 16 million and the Football League 19 million.

The decline in the number of English league football spectators (almost a quarter of the total between 1953 and 1977) was felt more acutely in the lower divisions than in the top division. Over the period First Division attendances fell by just under 15 per cent, while Second and Third Division attendances dropped by over a third and Fourth Division attendances by 55 per cent.

In the 1960s television coverage of football expanded significantly. Broadcasters concentrated on the top divisions so that through television the supporters of lower division teams were exposed to a competitive yardstick against which they could judge the standards of their local side. Many found the lower divisions wanting. At the same time cheap motoring and the construction of motorways meant that it became both feasible and economic to be a long-distance fan. In 1951 there were 2.4 million cars, a decade later it had risen to 6 million and by 1971 this had doubled to 12 million. Supporters found it easier to travel to games, but if they were going to travel, many preferred to visit a big club, where the standards of both the home and away teams were higher. As a result the small, less successful clubs felt the downturn in attendance more sharply.

This phenomenon can be illustrated by looking at the attendances of Manchester United and near neighbours Bury during the 1960s. In the 1959–60 season Manchester United's crowds were over four times larger than Bury's, but by the end of the decade the ratio had increased to over eleven times

Table 2.3
Average
attendance
during 1960s

	1959–60		1964–5		1969–70	
	Att. ratio	Div.	Att. ratio	Div.	Att. ratio	Div.
Manchester United	47,288	1	46,521	1	49,862	1
Bury	10,628	3	7,784	2	4,512	3
	4.44		5.98		11.05	
Leeds	21,877	1	37,490	1	34,613	1
York	7,507	3	7,185	4	4,274	4
	2.91		5.22		8.09	
Aston Villa	34,257	2	22,215	1	27,345	2
Walsall	11,570	4	6,754	3	5,428	3
	3.07		3.29		5.04	

(Table 2.3). This story was repeated in other cities such as Leeds and Birmingham. Leeds United drew less than three times the number of fans that York City did in 1960, but by 1970 the multiple had risen to eight times. Aston Villa drew three times the attendance of neighbouring Walsall in 1960, rising to five times by 1970.

The decline in attendances was not constant throughout the period. On the back of the euphoria of the 1966 World Cup, Manchester United's victory in the European Cup and the popularity of superstars such as George Best, football enjoyed a brief respite from declining attendances in the second half of the 1960s. In 1965–6 attendances totalled 27.2 million. In the year of the World Cup they rose to 28.9 million and peaked at 30.1 million the season after England's injury time win over West Germany. However, in the late 1960s and early 1970s the pattern of declining attendances re-established itself, this time accompanied by the emerging phenomenon of football hooliganism.

Football's nadir (1978–86)

English club football's finest period on the field coincided with the worst decline in attendances ever witnessed in its history. Despite success in the UEFA and Cup Winners' Cups, before 1977 England's only victor in the European Cup was Manchester United, but between Liverpool's two victories in Rome – 1977 against Borussia Münchengladbach and 1984 against Roma – the European Cup left England only once

(Liverpool were winners four times, Nottingham Forest twice and Aston Villa once). However, in the nine seasons after Liverpool's first success, English league attendances fell by 35 per cent. For the first time they were falling faster than prices were rising. Over the period attendances fell by 5 per cent on average per season while real prices increased by only 1.8 per cent.

During the late 1970s many outside football were coming to the view that football and social problems went hand in hand. In truth, these social problems (violence, the breakdown of traditional authority, inner city poverty, deindustrialization) can hardly be blamed on football clubs, and the unrest at football grounds was more a symptom of deep-seated social problems than its cause. None the less the clubs did not help themselves with their failure to modernize facilities and their apparent unwillingness to deal with problems such as racist abuse. Investment in facilities was virtually non-existent. Increasingly, it seemed as if football hooliganism was the main entertainment on offer at football grounds. To combat hooliganism both policing and crowd control measures became more intrusive. The arrival of away fans at matches became a highly organized police operation, and they were kept segregated from home fans. After the match away fans would be kept inside the ground while the home fans were forced to disperse, decreasing the risk of violence. Fences, which were later to be a major factor in the deaths of so many at Hillsborough, were commonplace. Chelsea even applied to electrify its fences, although the local council rejected this added refinement. In the first season after the Second World War police numbers averaged one per thousand fans but by the mid-1980s this had increased to as many as seventy-five per thousand.[12] The atmosphere in grounds and the threat, real or perceived, of football hooligan-ism had an impact on attendances and therefore revenues. The 1983 Chester Report identified fear of hooliganism as a major factor in people's decision not to attend matches.

Football's social problems also meant that clubs lost influence over the management of their own revenue generation. Government disquiet over the level of hooliganism led to pressure on the clubs to do something about it. The Prime Minister, Margaret Thatcher, knew little about football and cared even less, but was concerned that the perception of widespread national disorder would damage her government's reputation. At first there was encouragement for membership schemes to enable clubs to monitor offenders, but by 1986 there was pressure on the Football League to ban away supporters altogether. Luton Town, chaired by a Conservative MP, actually did ban away fans. The Football League negotiated with government on ever tougher measures to crack down on hooligans, many of which had adverse implications for club revenues. The government threatened draconian legislation if the clubs did not act. In the end, Luton withdrew its scheme and government plans were overtaken by events, notably the decline of hooliganism and the Hillsborough disaster.

During this time, football also became a vehicle for far right politics. Sociologists[13] have argued that the far right was attracted to football not only as a recruitment vehicle but also as a platform to disseminate its views in a simple and direct form into millions of homes. For example, in 1978 the National Front were leafleting outside many London football venues following the launch of the National Front Youth Newspaper *Bulldog*, which in the 1980s included a regular article entitled 'On the Football Front'.

English football was at its lowest ebb in 1985. During this season a young Birmingham fan died as a result of violence. Within a couple of weeks fifty-five people died during a fire at a Bradford City match and thirty-eight people died at the Heysel Stadium in Brussels before a European Cup Final between Liverpool and Juventus. The deaths at Heysel came as panicking Juventus supporters tried to escape an attack by English hooligans, causing a wall in the decrepit stadium to collapse. UEFA banned all English clubs from European competition for five years.

Recovery and rejuvenation 1987–

It is widely held that English football's recovery began with Italia 90 and Paul Gascoigne's famous tears. In reality the rejuvenation had begun about three years earlier, in 1987. Although the top division continued its downward trend, losing 13 per cent of its spectators between 1987 and 1990, the remaining divisions all grew strongly, particularly the Second Division (see Table 2.4). However, from 1990 onwards the top division grew much faster than the lower divisions, especially the lowest, which has again begun to lose spectators.

	All divisions	1	2	3	4
1987–90	18	–13	93	13	34
1990–98	27	41	21	25	–7

Table 2.4 Percentage changes in attendance 1987–98

The remarkable recovery of the Second Division between 1987 and 1990 was aided by the fact that during this time some teams with strong traditional support such as Manchester City, Sheffield Wednesday, Leeds, Newcastle and Chelsea were playing in the Second Division. However, this is not enough to explain such a dramatic reversal in the trend of attendances.

Football's recovery can be associated with wider trends in the economy and society. During the mid-1980s there was a significant consumer boom following the deep recession of the early 1980s. At the same time the long downward trend in cinema attendances halted and audiences started to grow again as people rediscovered a traditional form of entertainment, albeit housed in more comfortable multiplexes (see Table 2.2, page 46).

Changes also arose from within football itself. Post Heysel there was a change in the way that football fans represented themselves and thus were represented in the media, in cinema and even literature, creating a more positive image for the game and combating the fear of hooliganism which had deterred many spectators. In the immediate aftermath of the Heysel tragedy a group of Liverpool fans formed the Football Supporters Association (FSA). Their intention was to represent the fans who were interested in football, not the associated violence. At the same time that the FSA was being founded the remarkable growth in fanzines began.

Fanzines were magazines produced independently of clubs by their supporters, offering an alternative view to the mainstream media and club literature. Their production utilized the increasingly cheap photocopying and later in their development deployed the advances in desk top publishing. Fanzines provided supporters with a voice, allowing them to express their opinions on important topics, such as treatment by the police and stewards, and services that their club offered on match days, and presented an alternative image to the prevailing stereotype of the supporter as a violent, mindless thug. One of the most successful national fanzines, *When Saturday Comes*, was founded in 1986 and still thrives today. By the end of the 1980s it was estimated that there were over 200 fanzines selling in total over a million copies a year;[14] in 1998 there were over 600.

This new movement can perhaps explain why football's rejuvenation began, but the impact of the Hillsborough disaster should not be underestimated. The Taylor Report and subsequent court cases concluded that police incompetence combined with an antiquated stadium caused the death of ninety-six Liverpool fans attending an FA Cup semi-final.[15] Hillsborough was not a one-off but the result of the failure to heed the lessons of the many previous football disasters. In 1946 thirty-three people were crushed to death due to overcrowding at Burnden Park and the subsequent Hughes Report recommended limitations on crowd size and the licensing of grounds. Ibrox Park, the home of Glasgow Rangers, suffered two disasters. In 1902 at an England–Scotland match twenty-six people died and 500 were injured as a stand collapsed. Sixty-nine years later at the same venue sixty-six people were crushed to death at an Old Firm match.

The report by the late Lord Justice Taylor in the aftermath of Hillsborough made wide-ranging recommendations on safety within grounds, the most high-profile being the introduction of all-seater stadiums and the removal of –perimeter fencing. The government gave legislative force to the recommendations thus compelling the clubs to change the environment at football grounds once and for all. In response to the Taylor Report, Premier League clubs have spent an average £12m each on ground improvements. While this has reduced overall capacity, the number of seats has increased by over 200 per cent. Indeed several clubs such as Middlesbrough and Bolton have moved to brand-new purpose-built stadiums, and most grounds have been radically altered with the development of new stands. England now has the largest number of all-seater stadiums in Europe. Compulsory seating and the removal of fences have made a major difference to the atmosphere and have had an enormous impact on the attractiveness of football grounds.

Football in the 1990s has a completely new, fashionable image, and this has been reflected in increased attendances at matches as well as increased attention in the media, literary and cinematic worlds. For example, *Fever Pitch*, a football-based autobiography by Nick Hornby, became a best-seller and also a film. Several football nostalgia programmes were shown on television. Media personalities began to boast of their obsession with football, when once it would have been considered unmentionable. Perhaps the changing perception of football is most clearly illustrated by the relationship between football and politicians. Margaret Thatcher, football's *bête noire*, was replaced in office by John Major, an open fan of Chelsea. David Mellor, another Tory MP and former National Heritage Minister, began presenting 606, BBC Radio 5's post-match discussion programme. The Labour

Party, sensing the popularity of the sport, included a charter for football in their manifesto for their victorious 1997 election campaign. Within their first hundred days of power this spawned a committee for football charged with looking at issues of concern to fans, such as pricing policies and racism.

Football clubs have been well placed to take advantage of their increasing popularity. Following the Taylor Report most clubs have significantly upgraded their facilities, often enabling them to attract more fans and always enabling them to charge higher prices (see Figures 2.5 and 2.6, page 43). The resulting greater revenues have made it possible to fund a rise in wage levels which has helped to attract stars from overseas, and from the late 1980s onwards there was a significant increase in the number of foreign players in the English leagues. Higher revenues may also have helped to retain some English players who might otherwise have gone to play their football in countries such as Italy or Spain. It can be argued that a virtuous circle has been created. As more money has entered the game, improvements in stadiums and the attraction and retention of top playing talent have increased the popularity of the sport. This popularity in turn increases the revenue coming in via sponsorship, attendance and television rights.

A tempestuous relationship: football and television
Football and television have had a long and sometimes tempestuous relationship, but as we approach the millennium their futures are becoming increasingly intertwined. The first live transmission of a football game on English television was the 1937 FA Cup Final in which Sunderland beat Preston 3–1, watched by an estimated 10,000 people.[16] This followed the first radio broadcast, heard eleven years previously. Early transmissions focused on finals, and it wasn't until 1947 that a game other than a final was broadcast.[17]

The Football League did not sanction televised league matches until 1960. It was the fear of losing paying spectators that was at the heart of the League's reluctance. They believed that given a choice spectators would prefer to watch the game at home rather than go to the expense of attending the match. In practice the relationship between football and television is much more complicated than that. For certain fans televised football is a complement to attendance at live games. In other words, if a game is televised they will still attend the match, but will also record the game on video to watch later. As well as generating additional income, television provides an opportunity for marketing the product and increasing interest in the sport. A football game is much more of a televisual spectacle if there is a big crowd. Thus in many ways the interests of television and football clubs overlap. A balance between television coverage for marketing and income purposes and the deterrence of paying spectators must be struck, but recent history has shown that television income can be increased dramatically without adversely affecting attendances.

Initially, the League permitted only recorded highlights, and it was not until 1983 that live broadcasts of league games were sanctioned.[18] It was during the 1960s that English football's most famous and resilient television programme was born: on 22 August 1964 *Match of the Day* was broadcast for the first time, showing forty-five minutes of highlights of Liverpool beating Arsenal 3-2 at Anfield. At its peak *Match of the Day* attracted an estimated quarter of the population as viewers. ITV began to broadcast in 1968 with the *Big Match* on Sunday afternoons, in agreement with the BBC and the Football League.

When live broadcasts were first introduced in 1983 the total value of the television contract was £2.6m divided between the ninety-two clubs, giving each one £28,261. For the bigger clubs this was peanuts. For example, it amounted to only 1 per cent of Arsenal's turnover. By contrast television revenues are today a major source of income for top English clubs. In 1997–8 an average Premier League club received almost £7m. In 1997 14 per cent of Manchester United's revenue came from television. Even Third Division clubs today receive more than the top clubs gained from TV rights back in the early 1980s. Since then there has been a phenomenal increase in the value of television rights for English football. The rights to the Premier League alone were worth £49m per season in 1996–7 but will increase to £180m a season by 2000–2001, almost a 7,000 per cent increase on the £2.6m paid in 1983–4.

Figure 2.8
Premier
League[19] Live
Television Rights
1983–4 to
2000–2001

Figure 2.8 shows the number of live games broadcast per season and the price of the television rights from 1983–4 to 2000–2001, when the most recently signed deal expires.

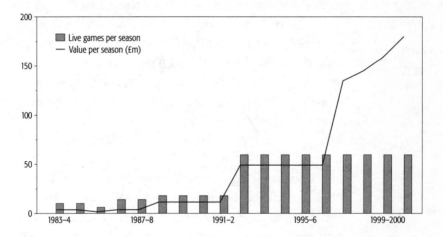

The current English Premier League television deal compares extremely well with those of its European neighbours. As Table 2.5 shows England's television contract is over 60 per cent bigger than that of any of the other 'big five' European footballing nations. This is in spite of the fact that Germany, Italy and Spain already offer pay-per-view services.

Table 2.5 Value of major European League television contracts 1997	UK	France	Italy	Spain	Germany
Value of TV contract p.a. ($ m)	300	185	140	170	125
Free	✓	✗	✓	✓	✓
Pay TV	✓	✓	✓	✓	✓
Pay-per-view	✗	✓	✓	✓	✗

Source: Deutsche Morgan Grenfell

The phenomenal rise in the value of English football's television rights is in part a response to the rise in its popularity as evidenced by growing attendances. This increases the value of football to commercial broadcasters, since larger audiences enhance the value of advertising slots. However, it was the introduction of satellite and cable pay television that radically altered football's fortunes. This created both competition for the rights and a more direct appropriation of the value of television rights from viewers (i.e. subscription revenue). The introduction of competition broke up the BBC/ITV 'cartel' agreement. Since ITV started transmitting football in 1968, television rights had always been shared by the BBC and ITV. The only departure from this was in 1978 when ITV, in an attempt to break up BBC's strong Saturday night schedule with *Match of the Day* at its heart, agreed an exclusive deal with the Football League. However, this coup, labelled 'Snatch of the Day' by the press, was ultimately unsuccessful. After questions in the House of Commons and the subsequent intervention of the Office of Fair Trading, the status quo was re-established.

The sharing agreement continued between 1983–4 and 1987–8 with the introduction of live football. Initially ten live games a season were shown, rising to fourteen in 1987–8. The football authorities were facing two buyers who colluded and had no alternative buyers to whom they could turn. ITV and BBC did not have to offer prices close to their valuation of the rights but just enough to make it worthwhile for the football authorities to sell them.

Indeed, in 1985–6, the football authorities refused to sell their products as they believed the price that the television companies were offering was too low. In a famous meeting of the club chairmen and television companies at the Café Royal in London in 1985, Robert Maxwell, then chairman of Derby, said, 'I'm a director of Central Television. I know more about this than anybody else. It's worth £90m. Don't give in to these mad people from television.'[20] The blackout lasted for half a season and did result in an increase in the total price for rights, which after the dispute rose by 20 per cent to £3.1m a season. However, at the same time the number of live games shown per season increased, meaning that the price per live game had actually fallen. Despite withdrawing the supply, the football authorities had achieved almost nothing.

The arrival of pay television heralded a new era. The creation of the Premier League and the TV agreements with BSkyB have been called 'one of the greatest corporate romances ever'.[21] Pay television not only offered competition for the BBC and ITV but also increased the value of television rights by enabling broadcasters to charge viewers directly for the privilege of watching the games. In 1988 the satellite broadcaster BSB (British Satellite Broadcasting) had entered the market. At that stage BSB could not reach enough of the population to exploit fully the potential of pay television, but their entry into the bidding for Football League broadcasting rights did contribute to the break-up of BBC's and ITV's cosy relationship. Competition forced the price up closer to the actual value to broadcasters. In 1988 ITV won the bid, signing a four-year deal to broadcast eighteen matches at a cost of £11m a season, a 350 per cent increase over the previous deal.

By the time the next renewal of television rights was due, Sky, which launched its UK satellite service in 1989, had won the battle of the satellite broadcasters and had merged with BSB to create BSkyB, adopting its dish technology instead of BSB's squarial. BSkyB saw the acquisition of football rights as key to their growth strategy. The rights were more valuable to them than to their competitors (the BBC and ITV) as they were able to charge viewers directly for watching and did not have to rely solely on advertising revenue. Football was the vehicle by which BSkyB aimed to penetrate the broadcast market.

In 1991 the FA published its *Blueprint for the Future of Football*, the central proposal of which was the formation of a

Premier League consisting of clubs belonging to the old First Division of the Football League. The creation of the Premier League ensured that more decision-making power and thus revenue could be concentrated in the hands of the top clubs. The first act of the new league was to set up an auction for the TV rights, with ITV and BSkyB the principal bidders. Clearly Sky were prepared to launch a substantial bid in order to promote their new services, but ITV were able to match broadly Sky's terms. Funded by the licence fee and without significant commercial income, the BBC was reduced to a bit part.

Sky invested a lot into preparing the deal, with Rupert Murdoch being personally involved in discussions with Rick Parry, chief executive of the Premier League. To help to allay the fear of industry regulators that league football would be entirely lost to terrestrial TV,[22] they cleverly aligned themselves with the BBC, who would continue to broadcast *Match of the Day*. By proposing to broadcast more matches and guaranteeing a minimum level of coverage Sky was offering the smaller clubs a better deal than the old ITV contract, which had tended to focus on the bigger clubs. Finally, Sky also had the strong support of Spurs chairman Alan Sugar, who headed up Amstrad, the electronics company that manufactured a large proportion of Sky dishes.

In the end Sky won, although not without claims of foul play and an attempt by ITV to strike down the deal with a High Court injunction. The new deal increased to sixty the number of live games that could be shown for a price of £49m a season, more than four times the previous annual fee paid by ITV and an 1,800 per cent increase on the 1983–4 deal. In order to broadcast this many matches, a significant alteration of the traditional fixture schedule was required, with matches being played on Sunday afternoons and Monday nights almost every week. The deal also allowed the BBC to broadcast highlights, ensuring the survival of *Match of the Day*.

Figure 2.9 charts the growth of cable and satellite television in the UK. By January 1998 there were 6.6 million

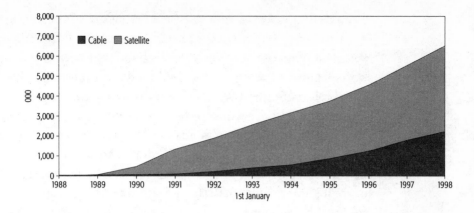

8,000
7,000
6,000
5,000
4,000
3,000
2,000
1,000
0

1988 1989 1990 1991 1992 1993 1994 1995 1996 1997 1998

■ Cable ■ Satellite

000

1st January

Figure 2.9 Cable and satellite subscriber households 1988–98

homes in the UK subscribing to cable or satellite television, approximately 28 per cent of all UK television households. Although cable's share has been growing steadily in the last few years, satellite delivery is dominant, making up 64 per cent of subscribers.

In the UK BSkyB is the dominant player in satellite television, with approximately 93 per cent of all pay TV households subscribing to a Sky programming package. Sky offers a basic package of general entertainment and news plus premium services including sports and films channels. In 1997 subscription to the basic package was around £13 a month and access to a single premium channel could double that figure. Of all Sky subscribers over 90 per cent subscribe to the sports channel.

In a few short years, pay TV has moved from being a loss-making, high-risk venture to become a large, profitable and still growing business. A great part of this success has been ascribed both by analysts and by BSkyB themselves to their football contract. In 1997 BSkyB had a turnover of £1.2bn, achieving profits of £374m, up by 26 per cent on the previous year. Direct-to-home (DTH) subscriptions are the most important source of revenue, representing some 72 per cent of turnover; of the remainder, cable subscriptions account for 12 per cent of turnover and advertising 11 per cent.

The acquisition of sports and film rights has been crucial

in the development of non-terrestrial television. Indeed at News International's annual general meeting in 1996, Rupert Murdoch, part owner of BSkyB, described the acquisition of sports rights as the 'battering ram' for the expansion of his global television network. He went on to say that 'Sport over-powers film and everything else in the entertainment genre ... Football, of all sports, is number one.'[23] The experience in the UK would appear to bear out Murdoch's views. In 1997 of the top thirty programmes on satellite, twenty-five were live football games.[24] Figure 2.10 shows the audience shares of the top five non-terrestrial channels. Sky Sports comes first, fol-lowed by Sky One, which is a general entertainment channel, and then Sky's two premium movie channels. The most popu-lar non-Sky channel is UK Gold, which shows classic British television programmes.

Figure 2.10
Audience share of top five non-terrestrial channels year to February 1997

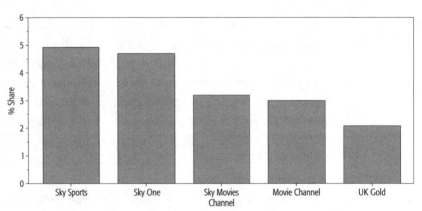

Source: Analysis of BARBdata. Skysports includes Sky Sports 1 and 2 for half-year share of viewing in non-terrestrial households.

Although Sky Sports does show a wide range of sports, an indication of the importance of football can be gained by looking at viewing figures. Figure 2.11 shows Sky Sports' average viewing share over the year to February 1997 and splits this into months when league football was available ('Football season') and when it was not ('Off season'). The figure shows clearly that Sky Sports' viewing share is much higher during the football season.

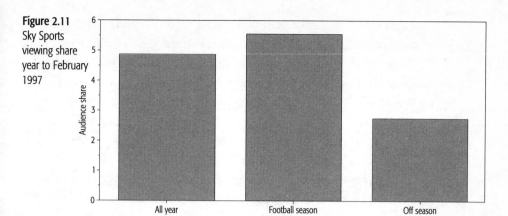

Figure 2.11
Sky Sports viewing share year to February 1997

Audience share

All year   Football season   Off season

In the 1992-3 season it was thought that BSkyB had a higher valuation of television rights than the terrestrial broadcasters, and thanks to their access to subscription revenues they were able to pay a higher price. However, in order for BSkyB to win the rights they only had to beat the bid of ITV, not necessarily paying anywhere near the value to themselves of the rights. As competition in pay TV started to emerge in the 1990s it became clear that the next TV contract would yield an even greater income for the Premier League.

In the competition for the most recent television contract (for 1997–8 to 2000–2001) it was reported that two media companies, Carlton and MAI, submitted bids as well as BSkyB. Thus in order for BSkyB to win the rights they had to beat not only the bid of free-to-air broadcasters but also that of the other proposed pay TV operators, who, like BSkyB, had a much higher valuation of the rights than the BBC and ITV. The result was an increase of more than 300 per cent in the cost of the rights. Again competition in bidding, this time between rival pay TV operators, forced the price closer to the broadcasters' valuation of the rights.

Premier League football is not the only provider of television rights revenues. European competition is an important source of television income for the top English clubs. UEFA negotiates the European Champions' League deal on a pan-European basis. In 1996–7 each club received £2m for entering the competition, plus £0.5m per win, £0.25m per draw, £1.3m for reaching the quarter-final, £1.5m for the semi-final and £1.75m for the final. In the European Cup Winners' Cup and UEFA Cup each home team negotiates its own deal.

The increase in popularity of football allied with the increase in television channels has led to a proliferation of the games shown, to the extent that even pre-season friendlies are now regularly being transmitted live. Table 2.6 shows the types of football broadcast in the 1996–7 season in England. However, in England, Premier League football is dominant both in terms of audiences achieved and rights revenue.

As in the past it is likely that future events in the broadcasting market will drive changes in the price of football's television rights. The next major development is the advent of digital television. It is expected that by 1999 there will be three digital television platforms. Sky launched its digital satellite service in October 1998, and will be followed by the digital terrestrial offering ONdigital and digital cable offered by cable companies, such as CWC, Telewest and NTL.

The introduction of digital television promises major changes to the broadcasting landscape. Digital television uses less bandwidth than the conventional analogue system of transmission. The introduction of digital will therefore increase the capacity of the cable and satellite networks from tens to hundreds of channels. Digital terrestrial television (DTT) is constrained by the need to fit around existing

Table 2.6 1996–7 TV Coverage in England		
BBC	Premier League (H); FA Cup (L&H); UEFA Cup (L&H)
ITV	European Champions' League (L&H); Coca-Cola Cup (L&H); Football League (H); Cup Winners' Cup (L&H)
Channel 4	Serie A Italy (L)
Channel 5	England Internationals (L)
Sky Sports	Premier League (L&H); Football League (L&H); FA Cup (L&H); Coca-Cola Cup (L&H); England Internationals (L&H); Spanish League (L&H)
Live TV	Cup Winners' Cup (L)
Eurosport	Cup Winners' Cup (L&H); UEFA Cup (L&H)

L: live; H: highlights

analogue transmission, but even so current plans allow for the launch of around thirty new services. The process of digitalization essentially involves reducing the information contained within the television picture into a format which can be processed by a computer. The advent of digital therefore brings television into the world of computing and telecommunication and enables the development of new additional interactive services alongside the conventional television pictures.

The Internet offers yet another opportunity for broadcasting football. At present, bandwidth and speed of access constraints limit the applicability of the Internet to the transmission of real-time video. A number of clubs already operate websites but these are at present little more than cross-promotional vehicles typically containing various pieces of background information, including facilities to order replica kits and other merchandising. This may change as new technologies such as high-speed cable modem access both speed up transmission and increase the volume of data which can be transferred. In March 1997 Leeds United broadcast live commentary of a match from its Internet site and considered broadcasting live pictures. This latter development was opposed by BSkyB and in the end a compromise deal was arranged which postponed the introduction of such services.

Historically the clubs and the leagues have resisted live broadcasting of football on the basis that it would adversely affect attendances. Thus live matches were not permitted until 1983 and before Sky only eighteen games a season were shown. The clubs now maintain that sixty is the upper limit beyond which attendances would be affected. However, there is no clear evidence that television coverage does on the whole adversely affect attendances. The first Sky contract increased live match coverage fourfold, but at the same time match attendances rose by 11 per cent. Recent studies have found that there was no clear negative effect on attendances when a game was shown on Sky.[25] It might even be argued that the

BSkyB coverage increased attendances by raising football's profile through its marketing campaign. However, shifting a game to a Monday night, as Sky often do, does affect attendances as it is harder for supporters to travel. In general it is not clear at what point increased TV coverage would affect attendances. During the 1990s attendances have grown not only with increased TV coverage but also with rapidly rising ticket prices. It would always be open to clubs to reduce admission prices in order to fill the ground with fans and at the same time generate more revenue from TV rights. As yet, few clubs seem to have a clear idea as to what balance this calculation might imply.

Yet technological advance is reaching a point where this is a calculation that the clubs need to make. Digital technology dramatically increases the number of available channels and therefore the ability to broadcast live football (among other things). The present BSkyB deal allows for the showing of sixty Premier League matches per season, out of a total of 380 matches played. The number of matches shown is constrained, at least in part, by the capacity limitations of existing analogue systems. The development of pay-per-view in the analogue environment is also in part limited by technical difficulties surrounding the implementation of authorization systems. In digital this capacity constraint all but disappears. With a maximum of ten games being played at any given time, it would require only ten channels to show all 380 Premier League games over the season.

The introduction of pay-per-view is likely to have profound implications for the value of live TV rights for football and for the process by which such rights are sold. As with satellite broadcasting, pay-per-view increases the value of rights because it enables broadcasters to extract more revenue from a given match. With new technologies encouraging the clubs to become the broadcasters themselves, pay-per-view will significantly alter the structure of the industry. The effect of digital television can already be seen with the BSkyB bid for

Manchester United. With the increase in broadcasting capacity that accompanies digital television, the largest returns will not go to those who control platforms (e.g. digital satellite) but those who control key content. Football is key content and BSkyB's bid can be seen as, among other things, an attempt to secure that key content. Rupert Murdoch's News Corporation, which owns a significant part of BSkyB, already follows this strategy with ownership of a string of US sports clubs and key television shows (e.g. Fox, a News Corporation Company, produces the X Files). These issues are discussed in more detail in Chapter 7.

Advertising and sponsorship

Advertising and sponsorship are becoming increasingly important sources of revenue for football clubs. Sponsors are attracted both to clubs (e.g. Sharp sponsors Manchester United) and to competitions (e.g. the Nationwide Building Society sponsors the Football League). Sportswear manu-facturers compete and pay clubs in order to provide their strip and thereby access the lucrative replica market. In addition there are the more traditional advertising opportunities offered by perimeter boards, programmes and tickets.

The attraction for commercial companies to associate themselves with football has a long tradition. Match programmes carried advertisements as early as the 1890s. Football's relationship with brewers also has a long history. For example, back in 1904 the construction of Spurs' White Hart Lane ground was greatly assisted by the proprietors of the neighbouring White Hart public house.

Advertisers also found establishing links with individual players useful, and there is a long history of players endorsing products. Immediately after the Second World War Denis Compton became synonymous with Brylcreem, Tom Finney with Shredded Wheat and Billy Wright with Quaker Oats. Rewards were good in comparison to the constraints that the maximum wage put on direct football earnings. For example,

Johnny Haynes of Fulham received £1,500 for three days' photographic work while earning an annual salary of only £1,000 as a footballer.[26]

Sponsorship was long resisted by the football authorities, who viewed such explicit commercialism as demeaning for the game. Offers of money by would-be sponsors became more and more frequent by the 1970s but time and again these were rebuffed.[27] The rules of both the FA and UEFA for many years banned any advertising on shirts. Even when sanctioned by the football authorities sponsorship often fell foul of broadcasting rules, particularly for matches covered by the BBC. The first sponsored English tournament was the Watney Cup, a pre-season event inaugurated in 1971. In 1976 Kettering Town became the first English club to have advertising on their shirts. The FA subsequently demanded the removal of the sponsor's name but a compromise was agreed with the shirts bearing only a single letter from the sponsor's name.

Corporate sponsorship and advertising really began to take off only at the beginning of the 1980s when the clubs found themselves in a severe financial crisis. They were permitted to organize sponsorship deals, and soon the major clubs were receiving a substantial boost to their income from sponsorship. As football's popularity grew from the mid-1980s (with increasing attendance and bigger television audiences), advertising and sponsorship revenues also increased. At club level the value of sponsorship and advertising is often related to success, since advertisers want to be associated with a winning side. In addition there are certain clubs such as Liverpool and Manchester United that have an inherently strong brand image irrespective of recent playing success. These brands have international appeal, as evidenced by Manchester United selling 40,000 copies of its club magazine in Thailand every month. Another example is the HSBC banking group, which has started an account in Mauritius which pays interest dependent on how many points Manchester United or Liverpool earn in a season.[28]

The League Cup was the first major tournament to be sponsored. In 1982 the National Dairy Council paid £500,000 a year to have the trophy named the Milk Cup. The competition is currently known as the Worthington's Cup, after interludes as the Coca-Cola Cup, the Littlewoods Cup and the Rumbelows Cup. The Football League was first sponsored in 1983 by Canon. Canon's sponsorship was seen as a success by the company, as it increased their brand awareness from 18 to 80 per cent over the period of the three-year deal. Table 2.7 shows the value of sponsorship of the top division since 1983. The original Canon deal was worth over £800,000 a season, and since then each new sponsorship contract (except the one with the *Today* newspaper, which was bankrupt at the time) has involved a major increase in value. The sponsorship revenue paid by Carling in the 1997–8 season was over ten times larger than the original deal signed with Canon.

Table 2.7
Premiership
(Division One)
sponsorship
1983–4 to
2000–2001

Sponsor	Date	Total value (£000s)	Annual average (£000s)
Canon	1983–4 to 1985–6	2,524	841
Today	1986–7	800	800
Barclays	1987–8 to 1992–3	10,050	1,675
Carling	1993–4 to 1996–7	12,000	3,000
	1997–8 to 2000–01	36,000	9,000

Source: The Football Trust

During the early 1980s clubs also began to strike individual deals for shirt sponsorship. For example, in 1981 Arsenal agreed to have JVC emblazoned on their shirts for £500,000 over three years.[29] As with other forms of sponsorship, the revenue received has been rising rapidly, especially for the top clubs. In 1987 Liverpool signed a deal with Candy worth £1.5m over three years, almost three times Arsenal's contract six years earlier. Table 2.8 gives the value of known club sponsorship deals in 1997.

Table 2.8 Club
sponsorship
deals in 1997

Club	Sponsor	Estimated value of deal (£000)	Estimated length (years)	Annual value (£000)
Chelsea	Autoglass	6,000	4	1,500
Newcastle	Newcastle Brown Ale	4,000	3	1,333
Liverpool	Carlsberg	1,250	130	1,250
Manchester United	Sharp	5,000	4	1,250
Aston Villa	AST	6,000	5	1,200
Leeds	Packard Bell	4,000	4	1,000
Tottenham	Hewlett-Packard	4,000	4	1,000
Wimbledon	Elonex	3,000	3	1,000
Manchester City	Brother	3,000	3	1,000
Coventry	Subaru	2,000	3	667
Everton	One-to-One	2,000	3	667
Nottingham Forest	Pinnacle Insurance	2,000	3	667
Sheffield United	Ward's Brewery	1,500	4	375
QPR	Ericsson	1,000	3	333
Wolves	Goodyear	1,000	3	333
Norwich	Colmans	250	1	250
West Brom	West Bromwich Building Society	500	3	167
Swindon	Nationwide Building Society	200	2	100
Millwall	Live TV	200	2	100
Watford	CTX Computer Products	250	3	83
Luton	Universal Salvage Auctions	140	2	70
Brentford	Ericsson	200	3	67
Bournemouth	Seward Rover MG	30	1	30

Source: Department for Culture, Media and Sport

In the mid 1990s sponsorship deals have been spreading
to more than just shirts. Middlesbrough and Bolton both play
in sponsored stadiums (Cellnet and Reebok respectively). In
1997 Birmingham City was reported to be considering including a sponsor's name in its title, a step already taken by a
Welsh club. Inter Cable Tel, entrants in the 1997–8 UEFA
Cup, were previously known as Inter Cardiff until they took
the name of their sponsors, a local cable company.

With rapid growth of the sports leisurewear market in the
late 1980s top football clubs found a new important revenue
source. The market for sports leisurewear was estimated to be
worth £3bn a year in 1997,[31] and replica football shirts have
become a major revenue generator in this market. Sportswear
manufacturers such as Nike, Adidas, Umbro and Reebok have
all invested heavily to attach their brand to successful clubs.
In 1996 Reebok agreed to pay Liverpool £6.5m a year to
supply their kit and have the replica rights. In the first year of

this deal Reebok achieved £40m in replica strip sales. Table 2.9 shows the top ten shirt sales in the 1996–7 season. Similar deals have been struck with Nike paying Glasgow Rangers £11m in a four-year deal and Umbro paying Manchester United £42m in a six-year deal.

Table 2.9 Top ten shirt sales 1996–7		
Manchester United	850,000
Liverpool	600,000
Newcastle	600,000
England	500,000
Rangers	500,000
Celtic	350,000
Arsenal	350,000
Tottenham	250,000
Leeds	230,000
Scotland	200,000

The base fee referred to above is not the only way that clubs receive income from these contracts. Kit deals are paid for in four ways: free kit supply for the club, a base fee, royalties on replica shirts sold and bonuses for performance. The split of revenue from a Liverpool Reebok shirt in 1997 is illustrated in Figure 2.12. There are certain termination rights connected with relegation, association with a competing brand, hooliganism and insolvency. This illustrates the importance of both success on the field and good behaviour by the fans to this income source. Indeed Reebok announced in 1997 that they were terminating their deal with Fiorentina in Italy due to fan violence. Sportswear firms do deals with individual players as well, particularly for boot sponsorship, and these contracts also have performance-related elements, which can include 'failure to compete at required level', and 'moral clauses' covering misdemeanours such as drug abuse.

Because of the large sums of money involved sportswear firms are demanding more and more control over the recipients of their investment. For example, in 1997 Nike tried to intervene in the transfer of Ronaldo to Inter Milan. They have also set up their own sporting promotions agency and signed a $200m deal with the Brazilian Football Association. This

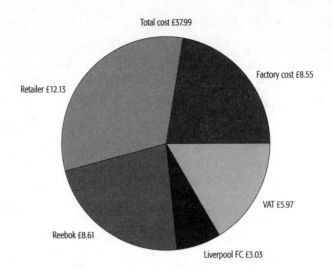

Figure 2.12
Revenue from sale of a Reebok Liverpool shirt 1996–7

Total cost £37.99

Factory cost £8.55

VAT £5.97

Liverpool FC £3.03

Reebok £8.61

Retailer £12.13

gives Nike the right to choose the opposition for and promote five Brazil friendly games around the world each season over the next ten years.

Stock market

Over the last few years there has been a large increase in the number of football companies that are quoted on the Stock Exchange (see Table 2.11, page 75) and much comment in the media on the wealth these flotations created for a few existing shareholders, including well-known club chairmen such as Martin Edwards and Doug Ellis. Whatever the rights and wrongs of individual deals, the issue of shares on the stock market is a legitimate activity of any limited company. However, share issues are just one way in which businesses can raise money.

Football clubs like any other business must secure financing to allow investment (e.g. in stadiums or players) and in some cases fund losses. There are a limited number of ways in which this can be achieved, and these are shown in Table 2.10.

Sponsor	Payback
Bank	Loan and overdrafts given to the club by banks in return for interest payments
Share capital	Shareholders, unlike lenders, participate in the ownership of the business. Shareholders are entitled to vote at the annual general meeting on issues relating to the management of the company and can ultimately fire the existing managers and replace them. Shareholders make a return on their investment either through dividends paid out annually from profits or through the increase in the share price which occurs when the company is seen to be financially successful. Shareholders take greater risks than lenders and therefore expect greater returns
Loans	Loans from non-bank sources, such as directors, which are paid for with interest
Supporters' debenture schemes	These are peculiar to sport. These schemes, in which a supporter will pay for the right to buy tickets in the future, were popular in the early 1990s when significant ground rebuilding was under way
Retained profits	Profits made by the club and not paid out in dividends to its shareholders

Table 2.10 Football clubs' financing options

Floating on the Stock Exchange can involve issuing new shares in the club and/or the sale of existing shares. If new shares are issued, then the proceeds from the sales go to the club for investment purposes and existing shareholders do not receive any money. If existing shares are sold, then the proceeds will go directly to the shareholders who are selling and no money will go to the club. Typically flotations involve both kinds of selling.

Share prices can fluctuate significantly. For most businesses the share price is influenced by news concerning the company's own activities, the prospects for the industry in general and the health of the wider economy. Football clubs' share prices are also influenced by events on the pitch. This is illustrated by Figure 2.13 depicting Manchester United's share price over the 1994–5 season. It shows that events such as Eric Cantona's attack on a Crystal Palace fan have a significant effect on the share price.

Often there are reports of millions of pounds being wiped off a club's value as a result of share price movements. However, the effect of share price movements on the clubs is limited. As shares represent the right to receive future divi-dends, the share price of a club reflects how profitable the market thinks that club will be in the future. Since the money a club receives from issuing shares is paid on issue, the subse-quent movement of share prices has no financial effect on a club. Generally the change in value of the club is only relevant

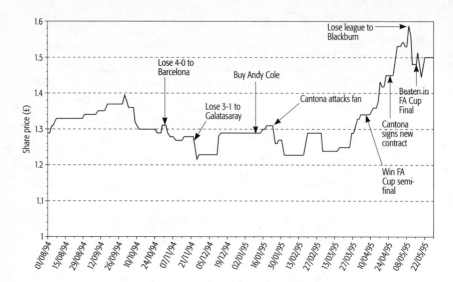

Figure 2.13
Manchester
United Share
Price 1994–5:
Event Study

to shareholders if they sell their shares. However, a falling share price indicates that investors see the future becoming less profitable. If the share price of a club collapses this usually indicates that the current management (both football and financial) is not deemed to be working effectively and this could lead to the removal of the management at the shareholders' request. It might also make it difficult for the club to issue shares again should it wish to raise money in the future.

Thus the flotation of a football club can impose a new discipline on it. In the past clubs were usually owned or controlled by successful businessmen, or by the fans themselves. These owners were more interested in winning competitions and trophies than in financial gains. When the owners of football clubs decided to raise money by selling shares to financial institutions, they were consciously transferring ownership to people primarily interested in financial performance rather than performance on the pitch. This suggests that Manchester United fans should have been at least as concerned when the club was floated as they are now at BSkyB's bid for the club.

Flotation also means that the club is in effect always up for sale. Any interested company can buy shares at any time on the Stock Exchange. The eventual owner of the club will be the organization who values it most highly. Thus if companies in related industries (e.g. broadcasting, media, sportswear) believe that a particular club will give its business more value than the current share price they will buy it. This is exactly what has happened with BSkyB's bid for Manchester United.

Table 2.11 lists the clubs that are currently floated on the Stock Exchange, the date they floated and their June 1998 market capitalization (which is the number of shares multiplied by the share price and is a measure of the size and importance of the company). Since flotation football shares have not been particularly successful and the reasons for this are discussed more fully in Chapter 8.

Table 2.11 English football clubs floated on the Stock Exchange 1998

Club	Float date	Market capitalization June 1998
Tottenham	October 1983	66.9
Millwall	October 1989	4.7
Manchester United	June 1991	411.7
Preston North End	October 1995	8.6
Chelsea	March 1996	13.1
Leeds Sporting	August 1996	47.6
Loftus Road (QPR)	October 1996	7.2
Sunderland	December 1996	31.8
Sheffield United	January 1997	13.7
Southampton	January 1997	18.6
West Brom	January 1997	9.1
Birmingham	March 1997	18.5
Charlton	March 1997	68.2
Burnden Leisure (Bolton)	April 1997	19.7
Leicester	April 1997	10.0
Newcastle	April 1997	106.7
Aston Villa	May 1997	55.5
Nottingham Forest	October 1997	23.2

The table shows that the sector is dominated by a few clubs and in particular Manchester United. Manchester United makes up over 40 per cent of the market capitalization and when you add the other two biggest clubs, Newcastle and Chelsea, together they make up over 60 per cent of market capitalization. This indicates that the market believes only a small number of clubs can make significant profits.

Other revenue sources
Pools and the Football Trust

The Pools was founded in 1923 by Littlewoods of Liverpool, soon to be followed by Vernons in 1929. They used football fixtures as a basis for their lotteries, entrants receiving a certain number of points for each result predicted correctly with a score draw receiving the highest amount. At its peak in 1950 Pools companies employed over 100,000 people and were ranked among the top ten industries in the UK. It was not until 1959 that the League established copyright over the fixtures and thus accessed a share in the Pools companies' profits. In 1960 the Football League received £170,000, which increased to £3m in 1981 plus £1m for Scottish football.[32]

The Football Trust was set up in 1979 and was originally funded by Littlewoods, Vernons and Zetters. They agreed to fund the Trust with 7.5 per cent of takings of their spot-the-ball competitions in a deal with the government which helped them avoid tax liabilities. The Trust invested around £100m during the 1980s in the improvement of grounds, schemes to suppress hooliganism and community football schemes. The Trust has also promoted research and disseminated data on football, but most of its money has gone into subsidizing activities associated with the larger clubs. In order to facilitate the prompt implementation of the Taylor Report the government agreed in 1990 to contribute £20m per year to the Trust and secured the agreement of the Pools companies to supply a further £12m per year. The money is allocated by the Trust for the improvement of facilities at football grounds, and by 1996 it had awarded £185m in grants, £132m of this going on measures directly associated with fulfilling the recommendations of the Taylor Report, this representing 28 per cent of the cost of the improvement schemes funded. Given a total estimated cost of implementing the Taylor Report of £600m, this has clearly been a substantial benefit for the clubs.

Supporters' clubs

In the past supporters' clubs were important contributors of revenue. For example, in 1960–61 Coventry supporters donated about £4,000, 7 per cent of the club's income in that year. In 1964–5 approximately £1.5m was donated by supporters' clubs and development associations, which amounted to 17 per cent of league clubs' turnover.[33] At that time the majority of fund-raising came from bar receipts from supporters' clubs. The 1975 Lotteries Act made it legal for clubs or supporters' clubs to run lotteries for the benefit of clubs. However, this was successful for only three or four years after the legislation was introduced, adding perhaps £50,000– £100,000 to clubs' income.[34]

Revenue maximizers?

Although there has always been an undercurrent of tension between the football clubs and their supporters, accusations that clubs are exploiting their fans, treating them only as cash cows for a cash-hungry business, have grown more strident in recent years. Indeed, this chapter has shown how the response of clubs to any problem has typically been to raise prices. None the less, any rational evaluation of football clubs must conclude that they have in the past devoted remarkably little effort to finding and exploiting all the potential income sources. Throughout most of the twentieth century football clubs scarcely advanced beyond the commercial practices of the 1890s.

Time and again it was developments elsewhere rather than internally driven initiatives that led clubs to find new ways of generating income. Football clubs and the football authorities did very little to seek out new sources of revenue – whether it be the Pools companies, television or sportswear – often resisting their development and always slow to recognize the potential benefit to football itself.

Like Mr Micawber, the clubs perpetually waited for something to turn up, while their businesses, beset with problems, struggled to survive. Miraculously, at the very moment when terminal collapse seemed imminent, not one, but three things happened. Firstly, the popularity of the game revived; secondly, changes in broadcast technology dramatically enhanced the value of television rights; and thirdly, the Taylor Report obliged the clubs to do what had long been necessary and even found a way for the government to subsidize over one-quarter of the cost. Blessed with this trinity of good fortune, the clubs started to take matters into their own hands. Most now have at least one marketing manager, charged with seeking out new sources of income. More than one club is planning to launch its own TV station and Manchester United has already created with BSkyB and Granada a cable channel (MUTV). Everywhere clubs are opening shops, developing brands and looking for new product lines to sell to the fans.

Several consequences follow from these changes. As football clubs look to expand their earning potential, the traditional mainstay, gate receipts, is becoming less and less important. Despite ever-rising prices big clubs now generate only about half their income in this way. However, this does not mean that attendances are not important any more. While clubs can earn revenue from many sources, the sources are closely interlinked. A decrease in popularity, possibly associated with poor form, will impact on all revenue sources of the club; a drop in attendances will likely cause a fall in merchandising, catering and eventually sponsorship revenue. A significant crowd also adds to the television experience and thus a poorly supported club will not be likely to feature on television regularly. These linkages are likely to make the income of clubs more volatile than in the past. Already we have seen that the gap between big clubs and small clubs has grown over the years. However, even when in the lower reaches of the Second Division, clubs such as Chelsea, Newcastle and Birmingham have remained big clubs because of their traditional support base. Nowadays developing technology enables fans, if they wish, to be more fickle, to change more rapidly between clubs than would have been feasible even twenty years ago, and the danger that a run of bad luck might cause a big club to turn into a small club is a greater threat today than it ever has been.

If clubs were once indifferent to maximizing income, many would argue that they have swung too far the other way. Abandoning Victorian business practices, they appear to have adopted marketing tactics usually associated with the worst kind of business-school strategy consultants. Many fans pine for the old-style management. But should the clubs maximize revenue? Partly this depends on how they spend the money. To the extent that income is required to survive in the competitive struggle of the League or to succeed in other competitions, then most fans agree that it is a price worth paying. However, if revenue maximizing is simply a means to maximize profits, the fans feel exploited and cheated. This reaction is probably true of the buyers of any product or service, but by virtue of its status as the 'National Game' the commercial exploitation of football creates an even greater public outcry. Even if it were to be accepted, it remains an open question as to whether blatant commercialism can succeed.

3 How football clubs spend their money

Everyone knows two things about the business of football: players are paid astronomical wages and clubs spend vast sums on transfer fees. But in fact, most players do not earn particularly high wages and net transfer spending (that is transfer expenditure in a given year less transfer income) is relatively small for most clubs and for the football leagues taken as a whole. The data in Table 3.1, taken from company accounts, is based on the reported wage expenditure and employment figures of football clubs in the 1996–7 season. Individual club data can be found in the appendix to this chapter, on page 121.

The average Premier League club in that season employed about 170 people and paid out about £11m in wages, salaries and employment-related benefits such as pension contributions. Thus clubs paid an average salary of £64,000 per year. As can be seen from Table 3.1, which divides the Premier League in two halves based on league position in that season, the less successful clubs employed slightly fewer people and paid slightly lower average salaries. Of course, not every employee is a footballer. The accounting data includes everyone on the payroll, from directors down to the car park attendants. Data on the salaries of footballers individually is not available, but a reasonable estimate of a first-team player's salary can be made if we assume that the first-team squad consisted of around forty players and the remaining staff were paid a salary in line with the national average. On this basis the average Premier League first-team player was paid just over £200,000 in 1996–7, with slightly more being paid to players in the top half of the division. In the Football League,

Table 3.1
Football
club wage
expenditure
1996–7

Division	Wage expenditure (£000)	Employees	Average wage (£)	Estimated first-team salary (£)[1]
Premier League (top half)	129,851	1,900	68,343	250,000
Premier League (bottom half)	77,045	1,375	56,033	158,000
First Division	75,321	2,178	34,583	73,000
Second Division	32,360	1,472	21,984	26,000
Third Division	8,884	512	17,352	17,352

Source: Deloitte & Touche, Annual Survey of Football Club Accounts

however, salaries do not appear nearly so generous. On the same basis we can estimate that first-team players in the First Division earned around £73,000 per year, a very high salary by most people's standards. But in the Second Division such players received around £26,000, in line with the national average, while Third Division players were paid around £17,000, about 20 per cent less than the national average.

Wage expenditure is by far the largest single expense for most football clubs. As can be seen from Table 3.2, in all but the top half of the Premier League wages consumed more than 50 per cent of income, and in the lower divisions they account for over three-quarters of all income. In fact, these figures underestimate the significance of wages for the top clubs because they include Manchester United, whose wage bill accounted for only 26 per cent of the club's income in 1996–7. When it is excluded from the first row of Table 3.2, the top clubs also spend on average over 50 per cent of their revenues on wages.

Table 3.2 Wage
bill and transfer
expenditure
1996–7

Division	Wage expenditure as a % of revenue	Net transfer fees as a % of revenue	Number of clubs for whom transfer expenditure exceeded the wage bill	Number of clubs for whom transfer expenditure was more than 50% of the wage bill
Premier League (top half)	48	11	0	4
Premier League (bottom half)	59	32	3	7
First Division	76	1	0	2
Second Division	75	–13	0	1
Third Division	89	–5	1	0

Source: Company accounts (note that a negative figure for net transfers as a percentage of revenue means that clubs were on average net recipients of transfer income)

Wages and Transfers in the Football Industry / 81

Transfer fees are less important than wages in the accounts of football clubs, even if from year to year individual expenditures may be quite large. Looked at for a single year, the Premier League spent 17 per cent of its income on transfers, much less than its wage spending, while Football League clubs spent even less than this. This is of course slightly misleading since averaging causes large net expenditures and receipts to cancel each other out. Teams in the bottom half of the Premier League seemed to devote a much greater proportion of their income to transfers, possibly trying to spend their way out of trouble. However, looking at all the divisions, it can be seen from the last two columns of Table 3.2 that in only four cases in 1996–7 did transfers exceed wage expenditure, while in only fourteen cases were transfers even half the size of wage expenditure.

Are football wages too high?

According to a report commissioned by the Football League in 1982, this is a question to which 'there can be no logical answer'.[2] Logical or not, it is a question upon which many have an opinion. The problem with such opinions is that they are usually based on mutually inconsistent concepts of value or worth. Many people suppose that there exists a fair or just wage, reflecting a 'reasonable' return for the effort and skill provided. Such notions have been held since at least medieval times and are encapsulated in the Victorian saying 'a fair day's pay for a fair day's work'. But who is to decide what is fair? The economists Adam Smith and Karl Marx both thought that value could be measured in terms of the labour input required in the process of production. Smith argued that wages would vary according to the skill, effort, hardship or risks associated with work, while Marx based his critique of capitalism on the notion that profits represented the expropriation of part of the just reward of the labourer. The labour theory of value, however, foundered on the inherent differences in the labour supplied by different individuals, so that by the late nineteenth century economists began to adopt a notion of value which reflected the scarcity of goods or services in question. This explanation of differences in value resolved the old paradox that water is useful (valuable) but has a low price, while diamonds are much less useful but have a much higher price. To an economist prices in the market-place reflect scarcity. Water (in England at least) is not usually scarce, but would have a very high price if it were. Diamonds command a high price because they are scarce. If diamonds were cheap, the demand would far exceed the available supply; their high price brings supply and demand into balance. Because it is plentiful (even more plentiful than the uses to which it can be put) water commands a low price in the market – and of course, where it is not plentiful, such as in an Arabian desert, water in fact trades at very high prices. In any market, the price mechanism (which Adam Smith called the Invisible Hand) brings supply and demand into balance. By the same token, the price (or wage) of a footballer would be expected to reflect the scarcity of the skills he provides.

Whatever view one takes of the proper wage of foot-ballers, it is hard to imagine that any player outside the Premier League or the top of the First Division is getting rich from his profession. In professional football careers are relatively short, averaging around five years, with even the best players seldom lasting more than ten. At the end of it, unless he is a superstar, the player has relatively narrow career options and limited qualifications.

Of course, a small number of individuals do earn very large salaries. One study[3] in 1998 reported that David Beckham was the highest paid British footballer, making £8.1m in a year. Only £1.35m (one-sixth of his income) came from his Manchester United salary, the rest coming from endorsements. Still, even his club salary amounted to around £26,000 per week. The same report rated Beckham only ninth in the world league of football earners, with Ronaldo of Brazil and Internazionale ranked first with an estimated income of

£20.5m per year (£390,000 a week). Other top Premier League players are said to be paid similar amounts by their clubs. Alan Shearer is reputed to earn £30,000 a week[4] and Jürgen Klinsmann, hired by Tottenham in January 1998 on a five-month contract to save the club from relegation, was said to be paid £40,000 a week.[5] When Paul Gascoigne moved to Middlesbrough it was reported that he would earn £1.5m a year over three years, equivalent to £29,000 a week.[6] While these sums are themselves enormous, rumours concerning wage demands have been even more extravagant. Robbie Fowler was said to be asking for £50,000 a week to stay at Liverpool,[7] while Chelsea refused to renew Ruud Gullit's contract as player-manager because they claimed he was demanding £3.5m a year.[8]

The growth in player salaries in recent years has been extraordinary. Only ten years ago the combined wages of David Beckham and Paul Gascoigne would have been enough to pay the salaries of any First Division club (including non-playing staff) apart from Tottenham, Manchester United and Everton. Even Tottenham, with the biggest wage bill of the time, paid only £5m in wages. The championship winners of that year, Arsenal, had a wage bill of a mere £2.3m, scarcely enough to satisfy a top striker nowadays. But is it that football players are paid too much now, or were they underpaid in the past? Before jumping to conclusions, it is worth considering what other top earners make on average.

Table 3.3 provides a comparison of salaries in different occupations. Mostly the figures relate to pre-tax salaries from direct employment and do not include income from secondary sources.[9] The annual salaries of football's élite, the twenty or so top players in the Premiership, are nowadays in excess of £1m per year, or £20,000 per week before tax. But this does not put them close to the highest paid earners in sports and entertainment. The top personalities in boxing and basketball, film and popular music all earn about ten times this amount. Most of these salaries are generated in the US, but sports with

Profession/Name	Estimated weekly earnings/income	Year
Table 3.3 Salary league table		
Boxing (Mike Tyson)	£875,000	1996[10]
Ronaldo	**£390,000**	**1998**[11]
Film star (Sylvester Stallone)	£385,000	1996[12]
Basketball (Michael Jordan)	£385,000	1996[13]
Motor Racing (Michael Schumacher)	£320,000	1996[14]
David Beckham (all earnings)	**£156,000**	**1998**
Rock star (Noel Gallagher)	£146,000	1995[15]
Baseball (Albert Belle)	£48,000	1996[16]
Alan Shearer (basic salary)	**£30,000**	**1996**[17]
Paul Gascoigne (basic salary)	**£28,846**	**1998**
David Beckham (basic salary)	**£26,000**	**1998**
American Football NFL commissioner	£19,230	1996[18]
Average major league baseball player	£15,385	1996[19]
Chairman of British Telecom	£13,530	1996[20]
Premier League (top half) squad member	**£4,800**	**1997**
Governor of the Bank of England	£4,365	1998[21]
Bruce Grobellaar	**£3,058**	**1994**[22]
Premier League (bottom half) squad member	**£3,050**	**1997**
John Fashanu	**£3,000**	**1994**[23]
City head of capital markets	£2,788	1995[24]
Managing director (large company)	£2,692	1996[25]
England manager	**£2,400**	**1995**
University vice-chancellor	£2,263	1995[26]
Prime Minister	£2,038	1997[27]
High Court judge	£1,885	1996[28]
Cabinet minister	£1,689	1996[29]
Hans Segers	**£1,673**	**1994**
Managing director (medium company)	£1,587	1996[30]
Premier League manager	**£1,400+**	**1995**[31]
First Division squad member	**£1,400**	**1997**
NHS chief executive	£1,077	1995
Managing director (small company)	£1,000	1996[32]
Doctor (GP)	£827	1996[33]
Barrister	£769	1996[34]
Head teacher	£731	1996[35]
NHS dentist	£711	1996[36]
Backbench MP	£655	1996[37]
University professor	£652	1997[38]
Second Division squad member	**£500**	**1997**
Average UK earnings	£411	1996[39]
Third Division squad member	**£334**	**1997**
Average full-time male manual worker	£300	1995[40]
Average UK pensioner	£161	1996[41]
Forty-hour working week at the minimum wage	£144	1998

a popular international following, such as Formula One motor racing, also generate incomes for the top performers which are much greater than those in English football. High sports salaries in the US include not just the top performers.

The *average* salary in US baseball exceeds $1m per year. In fact, in any comparison for similar jobs a US salary will typically be higher than a UK salary, and this relationship tends to be exaggerated at the top of the income ladder.

If we confine our attention to the UK alone, the wages of top footballers are certainly at the top of the rankings. In general the only British citizens who earn more than star players either work overseas or generate a substantial part of their income from products sold abroad. Those who come closest to these salary levels are the chairmen of major corporations such as British Telecom, and indeed if the value of share options they hold is included their income may be even higher. In addition there may be some individuals at the top of their professions, leading barristers, partners of accounting and consultancy firms or surgeons, who have large incomes which are not publicly disclosed.

But if the top twenty players are in the UK salary élite, the remainder are not so spectacularly paid. The salaries of two Premiership goalkeepers were revealed in a recent court trial. Bruce Grobellaar of Liverpool, probably among the highest paid goalkeepers in his time, earned £160,000 in 1994, while Hans Segers from Wimbledon, probably one of the worst paid goalkeepers in the Premier League, earned £87,000 in the same year. These are still high salaries, which are comparable with those of top professionals in the City or a High Court judge – and the England football manager. These top-earning players would be able to increase their income through sponsorship and endorsement deals, and they might also be able to make a career after retirement on the back of their football celebrity. However, few are as successful as John Fashanu, who developed business interests as a footballer and then became the host of a popular TV show.

The Premier League players are at the top of their profession; they are the select band capable of performing at the highest level out of the hundreds of thousands who play football in the UK. Below that, First Division players still do relatively well. The estimated first-team salary of £73,000 a year is £1,400 a week, equivalent to the earnings of a director of a small- to medium-sized company. However, once we reach the Second and Third Divisions salaries do not compare well with the professions, and players are paid little better than manual labourers. Thus the average Second Division salary of £500 per week is a little less than an NHS dentist earns and less than an average GP, barrister or head teacher. Not that anyone could argue that this is a poor return for playing a game which most players enjoy. Five hundred pounds a week is 22 per cent above the national average – scarcely enough to build up a significant nest egg for the long retirement period. There is then a big fall when we reach the Third Division, where salaries are not only below the national average but even less than the average full-time male manual earnings. Of course, playing football for a living is probably more enjoyable than working in a factory – but not because of the money.

From the maximum wage to £30,000 a week

Whether or not they are paid too much, one thing which is certain is that footballers are far better paid now than they ever have been. The origins of remuneration for playing football are furtive. The founders of the game never intended that it should become professional and the early footballers played solely for the love of the game. However, as soon as competition became important and successful teams began to attract paying spectators, the demand for winning led clubs to examine new ways of obtaining the services of the best players. Initially this took the form of inducements other than wages: playing expenses could be lavish, wages forgone from lost work time could be paid, and frequently a good player could be found a comfortable, well-paid job locally (just as in the twentieth century 'amateur' footballers in Communist countries were nominally workers in state industrial enterprises). The term 'shamateurism' was coined in 1896 to refer precisely to those individuals who claimed to be amateurs but in one form or another were paid for playing the game. When the FA Cup was started in 1871 virtually all players were still genuinely amateur. This is reflected in the identities of the Cup winners over the first few decades of the competition: The Wanderers, Oxford University, The Royal Engineers, and Old Etonians. However, professionals are recorded from 1876 onwards, and by the early 1880s professionalism was widespread.[42] This led the FA to pass a rule in 1882 allowing it to expel any club which paid a player more than expenses and the value of wages lost. Accrington was expelled in 1883 for paying a player and in 1884 Preston North End, one of the biggest clubs of the time, was accused of having paid its players. Preston's manager, Major William Suddell, admitted the charge claiming self-defence, since his main rivals Blackburn Rovers also paid their players. It was obvious to informed observers that the FA would be guilty of hypocrisy if it expelled Preston for doing something openly which most others were known to be doing secretly. The possibility arose that a breakaway professional league, beyond the control of the FA, might be formed. Amateurism had become unsustainable and in July 1885 the FA resolved to permit professionals, albeit under strict controls.[43]

In the early days, before the foundation of the Football League in 1888, a top footballer might earn between 30 shillings and £2 per week at a time when the weekly wage of an engineer, a skilled manual trade from which group most professional players were drawn, would have been around 30 shillings (£1.50 for a fifty-hour-plus week). The early professional was attracted as much by the short hours and pleasant working environment as by the money. With the advent of the Football League and the continuing rapid growth of interest in football, wages were bid to a range of £3–4 for the best players and £2–3 for the rest by 1893, and by the end of the century a top player could command as much as £6–7, at a time when skilled manual wages averaged around 35 shillings (£1.75) per week. However, at its foundation the League stated as one of its objects to obtain agreement on a maximum wage, and this was finally achieved in 1900 when the FA and the League agreed a maximum wage of £4 per week. This was still undoubtedly a decent wage for a working man at the time. As William Bassett, a professional player for West Bromwich Albion between 1886 and 1899, put it in 1905, 'Professional football players are a handsomely remunerated set of men.' Bassett himself later became a director and then chairman of West Bromwich Albion.

The maximum wage was justified by club directors on the grounds that continuing competition for players would ruin the clubs financially. As one commentator observed, 'Competition has been the ruin of many a business house.'[44] However, soon after the imposition of the rule the bigger clubs began to regret their decision and to campaign for repeal. At the same time numerous cases of infringement were uncovered and the FA handed out hefty fines to the offending clubs. A debate on the merits of free trade versus regulation ensued. Free traders argued that the competitive mechanism must decide: 'What must inevitably determine players' wages – all wages in fact – is the law of supply and demand.'[45] By contrast, those in favour of regulation emphasized that only in this way would football thrive: 'One does not altogether like the business or commercial atmosphere that surrounds football, but it is there, and if football has to be governed as a business, a maximum wage becomes a necessity.'[46] This debate mirrored a wider national debate on the merits of free trade versus protectionism, led by the Conservative politician Joseph Chamberlain. As Colonial Secretary he argued that Britain should retreat from its traditional policy of free trade and move towards a system of 'Empire Preference' favouring trade with India, Australia, Canada and other dominions. Chamberlain pointed to the threat of competition from newly emerging economies such as Germany, and argued that protection was necessary to preserve businesses at home. The debate reached its peak in the 1906 general election, in which Chamberlain's Conservatives were resoundingly defeated. By contrast, the FA, the League and the large clubs settled their differences and all agreed to abide by the maximum wage rule in 1909. This cosy consensus among the governing authorities outraged many of the players, who continued the campaign for free trade, and in 1907 the Players' Union was created. By 1908 it had 1,300 members and began to challenge the authority of the clubs, and even to consider organizing its own matches. The FA ordered all professionals to resign from the union in 1909 following threats of a strike. This was also a period of growing industrial unrest throughout the country as the trade union movement pushed for shorter working hours and minimum wages. Footballers found themselves involved in a general debate about how industrial relations should be structured and on the relationship between employer and employees. In general professional footballers, as individualists endowed with rare skills, have tended to eschew collectivist or egalitarian solutions to their industrial relations problems. However, in many cases this has also tended to weaken their bargaining power, enabling the clubs to pursue a 'divide-and-rule' policy. In 1910 an agreement was reached in which the Players' Union was recognized but it agreed to withdraw from the umbrella organization of the wider trade union movement, the Trade Union Congress. The union had little success over the next fifty years in confronting the massed authority of the football hierarchy and the maximum wage.

Football was suspended from 1915 to 1919 as a result of the Great War. The inflation which accompanied the war led to an increase in the maximum wage in 1920 to £9, a disappointment to many members, who then left the union and so encouraged the League to reduce the maximum in 1922 to £8, at a time when retail prices in general were falling. As Figure 3.1 shows, by 1920 the maximum wage had done no more than keep up with inflation. Individual players could earn more than the maximum wage: there were allowances for long service, and bonuses for league and cup success. However, few players could expect to earn substantially more than the maximum, and many were paid less. Between the wars there were few changes in the way players were paid, and the maximum wage was not altered. Clubs took a paternalistic attitude to the welfare of players, arranging housing and other important transactions on their behalf in exchange for continued deference. Babe Ruth, the celebrated American baseball player, visited England in 1930. In Liverpool he met Dixie Dean, who had scored sixty goals in the 1928 season, matching Ruth's sixty home runs in the same year. Ruth was amazed to learn that Dean was earning a mere £8 a week, at a time when he himself was earning the equivalent of around £300 per week.[47] Not surprisingly, football club directors preferred to compare footballers' wages with the earnings of skilled manual labourers in England. During this period average weekly earnings for those fortunate enough to have a job were £3 for a forty-six-hour week in manufacturing. No doubt the Depression was a major factor which kept the - maximum wage unchanged until the Second World War.

Figure 3.1
Salaries in the
English Football
League 1901–96

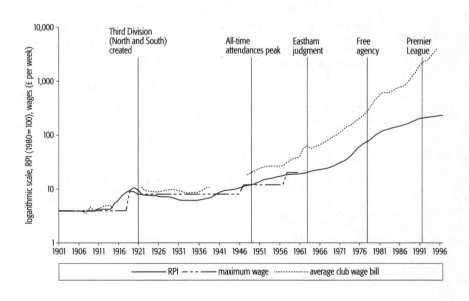

Falling prices enhanced the real value of player wages while high unemployment emphasized the comforts of professional football. During the Second World War football was organized on a regional basis and players, mostly conscripted to the army, were paid only expenses. Normal football resumed in 1945 and immediately there was a dispute between the Players' Union and the Football League, which was settled after a £9 maximum was agreed together with the introduction of bonuses: £2 for a win and £1 for a draw. The union demand for a minimum of £5 per week was rejected out of hand. In 1947, after arbitration by the Ministry of Labour, a £12 maximum and a £7 minimum (£10 and £5 during the summer) were agreed.

Many players were becoming increasingly dissatisfied with restrictions on their earning potential at a time when league football attendance was at an all-time peak and the clubs were making healthy profits. An interesting manifestion of this discontent is provided by the 'Bogotá affair'.[48] In 1950 seven British players, all representing top clubs and some recognized internationals, broke their contracts and went to play league football in Colombia. The players were paid well in excess of what they could earn in England. For example, Charlie Mitten claimed to have earned £3,500 in one year playing for Santa Fe, as opposed to the £700 or so he could earn at Manchester United. Clearly this was an extreme case. The non-democratic Colombian government was apparently using football as a means to suppress social discontent and thus was prepared to pay a premium to find the best players (the legendary Real Madrid player Alfredo di Stefano also moved to Colombia at the time). None the less, Colombia was not a rich country, and their ability to pay five times what an English club paid suggests that players had some legitimate grievances. Unable to adapt to the lifestyle abroad, in the end the players all returned to the UK, and were disciplined by the FA and Football League for breaking their contracts.

By 1952 the maximum wage had been raised to £15 per

week in the playing season and £12 in the summer, although in the mid-1950s the average professional player earned only £8 per week, compared to an average industrial wage of £10 per week. As can be seen from Figure 3.1, wages were achieving little more than keeping up with inflation at a time when football club finances remained healthy and the general standard of living was beginning to rise.

This not only caused discontent among the footballers, but also led clubs to try to find ways around the system in order to hold on to players. From Figure 3.1 it is clear that club wage bills were growing faster than inflation during the 1940s and 1950s. Sunderland was fined £5,000 in the late 1950s for making illicit payments, something it achieved by buying straw at inflated prices from a 'contractor', who then channelled the profit to the players.[49] Examples of this kind of evasion of the rules had been common since their creation. From the introduction of the maximum wage clubs broke the rules, to the extent that an amnesty had to be declared in 1908 in order to prevent the whole system breaking down. One ruse apparently used by Liverpool at the time was to employ their captain to check all the club's posters, a job with a salary. In 1919 Leeds City were expelled from the League for excessive payments to players, the club was closed down and all the footballers sold at auction.

The control of the wage system also led the Football League to impose restrictions on every aspect of players' remuneration. Thus in 1901 the League had actually attempted to outlaw win bonuses,[50] although these were subsequently sanctioned. The League specifed all forms of supplementary payments which could be legitimately made, including loyalty bonuses, appearance money, competition bonuses and so on. A government report on industrial relations in 1974 identified eighteen different kinds of bonus from a sample of just eight clubs. In addition to bonuses clubs were allowed to make payments for housing loans, displacement fees and so on. Thus even if a club did not want to evade the regulations (and many did) it is not difficult to imagine that it might by accident fall foul of this complex system of permitted and illicit payments.

The boom in football immediately following the Second World War started to create pressure for change. Postwar entrance prices were raised to two shillings while attendances reached an all-time high. From the 1950s onward the strength of the Players' Union started to grow. In 1958 it was renamed the Professional Footballers' Association and in 1960 the PFA, led by Cliff Lloyd and Jimmy Hill, then a player and later to become a TV pundit, ran a shrewd campaign which culminated in the threat of a strike if the maximum wage was not abolished. The Football League acquiesced in January 1961. Their decision was no doubt influenced by the changing legal climate, particularly the Restrictive Trade Practices Act of 1956, which forced companies to register agreements to restrict prices on the sale of goods, with a view to discouraging such practices. While applicable only to the sale of goods, the legislation suggested that the climate of opinion did not favour the restriction of open competition between businesses.

At last players started to achieve levels of wages which more accurately reflected their value to the clubs, leading administrators to criticize the players for their greed. Alan Hardaker, long-standing secretary of the Football League, commented in his autobiography, 'The agreement the players won has allowed them to take more out of the game than it has to give.' Hardaker also said that the clubs attempted to reach a 'gentleman's agreement' to keep wages down and not to exceed £50 per week. This agreement, if it existed, broke down immediately. Players' ability to obtain higher wages was aided by the end of the retain-and-transfer system (discussed in more detail below) which gave a club the right to prevent a player's transfer once he was registered with that club, and by the introduction of free agency. The retain-and-transfer system was successfully challenged in the courts in 1963, and free agency was agreed by the clubs in 1978. A free market in players had been established. Salaries rose quickly, particularly at the top end of the Football League. Between 1960 and 1964 average earnings for all players rose by 54 per cent and in the First Division by 61 per cent.

Rising wages coincided with, and were to a degree concealed by, the rapid acceleration of inflation in the 1960s and 1970s. However, the advent of free agency in 1978 led to a wage explosion in the late 1970s and early 1980s. Between 1977 and 1983 wage expenditure by clubs trebled in the First, Third and Fourth Divisions, while it more than doubled in the Second. This led to yet another report commissioned by the Football League into club financing, reflecting the perceived crisis in club profitablity. Free agency also brought about another major change: the advent of football agents. Traditionally the salary of a footballer was decided by the manager, who dealt with the player face to face. Such meetings could scarcely be called negotiations since the club controlled the right of the player to play professional football through the retain-and-transfer system, and most young footballers were so eager to become professionals that they accepted any offer made. With the lifting of the maximum wage discussions became more involved, at least for established players. The government report on industrial relations in football produced in 1974 stated that nearly 70 per cent of players whose contract came up for renewal said they did not always accept the club's first offer. In this detailed report no mention was made of agents acting on behalf of players, but by the early 1980s most top footballers were using them.[51] The most famous agent of current times, Eric Hall, began as a music business agent and reputedly has little interest in or knowledge of football itself. Interestingly, league rules forbid the clubs themselves to hire agents, although it is said that many do.[52]

Figure 3.2 illustrates the wage expenditure by clubs from the four divisions over the period 1978–97. It shows both the continuing overall rise of wages and their growing inequality. Since the advent of free agency the annual average increase of club wage expenditure has been 16.9 per cent, while over the same period general price inflation was only 6.2 per cent per year and average UK earnings rose by little more. Meanwhile, the gap between the wage bill of clubs expanded dramatically, as shown in Table 3.4. Even in the era of the maximum wage big clubs were able to pay more by having larger squads as well as having a greater proportion of the squad paid the maximum. But in 1956 the total wage bill of clubs varied remarkably little: the average First Division bill being only just over double that of a Third Division North club (then the lowest spending division).

The abolition of the maximum wage led to an initial widening of the gap, which continued to grow in the 1970s, so that by 1978 (when players achieved 'free agency' status) a First Division club spent on average nearly four times as much

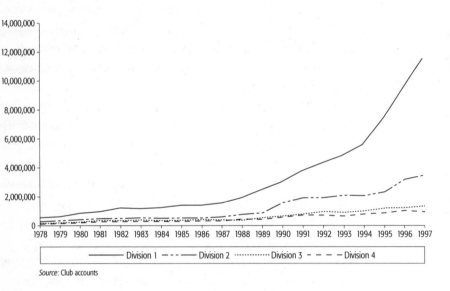

Source: Club accounts

Table 3.4
Average club
wage bill as
multiple of the
Fourth Division
wage bill

	1st Division	2nd Division	3rd Division
1956	2.16	1.47	1.35*
1965	2.42	1.83	1.44
1978	3.95	1.91	1.24
1997	12.26	4.24	1.88

*Third Division South divided by Third Division North
Sources: 1956 and 1965, PEP; 1978 and 1997, club accounts

Winners and Losers / 96

on player wages as a Fourth Division club. By 1995 this had risen to over ten times. The gap between each division has widened over the entire period, so that the gap between a First Division club and one in the Second has grown, as has that between a Second Division club and one in the Fourth.

Free agency increased the mobility of players and therefore helped to increase the competition for players among clubs. Since the advent of free agency three distinct periods of wage growth can be identified. First came the rapid acceleration immediately after free agency, coinciding with the 1979 general election win of the Conservative Party under Margaret Thatcher. Prior to 1979 governments had attempted through incomes policies to restrain inflation and preserve employment by holding down wage growth. The Thatcher government argued that it was no business of the government to interfere with the operation of the labour market: it was up to firms to negotiate wages they could afford with their employees, and if wages were set too high, then firms and employees would face the ultimate sanction of bankruptcy and unemployment. Following several years of restraint, this free market policy led to an explosion of inflation and wage rises. As the government set about controlling inflation through higher interest rates, this in turn led to the biggest recession in the UK since the Second World War, an increase in unemployment from 1 million to 3 million and the disappearance of large sections of British industry. During this period club wage bills rose by nearly 25 per cent per year in all divisions, and pushed several clubs to the edge of bankruptcy. The 1983 Chester Report pointed to the growing indebtedness of clubs and large accumulated losses, particularly in the lower divisions. However, between 1982 and 1986 there was a pause in the growth of wage expenditure – indeed a decline in real terms. The rise in wage bills began again only in 1987 (see Table 3.5). As support for and interest in football recovered, as club incomes started to rise, then so did the clubs' wage bills.

Table 3.5	1st Division	2nd Division	3rd Division	4th Division
1977–82	24%	18%	24%	24%
1982–6	3%	1%	2%	0%
1986–97	21%	19%	11%	10%

Average annual wage bill growth by Division

From 1992 – 1st Div = Premiership; 2nd Div = 1st; 3rd Div = 2nd; 4th Div = 3rd
Source: Club accounts

Since the 1980s footballers' salaries have become more and more a source of dissatisfaction among fans and observers of the game. This complaint has emerged as a consequence not just of the level of salaries, but of the share of salaries in the total expenditure of football clubs. In Table 3.6 the changes in the share of player wages since 1929 are illustrated. For example, in the First Division it has risen from 36 per cent of total income to 45 per cent in recent years. Notably, the lower divisions have always spent a greater share of their income on wages than the First Division, so that by the 1980s Third Division clubs were spending nearly three-quarters of their total income on the wage bill. What is also noticeable is that in the 1990s the share of the wage bill has fallen in all divisions, as clubs have been forced by the government to divert money into stadium redevelopment following the Taylor Report.

Table 3.6	1st Division	2nd Division	3rd Division
1929–39	36%	42%	53%
1947–60	30%	38%	45%
1961–70	38%	48%	53%
1971–8	46%	61%	67%
1979–88	51%	68%	72%
1989–97	45%	63%	66%

Footballers' wages as a percentage of total revenue by Division

From 1992 – 1st Div = Premiership; 2nd Div = 1st; 3rd Div = 2nd
Source: Club accounts

Controversy about the level of footballers' wages will continue to fill the pages of newspapers. In the US, where professional sports personalities have always been better paid, the complaints began much earlier and have grown louder as the years have gone by. This has helped the owners of teams to negotiate limits on payments through mechanisms such as salary caps. In the UK public outrage has generally been directed at the level of salaries paid to chief executives of public companies, particularly those of privatized utilities such as the water companies. So far footballers' wages have at least been accepted as a reward for exceptional talent. However, if salaries continue to grow, it will become increasingly likely that politicians will come under pressure to 'do something'. Whether or not this would be desirable is a matter discussed at the end of this chapter. First, however, we consider the other main form of expenditure on players.

Transfer spending from Common to Bosman

Many in the hierarchy of football regretted the move to recognize professionalism in 1885 but were persuaded to support it because it would at least allow clubs to assert control over the players. At its foundation in 1888 the Football League expressly set out the twin aims of imposing a maximum wage and preventing the movement of a player from one club to another without prior permission of the former. As we have seen, the imposition of a maximum wage was not achieved until 1900, but restrictions on the movement of players were created from the establishment of professionalism and the development of the retain-and-transfer system. This was based on the notion of a player's registration: only a player registered with the FA can play professional football. However, a registration can be held only by a football club. The essence of the retain-and-transfer system was that once a player had registered with a club that club held absolute discretion over the registration. If a player wanted to move to another club he could do so only with his current club's prior permission. Combined with the maximum wage, this meant that the football player was little better than a slave to football – albeit a relatively well-paid one. He was free to sell his talents at whatever price he could negotiate to any business outside football, but if he wanted to earn a living as a professional footballer he had little or no power to bargain over the terms of his employment, or to determine who his employer might be. At the end of each season a club would decide which of its players were to be retained and which would be made available for transfer (hence the name of the system). If any club wished to obtain the services of a player on the transfer list, it would have to offer a fee which satisfied the selling club.

This employment system is virtually unknown in any other kind of business activity. If it were found to be operating in any other industry and an employee challenged it in court it would almost certainly be found to be illegal. And yet sports businesses around the world have operated employment regulations along similar lines unchallenged by the courts. For example, from 1879 until 1975 US baseball teams operated a reserve clause system which allowed them to designate five players each year whom they would automatically retain, effectively maintaining monopoly rights over individual players. Numerous legal challenges by baseball players who found their careers beyond their own control failed in court. This is all the more remarkable since during this period the US had strict laws against restrictive practices.

The US Sherman Act of 1890 outlawed 'conspiracies' in restraint of trade. One example of a conspiracy deemed illegal was an apparently innocuous agreement among toilet bowl manufacturers to publish a standard price list through an industry trade association, a price to which in fact none of the manufacturers adhered.[53] While this was all illegal, an open agreement between the owners of baseball teams to respect each other's monopoly rights over the careers of their players was effectively deemed to be legal.[54] In the UK, where competition laws were not introduced until 1956, such restrictions were even easier to enforce. In 1912 the Players' Union attempted to challenge the retain-and-transfer system in court. In the case of Kingaby v Aston Villa, the plaintiff, a Villa player, claimed that a proposed transfer fell through because the defendant charged an excessive fee. He therefore demanded compensation for loss of employment. The judge ruled that even if the fee was excessive the club was within its rights given the original contract of employment between Kingaby and Aston Villa.[55] The legal defeat undermined both the finances and the credibility of the union, while strengthening the position of the clubs and the League. The transfer system went unchallenged for the next fifty years. The situation was nicely summed up in the fictional story of a football match by Arnold Bennett, also written in 1912. The hero of the story, Jos Myatt, is a full-back for the local team, a star worth £500 in the transfer market: ' "They" – the shadowy directors, who could not kick a ball fifty feet ... "they" paid him four pounds a week for being the hero of a quarter of a million people! He was the chief magnet to draw fifteen thousand sixpences and shillings [more than £375] of a Saturday afternoon into a company's cashbox ...'[56]

The real life consequences of the system could be harsh. Bill Shankly, before becoming a celebrated manager, was a well-known player, winning an F A Cup winners' medal with Preston North End in 1938. The interruption of the war stole from him what would have been his peak years, and while after the war he continued to play for Preston, the club soon told him his first-team career was over and offered him a three-year contract to bring on the reserves. Still wanting to play League football he turned it down, and in 1949 the club told him he would no longer be retained. Presumably they were trying to force his hand, since the club could demand an unrealistically large fee to deter other clubs. In fact Shankly accepted an offer to manage Carlisle United, but he was still not able to play for them, since Preston insisted on a fee for his registration and Shankly would not pay.[57] No doubt if Shankly had been a bit less stubborn, a compromise could have been arranged. But his inflexibility illustrated just how little real control the player had over his own career. There were many other instances of clubs demanding excessive fees for players whom they no longer wanted to retain and thus ending their careers prematurely.

If the intention behind the system was to restrain the expenditure on players, it can only be viewed as a partial success as can be seen from Figure 3.3, which illustrates the English domestic transfer record between 1905 and 1997. The most famous early transfer fee was the £1,000 paid by Middlesbrough for Alf Common in 1905 – unquestionably the world record at the time – in order to try to avoid relegation to the Second Division. It was the first four-figure transfer fee and, at a price which in today's money is equivalent to about £60,000, caused widespread outrage: how could any footballer be worth so much? One answer was provided by William Bassett: Middlesbrough did indeed avoid relegation and the annual income preserved by staying up was £4,000.[58]

Important landmarks were the first five-figure fee (1928, £10,890 paid by Arsenal to Bolton for David Jack), the first six-figure fee (1966, £100,000 paid by Everton to Blackpool for Alan Ball), the first seven-figure fee (1979, £1,180,000 paid by Nottingham Forest to Birmingham City for Trevor Francis) and then in 1996 the first eight-figure fee – £15m paid by Newcastle United to Blackburn Rovers for Alan Shearer. Table 3.7 illustrates the growth rate of transfers and

Figure 3.3
Record English domestic transfer fees 1905–97

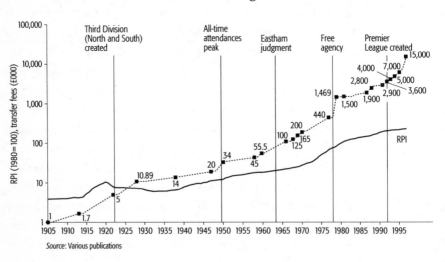

Source: Various publications

	Fee inflation	Retail price inflation	Inflation gap
Table 3.7 Transfer fee inflation and retail price inflation (annual averages)			
1905–13	6.86%	1.23%	5.63%
1913–22	12.73%	6.99%	5.74%
1922–38	6.65%	–0.93%	7.58%
1938–50	7.67%	5.20%	2.47%
1950–60	5.02%	4.05%	0.97%
1960–70	13.68%	4.06%	9.61%
1970–78	10.36%	13.20%	–2.84%
1978–88	17.46%	6.04%	11.42%
1988–97	20.50%	4.24%	16.26%

Calculated from transfer fee records in Figure 3.3

inflation over the entire period. Only between 1970 and 1978, a period when retail price inflation reached record levels, did transfer inflation fall behind retail price inflation.

From Figure 3.3 it is clear that there have been distinct phases in the growth of transfer fees. Before the First World War football was still expanding and fee inflation easily outpaced retail price inflation. Prices paid just after the First World War merely reflected the general price inflation caused by the war, but the early postwar years were still a time of growth in football. After 1938, however, fee inflation more or less matched the growth in retail prices. After the Second World War there was another jump in transfer fee levels reflecting the boom in attendances, but then fees rose only slightly faster than inflation until the Eastham judgment, which outlawed the old retain-and-transfer system. In 1963 George Eastham, a Newcastle player, wanted to move south for personal reasons, but the club refused to agree and put him on the 'retained' list. Challenging the retain-and-transfer system, Eastham took the club to court and the judge declared that the club was acting unlawfully 'in restraint of trade'. Effectively the judgment meant that a player had the right to play for any club, subject to respecting standard contractual terms.

At first the clubs reformed the retain-and-transfer system. Contracts were divided into an initial period of binding terms and then an option period (which could be no longer than the initial period). During the option period the club held the right to (a) retain the player as long as it offered terms at least as good as those offered by another club; or, if the club did not wish to retain the player it could (b) give the player a free transfer, or (c) demand a transfer fee by placing him on the transfer list. This was not freedom of contract, since the player's future was still decided by the club. However, in either case (a) or (c) the player could appeal against the decision and go to arbitration by an independent tribunal. The tribunal then made a binding judgment, which in general might be expected to lean in favour of the player. But even under arbitration the player might not get all he wanted at the tribunal and might forgo higher earnings available elsewhere while waiting for the tribunal to reach a decision. The option element in the contract was one-sided and in effect tilted the balance of bargaining power in favour of the club wanting to retain the player.

The government-sponsored Chester Report of 1968 favoured the introduction of complete freedom of contract (and a levy on transfer fees to prevent their spiralling growth). In 1974 the government's Commission on Industrial Relations produced a report which led to the creation of a negotiating committee with representatives from the PFA and the League and which met to discuss industrial relations, including the possible introduction of freedom of contract. The clubs maintained they needed a return on their investment in a player if he moved to another club. They also argued that transfer fees kept money circulating in the game and that their abolition would focus resources on the big clubs and force the smaller ones to become semi-professional. The possibility of liquidating a team for cash was also a factor which persuaded banks to provide clubs with overdrafts. The PFA accepted the argument that retaining transfer fees would maintain a greater number of professional players. After considerable procrastination by the clubs, 'freedom of contract' was instituted in April 1978 and the terms agreed then operated until 1998. In effect the option period was abolished. The new rules meant that when a player reached the end of his contract the club could (a) offer a contract on terms at least as good as the previous contract, (b) give the player a free transfer or (c) sell the player for a transfer fee. In any of these situations the player was entitled to move to another club if he wished and if another club wished to offer him a contract. The compensation to be paid in the case of a transfer was subject to negotiation, and in the event of disagreement the issue was referred to the Football League Arbitration Committee (FLAC), consisting of an independent chairman, and representatives from the League, the PFA and the Secretaries and Managers' Association. The committee invited each club to make a final offer and justify its position, and also consulted with the player. It then made a binding decision on the transfer fee to be paid. A recent study[59] of the operation of the FLAC showed that fees decided by them tended to be lower than transfer fees which had been agreed by the clubs, suggesting that arbitration was bad for selling clubs and good for buying clubs.

With the advent of free agency in 1978 there was a huge jump in the value of transfer fees. In 1977, one year before free agency, Liverpool paid a record £440,000 for Kenny Dalglish. Two years later the record rose to £1,469,000, paid by Aston Villa for Andy Gray. During the early 1980s there was a brief pause in the growth of transfer fees, just as there was in wage growth. In 1981 the record increased to £1.5m, the fee paid for Bryan Robson by Manchester United to West Bromwich Albion. That record was not broken until 1987.

By the 1980s football players were less and less confined to playing in their domestic leagues. Instead of a series of national markets, an international market for footballers, particularly at the top end of the scale, began to emerge. Although in the early years of football the English League was the world's largest and the biggest generator of revenue, and consequently English transfer fees were the highest in the world, by the 1980s foreign transfer fees were starting to pull well ahead and Italian and Spanish clubs were regularly paying fees in excess of those paid by English clubs. In 1982 Barcelona paid £4.8m for Diego Maradona and then sold him to Napoli for £6.9m in 1984. This remained the world record until 1992, but by 1988 there had been around twenty transfer fees paid in excess of £2m, including three English league players moving abroad: Gary Lineker (£2.75m) and Mark Hughes (£2.3m) to Barcelona and Ian Rush to Juventus (£3.2m).

As the attendances and income of English football clubs started to rise again from 1987 onwards so did the domestic transfer fee record. In 1987 Liverpool paid £1.9m for Peter Beardsley and in the following year Everton paid £2.2m for Tony Cottee. But the real buying power in football lay with the Italian clubs, and the top English players were attracted by the much higher fees (and wages) paid in Italy. After the Italia 90 World Cup players from the successful England team moved to the Italian league: Gascoigne (£5.5m to Lazi0), Platt (£5.5m to Bari in 1991 and £6.5m to Juventus in 1992) and Walker (£1.5m to Sampdoria). In 1992 AC Milan spent £10m on Jean-Pierre Papin and £13m on Gianluigi Lentini, a new world record. In the same year Sky TV signed a £304m deal with the new Premier League for TV rights and English domestic fees exploded: £3.6m paid by Blackburn Rovers for Alan Shearer in 1992, £3.75m paid by Manchester United for Roy Keane in 1993, £5m paid by Blackburn Rovers for Chris Sutton in 1994, £7m paid by Manchester United for Andy Cole in 1995. For the first time English football clubs started to buy players from all over the world; big signings were made from Italy, Brazil, France and Germany. But English clubs were also interested in less expensive foreign players, partly because of the inflation in domestic wages, and many started to be brought in from Eastern Europe, the former Soviet Union and traditional recruitment grounds such as Scandinavia. The English record once again became the world record in 1996 with the transfer of an English player, Alan Shearer, from Blackburn Rovers to Newcastle for £15m, but in 1997 the Spanish club Real Betis agreed to pay £21.5m for the Brazilian Denilson, even though he would not be released to play for them until after the 1998 World Cup. In the four years following the first Sky TV contract the transfer record has increased fivefold, an unprecedented rate and unsustainable over the long term.

In December 1995 a case brought by Jean-Marc Bosman, a Belgian player who wished to transfer from RC Liège in Belgium to US Dunkerque in France, came before the European Court. Under Belgian rules Liège were allowed to fix a fee for the player without negotiation and as a result the transfer had fallen through because Dunkerque could not afford the fee. The European Court decided that the transfer system restricted the freedom of movement of employees (footballers) in the European Union in contravention of Article 48 of the Treaty of Rome and ruled that a club could not demand a transfer fee for a player who had completed his contract.

The Bosman ruling referred to players moving between member states, but the implication of the judgment is that transfer fees for any player out of contract would not generally be legally enforceable.[60] Since the English system sanctioned transfer fees for players out of contract, it too was affected by the judgment. Tottenham Hotspur, a club which has for some years valued players' contracts as assets on the company balance sheet, immediately wrote down their assets by £7m to reflect the loss of value implied by the Bosman ruling.

In the immediate aftermath of the Bosman case English clubs continued to pay transfer fees for players purchased at the end of their contracts, just as before. However, in 1997 the FA agreed a new system with the English leagues to operate from 1998 onwards. Under the new system no fees will be payable for out-of-contract players over the age of twenty-four, although this will not prevent clubs demanding fees for players whose contracts have not yet expired. At the beginning of their careers players will sign a training and development contract up to the age of twenty-one, and the contract will also include general education and vocational training. Any player who moves club between the ages of twenty-one and twenty-four, having refused a new contract with his existing club, can be transferred only if a fee is paid reflecting the investment made by the club. In the case of a dispute the transfer fee will be decided by the FLAC.

Many clubs, particularly the smaller ones, complained that the Bosman ruling would do them long-term harm. Graham Kelly, then chief executive of the FA, said, 'If the transfer compensation system isn't allowed to continue in some form, the implications for the smaller clubs and the game as a whole will be very adverse.' Mike Bateson, then chairman of Torquay United, a club that oscillated between the Second and Third Divisions, said, 'I am damned if I'm going to put my money into a youth system just to let the bigger clubs snaffle up the product. The fat cats may get fatter but the scrawny ones down this end will die of starvation. A lot more players are going to be out of work.'

Although widely perceived as revolutionary, the Bosman judgment does not mean the complete abolition of transfer fees. It challenged the payment of fees only when a player's contract has expired, not fees paid for transfers during a contract or before it has run out. In these cases a fee can be legally justified as compensation for early termination of the existing contract, and in practice most transfers have always occurred before contract expiry. Since the trading of players within contract is unlikely to die out post-Bosman, one might legitimately wonder what all the fuss is about.

The real issues underlying the Bosman judgment have to do with the length of the employment contracts written in football. Imagine a world where no transfer fees of any kind were permitted. In such a world clubs would be unlikely to agree employment contracts which lasted longer than a single season for most players, since players would simply leave their current employment if they got a better offer. The club would gain nothing from signing long-term contracts and would in many cases be saddled with expensive players who had lost their form.

The ability to demand a transfer fee for a player who moves within contract makes it profitable for clubs to sign long-term contracts for the top players. They are then assets, which can be sold if the need arises. Because some players turn out to have valuable talents while some do not, employment contracts can be thought of as lottery tickets and every so often most clubs will hit the jackpot. Players are in general willing to sign long-term contracts because they provide greater security in what is a very uncertain career. Long-term contracts benefit the clubs because they create valuable assets and benefit the players because they insure their future. Indeed, generally speaking, the longer the contract, the better off the player is in the sense that he is exposed to less risk.[61] A long-term contract need not mean a fixed wage, since contracts can be renegotiated in the light of changing form. Typically a contract places a lower limit on what a player can earn, and the longer the contract the greater the value of this security. However, longer contracts are also expensive liabilities for the clubs, since the contract specifies a commitment to paying the player. Thus clubs will only sign long-term contracts if there is no more profitable alternative.

The transfer system pre-Bosman made short-term contracts a more profitable alternative because even if a contract lasted only a few years, the club could demand a transfer fee on termination. This was like obtaining a significant part of the benefit of a long-term contract (i.e. the expected increase in the value of the player) without having to pay for it (because the club was always entitled to something even when the contract expired). This meant that players had less job security and more uncertainty. The implication of this analysis is that post-Bosman the clubs will have to write longer-term contracts if they wish to realize the value of their investment in players. Clubs will then have longer-term liabilities in respect of their wage contracts, and will be forced to adopt a longer-term perspective in the conduct of their business. Many would argue that this would be no bad thing in general and will bring a benefit to players the clubs want to hire.

However, Bosman may also force some clubs to lower their expectations. If the pre-Bosman rules enabled some clubs to obtain players at a lower long-term cost than is possible post-Bosman, then clubs will be unable to maintain a team of the same quality without extra expenditure.[62] Clubs which are already only just breaking even financially will be forced to reduce the average quality of their squads post-Bosman as the clubs balance their books. This may mean a lower overall demand for top-class footballers. In other words, smaller squads, or fewer full-time professionals, are likely consequences of the Bosman ruling, and even if the judgment forces clubs to treat the players they employ better than before, it may well be that they will employ fewer of them.

In sum, the lower division clubs which bring on talented players can expect to generate transfer fee income from selling them while under contract, more or less as they have done since the nineteenth century. The top players will be worth more because they will be sounder financial investments, and so they will attract higher salaries and higher fees. The remainder will be likely to find themselves subjected to greater competition and relatively speaking their wages will fall behind those of the leading players. In effect this only re-inforces the trends which have been discussed in this chapter, both for wages and transfer fees.

Who benefits from the transfer system?

As has been pointed out already, freedom of contract led to a dramatic increase in the English transfer fee record, but what difference does this make to the clubs and the players involved? Every fee paid is matched by a fee received, so the net effect on football clubs as a whole should be zero. A proportion of the transfer fee, currently around 10 per cent, is taken by the player and a further 5 per cent is paid to the PFA to fund the Players' Cash Benefit scheme.[63] However, it is widely held that the most important aspect of the transfer system is that it redistributes income from the big clubs to the small clubs. Without transfers, it is argued, the large clubs would simply hire all the good players trained and developed by the small clubs, who would receive no compensation for their investment. As a result the small clubs would either face bankruptcy or give up training young players. Small clubs would be even less able to pose a competitive threat to the large clubs, either because they had less money to invest or because without their own youth development system they would be entirely reliant on the cast-offs of the big clubs.

Despite the theory that the transfer system redistributes income from the strong to the weak having been propounded for at least ninety years, the evidence to back it up has always been thin on the ground. The argument has several variants. Firstly, it might be supposed that clubs with higher league positions transfer income down to clubs with lower positions. Secondly, since it is possible for 'small' clubs to enjoy league success the theory might refer to clubs with large incomes (excluding transfer fee income) redistributing their income to clubs with smaller base incomes. Thirdly, the theory might relate to financial viability, so that clubs with large profits (before transfer income) subsidize those with small profits (or losses).

Examined purely on a divisional basis there is little support for the redistribution theory. Table 3.8 gives a break-down of the financial flows and movement of players between the divisions based on transfer data from published newspaper sources for the season 1996–7. It covers 234 players who were transferred for a fee.[64] The rows in Table 3.8(a) tell us where players transferred from a particular division went (where a known fee was paid). The rows in Table 3.8(b) tell us how much was paid in total to clubs in a particular division by the other divisions (or by Scottish and overseas clubs). Thus the last row of 3.8(a) shows how many players were acquired by each division, while the last row of 3.8(b) shows how much was spent in total by each division. In addition to movements within the professional English leagues, movements to and from Scotland and overseas are included. For example, from 3.8(a) it can be seen from the first row that Premier League clubs sold thirty-four players to the First Division, while from the first row of 3.8(b) it can be seen that Premier League clubs received a total of £16.9m for these players. From the second row of each part of the table it can be seen that fourteen players moved from the First Division to the Premier League, whose clubs paid a total of £16.5m. Thus it appears that the First Division had a deficit of £400,000 with the Premiership. In the same way it can be calculated that the Second Division had a surplus of £2.5m with the

Table 3.8

Transfers between the Divisions in 1996-7

(a) Number of player movements

		Movement of player to						
		Premier League	Division 1	Division 2	Division 3	Overseas	Scotland	Total
Movement of player from	Premier League	9	34	4	0	11	0	58
	Division 1	14	9	22	3	2	2	52
	Division 2	7	10	15	13	0	1	46
	Division 3	2	4	7	8	1	0	22
	Overseas	36	10	5	1	0	0	52
	Scotland	2	1	1	0	0	0	4
	Total	70	68	54	25	14	3	

(b) Financial flows (£m)

		Payment from						
		Premier League	Division 1	Division 2	Division 3	Overseas	Scotland	Total
Payment to	Premier League	20.6	16.9	0.2	–	17.3	–	55.0
	Division 1	16.5	4.3	2.4	0.1	0.5	0.4	24.2
	Division 2	2.7	4.0	1.5	0.5	–	0.1	8.8
	Division 3	0.8	0.5	0.9	0.2	0	–	2.4
	Overseas	59.4	4.3	0.3	0.1	–	–	64.1
	Scotland	4.5	0	0	–	–	–	4.5
	Total	104.5	30.0	5.3	0.9	17.8	0.5	

Source: Newspaper data

Premiership, while the Third Division received £800,000 in total from Premier League clubs and paid them nothing. Thus in 1996–7 money flowed from the First Division to the Premiership, while the sums of money trickling down from the Premier League to the Second and Third Division were relatively small. By contrast, there has been a large movement of cash out of England, as Premier League clubs have moved to acquire overseas players.

Adding up the columns of Table 3.8(b) indicates the total amount of money spent by a division and summing the rows shows you the total amount of money received. This information is presented in Table 3.9. It shows that the Premier League had a £50m deficit on transfer spending for the year, most of which went overseas; the First Division had a £6m deficit, while the Second and Third Divisions showed small surpluses. Averaged out around the clubs, these surpluses represent a negligible trickle down the leagues. The average surplus per Second Division club is £104,000, the average surplus per Third Division club is £62,500. For comparison, the average pre-tax loss per Second Division club in 1995 was £222,000 on an average turnover of £1.8m, while the average pre-tax loss per Third Division club in 1995 was £145,000 on an average turnover of £1m.

These results are not exceptional. Table 3.10 describes the income and expenditure on transfers by division for the years 1964–6.[65] During that period the then First Division showed a surplus on transfer fees, while the lower divisions actually showed a net deficit. It is striking to compare the ratios of spending between the top and bottom divisions over the two

Table 3.9 Income from and payment of transfers by Division 1996–7		Income from transfers (£m)	No. of players	Payment of transfers (£m)	No. of players	Balance (£m)
	P	55.0	55	104.5	70	−49.5
	1	24.2	52	30.0	68	−5.8
	2	8.8	46	5.3	54	2.5
	3	2.4	22	0.9	25	1.5

Source: Newspaper data

Wages and Transfers in the Football Industry / 113

Table 3.10		Income from transfers (£m)	No. of players	Payment of transfers (£m)	No. of players	Balance (£m)
Income from						
and payment of	1	1.234	160	0.915	34	0.318
transfers by	2	1.026	103	1.097	91	−0.071
Division 1964–6	3	0.586	74	0.91	156	−0.323
	4	0.311	47	0.235	103	−0.076

Source: Chester Committee Report

periods. In the 1964–6 period the First Division spent and received around four times as much as the Fourth Division. By 1996–7 the ratio had risen to twenty-five times in terms of income and over one hundred times in terms of expenditure. The gap in spending power between great and small measured by division has expanded dramatically. In neither case, however, is there support for the theory that the transfer system has a significant redistributive effect.

A more detailed examination of the various versions of the redistribution theory can be made using the data for forty clubs over the period 1978–97. Whatever definition of 'large' and 'small' clubs we select, we should observe that in any one season the large clubs tend to be net spenders in the transfer market while the small clubs should tend to generate a net income from transfer activity.[66]

Table 3.11 illustrates the relationship between being a net transfer spender or a net transfer income generator and three measures of size: size ranked by average league attendances, size ranked by league position and size ranked by profits. The first two rows refer to size measured by seasonal attendances. If redistribution was significant we should expect to observe mostly big clubs being net spenders and small clubs being net

Table 3.11 The		Proportion of clubs with net transfer income	Proportion of clubs with net transfer expenditure	Proportion of cases confirming the redistribution theory
relationship of transfer income	Clubs with lowest seasonal attendances	33%	17%	
to attendances,	Clubs with highest seasonal attendances	18%	32%	65%
position and	Bottom half of positions	32%	18%	
profits	Top half of positions	19%	31%	63%
	Loss before tax and transfers	24%	35%	
	Profit before tax and transfers	26%	15%	39%

Winners and Losers / 114

recipients. In fact, overall 65 per cent of cases showed the right combination of size and net transfer income required to confirm the theory. In 33 per cent of cases small clubs (with low average attendance) had positive transfer income and 32 per cent of large clubs were net transfer spenders.

The next two rows of the table show the relationship between league position and net transfer expenditure. The figures are remarkably similar to the first two rows, with 63 per cent of cases indicating support for the redistribution theory. Finally the last two rows in the table show the relationship between net transfer income and profitablity. While in the previous two instances large and small clubs were defined (either by attendances or by league position) to include 50 per cent of clubs in each category, there were over this period a larger proportion of loss-making clubs (59 per cent of the total) than profit-making clubs (41 per cent). The data suggests that loss-making clubs tend to be the net transfer spenders (indeed the losses may be caused by the transfer expenditure) while profitable clubs tend to be those which have a positive transfer income.

Table 3.11 does not lend much support to any version of the redistribution theory. The reason for this may be that all clubs tend to dip into the transfer market whenever they can in order to boost their standing, selling players only in times of financial crisis. The operation of the transfer market can be seen as a kind of insurance policy. For example, a bank will be willing to lend money to a club to maintain its current level of expenditure as long as it believes the club can raise income from transfers. Without the ability to sell players, a club would have to adopt a far more cautious policy. For example, a club can offer a young player a three-year contract, which is a significant financial commitment, with the knowledge that in case of financial difficulties he can be sold. Without the possibility of transfer income, a three-year contract might turn out to be an unacceptable liability: clubs might refuse to offer anything other than short-term contracts of a year or less. Indeed, this was the situation in the early days of professional football before the retain-and-transfer system was established, when players might be hired on one-year contracts or even on a match-by-match basis. Of course, the insurance aspect of the transfer market is in general more important for the small clubs which do not have the security of a large club with guaranteed season ticket income, a wide base of supporters, TV and sponsorship income and the likelihood of regular cup runs. But occasionally large clubs experience a collapse in performance and in such situations the ability to sell players may be an important aspect of survival. Transfer fees may help to reinforce the status quo by enhancing the ability of larger clubs to invest in players. If transfer fees benefited only the smaller clubs, one might have expected to hear complaints from the larger clubs about the unfairness of the system: there have been no such complaints. Certainly a bank will be more willing to lend money to a large club to finance its investment in player contracts than to a small club, many of which already operate on a semi-professional basis. If there were no transfers at all then all clubs would have to adopt a more cautious policy towards player contracts, which would generally be shorter. As a consequence footballers would be more mobile and it would be open to smaller clubs to acquire better players for shorter periods, giving them a chance to progress up the leagues. Of course shorter-term contracts would be disadvantageous to players because of the loss of security.

In practice transfer fees will not be abolished, and even after the Bosman judgment they will continue to play a significant role in football club finances. In order to ensure that they can realize a return on their investment clubs are likely to write longer, rather than shorter, contracts. This may actually benefit the players, who will be offered greater security (since the value of a player on the market can fall as easily as it can rise). Whether or not the small clubs will have the ability to finance long-term contracts remains unclear. If they cannot, it will be because they do not generate enough income against which they can borrow to pay contracted wages. Faced with this problem, a club may have to become semi-professional and it will be even less likely than at present that such clubs will be able to compete with the big ones.

The winner-take-all society

'Winning is everything, second is nowhere.' Every football manager, player and TV pundit says so. When football was an amateur game played because it was character-building, it was possible to play for the sake of playing. In professional football neither the management nor the fans can tolerate failure. In such a world, a free market has certain natural consequences.

The retain-and-transfer system combined with a maximum wage restricted the operation of the market and enabled clubs to keep down the cost of players. It also made football an egalitarian activity, so that a world-class star like Sir Stanley Matthews could earn little more in his career than a good Third Division full-back. There is no evidence that this affected the standard of play, for better or for worse. But it was patently unfair. It was unfair to football players collectively, who received much less than their worth to the clubs, but in particular it was unfair to the most talented players, who attracted fans but took no share in the revenue so generated. As well as the clubs, some professionals benefited from restrictions placed on the operation of the market, since clubs invested in large squads when players were cheap. Mostly these were players at the lower end of the ability scale and equivalent players today cannot expect to pursue a full-time professional career: over the century the number of full-time professionals in English football has fallen.

Abolition of the maximum wage and free agency have given the player more control over his career. For some, those with exceptional talent, this freedom has brought with it enormous increases in the financial rewards of football. For the remainder, however, with greater freedom has come

Wages and Transfers in the Football Industry / 117

increased uncertainty and limited growth in financial rewards. This phenomenon has been characteristic of many activities in the modern world, as was pointed out in a book called *The Winner-Take-All Society*.[67] In supermarkets shelf space is limited, and so only the leading brands can be displayed; brands which are almost identical in quality get no space at all. Defendants in court want the best lawyer, so those with a reputation can get all the business they want, while lawyers nearly as good cannot find clients. Everyone wants a standard software package, so one company, Microsoft, dominates the market even if there are alternatives which might be better. Everyone wants to own a house in the most desirable neighbourhood, so that houses in that neighbourhood sell at a large premium to similar houses with the wrong postal address. In practice the difference between the best footballer, breakfast cereal and lawyer and the second-best might be negligible, but the difference in revenue-generating capacity is enormous.

Of course in any given field the best have always attracted the highest rewards, but what has changed in the twentieth century has been the technological capacity to disseminate the leading products and the work of the best performers to consumers and audiences world-wide. Global mass production techniques and distribution networks have made the best consumer products available in every shopping centre around the world. Radio, cinema, television, cassette recorders, CDs and all the other forms of broadcast technology have enabled the best performers to sell their talents to a global audience. The winner-take-all society is a consequence of the technological capacity to make the best product in each industry available to the consumer combined with the individual liberty to pursue the best available deal. In the nineteenth century the best soprano or concert pianist could expect to perform to an audience of a few hundred thousand people at most over an entire lifetime. Today millions of consumers can obtain or hear the latest pop music as soon as it appears on sale in the shops.

Professional competitive sports are the example *par excellence* of the winner-take-all phenomenon. Unfettered markets and the ability to reach ever larger audiences create increasing competition for the services of the best players. Competition is most intense where talent is scarcest, and the rewards are more than proportionately greater. A top striker might score twenty goals in forty games, while a second-rater will only score fifteen (a 25 per cent difference), but this difference might be worth two or three times the salary (a 300 per cent difference). In the US this process is already far advanced, as can be seen in Table 3.3, which indicates the phenomenal salaries that the top sportsmen can earn. In football this process has really begun only recently, but it is likely to continue over the coming years.

Some question whether such differences are good for the health of the game or even of society as a whole. Historically, the market for players was heavily restricted but in recent years almost all these restrictions have disappeared. Even when wages were held down, the restrictions on transfers were only partially successful in holding down costs. Technology raised the capacity of clubs to generate income and so increased their willingness to pay for players' registrations. With the abolition of the maximum wage football wages have spiralled and with the introduction of free agency transfer fees have grown at unprecedented rates. Already the market has created millionaires in their early twenties, and in a few years current salaries may come to seem modest. Whether this is a good thing or not, there is every likelihood that the top stars will continue to see their earnings driven higher and higher by competition in the market. The laws on competition now prevent the kinds of competitive restraints which the Football League once used to hold down payments to players. In US sports they have looked to other methods, such as negotiated salary caps, to try to hold down the excesses, (these schemes are considered in more detail in Chapters 7 and 8). In Chapter 5 we will go on to analyse the relationship between the market for players and the playing success of football clubs. First, however, we consider the general principles of business strategy.

Appendix: Wage and transfer spending 1996–7

Table A1
Premier League

Club	League position	Staff	Wage bill (£000)	Net transfer spending (income) (£000)
Manchester United	1	412	22,552	–293
Newcastle	2	199	17,487	–1,436
Arsenal	3	145	15,279	3,476
Liverpool	4	205	15,030	7,520
Aston Villa	5	178	10,070	9,336
Chelsea	6	125	14,873	1,921
Sheffield Wednesday	7	206	7,571	4,355
Wimbledon	8	86	6,018	1,913
Leicester	9	179	8,914	4,709
Tottenham	10	165	12,057	1,528
Leeds	11	195	12,312	11,778
Derby	12	119	4,256	2,892
Blackburn	13	204	14,337	–8,533
West Ham	14	136	8,298	6,657
Everton	15	177	10,933	5,549
Southampton	16	66	4,776	4,875
Coventry	17	147	8,396	8,859
Sunderland	18	152	5,703	842
Nottingham Forest	20	179	8,034	8,868

Table A2
Football League
First Division

Club	League position	Staff	Wage bill (£000)	Net transfer spending (income) (£000)
Bolton	1	212	6,159	1,587
Barnsley	2	76	2,613	–273
Ipswich	4	128	4,321	–1,303
Sheffield United	5	126	3,560	2,966
Crystal Palace	6	115	5,340	–1,028
Portsmouth	7	98	3,308	905
QPR	9	145	6,659	3,556
Birmingham	10	95	4,900	–209
Tranmere	11	91	3,282	–1,265
Stoke	12	91	2,856	321
Norwich	13	90	3,831	–23
Manchester City	14	166	7,200	1,754
West Brom	16	95	3,095	938
Oxford	17	144	2,331	458
Reading	18	86	3,035	–275
Swindon	19	83	3,276	–449
Huddersfield	20	72	2,251	405
Grimsby	22	76	2,037	–1,044
Oldham	23	104	2,779	–1,514
Southend	24	85	2,488	38

Table A3 Football League Second Division	Club	League position	Staff	Wage bill (£000)	Net transfer spending (income) (£000)
	Bury	1	93	1,348	533
	Stockport	2	64	1,819	94
	Luton	3	85	2,842	−1,753
	Brentford	4	47	1,016	−531
	Crewe	6	74	1,052	−319
	Blackpool	7	115	2,006	163
	Wrexham	8	70	1,397	
	Burnley	9	130	1,675	884
	Chesterfield	10	48	1,013	−501
	Gillingham	11	63	1,036	−83
	Watford	13	70	2,423	−465
	Millwall	14	93	4,129	1,019
	Preston	15	149	2,145	−392
	Bristol Rovers	17	69	1,546	−1,041
	Wycombe	18	73	1,783	450
	Plymouth	19	53	1,301	−532
	York	20	48	1,019	−134
	Peterborough	21	76	1,973	
	Shrewsbury	22	52	837	−165
	Rotherham	23		1,106	−212

Table A4 Football League Third Division	Club	League position	Staff	Wage bill (£000)	Net transfer spending (income) (£000)
	Wigan	1	49	606	733
	Swansea	5	64	1,039	0
	Cambridge	10	40	842	−380
	Mansfield	11	47	691	
	Scarborough	12			31
	Scunthorpe	13	59	889	−188
	Leyton Orient	16	56	1,296	9
	Hull	17	76	1,091	−350
	Hartlepool	20	26	503	
	Brighton	23	51	1,127	
	Hereford	24	44	800	−75

Structure and strategy

Manchester United is a successful business: in the last decade its performance on the pitch has surpassed that of its rivals (at least domestically) and it has earned a lot of money for its shareholders. Liverpool, while less aggressive in its marketing and less profitable, is none the less very successful measured in terms of performance on the pitch. Newcastle United is in football terms a very big business but not a very successful one. Despite generating a large income from loyal fans it has failed to win any major trophies in recent years. Financially the club has often struggled, and since its flotation on the stock market in 1997 the club's management has been in turmoil.[2] Wimbledon, on the other hand, is a relatively small club that has fared remarkably well given the limited resources available to it. One function of business strategy is to analyse the performance of individual companies. This means more than simply looking at who has been the most successful or most profitable. In one sense, Wimbledon is as much an example of success as Manchester United. Business strategy is about understanding how a given business manages to extract the greatest possible effect from its resources. However, it is also important to explain why Wimbledon, for all its success, seems unable to attract the same levels of support as big clubs such as Manchester United or Newcastle. In that sense, Newcastle is actually more successful than Wimbledon. When looking at individual clubs, business strategy seeks to explain the relationship between the resources available to a business, its objectives and its performance. This means not only making the best of any given situation, but also deciding what is to be considered 'best'. For example, are commercial ends compatible with playing success, and what are the implications of adopting a more commercial attitude?

A second strand of business strategy is about understanding the performance of an industry taken as a whole. Industry analysis provides a benchmark for measuring the performance of individuals and is critical to explaining what is common to firms competing in an industry. Industry analysis is the basis for understanding the potential of firms, but it also has a wider significance. While certain conditions in an industry are more or less fixed, i.e. beyond the control of those in the industry (for example, the technology involved in building a football stadium), in many cases outcomes depend crucially on the interaction between competing firms. Thus the performance of a firm in an industry may depend as much upon the agreed rules of conduct between firms as it does on the behaviour of the firm itself.

The design of strategy

Strategy design involves three components: identification of objectives, identification of resources and capabilities, and identification of the constraints imposed by the business environment. A well-designed strategy is one which enables a firm to achieve its objectives given its resources by adapting optimally to its environment. The most convenient way to analyse this process is to distinguish between the industry and the market. The industry can be defined as the set of firms which use broadly similar technologies to supply the market, and the market can be defined as the set of consumers which a firm might potentially supply. For example, Manchester United and Independiente of Argentina are in the same industry (football) but not (at least presently) the same market, since each appeals to quite different potential supporters.[3] Liverpool FC and Aintree racecourse might be said to be in the same market, defining it broadly as the market for leisure pursuits, but clearly not in the same industries.

Strategy requires objectives. A business needs to define its objectives sensibly: Scunthorpe United cannot aspire to compete in the same way as Manchester United, but it can aspire to improve its performance by using its capabilities more effectively. Moreover, it is important to distinguish between the fundamental purposes for which the business exists (its long-term goals) and intermediate targets which are set so as to improve long-term performance. Long-term objectives can be stated simply: for example, maximizing shareholder value, maximizing league position. Long-term objectives set the tone for a business but provide only a hazy guide to the conduct of day-to-day activities. For example, a fundamental dilemma for football clubs is to determine the balance of profits and team performance in their long-term objectives. This dilemma cannot be resolved by strategic analysis, although the analysis of industry structure may give an indication of the likelihood of successfully achieving either goal in the long term. The implementation of a club's strategy must be revised in the light of changing circumstances, and is therefore much more concerned with the process of matching capabilities to the environment. The more practical aspect of strategy formulation involves analysing industry and company performance with a view to improving performance in the medium term by the adoption of specific business policies.

Industry analysis[4]

Company performance depends in part on the general conditions of the industry in which the firm operates. Comparison of different industries at any particular point in time reveals different levels of performance, measured by indicators such as profitability, return on capital employed, stock market valuation and so on. Table 4.1 illustrates the profitability of a selection of UK industries in 1994. It is clear from the table that the pharmaceutical industry was by far the most successful measured in terms of its profit margin, which was 22 per cent. This is an average over all the firms in the industry, some of which individually may have performed far better or far worse. By contrast firms in the engineering sector achieved only a 2 per cent profit margin on average. Industry analysis sets out to explain the different levels of industry performance by looking at industry *structure* and industry *conduct*.[5] Industry structure consists of those features of an industry which dictate the ways in which products can be produced and the ways in which they can be sold. Structure may arise naturally through the unfettered processes of the market, but in many cases it is at least in part determined by the intervention of government or industry regulators. Industry structure dictates to some extent how many firms operate in an industry and how big those firms are. Industry conduct concerns the way in which the firms in an industry choose to compete with each other, how intensive competition is and the pace at which the firms in the industry enter or leave the market. These conditions then determine the prices which firms choose to charge for their products and the level of expenditure that individual firms make either to improve their products and reduce their costs, or to encourage buyers to purchase their products. Above all, conduct concerns the intensity of rivalry between firms which are already in the industry and the competitive threat posed by firms considering entry. The combination of structure and conduct then determines the performance of the industry, the volume of products sold and

Table 4.1 Profit margins by industry group 1994

Industry group	Profit margin
Pharmaceuticals	22%
Breweries	12%
Transport	9%
Utilities	8%
Retail	7%
Health and household goods	6%
Printing, paper and packaging	6%
Food manufacturing	5%
Electronics and electrical	5%
Food retailing	4%
Oil	3%
Textiles and clothing	3%
Engineering	2%
Distribution	2%
Building and construction	2%

revenues generated, the costs associated with production and sales, the profitability of the industry and its growth rate.

In comparing the pharmaceuticals and engineering industries it is easy to note several aspects of the structure and conduct which influence the overall performance. In terms of structure, the pharmaceuticals business is dominated by a small number of firms who need to operate on a large scale in order to invest the large amounts of capital required for research and development. Demand for the products of the industry is generally insensitive to price because of the high value we place on our health. In terms of conduct, the industry is frequently protected from competition by patents which make imitation illegal, and even when patents expire relatively few companies have the necessary expertise to compete. All this means that successful pharmaceutical companies can expect to generate large profits from their products. In the engineering industry the capital required to set up in business is relatively low and demand is relatively price-sensitive since customers expect to shop around. This means that the conduct of firms in the industry is characterized by a high degree of competition and it is hard to make a profit under these conditions.

While the basic business unit in team sports is the club, the league authorities are more than a mere trade association. Leagues exist largely because the product (the sporting contest) cannot be produced without the co-operation of the competing participants. A minimum level of co-ordination is required to establish a viable competition. However, the activities of league organizers often go well beyond this necessary minimum. In practice they tend to create a particular form of competition calculated to be in the interests of all league members. The league rules themselves affect both the conduct of the clubs and the revenues, costs and profitability of the industry as a whole. Members of sports leagues are not unique in being affected by the rules established by higher authorities.[6] However, it is frequently argued that competition in the football industry is particularly sensitive to the structure of the rules laid down by the governing bodies. In the football leagues these governing bodies, as well as the UK government and more recently the European Court of Justice and the European Commission, have imposed rules which, by seeking to influence industry performance, have affected the structure and conduct of the industry. For example, rules concerning the movement of players were created by the FA, the Football League and subsequently UEFA and FIFA to control the structure of the game. These rules have been struck down successively by English courts and the European Court of Justice.

Industry performance and firm performance
A long-standing issue in business strategy is the extent to which the performance of an individual business can be attributed to industry factors or to firm-specific variations. This issue is critical to the formulation of strategy. For example, can it be said that some industries are intrinsically more profitable and therefore more attractive than others? This view might appear to be supported by the data in Table 4.1. However, it is unlikely that profitability is merely a consequence of the industry in which a firm competes. Within any industry some businesses are more profitable than others, and explanations for these differences must be found somewhere else. In the long run it could be argued that everything is determined by the industry if there exists a unique best practice which all firms are driven to adopt (although even in the long run it might be the case that more than one strategy can successfully co-exist). However, the long run may be a long time coming. In the interim there is scope for individual firms to outperform their rivals, for example, by adopting innovations faster than their rivals and thus obtaining a competitive advantage.

The success of football clubs in a league is one of the best possible examples of the differences in long-run performance between firms. The extent of the differences is quite striking. Since the foundation of the Football League in 1888 there have been ninety-nine League (and Premier League) Championships. Of these, forty-nine, just over half, have been shared by four clubs alone (Liverpool, Manchester United, Arsenal and Everton). Table 4.2 lists the twenty-three clubs that have won League Championships since 1888–9 out of the sixty clubs which have appeared in the top division. Strikingly few clubs have won a championship *only* once (Sheffield United, West Bromwich, Chelsea, Ipswich and Nottingham Forest). Furthermore, most clubs winning more than one championship have won their titles in close succession. Thus Huddersfield, Liverpool and Arsenal have all won three championships in successive years, while the championship has been won in two successive years by clubs on fourteen separate occasions.[7] Clearly winning the championship is not a random event: clubs that win are doing something systematically and consistently better than other clubs.[8]

	Club	Number of League championships won	Rank
Table 4.2 Football League Champions 1888–9 to 1991–2 and Premier League Champions 1992–3 to 1997–8	Liverpool	18	1
	Manchester United	11	2=
	Arsenal	11	2=
	Everton	9	4
	Aston Villa	7	5
	Sunderland	6	6
	Sheffield Wednesday	4	7=
	Newcastle	4	7=
	Blackburn	3	9=
	Huddersfield	3	9=
	Wolves	3	9=
	Leeds	3	9=
	Preston	2	9=
	Burnley	2	13=
	Manchester City	2	13=
	Portsmouth	2	13=
	Tottenham	2	13=
	Derby	2	13=
	Sheffield United	1	13=
	West Bromwich	1	19=
	Chelsea	1	19=
	Ipswich	1	19=
	Nottingham Forest	1	19=

An Outline of Business Strategy / 129

Competitive advantage flows from the combination of two factors. Firstly, a business must be in possession of a distinctive capability, some attribute which cannot easily be replicated by rival businesses. Secondly, the managers in the business must be able to apply that distinctive capability to competition in the market. A distinctive capability creates the potential for outperformance. It enables a firm to produce an equivalent output at a lower cost or to sell a similar good at a higher price than its rivals. Distinctive capabilities are by their nature exceptional attributes possessed by a business; however, these attributes need to be cultivated in such a way as to produce an exceptional performance. In football there are countless instances of exceptionally talented individual players failing to achieve their potential because of a failure to cultivate all of the other attributes (hard work, perseverance, judgement and so on) which are required of a top-class footballer. Much the same can be said of individual clubs. No doubt Manchester United was not the only club capable of achieving its current pre-eminence in the game. It began with certain advantages in terms of location, history and reputation, but there are a few other clubs which might reasonably be said to have possessed a similar potential but have simply failed to cultivate it properly. At the end of this chapter the various types of distinctive capability a football club might possess are discussed, while Chapter 6 is devoted to analysing some specific instances of distinctive capabilities which have been successfully exploited in English football.

But strategy is more than one firm seeking competitive advantage over its rivals. Even in a highly competitive industry managers need to seek out ways in which co-operation with rivals can improve the performance of the industry as a whole. Competitors typically find it extremely hard to come to mutually beneficial agreement. During the process of founding the Football League in 1888 William McGregor made many proposals, such as the equal sharing of gate income, which he believed would benefit all the clubs. In practice the clubs found it difficult to agree and settled on a formula which shared only a small part of total revenues. Many of the most important issues in football in recent years have concerned the search for ways in which the leagues can be restructured to make football as a whole more attractive and more successful: restructuring league competition and altering the division of income from TV and sponsorship.[9] Clubs have come together to discuss reforms intended to benefit the game as a whole but have found difficulties in reaching agreement because usually some clubs believe that they will lose out as a result. The strategy of competitive interaction involves looking for ways to ensure that potential gains can be realized by all in the industry, while restricting the opportunities of rival competitor groups. Despite this tension, the search for mutually beneficial arrangements is an important aspect of strategy.

One of the most famous writers on business strategy, Alfred Chandler, stated in his book *Strategy and Structure: Chapters in the History of the American Industrial Enterprise* that 'structure follows strategy'. By this he meant that great corporations succeeded by adapting the structure of their business to the pursuit of their chosen business strategy, which was itself a response to the opportunities and needs faced by the business. However, the dictum can easily be reversed. Strategy may follow from structure, the structure of the production process or the dictates of the market, which then determine which strategies can be successfully adopted by individual businesses. Rather than pursue a philosophical debate about the priority of one or the other, it is perhaps more useful to consider industry structure (and conduct) as one part of understanding the performance of a business unit, while company strategy is the other side of that process. The two strands are presented in parallel in Figure 4.1. This illustrates the different parallel stages in the analysis of business strategy and the major topics which are discussed under each heading. Issues relating to structure and conduct of competitors in the industry as a whole are represented on the left-

Figure 4.1
Industry analysis
and strategic
analysis

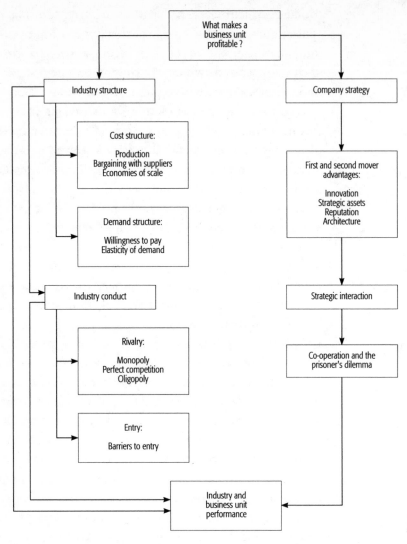

hand side while strategic decisions which can increase
profitability either by generating outperformance or
increasing industry profitability as a whole are represented
on the right-hand side. Structure and conduct provide the
basic framework which dictates the potential for generating
profits in a particular industry while strategy is about the
realization of that potential.

Industry structure

The fundamentals of industry structure depend on the nature of demand for the product or service being sold and the technology associated with bringing the product or service to the market. Firms need to understand the demand for their product in order to establish how revenues can be generated and to understand the technology in order to control costs. In that sense demand and technology can be thought of as independent forces which dictate the possibilities for achieving profits or any other measure of success.

Demand

Consumers in the market have a variety of opportunities for spending their income. The demand for any individual product or service arises through the process of budget allocation by each consumer. Whether the consumer's decisions are arrived at through some individualistic and rational process optimizing the allocation of income or are driven by custom and habit, a fundamental characteristic of markets is that higher prices will lead to lower demand and lower prices will lead to higher demand.[10] However, for some products demand may be relatively insensitive to price (inelastic) while for others it may be relatively sensitive. As we discussed in Chapter 2, the demand for football has been repeatedly shown to be insensitive to price changes.

Even if the demand for a product is relatively inelastic, this does not mean that sellers are able to command high prices. For example, the demand for food is relatively inelastic, but the ability of sellers to profit from this insensitivity by charging high prices is limited largely because there is competition in the supply of food. For example, in a situation where bread is the only food available and there is a single baker in the market, that baker would be able to charge a very high price to each consumer. Each consumer would be willing to pay a high price and in the absence of alternatives would have to pay a high price to obtain the bread. However, in any one market there are usually many bakers competing for customers, as well as many alternative sources of nutrition other than bread. Should an individual baker try to raise prices significantly, the customers are likely to go elsewhere. In other words, if demand for food as a whole is inelastic, the demand for the output of any one producer (such as a baker) will be relatively sensitive to the price set by that producer.

In the case of football, demand for the product is relatively inelastic both at the level of the industry taken as a whole and at the level of the individual club. This is because traditionally many fans have been loyal supporters, basing their allegiance on family ties, geography or tradition. For example, in *Fever Pitch* Nick Hornby describes how he came to be an Arsenal fan by accident, but having acquired a team he became a committed, even obsessive, supporter. For fans such as this price is likely to be a relatively unimportant consideration in the buying decision. This is a factor which works considerably to the advantage of football clubs.

Costs

Technology, which means simply the process by which inputs are turned into outputs, is probably the single most important factor in determining the structure of any industry. Technology determines the structure of costs in an industry. In selling its products the firm must be able to recover at least its production costs in order to survive, and these costs depend on the firm's technology. Some costs are fixed, meaning that regardless of the output sold by the business these costs do not change. Variable costs are those which change with the scale of output. If we think of football clubs as selling the rights to view matches, either at the ground or on television, then most of the costs are fixed, being incurred regardless of the number of paying spectators. In fact most of the costs are associated with the payments to the team.

Industrial development and increasing living standards over the last two centuries have to a large degree resulted from the ability to manufacture valuable commodities at low cost thanks to very large-scale production. Without mass production and economies of scale consumer goods such as cars or televisions could not be produced at affordable prices. Electricity and gas supplies rely on large-scale mining and extraction businesses to provide raw materials. Most construction work depends on large-scale steel and petrochemical plants to provide basic materials. The relative cost of food and clothing has fallen consistently over time thanks to the organization of cultivation and processing on a large scale. In most industries the exploitation of scale economies is essential to profitability. Yet this is not true of a game of football. Viewed as a product, football requires only the input of twenty-two players, a ball and a referee. This technology has not changed significantly over the last one hundred years. A game of football is the same today as it was when horses were the primary source of horse power and when it took eighty days to travel round the world. The most important changes in football have not been about the technology of the way the game is played, but about the way it is commercially exploited. The technologies which enable supporters to watch football matches have developed considerably since the foundation of the Football League. Developments in commercial exploitation have moved in step with changes in the technology of communication.

Industry conduct and the competitive environment

The process of competition is at the heart of understanding the business environment of the firm. Competition was memorably characterized as a process involving 'a creative gale of destruction'[11] by the famous economist Joseph Schumpeter. Schumpeter was impressed by the extraordinary dynamism of the capitalist system, its ability to consistently introduce new products and to expand markets. Prior to the industrial revolution productivity throughout the world had grown only slowly, and standards of living changed little from one century to another. With the industrial revolution came the free-trade doctrines of Adam Smith and the promotion of unfettered competition, first in England, then in the United States, and gradually across the whole world. While in reality governments have continued to play a significant role in economic activities, most industrial advances came through the development of new products by businesses driven primarily by the profit motive. Schumpeter argued that in a capitalist system firms and entrepreneurs are constantly looking for new profit opportunities. Profit opportunities are most easily found by creating new products for which there is a demand, and the lower the cost at which the product can be manufactured, the greater the potential market and the greater the profit opportunity. Furthermore, the search for profit produces competition for the innovator, as followers and imitators seek to share in the profitability of the new market. Thus the capitalist process brings a double benefit for the consumer, by encouraging the introduction of new products and by encouraging competition, which brings down prices.

However, viewed from the perspective of an individual firm established in a market (or its employees), this process is far from benign, since its tendency is to wipe out the profits which can be made. Any new product brought to the market can usually be sold at a profitable price as long as the firm retains a dominant market position. Furthermore, over time it can usually reduce costs by improving its production techniques. But competition drives down prices and therefore reduces the profitability of each unit of output which is sold. If competition is sufficiently intense, profits are eventually driven to a minimum, that minimum being the return on capital required to dissuade investors from pulling out of the industry altogether, but without offering a return high enough to attract new investors. Such conditions are enough to ensure the survival of a business but nothing more. The capitalist process thus offers opportunities to firms which are not yet established in a market, while posing a threat to those which already are. For this reason established firms have an incentive to find ways to limit competition. This can be achieved either by limiting the intensity of competition among existing firms in the market or by preventing new firms from entering the market and adding to the competitive pressure.

There are two important issues in understanding the competitive process. Firstly, there is the relationship between competitive intensity and industry structure. Intensity is influenced by both the structure of costs and technology and the nature of demand in the market.

Competitive intensity in a market is seldom static but develops over time, and the way in which it changes can be understood by looking at the relationship between competition and the environment. Secondly, there are the strategic decisions taken by firms within the competitive process which tend either to enhance or to diminish competitive intensity. Firms can still succeed in a market where competitive intensity is great, but every firm in a market can achieve a higher level of profit if competition is less intense.

One way to understand the competitive process is to think in terms of the product life cycle. As the competitive process advances it is possible to identify distinct stages in the development of demand and supply which fundamentally change the ways that firms compete and are characterized by different forms of competition. Table 4.3 illustrates three stages of the product life cycle: introduction, growth and maturity. Introduction is the earliest phase, which begins with the invention of a new product itself. In its early stages a new product is typically under development and not quite 'the finished article'. Its appeal may be limited to sophisticated or exceptionally enthusiastic consumers, while the majority remain sceptical about the product's potential. The growth phase occurs precisely when the product has reached a standard form which is convenient and therefore attractive to the less committed consumer. The product starts for the first time to reach a mass market, bringing with it economies of scale, lower prices and

Life cycle stage:	Introduction	Growth	Maturity
Industry characteristic			
Demand	High willingness to pay	Rapid increases in sales	Mass market
Technology	Non-standard	Product innovation	Process innovation
Products	Basic	Improved reliability	Quality focus
Manufacture and distribution	Specialized	Mass production	Flexibility with scale
Competition	Monopoly	Perfect competition	Oligopoly

Table 4.3 The product life cycle

deeper market penetration. The potential market for a product is limited by the population of consumers so that any product, however popular, must eventually reach saturation, at which point the growth of sales tails off and the product becomes mature. Table 4.3 characterizes the important differences in the product, the industry and the market as a product develops. These in turn help to determine the way in which competition develops between firms in the market. While not all industries will necessarily pass through each stage, the notion of the product life cycle provides a good illustration of the types of competition which are likely to occur in practice.

Introduction and monopoly

An innovator is, by definition, a monopolist. Often an innovator's monopoly power is protected by law in the form of a patent. This fact is striking since governments usually aim to impose limits on monopoly through competition law. In the US the Sherman Act prohibits any attempt to monopolize an industry and in the European Union the Treaty of Rome forbids abuse of a dominant position.[12] Monopolies are generally stigmatized because they are seen to be unfair and to give rise to unreasonable 'exploitation' of the customer. A monopolist is likely to charge prices that are excessively high and to restrict output to levels which are too low. A monopolist is usually able to charge different prices depending on the nature of the customer, a practice known as price discrimination. For example, a monopolist would seek to charge a higher price to a customer whose need is greater or whose ability to pay is greater. This leads to higher profits because the monopolist can bring new consumers into the market with discounted prices, while exploiting effectively the willingness to pay of the existing customers.[13]

Innovators are effectively licensed to charge high prices because of the perceived benefits which flow from innovation. Thus pharmaceutical companies are encouraged to devote significant resources to the development of new drugs because of the perceived benefit which they bring in the field of health care. During the life of the patent consumers are obliged to pay (directly or indirectly) more than would be necessary if competition were allowed to operate freely, but this is the price which is paid to encourage the innovation in the first place. In other words, the profits made by the monopolist under patent protection repay the original investment by the company in seeking to create the product.

Not all innovations are protected by patents, and patent protection is often quite weak, since imitators are often willing to break the law or to set up operations in countries which do not agree to be bound by patent laws. None the less, when a firm introduces a new product it starts with a strong advantage over potential rivals. At the same time, when a firm introduces a new product it has usually incurred significant development costs. The innovator faces a dilemma. Effective policies such as price discrimination can enable the innovator to recoup its investment quite quickly. However, in doing so the firm's profits act as a magnet to potential competitors, who will be prepared to make all the more effort to try to compete with the innovator. An alternative strategy for the firm is to try to maintain a dominant position in the industry. This requires both continued innovation and competitive pricing in order to preserve the firm's lead.

Research on innovators[14] has shown that this second policy is seldom successful.[15] More generally, innovators tend to be poor at acquiring the necessary business skills to develop their product into a mass market. A new product typically needs several years of development to become widely accepted. This means not only improving on the basic product

An Outline of Business Strategy / 139

itself but also enhancing the manufacturing process in ways that reduce cost and developing a distribution network to reach ever wider markets. In practice it is usually one of the early followers in the industry that enhances the initial product to the point where it becomes what is called the 'dominant design', the recognizable form which the product then takes into the future. For example, the typewriter was invented in 1874, but the original product little resembled what we would now recognize as a typewriter. However, in 1899 a rival firm came up with a design from which all subsequent typewriters, with remarkably few variations, were produced.

Growth and perfect competition

As a product develops into a standard recognizable form an industry typically enters into its most intensely competitive phase. By this stage the production process has been simplified to the point where mass production of a reliable product is feasible. Usually at this stage no single firm dominates the market, and more importantly the market is entering a period of rapid growth. This means that a firm coming into the market aims to become a major producer without being significantly handicapped by the established position of rivals. In the rush to create a mass market, scale is paramount in order to supply at a competitive cost. Scale also needs to be achieved quickly before rivals have time to match production levels. Firms at this stage typically invest huge amounts in plant and machinery to create capacity. In the drive to achieve scale economies the industry may start to suffer from excess capacity and prices in the market are driven down. What was an exclusive product becomes a commodity, and few firms are capable of sustaining anything above a bare minimum of profit in the market.[16] This stage approximates what is usually known in economics as 'perfect competition', a state where there are large numbers of firms supplying a homogeneous product to the market, prices are driven to the minimum feasible level and profits are negligible.

Maturity and oligopoly

The competitive phase cannot last for ever. Low profitability demands that some firms leave the market, either through bankruptcy or simply following a rational decision that there are better opportunities elsewhere. However, the competitive phase may last for a long time, because everyone knows that exit by others will relieve the pressure on profitability. Everyone holds out as long as possible in the hope that others will quit first. In some cases firms will be willing to 'invest' in sustaining losses now in the hope that they will be the survivors. Typically the survivors are those businesses which are the strongest, either in terms of efficiency or in product quality, a consideration which becomes increasingly important as an industry matures. Firms tend to invest in the development of the production technology in order to reduce costs (process innovation). Continued product development tends to focus on raising quality rather than fundamental change. Even though often only incremental in nature, this process continually pushes up the cost of competing effectively in the market, and so provides a greater incentive for the weak to quit.

In most industries a small number of businesses eventually come to dominate the market, a situation known as oligopoly. Most businesses are characterized by oligopoly, and indeed most of the world's marketed output is produced by a relatively small number of firms. In most markets fewer than ten firms produce more than 50 per cent of all output that is sold. In an oligopoly the potential profitability of firms is greater because of the potential benefits that firms can obtain from co-ordinating their behaviour in the market. This kind of behaviour is frequently illegal, since it amounts to firms acting in combination as if they were a giant monopoly, with all the perceived unfairness associated with monopoly. None the less, in some cases firms can find ways to limit competition and therefore improve their profitability.

Football and competition

The need for competition in football meant that there was no monopoly stage in the strict sense of the term. However, the first football clubs established dominant positions in their local markets for supporters and were from an early stage extremely profitable. Little accounting data is available from before the turn of the century, but in the years leading up to the First World War most clubs were able to make profits consistently, and on average football club profits exceeded 10 per cent of turnover during a period when interest rates averaged only 3 or 4 per cent.

The growth of football in general and the success of the Football League in particular led to a rapid expansion in the number of clubs, and most large towns found themselves capable of supporting at least one professional team. The original League quickly expanded from the twelve founder members in 1888 to fourteen in 1891, twenty-eight in 1892, thirty-one in 1893, thirty-two in 1894, thirty-six in 1898 and forty in 1905. This expansion was generally welcomed by the founder members since it expanded the available competition and hence the revenue-generating opportunities. However, most of the expansion involved the admission of teams from the north of England, with southern clubs relatively under-represented. Admitting teams from the south meant travelling longer distances for competition and also, by enabling southern clubs to compete regularly at the highest level, enhancing their competitive potential in the lucrative FA Cup.

The League was expanded to eighty-six teams in four divisions in 1922, and eighty-eight in 1923, since when the only change was the addition of four more clubs in 1950. The period from 1922 until the 1950s was one when competition took place largely among equals. Although there were big clubs, Third Division clubs were capable of attracting top players and large crowds and of competing on a level similar to that of the First Division. For example, when Notts County bought Tommy Lawton for £20,000 in 1947, breaking the

English transfer fee record, it was in fact a Third Division side. However, from the 1960s the inequalities between clubs started to grow. In 1950 the ratio of annual income of the First Division to the Third Division (North and South) was 2:1, by 1970 it was 5:1 and by 1995 it had reached 10:1. The increasing concentration of earning potential among football clubs mirrors a situation typical of many mature industries: in terms of income and expenditure a small proportion of clubs dominate.

Competitive advantage

A competitive advantage is something which makes a firm more successful (in terms of profitability or some other objective established by the firm) than its rivals. Much of the business literature concerns trying to understand why some firms are more successful than others in the oligopolistic phase of an industry (not surprisingly given the prevalence of oligopoly). The origin of a competitive advantage lies in a distinctive capability. Since the basis of the competitive process is imitation, competitive advantage can only be achieved when rival firms cannot imitate a particular skill or attribute. There are a number of ways in which a business may possess a distinctive capability.

Innovation

This may mean the capacity to create new markets, but in most cases it simply means the ability to generate incremental improvements to existing products. A firm may show a greater capacity to innovate than its rivals and successful innovations can generate huge profits. However, there is a price to be paid for innovation, in terms of research and development costs. Sometimes innovations are not successful. Even if an innovation is widely adopted it may not sell at a sufficiently high price to cover the investment made. Innovation is truly a distinctive capability only if a firm is capable of producing innovations at a lower cost than its rivals. Translating innovation into a competitive advantage is particularly difficult because it is not easy to protect valuable innovations from imitation. In the long run all innovations can be imitated and so businesses based on successful innovation have to be able to innovate repeatedly and consistently, a task which is beyond most firms.

Strategic assets

A better route to competitive advantage is simply to possess a monopoly over a necessary input in the production process. It might be some raw material which can be obtained only from a particular location owned by the firm, some specialized equipment or machinery which is produced by the firm, or a workforce which is less costly to employ than that of rivals. Easiest of all is to obtain a monopoly of raw materials such as a piece of land necessary to compete effectively for customers. Specialized equipment is more difficult to monopolize and requires the business to integrate backwards into another industry (i.e. buy up their suppliers) and obtain a competitive advantage there. Cheap labour as a strategic asset is usually associated with the national level of development – low-wage economies are an abundant source of low-cost labour – or with lightly taxed markets in which businesses have small social overhead costs to pay. Cheap labour need not mean unskilled labour. In many cases a low-wage country may have a well developed education system and so be able to supply highly skilled labour with low wage expectations. In all of these cases strategic assets are hard to imitate.

Reputation

This is a distinctive capability which comes from the estab-lished position of a product in the market. A good reputation makes a product more attractive to buyers because they are confident of what they are getting. Consumers who know the market well will be prepared to buy a reputable product since it is known to be better than the alternatives, while consumers who are relatively ignorant about what is available in the market are likely to choose a reputable product as a form of insurance. Reputation is like insurance because buyers pay a premium for what is perceived to be a guarantee relating to the experience of consumption. Reputation is a distinctive capability because it enables a firm to sell a similar product at a higher price. A reputation is hard to imitate because it takes time to acquire; it is an investment by a firm, which produces an income many years later.

Architecture

Imagine a consulting business founded on a close working relationship between the consultants and the client. Other firms might be able to supply exactly the same services, but the client is always likely to prefer working with the existing consultants, with whom it has an established relationship. This is a form of architecture, a distinctive capability based on personal relationships which cannot easily be imitated. This example is of external architecture (i.e. between two firms) and such relationships are the basis of the success of London as a financial trading centre or Silicon Valley as a centre for innovation in computing. Internal architecture is found where the nature of the relationships within the firm creates the ability to supply at lower cost or higher quality than rivals. This type of architecture might arise from a special relationship between management and workforce, perhaps because of a good understanding between managers and labour representatives, but in either case architecture refers to something which enables higher revenues to be generated without adding to costs. In other words, architecture cannot be attributable to particular individuals, or else those individuals would demand higher wages for supplying those specific skills.

Businesses in possession of distinctive capabilities are able to outperform their rivals: this is the meaning of competitive advantage. Possessing a competitive advantage simply means having the capacity to be more productive than rival businesses operating in the same markets. Measuring competitive advantage is generally a challenging problem. In principle it can be measured by a simple comparison of outputs and inputs. Suppose an industry consists of only two firms. Firm A takes inputs with a value of £100 and turns them into outputs which it sells for £150, while firm B takes inputs with a value of £50 which can be sold for £50 when turned into outputs (see Figure 4.2). The difference between the value of inputs and the value of outputs is called 'rent'. Firm A produces a rent of £50 while firm B produces no rent at all. This difference in the performance of firm A and firm B represents the competitive advantage of firm A, which is the same as firm A's rent in this example. If, however, firm B also produced a rent, then the competitive advantage of firm A would be measured as the difference between firm A's rent and firm B's. The fact that both firms were able to generate some rent would indicate that industry conditions are such as to make the industry attractive, regardless of the distinctive capabilities of any one firm. However, any rent which firm A generated above and beyond that amount which was common to both

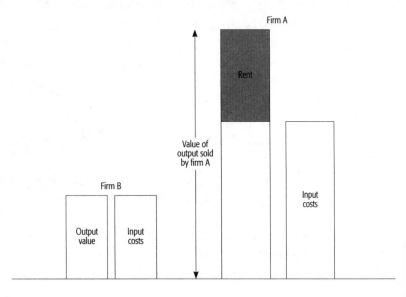

Figure 4.2
Measuring
competitive
advantage

firms would reflect competitive advantage. In other words, competitive advantage is a reflection of performance above and beyond that which can be achieved relative to an industry standard.

This notion is represented in Figure 4.3. Firm A is larger than firm B (measured by sales), so that the difference in rents needs to be set in the context of the difference in firm size. If firm A performed only as well as firm B, we would expect the value of outputs only to equal the value of its inputs (£100). This suggests that we can plot a relationship between size and *expected* performance, based on the industry standard. A measure of a firm's competitive advantage is its outperformance relative to its expected performance, given the industry standard. In this simple example with only two firms it is relatively easy to identify competitive advantage. In Chapter 5 we will look at ways of measuring competitive advantage when there are many competing firms, as in the football industry.[17]

Competitive advantage is not guaranteed simply by the possession of a distinctive capability. This is nowhere better illustrated than in the case of football, where various clubs

Figure 4.3
Competitive advantage relative to the industry

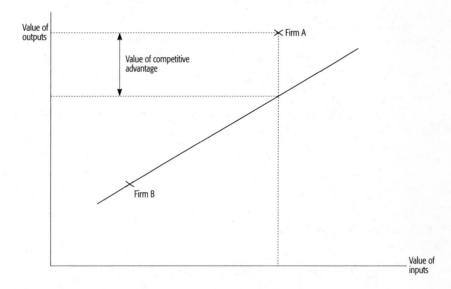

have held a strategic asset in the form of a rich benefactor prepared to plough money into the search for league success only for the money to be frittered away on players who do not live up to expectations. As in any business, the effective deployment of a distinctive capability requires an efficient management framework. Manchester United and Liverpool football clubs can field effective teams because they have large financial resources, but an integral part of their effectiveness in competition is an efficiently structured organization. Such an organization need not in itself be a distinctive capability, although in some circumstances it can be. More generally, however, it is simply the application of best practice to a given competitive environment.

Strategy in competition

In most industries competition is something that firms try to avoid. Competition between firms tends to lead to lower prices for consumers, reducing a firm's potential revenue. Competition encourages increased advertising budgets in order to win over consumers and increased expenditure on research and development in order to produce better products. Both these activities lead to increased costs. With higher costs and lower revenues profitability is reduced. Competition is good for the consumer but seldom good for the firm.[18] It is natural therefore that businesses should seek to find ways to limit competition. They can do two things. Firstly, firms can reach agreements among themselves to limit the extent of competition, to fix prices, restrict investment programmes or marketing budgets or otherwise enhance the capacity of all firms in the industry to reduce costs or increase revenues. Secondly, businesses that are already established in the industry can take action to prevent new firms entering the market to compete. In most industrial economies such practices are illegal. Governments have legislated against cartel arrangements which enforce restrictive practices among competing firms and against predatory behaviour aimed at keeping new firms out of the market, on the grounds that collusion and entry deterrence lead to outcomes which are analogous to monopoly and therefore unfair to consumers.[19] Before considering the legal aspect of anti-competitive behaviour in more detail, the potential for such actions needs first to be considered.

Co-operation, collusion and the prisoner's dilemma[20]

Co-operation between firms in the same industry is often called collusion. Simply wanting to collude does not mean that collusion will succeed. Imagine there are two firms selling the same product in a market and each has the choice of charging a high price or a low one. Low prices amount to competition and mean lower profits than each firm could achieve in a world of high prices. Choosing unilaterally to charge a high price would be unlikely to make sense to either firm, since each would expect the other to charge a low price and so compete away the other's customers. (If customers did not move to the lowest price then the two firms could not be said to be operating in the same market. This threat of substitution is why businesses have incentives to differentiate their products.) Hence the only way the two firms could reach a high price equilibrium would be if they entered a cartel agreement to charge high prices. However, the problem with a cartel is that each firm continues to have an incentive to charge a low price, effectively cheating on the agreement. In fact, cheating is the best response of each firm to the agreement. To see this, consider the profits that one firm makes, if the other firm cheats or does not.

Table 4.4
The prisoner's dilemma

The situation is illustrated in Table 4.4. If firm B does not cheat, then firm A has an incentive to cheat because by doing

		Firm B's choice	
		High price (not cheat)	Low price (cheat)
Firm A's	High price (not cheat)	(1,1)	(−1,2)
choice	Low price (cheat)	(2,−1)	(0,0)

Firm A's profit is the first figure in brackets, Firm B's profit is the second figure in brackets

An Outline of Business Strategy / 149

so it can make a higher profit (in this example, 2 instead of 1). Similarly, if firm B cheats, firm A also has an incentive to cheat, since in that case it makes a profit of 0 instead of –1. Thus cheating on the cartel agreement is the best response to any action by the other firm. The prisoner's dilemma (see the appendix on page 155 for the origin of this name) is one of the most studied problems in the fields of business strategy, political science and economics. Logic suggests that co-operative agreements will tend to break down, even if they are mutually beneficial. While this may sound contradictory, it is simply an illustration of a fundamental problem facing all institutions in society. While collectively we all have incentives to do one thing, self-interest may lead us to a different choice. Indeed, in society we recognize this fact by imposing laws in order to compel people to conform to the public interest. Laws against theft, murder or other anti-social activities exist because individuals cannot be trusted when acting alone to make choices which are collectively desirable. The problem in business is that the law operates in precisely the opposite direction. If firms could write contracts with each other (e.g. to maintain high prices) which could be enforced in the courts then they could get around the threat of cheating. But law forbids cartels so this is not possible.

Evidence on the operation of cartels tends to support the intuition of the prisoner's dilemma. Studying cartels is made difficult precisely because they are mostly illegal. However, cartels which operate beyond national jurisdictions, such as the Organization of Petroleum Exporting Countries (OPEC), illustrate the problems of cartel enforcement. OPEC shot to prominence in the early 1970s, following the oil embargo imposed by Arab states on Israel's allies in 1973. The shortage of oil that this precipitated led to a rapid rise in price. Further rises followed with the fall of the Shah of Iran in 1979 as the supply of oil from the Gulf of Arabia collapsed. While these shortages led to higher prices, OPEC tried to maintain the price increases when supplies returned to normal by entering into quota agreements that limited the amount that each member was allowed to supply to the market. As the prisoner's dilemma suggests, each member state found it in its interests to cheat on the cartel by overselling its quota. The result was that prices fell back to levels which in real terms (after allowing for inflation) were no higher than in 1970. The attempt to maintain an artificial shortage through quotas failed. Other examples of failing cartels can be found in research carried out into 'Trusts', groups of firms in the US which joined together to maintain high prices before the Sherman Act came into force in 1890. Time and again, recorded cartels in commodities such as sugar, salt, copper and so on collapsed because of cheating by cartel members.

Entry deterrence

Keeping firms out of the market is another potential way of raising profits by restricting competition. It is commonplace to argue that incumbent firms systematically drive new entrants out of the market or establish barriers to make sure that no entry takes place. In fact, for the large part such policies make little sense, because they are costly. To drive an entrant out of the market by predatory pricing means sacrificing one's own profit now for some hypothetical gain in the future. Apart from the fact that this gain might never materialize, predatory behaviour is usually too costly in the short term. This is not to say that prices do not fall when new firms enter the market, for this is the natural process of competition. However, setting prices low enough to guarantee that all firms make losses is not a good way to make money, even in the long term. Similarly, deliberately fixing low prices now to ensure that new firms do not enter the market in the future is also unlikely to be a profitable strategy. Sacrificing today's profit for an uncertain gain in the future only weakens the business now and provides no guarantee that new firms will not choose to enter. Entrants are more likely to make their entry decision on the basis of their expectation of the way market prices will develop post-entry, rather than on the basis of a belief that future prices will be the same as current prices. On this basis they are likely to calculate that the incumbent's incentive will lie with keeping prices up, not driving them down.

Practical entry deterrence occurs when incumbent firms take actions which are in themselves desirable from the firm's point of view and only have the effect of deterring entry as a secondary consequence. Thus a policy of investing in R&D, investing in marketing campaigns or building production capacity can all bring benefits to the firm if either they expand its potential market or enable it to reduce costs. They also have the secondary consequence that they raise the stakes for potential entrants, who must commit themselves to similar investments if they choose to enter the market. In such a situation incumbents, having already made the investment, view the prospect of competition with more commitment than an entrant. An incumbent will be willing (if not pleased) to sustain competition at lower prices, regarding the break-even point as that which enables them to recover their current costs, not their sunk, irrecoverable investment costs as well. By contrast entrants, planning their investment from scratch, will require prices to remain at levels which are sufficient to recover their entire costs, otherwise the venture is not attractive. Faced with this asymmetry, the entrant is likely to decide that entry is simply unattractive, because the incumbents will be prepared to compete more intensively than the entrant. The sunk costs of investment in demand enhancement or cost reduction create entry barriers, but only when they represent investments that the entrant would also be required to make; in other words, they form investments which any rational firm in the market would make, regardless of the issues surrounding new entry.

Strategic behaviour, sport and the law
Throughout the world sports teams and sports leagues are run as cartels. League rules restrict the operation of competition

between existing members, and new members are restricted from entering the league. From its foundation the Football League attempted to restrain competition. Minimum ticket prices were enforced until the 1960s. The major restrictions related to the transfer of players and the maximum wage that players could be paid. All these and other restrictions have been enforced with fines and ultimately the threat of expulsion from the League (Leeds City were expelled in 1919 for illicit payments to players). Were football clubs treated as ordinary businesses, such practices would have been deemed of dubious legality from the start. In practice they ran foul of British law only in the early 1960s, following the adoption of a tougher approach to competition around this time. Part of the reason that the authorities have been indulgent towards sports leagues is that the whole basis of operation of a league depends upon co-ordination, and it is clear that a well organized league with agreed fixtures is of more value to spectators than independent clubs meeting for fixtures on an *ad hoc* basis. Extending this notion the football authorities have tended to emphasize the 'good of the game' as the rationale for policy-making rather than the interests of individual clubs. Moreover, while clubs were self-evidently not pursuing profits as their main goal, competition authorities had little interest in interfering.

While the distribution of income among clubs remained fairly even this rationale found support from most League members. However, the growth in inequality from the 1960s onwards led to the eventual breakdown of the Football League and the creation of the Premier League in 1992. The cartel broke down because the members could not agree over the division of the spoils, primarily income from selling the TV rights. Further internal breakdowns might yet occur, but the shift of football clubs towards the pursuit of profit has also aroused the suspicion of the competition authorities. In the 1990s both the European Commission, which has jurisdiction in competition issues which involve trade between

An Outline of Business Strategy / 153

member states, and the Office of Fair Trading in the UK have shown an interest in the restrictive agreements entered into in the football industry and in 1997 an investigation into the sale of TV rights by football clubs began in the UK.

Appendix: the prisoner's dilemma

The prisoner's dilemma is probably the most famous example in Game Theory (a technique of analysis for dealing with situations where the decisions of individuals or firms are inter-related). Because of interdependence, rational individuals cannot base their plans on what they alone would like and must take into account the likely responses of others. In the prisoner's dilemma, by taking a view of rivals' responses individuals are led to make choices which appear sensible from a personal perspective, but lead to collective disaster. While people sometimes try to argue that there is a fault in the logic of the prisoner's dilemma (in fact there is not), we are surely all familiar with situations where we know there is a better outcome for everybody, but no one knows how to get to it. The prisoner's dilemma is simply a formalization of that intuition.

The original prisoner's dilemma is a story involving two criminals, Smith and Jones, who are being held in separate cells by the police. The police know that they have committed a serious crime but cannot prove it unless there is a confession by at least one of the prisoners. The police then offer the following deal to each one separately:

- If you confess to the serious crime while the other prisoner does not, we will ensure you receive a light sentence (say, one year).
- If you do not confess and the other prisoner does, we will ensure you go to prison for a very long time (say, ten years).
- If neither of you confesses, we will make sure that you are sent to prison on some trumped-up charge (say, two years).
- If both of you confess, then you will both go to prison for a long time, since we do not need the confession of one of you to convict the other. However, some allowance will be made for owning up so that the prison sentence will be less than the maximum (say, eight years).

The length of time each prisoner goes to prison, depending on the actions taken (for each prisoner 'confess' or 'not confess'), is called the payoff. If each prisoner tries to get the best payoff for himself alone, then the outcome will be that each prisoner confesses and so goes to prison for eight years, even though they would each be better off if they both chose not to confess and so went to prison for only two years. To see why both choose to confess, imagine you are Smith. Jones has two choices, confess or not confess. What is your best choice if Jones confesses? If you also confess you go to prison for eight years, while if you choose not to confess you go to prison for the full ten years: therefore you best choice is to confess, if Jones confesses. But what if Jones doesn't confess? If you also choose not to confess, you go to prison for two years, but you go to prison for only one year if you confess: once again your best choice is to confess. Thus regardless of what Jones chooses, your best payoff comes when you confess. However, the ranking of choices is exactly the same for Jones, so the best (selfish) choice is to confess, which is actually the worst possible outcome for Smith and Jones taken together, since they both end up going to prison for eight years. The key to this problem is that both Smith and Jones act selfishly, and believe that the other will also act selfishly, rather than valuing each other's interests.

Wages and league position

Between 1991 and 1995 Blackburn Rovers spent £26m on acquiring new players and a further £26m on paying their wages. Between 1991 and 1995 they rose from nineteenth in the old Second Division to become Premier League champions. It is undeniable that spending on players can affect playing performance, but sometimes the link appears unclear or to have broken down completely. For every Blackburn it is possible to point to a Middlesbrough or Wolverhampton, clubs which have spent prodigiously with limited rewards. Alternatively, clubs with limited financial resources such as Wimbledon or Coventry have managed to hold their own against more expensive rivals.

The playing performance of clubs attracts fans. More successful teams attract more support than less successful ones. Even if existing fans may remain loyal to their team regardless of performance, clubs find it harder to attract new supporters as their performance deteriorates. Similarly, teams which are successful attract a disproportionate share of the new fans coming into the game. However, success on the field is not the only factor which determines support. For example, in 1997 Wimbledon finished the season two places ahead of Tottenham. Wimbledon's home games were watched by an average of 15,156 spectators, while home games at Tottenham were watched by an average of 31,067. Largely because of this, Tottenham was able to realize income of nearly £28m for the season compared to a little over £10m for Wimbledon.

The primary purpose of business strategy is to understand the exceptional cases in any industry, the businesses which stand out above their rivals, but to do this one must first understand the regular cases. In this chapter we analyse two fundamental relationships. Each one concerns playing performance, measured here by league position. Firstly, we look at the playing performance of clubs in relation to their expenditure on players. Secondly, we look at the relationship between revenue and playing performance. These two relationships reflect the operation of two markets, the market for players and the market for supporting football clubs. Given these market relationships we can then go on to examine how some clubs outperform relative to the average in Chapter 6.

Footballers sell their services in a market. When a young talent emerges there are usually several clubs trying to persuade him to sign a contract. At the end of each contract the player may receive offers from a number of interested clubs, and it is common for players to be traded between clubs during an existing contract. Much of the day-to-day activity of a football club involves searching for new players and negotiating new contracts with existing players. In the days of maximum wage and the retain-and-transfer system, relationships between club and player were simple. Once hired, the footballer was more or less the captive of his club, and his wage was limited, no matter which club he played for. Since 1978, when the players were granted freedom of contract, they have been free to seek the best deal available. This has forced the clubs to offer terms which match what the player could expect to obtain elsewhere: the rule of the market.

Chapter 3 documented the growth of club wage bills as the market for players was liberalized. In this chapter we analyse the relationship between what individual clubs spent on wages in any particular year and their playing success measured by league performance. We begin by examining the expenditure of individual clubs in a particular year and correlating this with league position in that year. League position is obviously well known. Wage expenditure data can be obtained by inspecting the published annual accounts of football clubs because clubs are limited companies and must therefore file annual audited accounts at Companies House which are available for inspection by the public. Among the information that clubs must supply is the annual income (sales or turnover) and the annual wage expenditure. In recent years the accountants Deloitte & Touche have published convenient annual summaries of club accounting data.

Table 5.1 lists sixty-nine clubs for whom 1996–7 financial data was available. This represents three-quarters of the major professional clubs in England, and those missing are mostly from the Third Division[1]. In general we can see that not only do clubs in higher divisions tend to spend more money on wages than those in lower divisions, but clubs with higher positions in each division tend to spend more than those in lower positions. For example, clubs in the top half of the Premier League spent on average 52 per cent more than those in the bottom half (£13m compared to £8.6m). A similar picture emerges in the First Division, where clubs in the top half of the division spent 33 per cent more than those in the bottom half (£4.3m compared to £3.2m).

However, it is also possible to pick out instances where higher expenditure on wages did not lead to a higher position. In the Premier League the first four teams held the same ranks in terms of position as they did in terms of wage spending. However, Aston Villa, who came fifth, spent 8 per cent less on wages than Everton, who came fifteenth and only just avoided relegation. In Division One the champions, Bolton, spent 14 per cent less than Manchester City (the top spender in the division), who only managed fourteenth place. Barnsley gained promotion to the Premier League with a wage bill that was among the lowest in the division. Oldham actually spent more on wages than Barnsley and were relegated. In Divisions Two and Three wage spending appeared to have little to do with league position. For example, three of the biggest spenders finished in the bottom half of the division (Watford, Millwall and Preston).

Table 5.1 Wage expenditure and performance 1996–7

Premier League	Position	Wage bill (£000)	Division 1	Position	Wage bill (£000)
Manchester United	1	22,552	Bolton	1	6,159
Newcastle	2	17,487	Barnsley	2	2,613
Arsenal	3	15,279	Ipswich	4	4,321
Liverpool	4	15,030	Sheffield United	5	3,560
Aston Villa	5	10,070	Crystal Palace	6	5,340
Chelsea	6	14,873	Portsmouth	7	3,308
Sheffield Wednesday	7	7,571	QPR	9	6,659
Wimbledon	8	6,018	Birmingham	10	4,900
Leicester	9	8,914	Tranmere	11	3,282
Tottenham	10	12,057	Stoke	12	2,856
Leeds	11	12,312	Norwich	13	3,831
Derby	12	4,256	Manchester City	14	7,200
Blackburn	13	14,337	West Brom	16	3,095
West Ham	14	8,298	Oxford	17	2,331
Everton	15	10,933	Reading	18	3,035
Southampton	16	4,776	Swindon	19	3,276
Coventry	17	8,396	Huddersfield	20	2,251
Sunderland	18	5,703	Grimsby	22	2,037
Nottingham Forest	20	8,034	Oldham	23	2,779
			Southend	24	2,488

Division 2	Position	Wage bill (£000)	Division 3	Position	Wage bill (£000)
Bury	1	1,348	Wigan	1	606
Stockport	2	1,819	Swansea	5	1,039
Luton	3	2,842	Cambridge	10	842
Brentford	4	1,016	Mansfield	11	691
Crewe	6	1,052	Scunthorpe	13	889
Blackpool	7	2,006	Leyton Orient	16	1,296
Wrexham	8	1,397	Hull	17	1,091
Burnley	9	1,675	Hartlepool	20	503
Chesterfield	10	1,013	Brighton	23	1,127
Gillingham	11	1,036	Hereford	24	800
Watford	13	2,423			
Millwall	14	4,129			
Preston	15	2,145			
Bristol Rovers	17	1,546			
Wycombe	18	1,783			
Plymouth	19	1,301			
York	20	1,019			
Peterborough	21	1,973			
Shrewsbury	22	837			
Rotherham	23	1,106			

Source: Deloitte & Touche Annual Review of Club Accounts

Depending on which cases are examined Table 5.1 appears to tell any story the reader wants. Just by looking at the table it is hard to judge the strength or power of the relationship between wages and performance. What we want to be able to say is just how much influence wage expenditure is likely to have on performance, and we need some straightforward and simple way of representing this information. One way to do this is to draw a graph of wage expenditure against performance, as shown in Figure 5.1. League position is measured on the vertical axis while the total wage expenditure is measured on the horizontal axis[2] (the axes are scaled in logarithms to better illustrate the relationship). Each dot represents the combination of league position and wage expenditure for a particular club in 1996–7, and some of the clubs are labelled. Manchester United appear highest on the vertical axis, since they won the championship. Manchester United also appear farthest to the right in Figure 5.1, since they spent more than any other club on wages in that year. From the pattern of dots it can be seen that higher positions are generally associated with higher expenditure, and therefore most of the dots are located close to a diagonal line which runs from the bottom left-hand corner to the top right-hand corner. If all the dots lay exactly on this line, then we

Figure 5.1 Wage expenditure and performance sixty-nine clubs 1996–7

could say exactly how much a club had to spend to achieve a given league position. Since they do not, the relationship is not entirely predictable.

The line on Figure 5.1 is known as the 'regression' line.

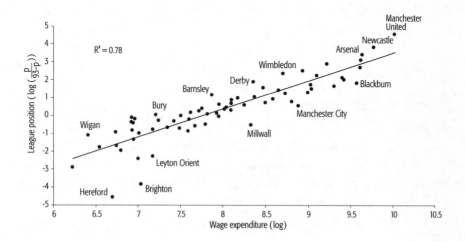

Regression was once thought of as an arcane statistical concept, largely because of the significant number of calculations required to estimate a regression line. However, the advent of personal computers and powerful spreadsheet packages such as Excel and Lotus have made regression a practical and accessible tool for anyone who can use a computer. To estimate a regression requires no more than a set of data typed into a spreadsheet package and a few seconds of computer time (the data in the appendix of this book, page 346, could be used to replicate Figure 5.1). A regression is essentially a calculation of the best 'fit' between two sets of data, between league position and wage expenditure in this case. It is an equation, a numerical representation of this relationship, allowing for the fact that any individual observation (club) need not conform exactly to the equation. For any individual observation the relationship between expenditure and performance can be broken down into two parts. First is that part which can be 'explained' by the regression, which is the vertical distance from zero to the regression line (remembering that the higher the vertical distance on the graph the higher is the league position). The second part is the unexplained variation, which is the vertical distance from the regression line to the actual position achieved (represented by each dot). This unexplained part (usually called the residual) can be either above or below the regression line, indicating that the regression has either over- or under-estimated the league position that the club should have achieved for its expenditure. Inspecting Figure 5.1 it is clear that for almost every club the vertical distance explained by the regression is much greater than the unexplained variation.

The proportion of the relationship which can be explained by the regression line is called the 'R^2' (R squared) of the regression.[3] This can be thought of as a measure of the reliability of the relationship and is also known as the 'goodness of fit'. In this case the R^2 is 0.78. Put another way, 78 per cent of the total variation in league position can be accounted for by wage expenditure. By most standards this is a high percentage: the correlation is very close.

While Figure 5.1 suggests that wage expenditure is important in explaining league position, there is a danger of placing too much trust in a single year's observations. How do we know that this was not just a freak year? Certainly, most clubs could point to some exceptional event, such as the loss of a key player, sacking of the manager, an unusually bad run of games, to explain a less than satisfactory performance. Pundits might also argue that individual clubs benefited from exceptional good fortune at one stage or another. At the moment we are not interested in particular stories relating to individual clubs, but it might also be that over time the relationship did not prove very reliable.

We could look at league performance and wage expenditure over time in several ways, but here we choose a particularly simple way. Since we have a complete accounting record for forty clubs from 1978 (the beginning of free agency) up to 1997, we relate the average wage expenditure to average league position achieved for each club over that period. This data is shown in Table 5.2. To measure average wage expenditure we have to take into account the fact that there has been considerable inflation in wage expenditure among all clubs since 1978. For example, when Liverpool were League Champions in 1979 the club wage bill was £690,000 (about the same as an average Third Division side in 1997), while in 1997 Manchester United spent £22.5m, nearly thirty-three times as much. If we simply looked at average wage expenditure over twenty years the average for each club would be weighted towards their expenditure in the later years, simply because every club was spending more by this time. To get around this problem the wage expenditure of each club in a particular year can be expressed as a multiple of the average for all clubs in that year. Thus Liverpool might spend two or three times the annual average, while Peterborough might spend less than half the average. By

Table 5.2 Wage
expenditure and
performance
1978–97

Club	Average league position	Wage spending relative to the average annual spending of all clubs
Liverpool	3	2.62
Manchester United	5	2.69
Arsenal	5	2.27
Everton	9	2.11
Tottenham	9	2.54
Aston Villa	10	1.65
Southampton	12	1.21
Coventry	14	1.34
West Ham	17	1.62
Leeds	17	1.62
Newcastle	20	1.69
Sheffield Wednesday	21	1.27
Blackburn	25	1.13
Leicester	25	1.08
Luton	25	1.09
Derby	26	1.01
West Brom	27	0.99
Oldham	31	0.69
Birmingham	32	1.07
Sheffield United	36	0.79
Barnsley	37	0.56
Bolton	43	0.76
Swindon	48	0.68
Bristol Rovers	49	0.42
Shrewsbury	49	0.39
Huddersfield	51	0.54
Plymouth	52	0.52
Hull	54	0.48
Reading	54	0.55
Brentford	55	0.45
Cambridge	56	0.38
Southend	57	0.44
Rotherham	58	0.40
Preston	60	0.47
Burnley	60	0.60
Wrexham	65	0.41
Bury	66	0.38
Peterborough	68	0.38
Mansfield	71	0.36
Scunthorpe	78	0.33

representing wage expenditure in this way an average can be constructed for each club over the period 1978 to 1997 without giving undue weight to spending in any particular year.

The clubs in Table 5.2 are ranked according to their average position over the twenty years. Liverpool was the most successful club over this period, averaging third position while averaging a wage spend which was over two and a half times the average. At the other end of the scale Scunthorpe averaged seventy-eighth position (i.e. mid-table in the Third Division) with a wage spend which was about one-third of the average for all clubs. It is clear from looking at Table 5.2 that the relationship between league performance and wage spending is even stronger over a period of time than for a single year. Few clubs ranked higher or lower in league position than they did in wage expenditure, and even in these cases the difference in the rankings was not that great.

The regression line for this data is shown in Figure 5.2. Once again we see a scatter of clubs around a regression line which indicates that higher wage expenditure is associated with higher league positions. Over this longer period of time clubs actually appear to lie closer to the regression line than they did in the single-year regression. This is confirmed by the fact that the proportion of the variation in league position which is explained by the regression line (R^2) is greater than before, at 92 per cent (compared to 78 per cent for the single year) of the total variation. This finding should not come as a surprise. If the performance of any individual club in any particular year is affected by random fluctuations or chance

Figure 5.2 Wage expenditure and performance forty clubs 1978–97

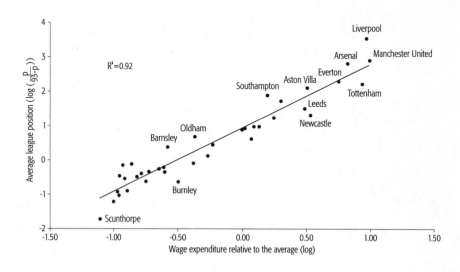

events, then over the years these effects should cancel out, so that the underlying relationship becomes clearer. Thus to the extent that the dot for any individual club deviates significantly from the regression line over a period of time (i.e. the unexplained variation), this deviation is unlikely to be attributable simply to luck (although twenty years of consistently good or bad luck is a possible explanation for over- or under-performance, it is not a very likely one). Before considering the interpretation of long-run deviations from the regression line for an individual club, it is important first to consider why the regression line indicates such a powerful relationship over a period of years.

Regression and the Market

What the regression line illustrates is the operation of the market for football players. In a world of free agency there is competition among clubs to obtain the best players. Because talent is scarce, the best players are offered the highest salaries, and the best teams are those filled with the best players. If wage expenditure translated exactly in league performance (i.e. the R^2 of the regression was 100 per cent), it could be said that the market for footballers was 'efficient', which in this context would simply mean that you get exactly what you pay for. (This might also make football rather less interesting, and we are not suggesting that efficiency is necessarily a good thing.) Given that the market is not perfectly efficient, how close to efficiency can we say it is? Being able to explain 92 per cent of the variation in average league position sounds quite close to efficiency. A useful comparison to make is with the period before the abolition of the maximum wage.

Table 5.3 gives the data for twenty-eight clubs over the period 1950–60, the eleven years leading up to the abolition of the maximum wage. The maximum wage restricted the amount that clubs spent by limiting the payments to the top players. In principle a club might spend an unlimited amount to accumulate an enormous squad, but in practice there were diminishing returns to scale, particularly in an era when the fixture list was far less congested. Because wage spending was constrained, the variation in wage spending relative to the average was much smaller in this period. Whereas between 1978 and 1997 Liverpool spent an average of nearly eight times as much as Scunthorpe United, between 1950 and 1960 the biggest spender (Tottenham) spent less than three times the average of the lowest spender (Oldham). What is also clear from the table is that while the clubs in the highest positions tended to spend more than those in the lowest positions, clubs in relatively low positions could easily spend just as much as those with much higher average positions. For example, Coventry achieved a rank of fiftieth on average with an average wage spend equal to the average of all clubs, while

Table 5.3 Wage expenditure and performance 1950–60

Club	Average league position	Wage spending relative to the average annual spending of all clubs
Manchester United	4	1.22
Arsenal	7	1.25
Burnley	8	0.89
West Brom	9	1.22
Bolton	10	1.01
Tottenham	10	1.52
Newcastle	11	1.35
Preston	12	1.10
Aston Villa	14	1.32
Sheffield Wednesday	19	1.23
Everton	20	0.85
Birmingham	20	1.31
Liverpool	21	0.81
Luton	24	0.97
Sheffield United	25	0.84
Blackburn	26	0.96
West Ham	29	1.22
Bristol Rovers	35	0.94
Hull	41	0.97
Barnsley	42	0.67
Bury	43	0.61
Brentford	43	0.82
Plymouth	44	0.88
Southampton	45	1.00
Coventry	50	0.92
Reading	53	0.79
Oldham	59	0.56
Swindon	59	0.62

The Structure of the Football Business / 167

Bolton spent almost exactly the same amount and achieved an average league position of tenth. The difference between these two levels of performance is equivalent to a position in mid-table of the old Third Division compared to mid-table in the old First Division. Manchester United, the most successful club of the period, managed an average league position of fourth with the same level of spending relative to the average as West Ham with a league position of twenty-ninth. The table also shows that there are several other cases involving large differences in what clubs could achieve for a given level of wage spending.

The regression line for this data is illustrated in Figure 5.3. Compared to Figure 5.2 the dots are much more widely spread, and consequently the percentage of the variation in league position which is explained by the regression line is much lower, the R^2 being 50 per cent. Wage expenditure did matter in the 1950s, but it was much less important than it has become in the era of free agency. Clubs which paid more money could in general attract the better players, although obtaining them on the transfer market was made more difficult and more expensive because of the restrictions on the rights of players to move club. Not all footballers were paid the maximum wage, and clubs in lower divisions might not

Figure 5.3 Wage expenditure and performance twenty-eight clubs 1950–60

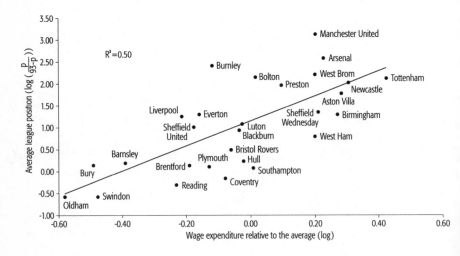

have any players on the maximum, but in general the maximum wage was so low that most clubs could afford to pay this amount to at least a few of their players, and were therefore as capable as the big clubs of attracting stars. The limit on wages meant that outspending rivals generally implied larger squads, which quickly ran into diminishing returns.

This comparison indicates that relatively speaking the market for players has become much more efficient since the introduction of free agency. Since then wage spending translates much more reliably into league position, which is precisely what we should have expected. Once the restrictions on players' salaries and mobility were removed the market was able to operate efficiently. In other words, the buyers and sellers were free to make the deals which suited them best. In general we expect that in a free market the seller will obtain a price which reflects the quality of what is being sold, and the buyer will have to match the best price offered by any other buyer. Thus on average we would expect better players to obtain higher wages. While in individual instances a buyer might pay more or less than the going rate, we would not expect this situation to persist over a long period of time. In the context of football, 'better' generally means possessing talents which are more likely to win matches. Thus the highest wages are paid to players whose teams win more matches and therefore achieve the highest league positions. Clubs demand such players either because their objective is playing success or because they believe their ultimate objective (profits, prestige, etc.) can only be achieved through playing success.

Of course, the freedom to buy and sell does not in itself guarantee an efficient market. Some markets will operate very inefficiently if left to themselves. Efficient markets can be thought of as those in which the process of competition determines the price of a good or the wage of a worker so that supply and demand are brought into balance. In an inefficient market there exist either buyers who would be prepared to pay more or sellers who would be willing to sell for less but for some reason are unable to do so. Cases of 'market failure' can arise for a number of reasons.

Monopolies are generally inefficient because the seller has excessive power to control the price while the case where there is only a single buyer in the market (monopsony) can also be shown to be inefficient. The situation before 1978 has often been described as one in which the clubs held monopsony power, being able to control the careers of players on their own books. Take for example the case of Bill Shankly mentioned in Chapter 3: his club did not need his services but he was still willing to play league football and there were clubs which would have hired him. With a willing seller and a willing buyer there is a clear gain to each side from trade, and so trade is efficient. Monopsony power could prevent efficient trades. In a world of free agency Shankly's club would not have been able to prevent this transaction. This effect may well have contributed to the relative inefficiency of the market observed between 1950 and 1960.

Another important factor which can interfere with the efficient operation of markets is a lack of information on the part of buyers or sellers. It is difficult to set a price which reflects the true worth of what is being sold if its qualities cannot be easily observed by one side or the other. Examples of this phenomenon abound. Purchasing a second-hand car is always a risky business because it is hard to tell whether it is in good condition. Superficial embellishments can make a car appear sound when in fact it is close to being a wreck. Buying a genuine Persian carpet requires an expertise which most potential buyers lack, and therefore they either do not buy at all or have to rely on an expert. Many of the best examples of information asymmetry relate to employment relationships. In recent years there has been a great deal of controversy concerning the remuneration of senior executives, mostly in large corporations. Chairmen and directors are often extremely well paid, and their salaries have risen rapidly since the 1970s. And yet it is difficult for shareholders to gauge whether they are getting value for their money. How can the performance of a company chairman be measured? If one could observe how much work he did, it would be possible to devise a scale of wages to reflect the effort contributed. But this is not possible. Suppose the chairman of one large corporation was observed playing golf with the chairman of another. Without actually participating in the round of golf it would be impossible to form a view on whether the chairman was simply playing golf or laying the groundwork for a valuable deal. In the event of being unable to monitor the precise contribution of an employee, companies tend to reward their staff on the basis of outputs: incentives which relate to company performance such as the granting of share options or bonuses based on company profits. These mechanisms can be very powerful, but they can also be quite blunt instruments, rewarding people for achievements which were not their own or failing to reward genuine contributions which could not be directly observed.

Such problems are not characteristic of professional football. Footballers' efforts are easily observed, in terms of both intrinsic ability and application, and therefore it is relatively easy to place a market value on the contribution of each player. Not only can such judgements be made by the performance of the player on the field, but also these performances are sufficiently regular so as to permit periodic reassessments. Nor are such judgements made behind closed doors; because football is a spectator sport it is possible to obtain evidence on several players at many different points in time. This does not require the manager to go to watch every player whose services he might wish to acquire. With scouts and videos a manager can in principle accumulate a large amount of information on the players he tries to hire without ever going to watch them himself. The key to assessing the worth of a footballer is to make comparisons, to be able to compare the skills of two players. While different players have different talents, the manager needs to be able to come to an overall judgement on which ones will make the greater contribution to the team. This judgement (even if sometimes incorrect) can be made because of the observability of the talents and efforts of players.[4]

More than money

In a world of free agency, wage expenditure is the single most powerful factor which accounts for variations in team performance. The market for players is the mechanism by which the value of the player on the pitch is translated into the wage rate for each player. This wage rate changes from year to year and depends on what every other player is getting. As in the winner-takes-all story, the greatest rewards go to the greatest talents.

If the market is completely efficient, in the specific sense that players are paid no more and no less than they are worth, measured by their contribution to the performance of the club on the pitch, then wage expenditure alone should capture all the variation in league performance. This is a powerful conclusion. For example, consider the difference between a successful striker with an outstanding goal-scoring record and a run-of-the-mill centre forward. A team that employs the more talented player should do better than a team employing the less talented player. If we measure talent by, say, the number of goals per game, then this measure would on its own be a good predictor of team performance. Now suppose we knew the strike rate of every forward in the league, then this indicator should also be a good predictor of league performance. But now consider what would happen if instead we used the wages paid to strikers to measure performance. If the market works efficiently, using wages should capture the differences in the players' strike rates. Otherwise some players would be underpaid and therefore could profitably be poached by rival clubs, and some players would be overpaid, implying that their employers would be looking for (and able to find) a cheaper yet equally effective striker.

Players differ in quality in more ways than in simple goal-scoring ability, and the variation in wages should be accounted for by many different factors. However, the variation in wages should account for all the variation in performance in an efficient market, otherwise, as before, some players are being overpaid and some are being underpaid. It is possible to identify many quantifiable characteristics by which players differ. We can test the extent to which the market actually is efficient by seeing whether or not these other factors contribute anything to the explanation of league performance *once the effect of wage expenditure is allowed for*. If they do, we have evidence that the market is inefficient in some way. If they do not, then while we have not proven that the market is efficient, we have evidence to support that hypothesis.

The relationship between wage expenditure and league performance was illustrated using the statistical technique known as regression analysis. Regression analysis can be extended from the case where a single factor is used to explain variations to the case of multiple regression, where many factors can be included. Multiple regressions can include any factors on which data can be collected, the only condition being that they must in some way be quantifiable. As well as testing for the efficiency of the market, the purpose of looking at these factors is to obtain the most complete explanation possible for the performance of football clubs.

Extending the regression analysis to include other factors can be done only if those other factors are in some way quantifiable. Once found, such quantifiable factors can in principle be used to formulate the policies of football clubs. In theory at least, if these relationships exist then the future performance will be predictable. For example, if we choose a level of expenditure from the horizontal axis of Figure 5.2, we can obtain an estimate of the league position which should be achieved on average by looking at the corresponding point on the regression line which can be found on the vertical axis.

Table 5.4 The effect of spending on league position based on the regression from Figure 5.2	Spending as a multiple of the average for all clubs	League position	Division
	2	7	Premier
	1.5	13	Premier
	1	5	First
	0.5	12	Second

Some examples are provided in Table 5.4, which indicates the long-run average position associated with different levels of wage expenditure as a multiple of the average for all clubs. What we are also interested in discovering is whether some clubs are able to sustain an above-average performance after allowing for all the factors we can quantify. These clubs can be said to possess some form of competitive advantage, since what makes them successful cannot be imitated because what makes them successful is not known.[5] This is considered in more detail in the next chapter.

Eight further factors are considered here. They are the net annual transfer spending by clubs, the number of players used in first-team league matches in a season, the proportion of squad members who were home-grown players, the squad size, the number of players in the team who have represented England at international level, the length of tenure of the manager, the proportion of first-team appearances accounted for by black players and the playing history of the club. These variables are summarized by year and by club in Tables 5.5 and 5.6.

Transfers

Transfer spending is a surprisingly poor predictor of performance. If it is included together with the club wage in a performance regression, it adds almost nothing to our ability to explain league position. Partly this is because transfer spending and wage spending are closely correlated.[6] Higher spending to obtain players usually leads to higher spending on wages as well. This can be seen by examining the correlation coefficient between wages and transfers for the sample of clubs used so far. The correlation coefficient is a number which must lie between 1 (perfect positive correlation) and –1 (perfect negative correlation). A correlation coefficient of 0 implies no correlation at all. The correlation coefficient between wages and transfers is 0.56, which implies a positive relationship, and one which is relatively close, although by no means exact. When transfers are high, wages also tend to be high. This suggests that we might try substituting transfer spending in the performance regression instead of wages (i.e. allowing transfers to determine league position rather than wages). However, when we do this the R^2 of the regression falls from 0.92 to 0.16.[7] The reason is that although transfer spending is closely related to wages, it is less closely related to league position in any given year. Transfer spending is an investment which may take several years to pay off, and at the time the investment is made there is no way of predicting in which year the benefits will show through. It is not possible to

Table 5.5 Data on club and player characteristics by year[8]

Year	Average annual spending on transfers (£000 1997)	Average managerial tenure (years)	Average number of players appearing in first-team matches over the season	Average number of professional players employed	Average number of home-grown players	Number of black players[9]
1978	54	2.7	22	25	14	4
1979	266	2.4	23	26	14	8
1980	245	3.1	23	28	15	12
1981	156	3.5	22	28	14	14
1982	196	3.3	22	29	14	16
1983	19	3.0	23	28	14	18
1984	61	3.2	23	23	11	23
1985	28	2.6	23	24	11	31
1986	100	2.8	23	22	9	36
1987	121	2.7	24	25	10	31
1988	81	2.6	25	26	9	31
1989	87	2.9	25	10	10	39
1990	424	2.7	25	28	10	48
1991	261	2.7	25	29	11	46
1992	398	2.4	26	30	11	54
1993	699	2.6	27	31	11	52
1994	536	2.7	27	31	11	
1995	1,020	2.4	26	29	10	
1996	2,379	2.4	29	30	12	
1997	1,596	2.4	28	30	11	

The Structure of the Football Business / 175

Table 5.6	Club	Average annual spending on transfers (£000 1997)	Average tenure of incumbent manager (years)	Average number of players appearing in first-team matches over the season	Average number of professional players employed	Average number of home-grown players	Average number of England internationals	Average number of England international caps awarded
Data on club and player characteristics by club	Arsenal	1,401	4	22	33	21	3	12
	Aston Villa	1,290	3	24	31	15	1	3
	Barnsley	−99	2	24	26	11	0	0
	Birmingham	16	2	29	28	13	0	0
	Blackburn	1,284	3	23	27	9	1	3
	Bolton	219	3	23	26	11	0	0
	Brentford	−25	2	26	24	6	0	0
	Bristol Rovers	−272	2	25	24	11	0	0
	Burnley	106	2	25	27	11	0	0
	Bury	−10	2	24	23	5	0	0
	Cambridge	−170	2	27	24	6	0	0
	Coventry	779	3	25	31	14	0	0
	Everton	1,954	3	23	30	12	1	5
	Huddersfield	−26	3	24	25	9	0	0
	Hull	−165	2	25	25	12	0	0
	Leeds	1,812	3	25	32	16	1	2
	Leicester	149	2	25	31	15	0	0
	Liverpool	2,864	3	20	34	12	3	14
	Luton	-408	3	24	29	17	0	0
	Manchester United	1,261	4	23	40	22	3	13
	Mansfield	−93	3	25	22	7	0	0
	Newcastle	2,201	2	25	32	14	1	2
	Oldham	−223	7	25	27	12	0	0
	Peterborough	−13	2	26	22	6	0	0
	Plymouth	−75	2	25	25	10	0	0
	Preston	−140	2	26	26	9	0	0
	Reading	−73	3	24	23	7	0	0
	Rotherham	−35	2	24	24	10	0	0
	Scunthorpe	−80	2	25	22	6	0	0
	Sheffield Wednesday	709	3	24	30	14	0	2
	Sheffield United	179	3	27	29	9	0	0
	Shrewsbury	−105	2	24	23	8	0	0
	Southampton	844	5	24	29	16	1	5
	Southend	−315	2	24	23	7	0	0
	Swindon	−197	2	24	25	7	0	0
	Tottenham	1,192	3	25	36	21	2	10
	West Brom	9	2	26	30	12	0	1
	West Ham	1,086	6	24	30	15	1	3
	Wrexham	−60	3	25	23	11	0	0

allocate the benefits of transfer spending to any particular year even with the benefit of hindsight. In general the transfer payment associated with a player is fixed at the beginning of his contract and does not vary with subsequent performance. This means that transfer spending involves a gamble on future performance which may or may not pay off.[10]

One important reason why transfers are a relatively poor predictor of performance is related to the notion of market efficiency. While the market for transfers is relatively active, most players do not move in a single season. Relying on transfer spending to explain performance means using information about only those players who were actually transferred, ignoring the effect on performance of those who were not. In any individual year a club may spend a large amount on transfers and occasionally even more than its annual wage bill. However, such sums are to some extent balanced by sales of players made in other years. While the big clubs tend to be net buyers and the small clubs tend to be net sellers, for any individual club wages loom larger in total player spending when averaged over time. This is illustrated in Table 5.7.[11] Even clubs, such as Newcastle and Blackburn, which have been revived by extensive buying in the transfer market in the 1990s devote around two-thirds of their player budget to paying the wage bill.

In practice, it simply isn't possible to attract big stars without ending up paying high wages as well. Clubs which have a positive transfer fee number are net buyers in the market, while those with negative numbers are net sellers. Most of the net buyers over time spend on average about 90 per cent of their budget for players on wages. Big spenders such as Liverpool and Manchester United still spent between two-thirds and four-fifths of their budget on wages over the period 1978–97. Over the years transfer spending even by the big clubs tends to cancel out.

Players used

It is frequently observed that stable teams tend to be more successful. Thus it might be expected that a club with a relatively lower player turnover will do better than a club with a relatively high turnover, assuming that each club paid out the

Table 5.7 The share of wages in total player spending 1978-97	Club	Average annual wage bill (£000 1997)	Average transfer spending (£000 1997)	Wage bill as a pecentage of total player spending
	Newcastle	4,405	2,317	66%
	Liverpool	5,803	2,864	67%
	Leeds	3,817	1,812	68%
	Everton	4,351	1,954	69%
	Blackburn	3,263	1,284	72%
	Aston Villa	3,590	1,290	74%
	Southampton	2,434	844	74%
	West Ham	3,289	1,086	75%
	Arsenal	4,946	1,401	78%
	Coventry	2,777	779	78%
	Sheffield Wednesday	2,927	709	81%
	Tottenham	5,253	1,192	82%
	Derby	2,310	502	82%
	Manchester United	6090	1,261	83%
	Bolton	1,545	219	88%
	Burnley	1,020	106	91%
	Sheffield United	2,503	177	93%
	Leicester	2,351	149	94%
	Birmingham	2,024	16	99%
	West Brom	1,743	9	99%
	Bury	687	−10	102%
	Peterborough	767	−17	102%
	Huddersfield	1,031	−26	103%
	Brentford	817	−25	103%
	Rotherham	703	−35	105%
	Reading	1,169	−73	107%
	Plymouth	955	−75	108%
	Wrexham	692	−60	109%
	Barnsley	1,076	−99	110%
	Swindon	1,536	−197	115%
	Scunthorpe	591	−80	116%
	Oldham	1,493	−223	118%
	Shrewsbury	683	−105	118%
	Preston	875	−140	119%
	Hull	843	−165	124%
	Mansfield	600	−126	127%
	Luton	2,011	−430	127%
	Cambridge	703	−170	132%
	Southend	1,011	−315	145%
	Bristol Rovers	821	−272	150%

same amount in wages. If the same players appear together regularly over a season, they are likely to develop a better rapport with each other. In general managers recognize this advantage and where possible try to maintain a stable team. In the regression analysis the smaller the number of players used in a season the higher the league position tends to be.

This is illustrated in Table 5.8, which shows the average number of players making first-team appearances in a season for clubs achieving a specific league position over the period 1978–97 from our sample of forty clubs. On average over this period a team winning the First Division had only nineteen players making first-team appearances, while a club coming twentieth used on average twenty-six players, and mid-table teams used on average around twenty-three or twenty-four players.

The ability to maintain a stable team is partly a matter of the consistency of individual players and a coherent strategy on the part of the manager (and indeed keeping the same manager in the job). However, injuries also play a significant part in the success of teams, and to some extent the number of players used is therefore a matter of good fortune, largely beyond the control of the club and the manager.

Table 5.8 First Division positions 1978–97, average number of players used and number of players used relative to the average of all clubs for each year

League position	Number of players making first-team appearances in a season	Number of players making first-team appearances as a percentage of the average number of first-team appearances for all clubs
1	19	83%
2	21	90%
3	22	94%
4	22	95%
5	22	93%
6	23	97%
7	24	101%
8	24	102%
9	23	98%
10	24	103%
11	25	106%
12	23	99%
13	26	110%
14	25	108%
15	26	109%
16	26	110%
17	25	105%
18	25	106%
19	24	101%
20	26	112%

Home-grown players

Every club hires its players in one or two possible ways: either a player is bought from another club (outright or leased on a loan) or he signs with the club without ever having registered with another club: in other words he is home-grown. On average about 45 per cent of players in the leagues are home-grown, with clubs in higher league positions tending to develop a greater proportion of home-grown talent than those in lower league positions, reflecting not just larger squad sizes but also more extensive youth development policies. Home-grown talent might be thought of as cheaper than buying players in the open market because there is no transfer fee. However, producing home-grown players requires investment in a youth development programme which is itself expensive. In an efficient market individual clubs would invest in developing home-grown talent to the point where the cost of that development just matched the cost of buying extra talent from outside.

Similarly, if players expected to obtain a higher return on their abilities by moving to another club, they would seek to sign shorter contracts in order to move on more quickly. In doing so this would reduce the supply of home-grown talent, which would in turn lead to the wage rate for such talent being driven up. Alternatively, if home-grown talent received a higher return than players who moved clubs, players would be less willing to move, increasing the bargaining position of clubs and driving down their wages. Ultimately the wages paid to home-grown and bought-in players of equivalent ability should be driven to equality in an efficient market. If the market is efficient we should therefore expect that after adjusting for the wage bill, the performance of teams with an above average proportion of home-grown talent will be no better or worse than that of teams with a below average proportion of home-grown talent. This hypothesis is in fact confirmed by the regression results, which show that the proportion of the team made up by home-grown talent makes no significant difference to the league performance of a club, once the effect of wage spending has been included.

Squad size

A club which can afford to maintain a larger squad (i.e. players available for use in the first team) can generally expect to do better than a club which can afford only a small squad, assuming players have comparable levels of ability. A larger squad can give the manager a greater range of possible playing strategies based on the different talents of individual players, while when there are injuries a club with a large squad may be able to adapt more easily. However, larger squads cost more money in terms of player salaries. Investing in large squads is thus a similar kind of activity to buying better players. We might therefore expect that the effect of larger squad sizes is captured simply by the wage expenditure of clubs, just as the quality of players is reflected in the wage expenditure. This is in fact the case. From the regression it can be shown that there is no additional effect on league performance attributable to the size of the squad maintained by each club, given that the clubs' wage expenditure is already accounted for.

England players

Teams with more players who have played international football are more likely to win games than other sides. International recognition is often a consequence of club success. To measure these effects data was collected on players who had represented England at international level. While this of course leaves out many other international players, restricting the analysis to these players avoids difficult comparisons in the status of international caps for different countries, while including a large enough number of players to allow any effect to be measured.

In the regression analysis clubs which employ footballers who have represented England do appear to perform better than those who do not. But the regression also suggests that it is just as likely that these players have achieved international recognition because of the success of the club in the league as that the club is successful because it employs exceptionally talented international players. Statistically the two measures, league position and the number of international players at a club, are determined simultaneously and it is not possible to say that one causes the other. This is not the case with wages. While statistically position is affected by wages, tests show that wages are not directly affected by position (even though players receive bonuses, these bonuses are written into their contracts, which are determined by their ability, which in turn determines league position).[12]

This finding is consistent with the operation of the market. Players who represent their country at international level are generally of a higher ability than the average player, and in an efficient market such players will be paid a wage which reflects this ability. Thus the wage bill of the club will reflect the ability of international squad members and the presence of internationals will have no effect beyond that measured in the wage bill. If the market were not efficient, a club could concentrate on hiring internationals and achieve a higher level of performance for a given expenditure than a club buying talented players who were not England internationals. The data suggests that such a strategy is unlikely to succeed.

Managerial tenure
In the analysis of club performance managers are like players. They bring to the development of the team skills which affect league position, but these skills have to be paid for in the wage bill of the club. There is as much a market for managers as there is a market for players, and each manager can be expected to obtain a market return for his skills. Managers who are successful tend to have a longer tenure. However, simply awarding longer tenure is not a recipe for success. As in the case of England internationals, the length of tenure is

jointly determined with league position rather than causing it. If this were not the case, then a club could improve its league performance simply by holding on to its manager for longer. It is often said that clubs fire managers too quickly, but it may also be the case that clubs are on occasion too loyal to managers, retaining them when it would be better to fire them. If it were possible to predict an improvement on performance simply by always retaining a manager longer (or firing him sooner), the market would be shown to be inefficient. This is not the case.

Race[13]

Market efficiency would also imply that race had no effect on the performance of a club, since even if black players differed systematically in their abilities these should be accounted for in the wage rates of players. In fact black players who have played in the football leagues are different from their colleagues. Some data on black players compared with a random sample of white players is shown in Table 5.9. Firstly, as is well known, they have tended to play more in forward positions and are less likely to be goalkeepers. Not surprisingly therefore black players tend to score more goals. However, they also tend to have longer careers, make more league appearances and make more international appearances. On the face of it this would suggest that the average black player is better than the average white player. In an efficient market black players would on average receive higher wages if they have higher ability. Racial discrimination is a form of market inefficiency. If there was discriminati0n, then black players of a given ability would be paid less than white players, and it would also follow that teams with an above average proportion of black players would achieve a higher level of performance for a given wage expenditure compared to other clubs. Regression analysis using data on black player appearances between 1978 and 1993 indicates that this is in fact the case, suggesting that there is evidence of discrimination.

Table 5.9	Black players born 1957–74	Non-black players born 1957–74
Sample size	193	193
Year born	1964.7	1964.7
% born overseas	11.4	4.7
% born in the North	22.3	53.9
% born in the Midlands	20.7	15.0
% born in the South	46.4	26.4
Year playing career started	1983.7	1983.8
Last year of playing career	1990.0	1987.7
Career length (years)	6.3	3.9
Number of clubs represented	3.0	2.1
League appearances	147.6	95.4
Goals scored during playing career	25.1	11.8
% who represented their country	35.8	22.8
% playing in defence	26.5	32.1
% playing in midfield	15.0	26.4
% playing in affack	58.5	33.2
% goalkeepers	0.0	7.8

Table 5.9
Playing careers

History

Quantifying the effect of history might be thought to be rather difficult, but in fact most fans, players and club officials are well aware of their own club's history, and the history of the game constitutes an important part of the attraction of football. In looking at the long-run performance of clubs, history can be quantified as the succession of league positions achieved from foundation to the present time. While this might seem a little different from the conventional notion of history, each year's league position can be thought of as summarizing the events which occurred in that year. History in this sense is connected to current performance, but the connection appears to be a negative one. Teams with relatively high league positions tend to fall back, while those with relatively low league positions tend to improve. Statistically, every club is attracted towards the mean. The implication of this is that if there were no other factors affecting league performance from year to year (such as wage expenditure, transfer spending and so on), then in the long run each club would achieve an average league position which is the mid-point of all possible positions (forty-sixth out of ninety-two). This does not mean that in every year all clubs would be bottom of the

Winners and Losers / 184

First Division, rather that on average clubs would expect to do no better than any other club, as one might expect.[14] In reality clubs do spend money and so we only observe the process of attraction towards the mean combined with other factors. What it means in practical terms is that a winning history is not sufficient to guarantee future success.

In considering the relationship between wage expenditure and league position we have looked at a number of additional factors which may also be related to league position and which can be accounted for through regression analysis. These are summarized in Table 5.10. Overall the effect of these other factors does little to change the underlying relationship between wage expenditure and performance. There are no doubt other factors which might be added to the analysis in order to obtain an even better fit between the choices of football clubs and their performance on the pitch, but it is unlikely that anything would approach the significance of the wage bill.

The significance of the wage bill arises through the operation of the market for players. The market ensures that each club can in general obtain only the league position which is warranted by the talent it pays for. In other words, most of the value which a player generates by his performance accrues to him through the process of competitive bidding for talent.

Factor	Effect on league position
Wage expenditure	Tends to improve it, strongly significant
Transfer expenditure	Tends to improve it, little additional impact once wages accounted for
Players used	More players leads to poorer performance, probably the effect of injuries
Home-grown players	No effect after controlling for wage expenditure
Squad size	No effect after controlling for wage expenditure
England internationals	Successful teams tend to have more England internationals, but does not appear to be cause and effect
Managerial tenure	Successful teams tend to have more managers whose tenure is longer, but does not appear to be cause and effect
Race	More black players tends to lead to better performance even after allowing for wages, indicating some evidence of discrimination
History	Without consistent wage spending clubs in high positions tend to gravitate towards the mid-point of league positions (i.e. bottom of the First/top of the Second Division)

Table 5.10
Factors affecting league performance

In the next chapter we will consider examples of clubs which appear to have been able to beat the market by obtaining a level of playing performance greater than the club's wage expenditure would warrant. This achievement clearly reflects an important kind of competitive advantage for a football club. First, however, we examine the other relationship introduced at the beginning of this chapter, the relationship between league position and revenue.

Revenue and league performance

Just as there is a market for players there is a market for supporters. Teams which enjoy greater playing success tend to generate more income. More successful teams are better at attracting fans and at maintaining their loyalty. A successful team will tend to attract greater attendances at matches played against any given rival, or played at any particular stage of any particular competition. Paying fans attending matches have been the main source of income for football clubs throughout most of their history, but in recent years clubs have developed new sources of revenue. Broadcast rights, sponsorship and merchandising have provided additional income, but they too are affected by the playing success of the clubs. Teams with better playing records are televised more frequently and receive a greater share of broadcast revenues. Corporate sponsors are willing to pay more to be associated with successful teams and successful teams are able to sell more merchandise.

In general one might expect that the market for spectators would be a lot less efficient than the market for players, since footballers are likely to be mobile and willing to play for the club which offers the highest wage, while football supporters will be loyal and remain true to their club regardless of playing success. However, this is not the picture which emerges from an examination of the data. Table 5.11 shows the league position and revenue of league clubs for the season 1996–7. As one might expect clubs in the higher divisions tend to have larger incomes. Also, clubs in the top half of any division tend to have a larger income than those in the bottom half. But it is also clear from the table that there are many exceptions. For example, Everton in 1996–7 came fifteenth in the Premier League with an income of nearly £19m, while Wimbledon

Table 5.11
Revenue and performance 1996–7

Premier League	Position	Revenue (£000)
Manchester United	1	87,939
Newcastle	2	41,134
Arsenal	3	27,158
Liverpool	4	39,153
Aston Villa	5	22,079
Chelsea	6	23,729
Sheffield Wednesday	7	14,335
Wimbledon	8	10,410
Leicester	9	17,320
Tottenham	10	27,874
Leeds	11	21,785
Derby	12	10,738
Blackburn	13	14,302
West Ham	14	15,256
Everton	15	18,882
Southampton	16	9,238
Coventry	17	12,265
Sunderland	18	13,415
Nottingham Forest	20	14,435

Division 1	Position	Revenue (£000)
Bolton	1	7,653
Barnsley	2	3,658
Ipswich	4	6,226
Sheffield United	5	5,133
Crystal Palace	6	7,856
Portsmouth	7	4,351
QPR	9	7,497
Birmingham	10	7,622
Tranmere	11	3,464
Stoke	12	5,026
Norwich	13	6,271
Manchester City	14	12,727
WBA	16	6,073
Oxford	17	2,225
Reading	18	3,311
Swindon	19	4,695
Huddersfield	20	3,745
Grimsby	22	2,152
Oldham	23	3,098
Southend	24	2,449

Division 2	Position	Revenue (£000)
Bury	1	1,889
Stockport	2	2,945
Luton	3	2,955
Brentford	4	1,921
Crewe	6	1,406
Blackpool	7	2,432
Wrexham	8	1,732
Burnley	9	3,701
Chesterfield	10	3,222
Gillingham	11	1,940
Watford	13	2,963
Millwall	14	4,054
Preston	15	3,847
Bristol Rovers	17	1,374
Wycombe	18	3,218
Plymouth	19	2,297
York	20	1,064
Peterborough	21	3,452
Shrewsbury	22	869
Rotherham	23	799

Division 3	Position	Revenue (£000)
Wigan	1	909
Swansea	5	1,180
Cambridge	10	784
Mansfield	11	985
Scarborough	12	809
Scunthorpe	13	1,072
Leyton Orient	16	1,462
Hull	17	799
Hartlepool	20	762
Brighton	23	1,102
Hereford	24	1,035

came eighth but only generated an income of £10.4m. However, when we look at the regression line for the relationship between league position and income (Figure 5.4) the proportion of the variation in income which league position can explain is 82 per cent (this is the R^2), which is comparable to the 78 per cent of variation in league position which could be explained by wage expenditure.

A similar story emerges when we look at the relationship between revenue and league position over the period 1978–97 for the same forty clubs which were considered in the previous sections. Table 5.12 shows the average league position and revenue relative to the average for each club over the nineteen-year period. As with wage expenditure, when we look at clubs over any period of time it makes more sense to express income relative to the average of a particular year, since over time the income generated by football clubs has expanded rapidly. Clubs with higher average league positions tend to have higher revenues relative to their rivals. When this relationship is plotted as a graph as in Figure 5.5, we see from the regression line that 89 per cent of the variation in incomes relative to the average is explained by league position. If anything, this suggests an even closer relationship between income and league success than the data for the same period

Figure 5.4
Revenue and performance Sixty-nine Clubs 1996–7

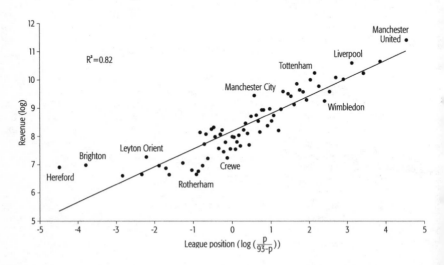

Table 5.12	Club	Average league position	Revenue relative to the average annual revenue of all clubs
Revenue and performance 1978–97	Liverpool	3	2.90
	Manchester United	5	4.22
	Arsenal	5	2.60
	Everton	9	2.15
	Tottenham	9	3.39
	Aston Villa	10	1.91
	Southampton	12	1.25
	Coventry	14	1.05
	West Ham	17	1.64
	Leeds	17	1.41
	Newcastle	20	1.75
	Sheffield Wednesday	21	1.25
	Blackburn	25	0.71
	Leicester	25	1.04
	Luton	25	1.10
	Derby	26	1.19
	West Brom	27	1.00
	Oldham	31	0.57
	Birmingham	32	0.75
	Sheffield United	36	0.71
	Barnsley	37	0.37
	Bolton	43	0.61
	Swindon	48	0.56
	Bristol Rovers	49	0.34
	Shrewsbury	49	0.23
	Huddersfield	51	0.37
	Plymouth	52	0.66
	Hull	54	0.27
	Reading	54	0.41
	Brentford	55	0.40
	Cambridge	56	0.33
	Southend	57	0.39
	Rotherham	58	0.29
	Preston	60	0.39
	Burnley	60	0.43
	Wrexham	65	0.35
	Bury	66	0.24
	Peterborough	68	0.29
	Mansfield	71	0.23
	Scunthorpe	78	0.24

and the same clubs showed between league position and wage expenditure (compare Figure 5.2).

Table 5.13 shows the relationship for twenty-eight clubs over the period 1950–60. In Figure 5.6 the relationship is graphed, and we find that 62 per cent of the variation in income relative to the average can be explained by league position.

The Structure of the Football Business / 189

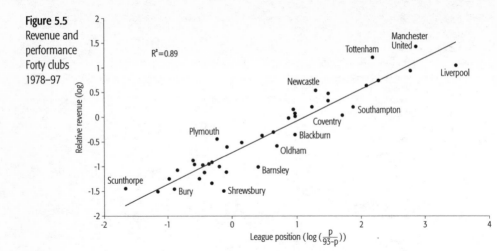

Figure 5.5
Revenue and
performance
Forty clubs
1978–97

All this suggests that support, at least measured by income generated, is about as fickle as the average player: both are driven by success. Successful players move to the clubs who pay the most, and fans shift towards supporting successful clubs. This is not an entirely fair characterization of all football supporters. Many fans do remain loyal to a club through thick and thin. These fans might be thought of as the hard-core of any club, its most reliable source of income. However, beyond the hard-core there are many supporters who are willing to switch allegiance towards more successful teams. This may not be mere fickleness, but may actually reflect a greater interest in the quality of the football played rather than the fortunes of any one club. This effect is likely to be particularly damaging when a club is relegated to a lower division. Another important aspect is that each year some fans give up watching football while new ones begin attending matches. The newcomers are likely to be disproportionately drawn to the more successful clubs, if only because these are more familiar to them. Thus over time, if a club is not successful, it will find its fan base dwindling to the level of hard-core support. All these effects relate to income generated by match attendances. Other sources of income are likely to be much more sensitive to playing success since they are much less dependent on supporter loyalty. Broadcast income is likely to be highly dependent on the perceived quality of the team, which is in turn likely to be closely correlated with playing success; sponsors want to be associated with successful teams and so on. Thus in the end it is perhaps not surprising that club revenues tend to be just as sensitive to playing success as playing success is to wage expenditure.

Just as we considered other factors which might explain league position, we can look at other factors which explain revenues. In fact the contributions from the various sources discussed in Chapter 3 might be included in any explanation of revenue generation. However, most of these sources themselves depend on playing success measured by league performance. The other obvious source of income opportunities is

	Club	Average league position	Revenue relative to the average annual revenue of all clubs
Table 5.13 Revenue and performance 1950–60			
	Manchester United	4	1.49
	Arsenal	7	1.95
	Burnley	8	1.00
	West Brom	9	1.01
	Bolton	10	1.01
	Tottenham	10	1.63
	Newcastle	11	1.39
	Preston	12	0.93
	Aston Villa	14	1.61
	Sheffield Wednesday	19	1.05
	Everton	20	1.58
	Birmingham	20	0.86
	Liverpool	21	1.03
	Luton	24	0.81
	Sheffield United	25	1.03
	Blackburn	26	0.82
	West Ham	29	0.80
	Bristol Rovers	35	0.86
	Hull	41	1.00
	Barnsley	42	0.47
	Bury	43	0.57
	Brentford	43	0.59
	Plymouth	44	0.74
	Southampton	45	0.73
	Coventry	50	0.61
	Reading	53	0.59
	Oldham	59	0.39
	Swindon	59	0.55

The Structure of the Football Business / 191

cup competition, from the FA Cup and various incarnations of the League (currently Coca-Cola) Cup to the big European club competitions. As discussed in Chapter 3, success in these competitions adds to income, but in general the league is far more important in generating revenues.

Two fundamental relationships

This chapter has examined two relationships: the first between wage expenditure and league success, the second between league success and revenue. Both these relationships are perhaps much closer than people generally suspect, but each reflects the operation of a market. Broadly speaking these markets can be considered approximately efficient. That is to say, while an expensive team will not always beat a less expensive one, over the long term and on average the relationship between wage spending and league performance is quite close. Similarly, successful teams over the long term are likely to attract more revenue.

From the point of view of business strategy we are interested in finding cases where individual clubs have succeeded in outperforming the market over a sustained period of time and to understand how such achievements came about. Competitive advantage in football means being able to do

Figure 5.6
Revenue and performance
Twenty-eight Clubs 1950–60

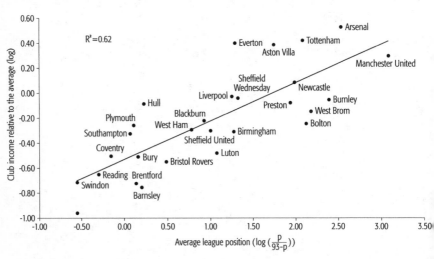

better than the relationships implied by the regression lines in this chapter suggest. We will now look at some examples of clubs which have done exactly that.

Competitive Advantage in Football

6 Added value, distinctive capabilities and competitive advantage

The relationship between investment in players and success in competition for a football club manager is not dissimilar to that between investment in shares and financial returns for a stock market investor. A sum of money invested in shares will rise on some days and fall on others, producing a volatile pattern of daily investment returns. Over the long term these ups and downs will tend to cancel each other out, leaving only a long-run trend in the value of the investment. The trend performance of any particular investment manager can be compared with the average performance of the market as a whole over a given period of time. Given a long enough period of time, even though each manager will experience daily ups and downs, very few managers will consistently maintain a performance out of line with the average. Researchers in financial markets have explained this tendency using the notion of market efficiency, by which they mean that the selling price of an asset at any point accurately reflects the expected returns from that asset, given the information available at that date.

If financial markets are not efficient, then there must be predictable ways to earn above average returns, which for an investor would be like owning a 'money machine', a mechanism which automatically guarantees a profit under all possible circumstances. A money machine in the financial markets would make a guaranteed profit simply by following a consistent investment rule. In a competitive market it is hard to see how such a machine could exist. A predictable investment rule (for example, to invest in the shares of a particular company such as BP) could easily be imitated. As investors tried to follow the rule and buy BP shares they would find the price of the shares was rising, so that the potential profit from the investment would diminish. This process would continue until all of the above-average return was competed away. In financial markets trading takes a matter of moments, so that the process of competing away above-average returns is almost instantaneous.

While the market does not operate as quickly in football, a similar story can be told for football clubs and their managers. Like investment managers they must compete in a market where there are many rivals searching for profitable opportunities. A profitable opportunity demands the buyer should be able to acquire the investment from the seller at a price which is lower than the expectation of its true value: in other words, the seller must be making a mistake. In practice mistakes do occur, but it is not plausible to say that they are the norm. This does not mean that in an efficient market there is no point in trading. Owners of assets sell them when they want to use the proceeds to buy goods and services. Football clubs sell players when they need to fund new investments or to raise cash to repay debts. In an efficient market, however, the price at which the transaction occurs in itself yields neither a profit nor a loss.

Footballers, of course, are not quite the same as financial assets, even if some clubs treat them as assets on the balance sheet.[1] Financial assets are generally pieces of paper which represent ownership of objects or rights. Even if the club owns a player's registration, it cannot own the player himself, nor can it nowadays refuse to surrender the registration if at the end of his contract the player chooses to leave the club.

The value of a financial asset to one investor is usually pretty much the same as it is to any other investor. Shares in Glaxo or ICI have the same worth to almost anyone who owns them. Footballers, however, may have different values to different clubs. This means that trades can be profitable to both buyer and seller. The difference here is that professional investors buy assets only for the financial returns they provide and have little interest in the performance of the underlying assets (e.g. the actual businesses of Glaxo or ICI) other than their financial performance. In football the performance of a player in relation to other players is crucial to the investment. For example, it might be that Tottenham believed that Les Ferdinand is more valuable to them than he is to Newcastle because he would play better with one of their current players, such as Chris Armstrong.

However, this argument is often overstated. While it is obviously true that most players perform better when their team-mates are of a higher quality, this does not imply that the value of two players taken together will be greater than the value of each player separately. In football there is little evidence from the market that the whole is greater than the sum of the parts. If it were really the case that the value of a particular footballer was significantly affected by who he played with, then footballers themselves would find it profitable to sell themselves as partnerships.

For example, if the England striking partners of recent years, Shearer and Sheringham, were really more valuable as a pair than as two individuals located at different clubs, then they would presumably try to earn more by selling themselves as a strike partnership. Rather than negotiate individual contracts at different clubs they would offer themselves as a pair to the club prepared to bid the most and divide the income between them. While a partnership deal of this sort might be complex, it would be no more so than the kinds of partnership deals signed between highly skilled individuals such as leading barristers and accountants. The most likely explanation for the fact that such deals never seem to occur in football is that a top player will perform no better with one individual of a given talent than with another. If it is the case that Shearer plays better with Sheringham than with some other players, this is merely a reflection of the fact that Sheringham is himself better than those other players. Shearer is likely to perform as well with any other footballer equally as good as Sheringham. The fact that partnership deals are almost unheard-of in football strongly suggests that there is no predictable benefit associated with strike partnerships, or midfield or defensive units, other than the qualities of the individual players themselves.

Notwithstanding some of the differences, football players share many of the same characteristics as financial assets. In England the accounting firm Deloitte & Touche have advocated that clubs should value players' registration as assets on their balance sheets and have persuaded several clubs to adopt this practice. The Bosman ruling caused some clubs to review this policy: Tottenham wrote down their valuation and Sheffield United discontinued the practice altogether. However, in December 1997 the Accounting Standards Board issued a ruling known as FRS10 that will require all companies to treat 'intangible assets' in the same way as they treat assets like plant and machinery. Intangible assets include valuable rights such as franchises, licences, brand names, and in the case of football players their contracts. This new method of valuing players is scheduled for introduction in 1999, although many clubs may try to get around it in some way since it is likely to involve them in paying more tax.

If players can indirectly be treated as assets, then it is possible for investors to buy and sell stakes in these assets rather like company shares. This already happens in Argentina. For example, in 1997 Diego Maradona's contract was owned by Multimedios America, a broadcasting company which then rented his contract to Boca Juniors, a leading Argentinian club. Also in 1997 Boca Juniors launched a £15m investment fund based on players' contracts. The fund buys the contracts of players aged under twenty-six who are signed to play for the club, and if the player is subsequently sold for a profit Boca and the fund shareholders split the profit 50:50.

In essence this is a way for investors to make money out of football (in return for putting the money in up front) without investing in the clubs themselves. If most of the returns in football go to the players because they are the valuable assets, then it is likely that there will be more funds of this type in the future.

The previous chapter established the two fundamental relationships which drive the performance of clubs. Clubs invest in players, paying a wage rate which is largely determined by the market, at least since the advent of free agency. Clubs must pay the going rate for a player, since otherwise there are plenty of competing clubs around prepared to offer better terms. The playing performance level of a club is largely determined by the amount of money it spends on players, and the revenue that a club generates in turn depends on its playing performance. The combination of these two relationships dictates the potential for each club. Clubs with an above-average revenue-generating capacity will be able to afford more expensive teams and can therefore expect in the long run to be more successful. Similarly clubs which are able to achieve an above-average performance from a given expenditure on players can earn more money and finance ever higher positions in the league.

Few clubs possess what might be thought of as 'natural' advantages. Consider location, for example. In US leagues location can be a very significant advantage. If you live in New York there are only two baseball teams you can go to watch within a ninety-mile radius (the Yankees and the Mets), which gives these two teams a very strong natural advantage over rivals based in less densely populated areas. By contrast there are forty-three professional football clubs within ninety miles of Manchester, and twenty-five within fifty miles. According to the 1995 Carling Premiership Fan Survey one in six fans travels more than fifty miles to watch their team and in some cases distances covered are much greater. While it may be true that teams from rural areas or distant from the major metropolitan conurbations (such as Shrewsbury, Wrexham or Plymouth) are unlikely ever to be able to attract a level of support which would enable them to compete with metropolitan clubs, among the metropolitan clubs it is not local population which appears to determine success.

The relationship between population and league success is illustrated in Table 6.1 and Figure 6.1. Table 6.1 is based on the 1991 census and shows the total population living within a ten-mile radius of each club's ground. Although Arsenal had the biggest local population and also won the championship

Table 6.1 The relationship between performance and population within ten miles of the ground 1991

Club	Population	League position
Arsenal	1,198,098	1
West Ham United	1,009,896	22
Brentford	1,007,919	50
Tottenham	945,996	10
West Brom	573,949	43
Aston Villa	501,837	17
Manchester United	489,834	6
Birmingham	452,058	56
Oldham	366,162	21
Bolton	329,931	48
Leeds	326,156	4
Liverpool	320,218	2
Everton	314,647	9
Newcastle	294,162	31
Rotherham	248,577	67
Sheffield	229,011	13
Sheffield Wednesday	223,721	23
Huddersfield	216,617	55
Bristol Rovers	197,256	33
Blackburn	171,293	39
Coventry	165,297	16
Gillingham	158,727	85
Leicester	150,652	42
Luton	140,291	18
Southampton	136,861	14
Southend	128,020	46
Reading	114,745	59
Hull	105,488	44
Burnley	104,779	74
Plymouth	80,684	38
Cambridge	58,381	45
Wrexham	54,589	92
Lincoln	41,536	84
Scunthorpe	40,059	76
Shrewsbury	34,313	62

that year, many clubs appearing near the top of the table have enjoyed limited success. Brentford enjoys the third largest catchment area but was last in the First Division in 1947. West Ham, with the second largest catchment, has never come higher than third in the First Division, while West Bromwich Albion, with the fifth largest catchment, has struggled to compete with the top clubs in the postwar era.

Figure 6.1 shows a regression line relating population to league position. While there is clearly some relationship, it is evidently quite weak (the R^2 is 0.36), and cannot explain why clubs such as Liverpool and Manchester United have enjoyed such a high degree of success. Without the kind of natural advantage created by a captive local audience, long-term out-performance requires a club to possess some special character-istics. From time to time a club may achieve a run of success or enjoy an exceptional windfall which leads to a period of above-average performance, but usually such periods are short-lived. To achieve a consistently above-average perform-ance requires some kind of distinctive capability. This capabil-ity needs then to be effectively managed so as to turn into a competitive advantage. The two great examples of sustained competitive advantage in English football since the Second World War are Liverpool and Manchester United.

Table 6.1 The relationship between performance and population within ten miles of the ground 1991

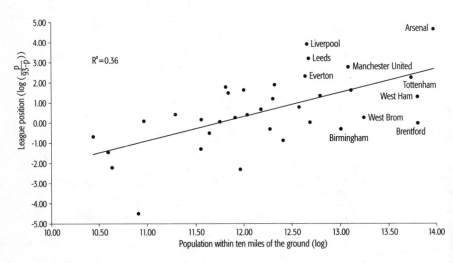

Liverpool are the most successful team of all time measured by the number of Football League Championships won. Between the end of the Second World War and 1990 they were League Champions on fourteen occasions out of a total of forty-four competitions, i.e. on average Liverpool won the championship about once every three years. They are also the most successful English side in terms of European Cups won and among the most successful in all other major competitions. Between 1977 and 1989 Liverpool dominated English football almost to the exclusion of other teams. Moreover, before the expulsion of English clubs from European competition in 1985, English clubs dominated European competition, so that Liverpool dominated what was arguably the strongest league in Europe at the time.

Manchester United became the country's best supported team from the 1960s onwards. Under the charismatic leadership of Sir Matt Busby the club developed sides which were both exciting to watch and successful in competitive terms. Busby achieved successes throughout the 1960s, culminating in victory in the European Cup in 1968, the first English club to achieve the feat. His team contained some of the most famous names ever to play in English football: Denis Law, George Best and Bobby Charlton. When Busby retired in 1971 the club struggled to maintain a comparable level of performance on the pitch, despite spending more than any other club on acquiring and maintaining players. By the standards of its own history and by the standards set by its rivals, Manchester United's performance in the domestic league and in international competition between 1971 and 1990 was poor (the club's only major successes were in the FA Cup). What was remarkable about the club in this period was that it remained the best supported club in the country, with a significant international following. This enabled the club to remain financially secure throughout the lean years and ultimately able to finance its remarkable resurgence in the 1990s.

Both these clubs differ from their competitors. Various

competitors have achieved success. Two of their greatest rivals, Arsenal and Everton, have each won the League Championship more than once in the postwar era and other clubs such as Nottingham Forest and Ipswich have won it on single occasions. But none of these clubs has managed to sustain a run of success over such an extended period. The ability of Liverpool and Manchester United to sustain an above-average level of performance (either in terms of playing honours or in terms of support) without other clubs managing to imitate them successfully naturally leads us to ask how they managed to achieve this feat.

In Chapter 4 it was suggested that consistent outperformance in business derived from the possession of a distinctive capability, something which cannot easily be imitated by rivals, and which can then be successfully exploited in the commercial market. Possession of a distinctive capability is essential because in open competitive markets the process of imitation will compete away any other kind of temporary competitive advantage. It was suggested that there are four possible types of distinctive capability: a strategic asset, innovation, reputation and 'architecture'.

In the case of football, strategic assets and innovations are likely to prove transitory. A strategic asset is a scarce resource which provides an advantage in competition and which, once possessed by one firm (club), cannot at the same time be enjoyed by another. The classic example in the business world is an input in the production process such as a raw material which is monopolized by one firm. A fine mineral spring for the production of bottled water or a quarry which is the only source of a particular ore might be good examples. In football a strategic asset might be a particularly successful player or manager who commits himself to a club regardless of offers from outside. Such a person would usually offer themselves on the market and accept the highest bidder, who can then expect to receive little more in return than the amount spent on the acquisition of the scarce talent. A strategic asset might be thought of as an exceptional talent which for one reason or another is either not considered valuable elsewhere or elects to stay put despite better offers from other clubs. In possession of such an asset, a football club can achieve far more than might normally be expected given their initial resources. The classic example of a strategic asset is Brian Clough, one of the most exceptional managers of his generation, who was once described as 'the only manager to win the First Division with two provincial clubs'.[2] However, the first point to make about an asset like Brian Clough is that his effect on performance is unlikely to last long beyond his tenure. As will be discussed below, the magic of Brian Clough lay in his ability to get more from players than other managers ever could: once he left, the performance of his players and his clubs returned to their 'natural' level.

Innovation in football is a rather unlikely source of competitive advantage. Tactically there have been many changes in the way football has been played over the years, and each innovation has typically been associated with a particular club or manager. However, an innovation which produces success will, thanks to the process of competition, be quickly understood and imitated. In business product innovations are considered so valuable to society that innovators are protected from competition by patents. There is no analogous way to protect playing innovations in football, and hence these can seldom be the source of a long-term competitive advantage.

Distinctive capabilities such as reputation and architecture are much harder to imitate. Manchester United's reputation is a consequence of its long history and the dramatic events associated with it. Such a history can only be acquired at the end of a long wait – if it can be acquired at all. While other clubs seek to emulate its achievements by creating their own mythology, United can enjoy the fruits of its reputation, which are the ability to attract significantly more revenue for a given level of performance on the field than any of its rivals.

Liverpool's success stemmed from a unique organization structure, sometimes associated with the managers (Bill Shankly and Bob Paisley), sometimes with the players (Kevin Keegan and Kenny Dalglish), sometimes with the relationship between team and supporters (the Kop) and sometimes with its institutions (the boot room). What is significant about these explanations is that ultimately none of them is totally convincing on its own, but that taken together they amount to a powerful source of competitive advantage, distinctly associated with Liverpool and never emulated elsewhere.

Brian Clough, Manchester United's reputation and Liverpool's architecture: these are probably the three best illustrations of the underlying concepts of distinctive capabilities and competitive advantage. But there are lesser examples as well, which are briefly considered at the end of this chapter.

Brian Clough: a strategic asset
The achievement

Brian Clough's success as a manager is associated with his tenure at Derby County between 1967 and 1973 and at Nottingham Forest between 1975 and 1993. Both elected to the Football League in 1892, these clubs are twenty miles apart and therefore compete for each other's fans. Each has historically hovered between the upper reaches of the Second Division and the lower reaches of the First Division; before Clough neither had ever won the League Championship. With a combined footballing age of 193 years BC (before Clough) the two clubs had won a major trophy, the FA Cup, on only three occasions (Derby once in 1946, Nottingham Forest twice, 1898 and 1959).

Over twenty-four years as a manager Clough won twelve major trophies, including the First Division Championship twice, the European Cup twice and the League Cup four times. The only major trophy which eluded him was the FA Cup. His reign as manager of Nottingham Forest between

1975 and 1993 was the sixth longest of any manager with a single club. His success with Forest was in itself remarkable. When he took over they had just spent two years in the Second Division, having struggled to survive in the First Division during the 1960s. Under Clough Forest won the First Division Championship title in 1978, immediately following promotion from the Second Division, the only side ever to achieve this feat. They won the European Championship (the most prestigious competition for a European club) twice in succession and also the Super Cup (a match between the winners of the European Cup and the European Cup Winners' Cup). They also won the League Cup four times and a string of other cup competitions. During Clough's tenure the club never finished in the bottom half of the table until the last year of his reign. In 1993 they finished bottom of the inaugural Premier League and he decided to retire. Since then the club has again struggled to sustain itself at the highest level and was relegated to the new First Division in 1997.

Clough's record at Nottingham Forest would on its own be enough to distinguish him as one of the great managers, but he also achieved success with Derby County as manager between 1967 and 1973. During most of the postwar period the club had languished in the Second Division. Clough took them into the First Division in 1969 and they won the championship in 1972. In the following year Clough resigned following a disagreement with the board of directors, but much the same squad as Clough had assembled won the League Championship again in 1975. Between 1967 and 1993 the relative performances of Derby and Forest can be largely attributed to the presence of Clough. Figure 6.2 compares the relative positions of the two clubs between 1967 and 1973, when he was at Derby, and Figure 6.3 compares the relative positions between 1975 and 1993, when he was at Nottingham Forest.

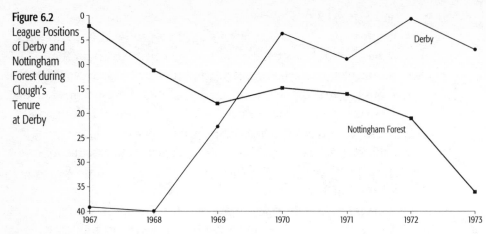

Figure 6.2
League Positions of Derby and Nottingham Forest during Clough's Tenure at Derby

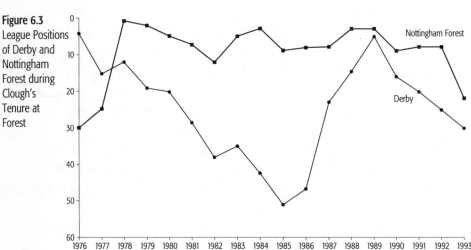

Figure 6.3
League Positions of Derby and Nottingham Forest during Clough's Tenure at Forest

Measuring outperformance

That Clough achieved success is unquestionable. However, in our analysis we are more interested in the relationship between this performance and the resources available to him. Clough's time at Derby can be illustrated by a series of yearly regressions for the six seasons he managed the club (Figures 6.4–6.9). In each year of his tenure apart from 1968–9 the league performance of the club lay above the regression line, indicating a better performance than the wage expenditure alone would have justified. Just as important in assessing this

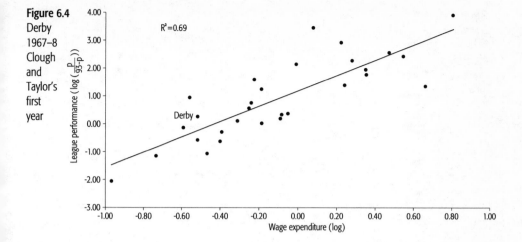

Figure 6.4 Derby 1967–8 Clough and Taylor's first year

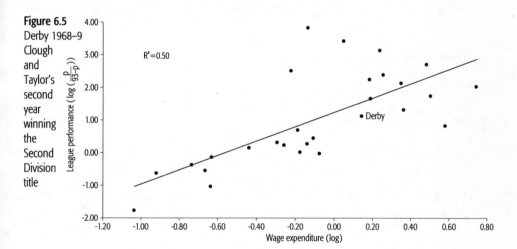

Figure 6.5 Derby 1968–9 Clough and Taylor's second year winning the Second Division title

achievement is Figure 6.10, which shows the relationship over these years between Derby's performance in the League and its revenues. As a 'provincial' club, Derby never generated the level of income that its performance might have been expected to create. Clough was persistently faced with financial pressure at Derby but still managed to compete with the top clubs. Not that Clough was entirely devoid of financial resources, as can be seen by his transfer spending over the period (Table 6.2), which amounted to some £650,000 net over the six years. During this period only Manchester United, Aston Villa

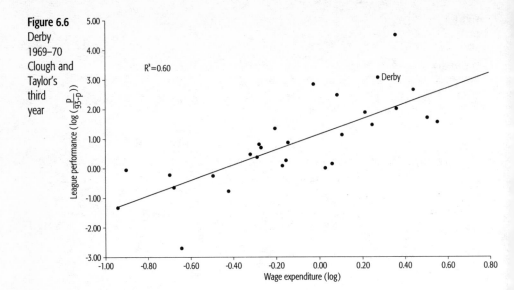

Figure 6.6
Derby
1969–70
Clough and
Taylor's
third
year

League performance $\left(\log\left(\frac{p}{93-p}\right)\right)$

$R^2=0.60$

• Derby

Wage expenditure (log)

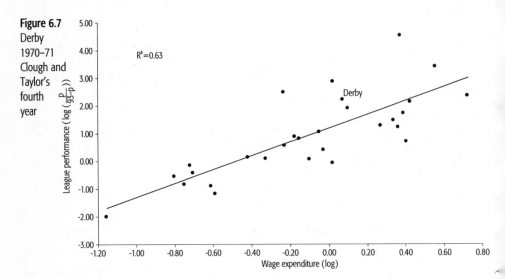

Figure 6.7
Derby
1970–71
Clough and
Taylor's
fourth
year

League performance $\left(\log\left(\frac{p}{93-p}\right)\right)$

$R^2=0.63$

Derby

Wage expenditure (log)

and West Ham spent more. However, it is as well to remember that this investment left in place a squad which went on to win the league title again in 1975.

Judged only on his Derby years, Clough would be considered one of the more successful managers of the postwar era, but not one of its greatest. Furthermore, much of the credit

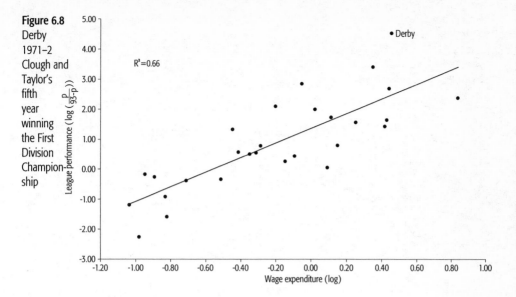

Figure 6.8
Derby 1971–2 Clough and Taylor's fifth year winning the First Division Championship

$R^2 = 0.66$

X-axis: Wage expenditure (log)
Y-axis: League performance ($\log(\frac{p}{93-p})$)

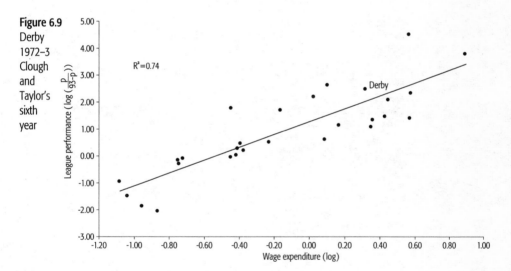

Figure 6.9
Derby 1972–3 Clough and Taylor's sixth year

$R^2 = 0.74$

X-axis: Wage expenditure (log)
Y-axis: League performance ($\log(\frac{p}{93-p})$)

might reasonably be given to Peter Taylor, nominally his assistant but in reality his partner in management until 1982. The League Championship victory of 1972 was a particularly close-run thing. At the end of the season Derby had finished all their matches and both Liverpool and Leeds had a game left to play. Each club was a point behind Derby: Liverpool

Competitive Advantage in Football / 209

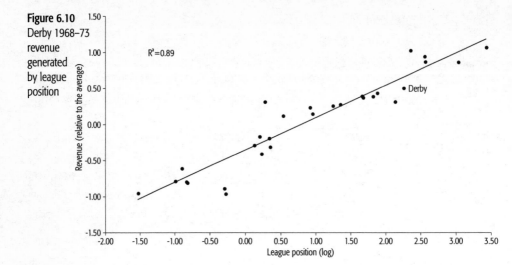

Figure 6.10 Derby 1968–73 revenue generated by league position

$R^2 = 0.89$

Revenue (relative to the average)

• Derby

League position (log)

Table 6.2 Transfer spending over the years 1968–73

Club	Transfer spending (£000 1973)
Manchester United	926,617
Aston Villa	725,450
West Ham	694,674
Derby	655,741
Tottenham	624,433
Liverpool	507,910
Coventry	345,128
Everton	277,090
West Brom	190,020
Southampton	149,510
Plymouth	130,755
Arsenal	125,373
Reading	61,654
Hull	52,740
Luton	52,155
Swindon	48,148
Sheffield Wednesday	37,228
Blackburn	21,849
Brentford	10,767
Preston	−24,867
Barnsley	−28,224
Sheffield United	−30,002
Oldham	−84,538
Bristol Rovers	−86,036
Bolton	−101,965
Bury	−193,035
Burnley	−703,078

needed to win and Leeds needed only a draw. Before the final matches the bookmakers were giving 8–1 odds against Derby being champions. In the event both Liverpool and Leeds lost. Leeds were particularly unfortunate, since their last game followed only three days after they had won the FA Cup Final and they only lost their final game 2–1.

Clough's greatest achievements, however, were with Nottingham Forest. Figure 6.11 illustrates his remarkable success in league competition between 1982 (the earliest date for which wage data is available[3]) and 1992. During these years Clough teams matched the performance of clubs which were spending around three times the average wage spend of all clubs, while he himself was only spending about one and a half times the average. In today's terms this is the difference between spending about £14m a year compared to £7m. Valued over a ten-year period, this achievement is equivalent to a difference of £50–£100m in the required spending, making Brian Clough an extraordinarily valuable asset. Furthermore, this achievement came after the break-up of his partnership with Peter Taylor. Clough's net transfer spending over this period was also extremely modest, a net £134,000 in 1993 money over ten years and considerably less than his main rivals (see Table 6.3). Interestingly, Nottingham Forest

Figure 6.11
Nottingham Forest under Clough 1982–92

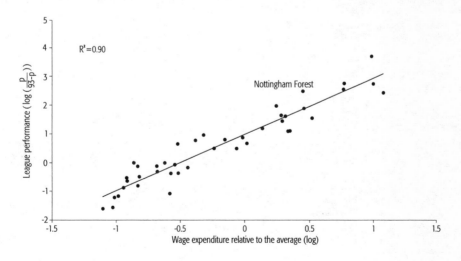

during this period appears to have been a better revenue generator than Derby was during his tenure there, as is illustrated by Figure 6.12. Forest lies exactly on the line, suggesting that its income on average was exactly what one might have expected given its league performance.

These figures and tables are a quantified representation of the outperformance achieved by clubs under the management

Table 6.3
Aggregate real transfer spending 1982–93 (in 1993 prices)

Club	Transfer spending (£000 1993)
Manchester United	16,123
Liverpool	15,837
Leeds	10,135
Tottenham	9,826
Everton	8,293
Arsenal	6,650
Blackburn	6,630
Southampton	5,172
West Ham	3,730
Sheffield Wednesday	3,635
Sheffield United	2,816
Newcastle	1,173
Plymouth	1,018
Brentford	748
Cambridge	275
Burnley	251
Aston Villa	157
Nottingham Forest	134
Bolton	109
Coventry	−112
Southend	−170
Peterborough	−182
Bury	−268
Scunthorpe	−300
Reading	−374
Rotherham	490
Mansfield	−693
Hull	−971
Wrexham	−1,141
Preston	−1,213
Oldham	−1,393
Shrewsbury	−1,509
Huddersfield	−1,605
Watford	−1,903
Barnsley	−1,975
Birmingham	−2,078
Swindon	−2,622
West Brom	−2,649
Bristol Rovers	−3,103
Luton	−3,726
Leicester	−3,891

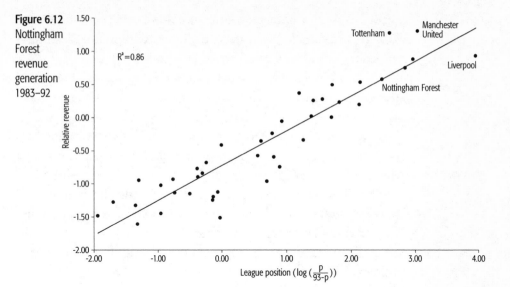

Figure 6.12
Nottingham
Forest
revenue
generation
1983–92

$R^2 = 0.86$

Relative revenue

Tottenham •

Manchester
United •

Liverpool

Nottingham Forest

League position ($\log(\frac{p}{93-p})$)

of Brian Clough. But what was his distinctive capability, and why did he not sell it to clubs capable of bidding more for his services?

Clough as manager

Much has been written about Brian Clough and his behaviour as a manager, and only a brief summary of salient points will be given here. Clough went into management following a premature end to his playing career. Like most successful managers in English football he had been a successful player, scoring 204 goals in 222 matches. At 0.92 goals per game, his is the best postwar strike rate by some margin. For example, prodigious goalscorers of the 1980s, such as Ian Rush and Gary Lineker, had strike rates of only just over 0.5 goals per game. It is unlikely that any player with a career of more than fifty games will ever beat Clough's achievement. However, most of his career was spent in the Second Division. He played only three First Division games, he was capped only twice for England, and in the view of his detractors he did not have the ability to play at the highest level. Seldom modest in describing his own talents, Clough always resented his lack of recognition as a player. His outspoken comments unquestionably irritated many, and these characteristics may indeed have affected the judgement of potential employers.

When his playing career finished he was put in charge of the youth team at his club, Sunderland, until in 1965 he was appointed manager of Hartlepool United, a struggling and impoverished Fourth Division club. At thirty years of age he was the youngest manager in the Football League. Clough was the manager, but he was hired as a team to work with Peter Taylor. Taylor was seven years his senior and the two had played together at Middlesbrough when Clough was a young striker and Taylor was his mentor. Taylor himself aspired to be a top manager, but recognized the potential of their partnership and, more modest than Clough, was prepared to accept the nominally lesser role. Their achievements at Hartlepool were not spectacular, but they were a significant improvement on what had gone before. Counting from the first full year after their arrival and allowing them credit for the promotion to Division Three which their team achieved immediately following their departure, their average position was equivalent to third in the Fourth Division. This compares with the club's average position of twenty-first place in the Fourth Division in the eight years before Clough and Taylor, and eighteenth place in the eight years after they had gone. Clough and Taylor created a sense of excitement during their brief tenure. The partnership changed the attitude to football at the club and in the town, encouraging support, promoting ground improvements and developing new players. One characteristic of Clough's management style which was already emerging was his relationship with players, who became completely dependent on him. Unlike many managers he did not thrive on conflict, rather he demanded complete subordination. John McGovern, a player who worked for Clough for nearly twenty years, at Derby and at Forest as captain, was first discovered by Clough at Hartlepool.

When Derby hired Clough, he insisted that Taylor came

with him as assistant. They immediately replaced the majority of the team with their own signings. A notable feature of their policy on signing players was the many different types of footballer they were attracted to: players in the twilight of their careers and unproven youngsters, unsung journeymen and players with extraordinary talents, players who were conformists and some who were hell-raisers. No obvious pattern or policy can be detected in their signings, except that most of them tended to perform better for Clough (and Taylor) than they ever had or ever would for any other club. Part of this had to do with spotting what other people could not see, often qualities which are not in themselves footballing skills, e.g. leadership, willpower, determination. Clough and Taylor called this 'moral courage'.

Often they found a way to motivate a player who had not been well motivated elsewhere. Some of their footballers had alcohol problems (common enough in the game) and Clough and Taylor would somehow get them to keep it under control, not directly attacking the habit, nor alienating the players with a lecture, but developing their motivation in the direction of football and away from alcohol. But Clough possessed more than just an ability to deal with difficult players.

The division of labour between Clough and Taylor is a matter of some dispute. Clough was unquestionably the front man, generally running the training sessions, picking the team and dealing with the media; Taylor spent most of his time searching for new talent, at which he was remarkably successful. Their partnership broke up in 1982 and Taylor later went back into management at Derby. In 1983 the two men fell out and never spoke again; however, their relationship continued in the media, with each claiming a greater share in their combined achievements. It is certainly the case that Clough on his own never achieved as much as he had with Taylor, but it is also clear that Nottingham Forest continued to perform well above what might have been expected.

Clough and Taylor's success at Derby was founded upon a close relationship with the players but a very poor relationship with the directors of the club. In fact Clough and Taylor both despised directors and club chairmen. Clough always made it clear that he was in charge and that he considered the directors little more than a nuisance, even though he needed their money to buy players. Historically club directors have been able to obtain little more than local respect and prestige from their job, given the limitations on financial returns and the often critical financial position of clubs. Thus local celebrity was a privilege for which they had to pay large sums in order to keep a club afloat. It is not surprising that a manager who openly despised and criticized the directors did not forge a healthy relationship with them. Clough and Taylor walked out at Derby after a confrontation with the chairman.

There followed the least successful period of their career. Nine months of high spending with Second Division Brighton led not to promotion but almost to relegation. In July 1974 Clough moved to Leeds United while Taylor stayed on at Brighton. One of the most successful teams of the period, the Leeds side had been created by Don Revie, who had just moved to become the England manager. The team was full of international stars – Bremner, Lorimer, Hunter, Clarke, Giles and others – and had just won the First Division Championship for the second time in six years. Faced with a settled and successful side full of large egos, Clough decided to take them down a peg. He told them that he didn't like the way they played. In truth their style of play was quite differ-ent from his own; he generally espoused a tactical passing game, more continental than the British style which involved aerial dominance and large, aggressive players, a style of which this Leeds team was probably the archetype. However, he conveyed this message in a fashion which was apparently calculated to offend. It did, and the players made this clear to anyone who asked. At the same time the results at the begin-ning of the 1974–5 season were not at all satisfactory, and the directors became uneasy. After only forty-four days in the job, Clough was fired.

Clough was hired by Nottingham Forest in January 1975, when the club was failing in the Second Division and facing financial difficulties. Forest was the only Football League club which had not turned itself into a limited company, but was a club in the legal sense and therefore with much weaker financial powers than most club companies. Clough inherited a squad which included some of his future leading stars: Martin O'Neill, John Robertson, Ian Bowyer, Tony Woodcock and Viv Anderson. But when he re-established his partnership with Taylor six months later a stream of new talent was injected. At first the players came at relatively low prices: John McGovern, Archie Gemmill, Larry Lloyd, Peter Withe, Frank Clark and Gary Birtles. However, in 1979 Forest broke the £1m barrier for transfers in signing Trevor Francis. With this group of players Clough and Taylor achieved their greatest successes. The major honours they won and the transfer of stars who emerged under them brought large sums of money into the club for the first time in its history. Clough and Taylor insisted on controlling how the money was spent; given the weakness of the club's organization, and its obvious dependence on the management team, it would have been hard for the club to resist. Eventually Clough's involvement with financial affairs led to accusations of corrupt transfer dealings, although these have always been denied by Clough.

But what was the secret of their success? A talent for spotting good players was something which to some extent Clough clearly shared with Taylor. In his solo period Clough acquired players such as Stuart Pearce, Des Walker, Neil Webb and Lee Chapman, all at modest fees, all subsequently sold for very high prices. He signed Roy Keane from an obscure Irish team for £20,000 in 1990 and sold him to Manchester United in July 1993 for £3.75m.

Comments made by players[4] illustrate Clough's (and Taylor's) ability to get the best out of individuals.

John Robertson: 'If it hadn't been for those two, I might have ended up a tramp and a boozer.'

Ian Bowyer: 'From that first game at Tottenham I never felt pressure from Clough to win a game – but I always felt under pressure to give my all for him. . . His in-depth knowledge was amazing: he just knew if you'd ducked a tackle or a header in the match and you dreaded the sharp edge of his tongue.'

Trevor Francis: 'He was by far the best manager I played for. His presence transformed players. He made me a better player by teaching me how important it was to incorporate my style of play into the team pattern that was unchanging. Play it simple.'

Clough is a man of extremes. He could be extremely harsh to players at certain times, humiliating them in front of everybody. After signing Peter Shilton for Forest at a fee of around £1m, he then made him serve drinks in the bar to all the other players just to show that there were no favourites. Similar treatment was handed out to Francis when he joined the club. Injured players were given little or no sympathy. When he left Steve Sutton out of an international tour at the last moment because of the arrival of an expensive new signing, his only words to the disappointed youngster were 'That's the way it goes, Sooty.' Explaining strategy to Martin O'Neill he would observe, 'What's the point of giving the ball to you when there's a genius on the other wing?' But Clough could be extremely generous. He was the first manager to introduce the mid-season break (a brief holiday in a foreign resort) into football to ease the heavy winter schedule. In a crisis he would offer fatherly support to players, and most who played for him speak of him much more in admiration than from fear.

In terms of training methods Clough always insisted on basic ball skills and game tactics, rather than the athletic training which has always been a British tradition. His methods were always viewed by players as the least strenuous in the football leagues. He himself said, 'I don't believe in too much coaching; either a player can do it or he can't.' Instead he spent time describing the style he wanted his players to adopt. He emphasized the simplicity of the game and the importance of getting the basics right. To achieve this he would simply watch a player's every move. He insisted that each should concentrate on the skills which he had and not worry about those at which he could never expect to excel.

Perhaps the most famous aspect of his management style was his unpredictability. Players usually found themselves both criticized and praised when they least expected it. But on occasions his methods were simply bizarre. The night before the League Cup Final against Southampton in 1979 Clough and Taylor relaxed the team by getting them to drink champagne all evening; playing with hangovers, they won. Time and again the recollections of players focus on the unpredictability, a feeling of always having to be on one's toes.

Taken as a whole much of Clough's success might reasonably be attributed to good practice, and it is perhaps surprising that some of his basic points have not been more widely appreciated in football. Other elements of his management technique are harder to account for. Not all of them bred success; along the way there were failures (such as at Leeds) and these must sometimes be attributed to more than just bad luck. But how is one to disentangle the good from the bad? It is hard to imagine writing a management textbook which could train managers to emulate his methods. Brian Clough is a larger-than-life character, perhaps the most exceptional personality of his era in English football. To suggest that another manager might imitate him is to realize the impossibility of doing so. On the one hand, it would be hard to select the exact elements which constituted the primary sources of his success. On the other, to attempt to imitate him lock, stock and barrel would amount to trying to clone his personality, a feat rendered more or less impossible by his very unpredictability.

This is what made Brian Clough a distinctive capability, a strategic asset for the clubs for whom he worked. He could do things which others could not for reasons which are not altogether clear. If they were clear, they could, and would, have been imitated. But what of his value to the clubs which he managed? The central question is why a manager of such exceptional talent worked only for relatively low-ranked clubs such as Nottingham Forest and Derby County. In the market for football managers as well as players the best talents tend to command the highest prices and to work for the largest, most powerful clubs. What made Brian Clough a strategic asset for first Derby and then Forest was his inability to work with others. For this reason he quit Derby. His failure to survive at Leeds signalled to every big club that they would not be able to handle him. There is little evidence to suggest that one of the most successful managers in the history of English football received a constant stream of offers from the other big clubs.

The fact is that the directors of such clubs would not have wanted him. Clough had to settle for a relatively minor club where he could be the dominant force. Clough's greatest ambition was to manage the England team. During his management career he was much more successful in terms of club competitions than the managers who actually held the England job (apart from Don Revie, who had created the Leeds team which won two league titles, the FA Cup and League Cup once and the Fairs Cup twice; Revie turned out to be a disastrous England manager). However, the Football Association never asked him to do the job, because they were always afraid that they could not handle him. In a sense this was perhaps Brian Clough's tragedy; but to Nottingham Forest it was the source of a tremendous competitive advantage which gave the club its most successful era in its history.

In the end, Brian Clough's own explanation of his success illustrates perfectly just why he was a strategic asset:

> *They tell me people have always wondered how I did it. That fellow professionals and public alike have been fascinated and puzzled and intrigued by the Clough managerial methods and technique and would love to know my secret. I've got news for all of them – so would I.*[5]

Reputation: Manchester United

Manchester United (then known as Newton Heath) entered the Football League in 1892 and was almost bankrupted in 1902. The club was saved primarily by a wealthy local brewer, J. H. Davies. He had ambitions to create a major footballing power and invested heavily, particularly in the development of the ground at Old Trafford, which from its completion in 1910 became one of the leading stadiums in the country, perhaps the most important one in the north of England, hosting FA Cup semi-finals and final replays from its earliest years down to the present. Under Davies the club became known as 'moneybags United' and was officially censured by the League and the FA in 1910 for misrepresenting its financial position. Also around this time Manchester United became the centre of controversy over players' pay and the formation of a players' union, particularly as a result of the efforts of Billy Meredith, one of the club's most famous footballers. The club also enjoyed league and cup success in this era, winning the First Division Championship in 1908 and 1911 and the FA Cup in 1909.

Between the wars the club sank into relative obscurity, moving between the First and Second Divisions and failing to win any honours. During the Second World War Old Trafford was badly damaged by German bombing raids and after the war the club faced a crisis. Apart from rebuilding a team, the club needed to rebuild its stadium. The directors gambled in appointing a leading pre-war player, Matt Busby, as manager.

While playing home games at rivals Manchester City's Maine Road ground, Busby developed an exciting team which had shown some promise before the war. He achieved almost immediate success by winning the FA Cup in 1948, and his team were runners-up in the First Division on three occasions in the late 1940s. The team also had a reputation for playing exciting football and producing high-scoring games. Success enabled the home ground at Old Trafford to be rebuilt by 1949 and finally Busby's team won the league in 1952. One other advantage that Busby inherited from the pre-war era was a youth development programme. It is notable that during its most successful periods Manchester United has always developed most of its own talent, rather than relying on clever purchases in the transfer market. As Busby said, 'If my club decides to buy a player, we do so only because every other method of filling a place in the United team has failed.'

Busby also made it 'his' club. From the very beginning he insisted on management control, an unusual situation at a time when it was normal for the directors to select the team and decide upon transfers. Before the war managers were generally more like trainers. A football club resembled a military unit, players taking orders without question from the manager, who in turn received orders from the directors. Busby started the long process of breaking down this antiquated approach to management, and took revolutionary steps such as consulting the team about decisions, asking their opinions, and insisting that it was the management, not the directors, who were best placed to make footballing decisions.

After winning the championship Busby had to rebuild his team with younger players. The Busby Babes, as they were known, were an outstanding collection of young talent and won the league in 1956 and 1957, a remarkable achievement for a side populated with players in their early twenties. Like Busby's earlier team they did it playing the most exciting football in England. Busby and the club also took the momentous decision to enter the newly inaugurated European

Championship at a time when much of the English football establishment maintained the view that because it was 'our game', competition with foreigners was beneath them. Technological advance, in the form of scheduled passenger airline services and above all floodlighting, made regular competition with European clubs feasible for the first time, and television promised to make it profitable.

Manchester United were defeated in the semi-finals at their first attempt in 1957 and then in 1958 reached the semi-finals again. They beat Red Star Belgrade over two legs, 2–1 at home and then 3–3 in Belgrade on 5 February 1958. On the return flight the next day the plane stopped to refuel at Munich. Trying to take off in a blizzard the plane crashed, killing eight of the young squad which would probably have dominated English football for the decade. Fifteen others died in the crash, and Busby himself was severely injured and only just survived after intensive care. The tragedy was felt, not just by Manchester United fans or even in England alone, but internationally. Without question it changed the attitude of many towards the club and certainly made it a household name, though this is not to argue that Manchester United benefited from the crash, since the club might have been even more successful had its young team survived.

To see how Manchester United developed under Busby it is convenient to divide his tenure into two periods. The Munich disaster was undoubtedly a watershed for Busby and the club, but the following few years were also a turning point in the structure of football with the abolition of the minimum wage in 1961 and the Eastham judgment in 1963. Figures 6.13 and 6.14 illustrate the two fundamental relationships, between wage expenditure and league performance and between league performance and revenue, for the years 1950–61. As can be seen from Figure 6.13, in this period Manchester United achieved a remarkably high level of league performance given a relatively modest wage expenditure. In terms of average league position they were the most successful team of the period despite being outspent by half a dozen clubs. However, during this period the club was not a great income generator. Figure 6.14 shows that Manchester United actually lies below the regression line in terms of revenue generation from league performance, indicating that an average club blessed with Manchester United's exceptional league performance would have expected to achieve a significantly higher level of revenues. In terms of both relationships, however, this was still a period when the role of the market was limited, when the gap between the biggest and the smallest in terms of income or expenditure was relatively small, so that the explanatory power of the regression lines was much weaker than it is today.

After he recovered from the crash Busby went back to rebuilding his team. In fact his remaining squad was so strong that Manchester United reached the final of the FA Cup in 1958 and were runners-up in the league in the following year. But it took a few years to become real contenders again. The acquisition of Denis Law in 1963 for a record £115,000 and the emergence of George Best from the youth development scheme in the same year combined with the maturing Bobby Charlton to create one of the most potent, and also most

Figure 6.13
Wage expenditure and league performance 1950–61

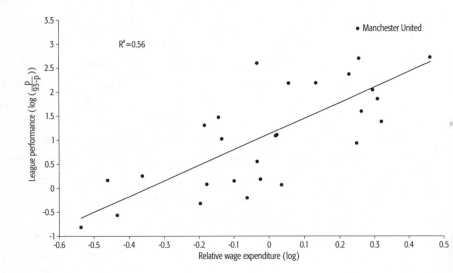

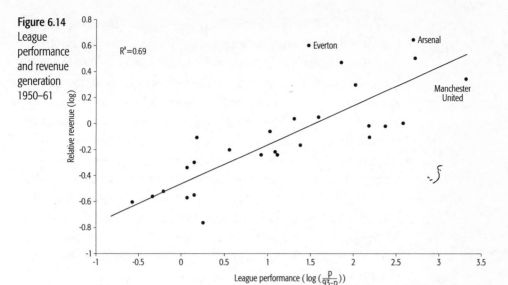

Figure 6.14
League
performance
and revenue
generation
1950–61

Relative revenue (log)

$R^2=0.69$

Everton

Arsenal

Manchester
United

League performance ($\log(\frac{p}{93-p})$)

admired strike forces in the history of football. They won the
FA Cup in 1963, were runners-up in the league in 1964 and
then won it in 1965. They repeated the feat in 1967, and in
1968 Busby achieved his final ambition when Manchester
United became the first English team to win the European
Cup.

It is sometimes said that during this period Matt Busby
and Bill Shankly struck a secret agreement to keep players'
wages down: if so, it would appear that only Shankly kept
his side of the bargain. The difference between the teams
produced, of course, was notable. The Manchester United
of Charlton, Law and Best is one of the most celebrated teams
in the history of football, so it may not be so surprising that
the team was costly. Taking the period 1962–71, Manchester
United's performance looks rather different from that of the
earlier period. In Figure 6.15 it is clear that although the club
continued to have one of the most successful league records, it
became more dependent on wage expenditure compared either
to the early Busby years or to the emerging power of
Liverpool. Thus while United was spending twice the average
of any other club, Liverpool was spending no more than the

Competitive Advantage in Football / 225

average for roughly the same average league position. During this decade each club won the First Division title twice. If anything Manchester United was achieving less in terms of league performance than an average club spending the same amount might have expected based on the regression line.

But with a team peopled with such extraordinary talents United became a strong revenue generator. As Figure 6.16 shows, during this period the club's revenue generation placed it above the regression line, somewhat more successful in this respect than its major rivals. The Manchester United legend was well and truly established, to the point where *current* league performance became less important in determining the level of support for the club. This was also the period when the dominance of the 'Big Five' (United, Liverpool, Everton, Arsenal and Tottenham) started to become clear. In Figure 6.16 these five are clustered together, combining the highest league positions and the highest levels of income. It was in this era that the market for players began to create significant differentials among footballers. By the late 1960s a club needed to have a significantly above-average income in order to be able to afford the star players.

Figure 6.15
Wage expenditure and league performance 1962–71

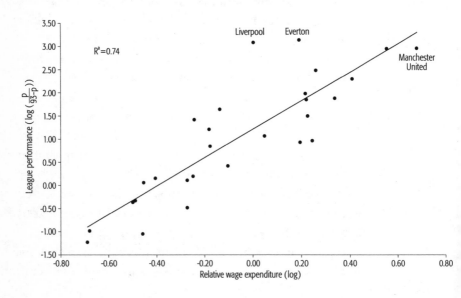

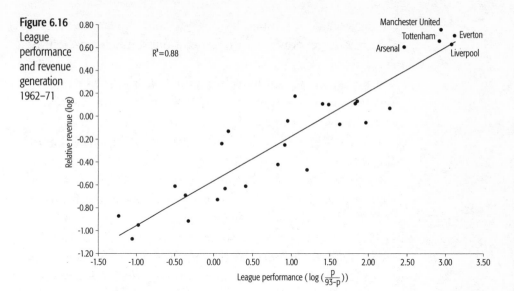

Figure 6.16
League performance and revenue generation 1962–71

$R^2 = 0.88$

Relative revenue (log)

League performance ($\log\left(\frac{p}{93-p}\right)$)

Manchester United
Tottenham
Arsenal
Everton
Liverpool

Sir Matt Busby (as he became) is in the view of many the greatest ever manager in English football. Manchester United today is still essentially the institution he created, although he retired in 1971. Busby himself might be thought of as a supreme strategic asset, since he took what was at the time a middling club and turned it into a world-ranked one, with scarcely better resources than any other manager. There are many parallels with a manager such as Clough. Although less prone to extremes and less outspoken and arrogant in public, Busby made it clear to the directors from the start that he was in charge. He was always very close to his players, just as Clough's were to him. Both were managers committed to building sides which not only won but were attractive to watch.

Busby's more emollient approach to management enabled to him to remain at the same club as manager for his entire career, and this also meant that something was left behind when he retired. During his tenure he built three outstanding championship teams and in the process caused Manchester United itself to be associated with a particular style of play. As a result of the youth system, created before the war but

Competitive Advantage in Football / 227

enthusiastically developed by Busby, the club was able to pass on from one generation to the next a particular approach to the game.

After Busby the club experimented with a series of managers but enjoyed little playing success over the next twenty years. The club's wage and revenue performance between 1972 and 1990 is illustrated in Figures 6.17 and 6.18. Figure 6.17 shows that the club's performance on the field lay significantly below the regression line while Figure 6.18 shows that its revenue generation over the same period lay significantly above the line. Despite a chronic lack of league success (three FA Cup victories provided some consolation), the club was able to finance the most expensive team in the country thanks to its extraordinary ability to generate income. In every year between 1972 and 1992 the club was among the top five spenders on playing talent measured by the wage bill. On one occasion it was the biggest spender and on six occasions it was the second biggest. The club became a heavy spender in the transfer market, and a succession of managers came and went, each succumbing to the pressure for league success. Busby himself was criticized for becoming an *eminence grise*

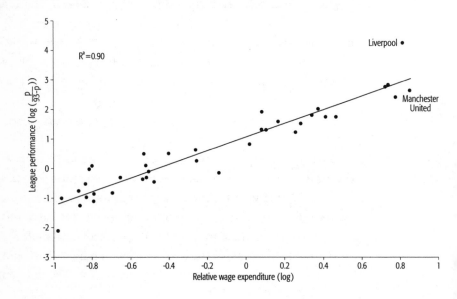

Figure 6.17
Wage expenditure and league performance 1972–90

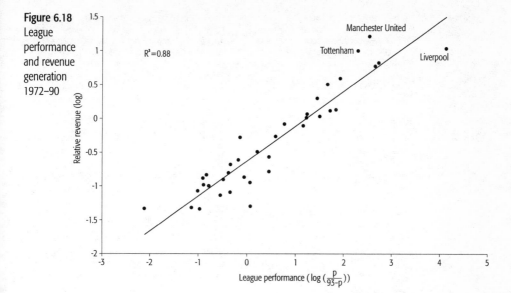

Figure 6.18 League performance and revenue generation 1972–90

(y-axis) Relative revenue (log)

$R^2 = 0.88$

Manchester United

Tottenham ●

Liverpool

(x-axis) League performance $\left(\log\left(\frac{p}{93-p}\right)\right)$

looming behind every manager. However, throughout all these disappointments Manchester United remained the most famous and the best supported club in the country.

The extent of this support is illustrated in Table 6.4, which compares the league performances and match attendances at Manchester United and Liverpool from the retirement of Sir Matt Busby until their next championship, won under Alex Ferguson. In each year the two clubs were always the first and second best supported clubs in league football, apart from 1982 and 1991 when respectively Tottenham and Arsenal appeared in the top two. These were the glory years of Liverpool: eleven league titles in twenty years, runners-up on every other occasion apart from two. In fact, when Liverpool came sixth in 1992, it was their worst league position since 1965. Yet despite this convincing superiority on the field, Liverpool attendances were consistently smaller than Manchester United's. United were the country's best supported league team in every year between 1973 and 1992, apart from a brief interlude in 1987–8 and 1988–9 when Liverpool attracted slightly higher gates. To illustrate the scale of the difference in support, the total number of tickets sold for home

Competitive Advantage in Football / 229

Table 6.4
Manchester United and Liverpool, comparison of league position and league attendances 1972–92

Year	Liverpool average league gate	Rank in Football League attendances	Liverpool league position	Manchester United average league gate	Rank in Football League attendances	Manchester United league position	Ratio of Manchester to Liverpool attendances
1972	47,687	1	3	45,999	2	8	96%
1973	48,127	2	1	48,623	1	18	101%
1974	42,332	2	2	42,712	1	21	101%
1975	45,966	2	2	48,389	1	23	105%
1976	41,623	2	1	54,750	1	3	132%
1977	47,221	2	1	53,710	1	6	114%
1978	45,546	2	2	51,860	1	10	114%
1979	46,407	2	1	46,430	1	9	100%
1980	44,586	2	1	51,608	1	2	116%
1981	37,547	2	5	45,071	1	8	120%
1982	35,061	3	1	44,571	1	3	127%
1983	34,758	2	1	41,695	1	3	120%
1984	31,974	2	1	42,534	1	4	133%
1985	34,444	2	2	42,881	1	4	124%
1986	35,271	2	1	46,321	1	4	131%
1987	36,286	2	2	40,594	1	11	112%
1988	39,582	1	1	39,152	2	2	99%
1989	38,574	1	2	36,448	2	11	94%
1990	36,589	2	1	39,077	1	14	107%
1991	36,038	3	2	43,218	1	6	120%
1992	34,799	2	6	44,984	1	2	129%

league matches over this period was 17.4 million at Liverpool and 19.7 million at Manchester United, some 13 per cent higher, despite a consistently weaker league performance.

This support was critical to the long-term survival and prominence of the club. While it is true that Manchester United continued to play attractive football throughout its relatively lean years, this alone cannot account for the sustained interest in the club. Manchester United is distinguished as being a club which does not appear to draw its support primarily from its local area. In Manchester itself it is said that City is the most popular team; but United is supported all over the country. Moreover, in international terms United is probably the most well recognized English football club. In that sense it is like a brand name such as Coca-Cola, Marlboro cigarettes or Nescafé. Although competing in markets crowded with superficially similar products, these brand names, and others like them, are characterized by the fact that consumers have a strong tendency to rely on them in preference to their rivals. There are any number of cola drinks or cigarette brands in the world, and in blind taste tests consumers may be unable to distinguish a cola drink from genuine Coca-Cola, or Marlboro tobacco from any other brand, but the established brand names can still sell at higher prices than their rivals and continue to dominate the market. In a sense this is what Manchester United achieved; despite a lower level of league performance than its major rivals, it was still able to attract more customers than them.

There are perfectly rational reasons for consumers to make choices based on brand image, even if sufficient research could show that they are paying higher prices for equal products. Firstly, choosing a brand name is generally simpler. If consumers had adequate information, they might choose to buy a better value brand of coffee each week, or choose to see a different football match. However, information processing is very costly, so it makes sense to go to see a team with an established track record. Few clubs in postwar England have had a better track record than Manchester United, even if this argument was beginning to wear a bit thin by the early 1990s.

Secondly, choosing a brand name is often a safer decision than gambling on a less well known alternative choice. Brand names represent a long history of product development and promotion. The owners of a strong brand have a big incentive to try to maintain that image, while owners of products without such an image have less to worry about if they let the customer down. In that sense, Nescafé will always be committed to maintaining the quality of their coffee and Manchester United will always be committed to attractive winning football, since to stop doing so would be to throw away a valuable image built up over many years. To fans considering the choice of club to support over a lifetime this is a comforting thought.

Thirdly, given that many people choose to support their local team, those who choose a non-local team are to some extent exceptional, and are clearly making a decision based on alternative criteria. One likely criterion for such a choice is likely to be history and image, and most dispassionate observers would argue that on this basis Manchester United is the most attractive club. Finally, given that for most supporters there is usually a fairly large number of local teams to pick from, the actual choice of club can be a random decision based on experiences early in one's youth (a point very well made by Nick Hornby in *Fever Pitch*). A decision such as this is likely to be influenced by the most popular team around at any point in time. Thus to some extent Manchester United is well supported because it has always been well supported.

The ultimate consequence of Manchester United's reputation was the ability to sustain itself through the lean years. By 1992 the club had gone twenty-five years without a league championship. In a similar position most clubs would have suffered financially. Manchester United, however, was still able to spend large sums on wages and, when required, transfers. Eventually Alex Ferguson built a championship-winning team, and went on to win the inaugural Premier League Championship. This success opened the floodgates, with four championships in the next five. The change in

Figure 6.19
Wage expenditure and league performance 1991–7

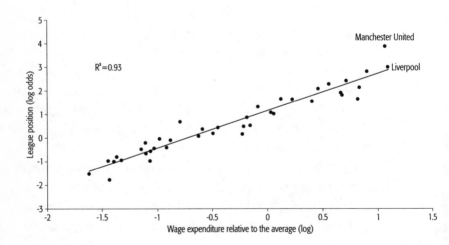

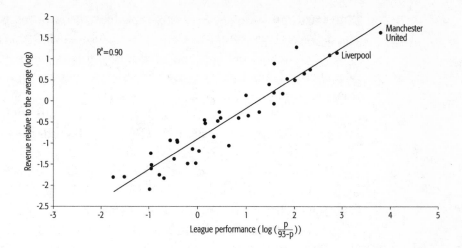

Figure 6.20
League performance and revenue 1991–7

fortunes is illustrated by Figures 6.19 and 6.20. In terms of league performance Manchester United and Liverpool have reversed their roles, with Liverpool spending more than any other club and underperforming while Manchester United has significantly outperformed. As can be seen from Figure 6.20, United's revenue generation is in fact no better than might have been expected given such an outstanding performance in the league. In a sense, reality has caught up with the myth. With continuing high levels of support and a winning team, the club has become the most profitable football business England has ever seen.

Architecture: Liverpool

Liverpool is not like Manchester United. Its support comes primarily from the city itself, and even there it has to compete for the fans' loyalties with another major club, Everton. It has seldom attracted the same degree of interest, support or recognition among neutrals. Liverpool Football Club is really only famous for one thing: winning. Elected to the Football League in 1893, the club won two First Division Championships before the First World War (1901 and 1906), two just after (1922 and 1923) and their fifth in 1947, the first postwar championship. Then the club started to slide and by 1954 had been relegated to the Second Division. In a period when its closest rivals, Everton and Manchester United, thrived, Liverpool seemed unable to compete. As was the case with Manchester United, its renaissance was associated with a new manager, Bill Shankly. Born in 1913, Shankly was a contemporary of Busby's (1909). Both came from small mining villages in Scotland, and Shankly was also a famous player in his time (at Preston North End). He left Preston in 1949 to become manager first of Carlisle (1949–51), then Grimsby Town (1951–3) and then Workington (1954–9). These were all lesser clubs, and although in the 1950s the difference in quality between the divisions was much smaller than it is today, Shankly really wanted to manage a club which had the financial resources, and ultimately the level of potential support, which could sustain a winning First Division side. In 1959, after his long apprenticeship, Shankly was hired by an ailing Liverpool.

Shankly transformed Liverpool. Within three years they were back in the First Division, after five years they won the First Division Championship. A year later they won the FA Cup and then in 1966 the First Division Championship again. Like Busby, Shankly inherited some key personnel who would figure heavily in the club's future success: Bob Paisley, Joe Fagan and Ronnie Moran. But it was Shankly's inspiration which turned the club around. His distinguishing feature, both as a player and as a manager, was his commitment. He made it clear to everyone around him that he was completely focused on one thing, winning, and showed little tolerance for anyone involved with the club who did not share this view. Throughout most of his career he was at loggerheads with club directors, whose interference he strongly resisted and whose contribution he apparently despised (though he used their money often enough). Shankly, like Busby and Clough, placed his relationship with his players at the centre of his strategy, giving and receiving total loyalty. He considered injuries a betrayal, demanding that even serious ones be overcome with willpower. His coaching methods emphasized simplicity and above all passing the ball. His own comments illustrate the extent of his commitment:

> *I'm possessed with a killer instinct, which in my playing days paid dividends, without using shady tactics, I made sure that my immediate opponent drew a blank. I used to think that it would be better to die, than lose. To enable me to reach the top and keep there, I went to all extremes, no women, no smoking, early to bed, good food, this went on for years, but it was worth while.*[6]

After his side of the mid-1960s began to age Shankly started to put together a second great team, many of whom came through the club's youth development system. Like other truly outstanding managers, he was capable of repeating the trick and his new team won the First Division title again in 1973. This was the beginning of the most successful run of league performance ever achieved by an English club. But just at that point Shankly retired, a hero to the team and the supporters, one of the great managers. When Busby left Manchester United they struggled, even being relegated for a season to the Second Division. Both Nottingham Forest and Derby County briefly flourished after Brian Clough left, but soon struggled. After a successful decade under Shankly, Liverpool got even better. Some might argue that it was his team which achieved some of the great successes of the late 1970s, but by the beginning of the 1980s, a decade in which Liverpool won six First Division titles and numerous other honours, the Shankly squad had retired. Bob Paisley, Shankly's successor, is the most successful manager in the history of English football measured by trophies: six First Division Championships, three League Cups, three European Cups and the UEFA Cup – all this was achieved in a relatively short career as manager from 1974 to 1983.[7] But when Paisley retired the success continued under first Joe

Fagan and then Kenny Dalglish, who became player-manager.

If Liverpool's success cannot be wholly attributed to Shankly, it certainly cannot be attributed to any other single individual. All the managers during these years played a role, but none was pivotal. The same can be said of the players. Individual talents made a huge difference to the club's success and players such as Kevin Keegan and Kenny Dalglish commanded enormous loyalty from the fans, but over the years stars came and went and the winning continued.

Liverpool's success was much more than a matter of spending. The exceptional quality of their success is illustrated in Table 6.5, which shows the total annual wage bill of Manchester United and Liverpool over the years 1972 to 1990. Taking the period as a whole, Manchester United actually outspent Liverpool by about 6 per cent.[8] Liverpool did not simply buy success in the market place. League positions can be bought by spending more money than rivals, but the level of success achieved by Liverpool would have cost two or three times more than the club actually spent. The point can also be seen from Figure 6.17, which covers the years 1972 to 1990. Liverpool simply stand out far above the competition in

Table 6.5
Liverpool and Manchester United annual wage bill 1972–90 (£)

Year	Liverpool	Manchester United	Ratio
1972	209,322	342,027	61%
1973	286,639	289,052	99%
1974	366,000	328,000	112%
1975	347,000	354,000	98%
1976	488,000	439000	111%
1977	576,000	522,000	110%
1978	766,000	630,000	122%
1979	699,000	702,000	98%
1980	1,000,000	849,000	118%
1981	1,230,000	1,092,000	113%
1982	1,557,000	1,503,000	104%
1983	1,375,000	1,554,000	88%
1984	1,436,000	1,941,000	74%
1985	1,974,000	2,806,000	70%
1986	2,198,000	2,576,000	85%
1987	2,259,000	2,666,000	85%
1988	2,924,000	2,543,000	115%
1989	2,796,000	3,012,000	93%
1990	3,917,000	3,909,000	100%

terms of performance relative to wage expenditure. So how did they achieve it?

Shankly himself emphasized again and again that no individual was more important than the club and that what mattered was the collective effort. While all players pay lip-service to this philosophy, in most clubs it does not quite ring true. Manchester United in particular has always tended to be a team of stars with each player competing for the limelight, and in the 1960s and 1990s this worked well. A player such as Eric Cantona, brilliant, individualistic, erratic and egotistical, produced his best for Manchester United, but it would have been hard to imagine him ever fitting into a Liverpool side. In the 1970s Liverpool dominated the opposition by a collective effort which tended to downplay the contributions of individuals. Heroes to their fans, the Liverpool team were often seen by the neutral as part of a grim machine grinding out results. This might also explain why Liverpool was a relative underachiever in terms of income generation during its most successful years. As Figure 6.18 illustrates, its income was well below what an average club might have expected to earn for a similar standing in the league. When Liverpool finally managed to achieve higher gates than Manchester United in the 1987–8 and 1988–9 seasons the Liverpool team of that period were not only successful but playing more adventurous football under Kenny Dalglish. With stars such as John Barnes and Peter Beardsley, the team attracted an even wider following. In the barren 1990s, the Liverpool team have continued to play attractive football, but without the consistency of results.

Just as the industrial success of Japan in the 1960s and 1970s spawned a generation of research into the genesis of the country's achievements, so the dominance of Liverpool led to a large amount of speculation about the secret of their success. These speculations have been hampered by the club's reticence when it comes to talking about it (although club officials are usually prepared to talk to journalists on all other issues, this subject of discussion is actively discouraged). The most widely quoted explanation for Liverpool's success is 'the boot room'. The boot room was simply that, a store room for boots and other sports equipment, traditionally maintained by Ronnie Moran, Roy Evans and other trainers at the ground from the earliest of days of Shankly's tenure.

One insider described it thus:

> *This great institution was where so much of Liverpool's preparatory work was done and yet Shankly himself spent comparatively little time there. Tom Saunders confirms that 'Bob Paisley, Joe Fagan, Ronnie Moran, Reuben Bennett and myself would come into Boot Room on Sunday and talk about the matches we'd been involved with. . .' Tactically a lot of Liverpool's work was done in the Boot Room. . . For many years the Boot Room had been the heart of the club.*[9]

So what went on in the boot room? Usually the trainers would meet on a Sunday, discuss tactics, games, players, opponents. Players were not allowed in. After a match on Saturday the opposing manager would be invited in for a drink, as an exalted guest at the high table of an exclusive college, largely, it would appear, with the sole purpose of extracting some kind of psychological advantage. There is no doubt that Liverpool were always meticulous in their preparation. According to Graeme Souness, club captain in the mid-1980s and manager in the early 1990s,

> *What Liverpool have that other clubs do not is continuity and that stems from a set of volumes stored at the ground and kept up to date without fail every day. It is the football bible as far as the Anfield backroom staff are concerned and contains the answer to almost every problem and every situation which could arise in the day-to-day running of a successful club. Every detail is noted,*

from the temperature and ground conditions to the
physical and mental state of the players. Injuries are
logged, including how and why it happened as well as
how it responded to treatment. There are volumes and
volumes, maintained ever since Joe Fagan first introduced
them under Bill Shankly.[10]

The boot room might be thought of as representing the
institutionalized knowledge about running the club, a kind
of collective memory.

During Kenny Dalglish's tenure the actual boot room
was demolished as part of a rebuilding programme and
Dalglish has been accused of destroying it as an institution. In
his autobiography he denied this strenuously.

> *It was an institution, one I would never have meddled*
> *with. . . It was a symbol of Liverpool's approach to the*
> *game, the thinking and planning that brought victories.*
> *Other clubs tried to emulate the Boot Room – every club*
> *has its own place where you can have a drink afterwards –*
> *but it's the people who count. They are more important*
> *than the place. Other clubs could recreate the setting but*
> *you can't recreate Ronnie, Roy, Bob and Tom. They were*
> *unique.*[11]

The boot room then appears to have been some kind of
data base for the club, not merely of facts and figures about
past performances, but a record of the club's 'spirit', its
attitudes and its philosophy. This cannot merely be recorded
in written volumes but has to be embodied in the conduct of
the club. If it could simply be written down, then it could
easily be imitated. The boot room might be thought of as the
equivalent of 'reputation' in the context of an organization, an
established set of traditions which oblige newcomers to adapt
themselves to fit in, largely because the very success of the
organization makes rebellion or radical departures lack

credibility. Sir Matt Busby created a reputation for the fans at Manchester United, but despite his continued involvement in the club the team of his successors appeared unable to recapture his winning ways. United continued to develop fine individual players, but the club's individualistic ethos seemed to militate against a sense of shared experience passed on from generation to generation. Bill Shankly's collectivism achieved just that, a means by which the club itself, not just the individuals, could learn.

The notion of the boot room fulfils the prerequisites for a distinctive capability. It is something which is not very precise and cannot be written down as a formula, and it is therefore difficult to copy. On the other hand, it seems sufficiently clear as a concept that we can understand what it means, even if we would not know how to go about emulating it. Possession of this distinctive capability can therefore become a source of competitive advantage. As a strategist might say, the difficulty lies not in the concept but in the implementation. Another important aspect of the boot room is that it is a distinctive capability of the club, not of the individuals involved. Just as the performance of great players added to the reputation of Manchester United (as well as bringing fame to the individuals) the contribution of those people involved in the boot room, while creating a certain mythology about their own role, primarily served to enhance the club by preserving its collective memory. A name one might give to this kind of distinctive capability is 'architecture', a source of competitive advantage derived from the network of relationships inside an organization, which not only benefits the individuals involved but also enhances the organization itself.

The boot room is like any distinctive capability: its mere possession does not create a competitive advantage, it must also be harnessed. When Kenny Dalglish resigned unexpectedly in 1991 he was replaced by Graeme Souness. Expected to continue the traditions of the club, Souness turned out to be an iconoclast. Despite his recognition of what it had done to the club, he seemed prepared to dispense with the institution of the boot room. He also felt the team he inherited needed replacement and set about dismantling it. Souness claimed that Liverpool was becoming ossified and needed rejuvenation; his critics claimed that he thought he was bigger than the club and had no respect for its traditions. In any case, his methods did not yield instant success on the pitch. With considerable acrimony, he was fired in 1994, the first manager not to retire of his own volition since Shankly's arrival thirty-five years earlier. He was replaced by the model boot room personality, Roy Evans, supported by Ronnie Moran, who first signed with the club in January 1952. Evans failed to win a trophy, and was replaced in 1998 by Bernard Houllier, the first outsider to manage the club since Shankly himself. It remains to be seen if the Liverpool architecture is a distinctive capability that can be revived once it has been neglected.

Deep pockets as distinctive capabilities
In a competitive environment firms cannot be expected to outperform their rivals systematically. Any competitive strategy which is successful is likely to be rapidly adopted by rivals, thereby neutralizing its advantage, and the more competitive the market, the quicker the process of imitation is likely to work. Football is an extremely competitive industry and so the opportunities for outperforming the market are limited. This means that in pure business terms the opportunities for making profits are limited, but it also means that in sporting terms the playing performance of a club is largely dictated by the current financial resources available to it, financial resources which are themselves dictated by the level of performance of the team. The Premier League Championship can be bought, but it is expensive. One way to competitive advantage is simply to find someone prepared to inject the necessary financial resources, as Blackburn Rovers did. This is a form of distinctive capability in itself, the distinctiveness arising from being the chosen one. Presumably Jack Walker

could have selected any club to be recipient of his largesse; all would have accepted, and all would have prospered under him. In 1997 a similar kind of process was begun by Mohammed al Fayed who selected Fulham as the vehicle for his ambition to own a top English football club.

This kind of distinctive capability seems different from the others discussed in this chapter. This is partly because the work of Brian Clough, the reputation of Manchester United and the architecture of Liverpool were created not just by talent but by hard work over a long period of time. To be selected by Mohammed al Fayed does not appear to require a great deal of effort, merely to be in the right place (i.e. close to Harrods. In fact Chelsea is closer, and it appears that Mr Al Fayed had talks with its owners first, but the dominant shareholder, Ken Bates, was not interested in sharing control.) However we may feel about the different ways that money can be generated, Manchester United and Fulham are similar to the extent that each club has more money available to spend than similar rivals. In the case of Manchester United its extra revenue comes from a large and loyal base of fans, in the case of Fulham the extra revenue comes from a single person. In practice, Manchester United's distinctive capability is likely to be more reliable over the longer term, given that it is not dependent on the goodwill of a single individual. Both these examples are different from Brian Clough and Liverpool, which outperformed the market by extracting an above average level of performance from the players in their teams.

The examples selected in this chapter concern sustained outperformance over a lengthy period of time. This is because in any activity where chance plays a role, a temporary period of outperformance may be attributed to luck. No one could credibly argue that Liverpool's success over eighteen years was simply good fortune: we can be sure that there existed some kind of distinctive capability which was causing them to out-perform. To identify further examples is more difficult, since they involve less sustained periods of outperformance and therefore are more open to question. If we go back to the pre-war period, the case of Herbert Chapman, who led both Huddersfield Town and Arsenal to successive league championships, suggests itself as another example of a strategic asset. Arsenal has been one of the most successful clubs of recent years, winning three championships since 1988 under two different managers. It has also been one of the most successful revenue generators. This has enabled the club to fund an increasingly expensive squad. In fact, much the same can be said of all the major London clubs: Tottenham, Arsenal and Chelsea are all capable of attracting substantial income largely because of their location which allows them to develop a large and relatively affluent base of fans. The success of these clubs might be attributed to a strategic asset (i.e. location in London, and in the case of Chelsea in one of the wealthiest parts of London) combined with reputation (they were among the earliest clubs in London).

Another London club, Wimbledon, might be cited as another example of architecture. Wimbledon were an amateur team outside the Football League until 1978 but rose rapidly on admission to the Fourth Division. They reached the First Division in 1986, since when they have never been relegated and have generally achieved positions in mid-table or higher. Interestingly, Wimbledon have consistently developed an image of themselves as 'The Crazy Gang', a team loved by no one who is not a supporter, loyal only to themselves, self-appointed tormentors of the football aristocracy. Wimbledon, playing in a completely different style to Liverpool, have managed to sustain a Premier League level of performance with a Second Division budget, and have done so for more than a decade now. This is illustrated in Figures 6.21 and 6.22. Figure 6.21 illustrates the club's exceptionally high level of performance from its wage expenditure, standing further above the regression line than any other club over a similar period. However, Figure 6.22 illustrates that it needed to do this just to maintain its position in the league. Its revenue

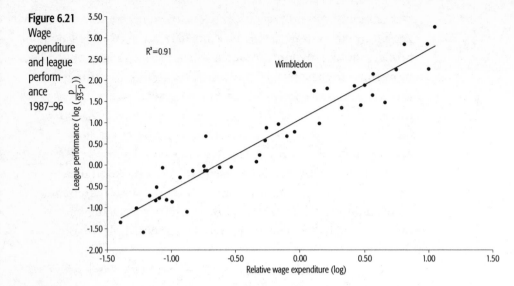

Figure 6.21 Wage expenditure and league performance 1987–96

League performance $(\log(\frac{p}{93-p}))$

$R^2=0.91$

Wimbledon

Relative wage expenditure (log)

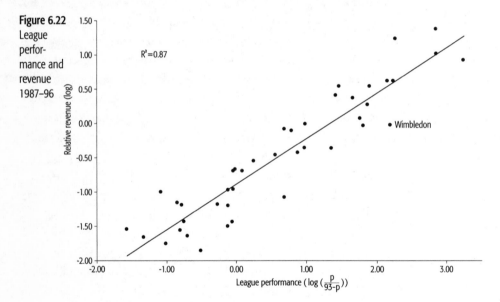

Figure 6.22 League performance and revenue 1987–96

Relative revenue (log)

$R^2=0.87$

Wimbledon

League performance $(\log(\frac{p}{93-p}))$

generating abilities place it about as far below the regression line as it lies above it in Figure 6.21.

This chapter set out to provide a detailed illustration of the three principal sources of competitive advantage for a football club. The distinctive capabilities known as strategic assets, reputation and architecture were illustrated using the exceptional examples of Brian Clough, Manchester United and Liverpool. No doubt there are other possible examples, but such examples are generally less clear. One can think of other successful managers (eg. Don Revie, Ron Saunders or Howard Kendall), teams with strong reputations (Tottenham, Newcastle or Chelsea) or teams with reputations for a particular style of play (Tottenham again, or in a negative context Wimbledon). But in general these cases are exceptional to a lesser degree, the success that was associated with them was less pronounced and the period over which success was maintained was generally shorter. It would be foolish to imagine that there could be lots of examples precisely because distinctive capabilities are scarce. Most teams perform in line with the money they spend on players and occasional instances of outperformance are usually matched by periods of underperformance. Distinctive capabilities are by their nature rare things, which is why they permit their owners exceptional opportunities to outperform rivals consistently.

Co-operation and Collusion

Competition and co-operation

In all industries most firms have an incentive to collude with each other. Unless a firm believes that it can force all the others out of the industry and become a monopolist in its own right, it has an incentive to co-operate with its rivals. Even if it can eliminate the competition, such actions are often costly to the firm, so that it may still be more profitable to collude. By eliminating the effects of competition without eliminating competitors a firm can increase its profits. Collusive agreements can increase profits in three ways. They can enable firms to raise prices and restrict industry output; they can resist competitive expenditures such as advertising or research and development; and they can define limits to competition for necessary inputs such as labour or raw materials. The incentive to collude is extremely powerful. In the memorable words of Adam Smith: 'People of the same trade seldom meet together, even for merriment and diversion, but the conversation ends in a conspiracy against the public, or in some contrivance to raise prices.'[1]

If collusion is good for firms, it is seldom good for their customers or suppliers. Consumers pay more and suppliers get paid less than they would under free competition. Collusion, like monopoly, redistributes wealth from consumers and suppliers to the colluding firms. It may also have serious adverse consequences for society as a whole because by limiting innovation collusion will reduce the amount of investment by firms and limit research and development into new products and new techniques. These adverse effects of collusion and monopoly have been recognized since the end of the Middle Ages, but the first country actually to legislate against them was the United States under the Sherman Act of 1890, which outlawed both 'the intent to monopolize' an industry and 'conspiracies in restraint of trade'. Violation of the Sherman Act can lead to sizeable fines, damages and even prison sentences for the executives involved.

Legal prohibitions in England have historically been somewhat weaker, and there was no specific legislation dealing with collusion until the 1956 Restrictive Trade Practices Act. This Act and its successors required firms entering restrictive agreements to register them with the Restrictive Practices Court. The law presumed that such agreements were not permissible unless the firms could prove that they were in the 'public interest'. Defining the public interest is of course a tricky job, opening up a loop-hole through which a group of firms (known as a cartel when they collude) might escape the force of the law. Furthermore, even if agreements are found not to be in the public interest, the only sanction against the firms is an order for them to desist. There are no fines or penalties under the law, which some might argue limits the threat posed by the law to potential cartel members.

In 1997 the new Labour government decided to adopt the framework of competition policy in force in the rest of Europe under the Treaty of Rome, which already applied to British businesses involved in trade within the borders of the European Union. The Treaty of Rome lays down rules on competition which are quite similar to the prohibitions in the Sherman Act. In particular Article 85 prohibits agreements which restrict or distort competition, thus covering collusive agreements, and Article 86 prohibits 'the abuse of a dominant position', implying severe restrictions on the activities of monopolists. These rules give the competition authorities powers to impose fines of up to 10 per cent of turnover of the companies found in breach of the law.

Competition in team sports is not feasible without collusion among the competitors, and this basic fact renders team sports companies almost unique in the business world. A competitive team sport cannot be produced and sold to the public unless two teams agree to stage a match. In the jargon of economics, competitors in team sports such as football are also complements in the production process: unlike in any other industry competitors need each other in order to produce what they sell. Thus, in the case of a football match the clubs have to both co-operate and compete. The competition between clubs to win the game provides the spectacle, but co-operation is required to ensure that the fixture takes place on an agreed date with rules and regulations accepted by all participants. The dual nature of sporting competition has presented the competition authorities with a severe dilemma over the years.

Most team sports businesses are co-ordinated through a league structure, with a governing body in charge of the rules. In England football developed with two governing bodies, the Football Association and the Football League. The FA represented the game at national level, determined the rules and authorized the activities of league competitions; the Football League administered the league competition among the top clubs, arranging the fixtures and adding supplementary rules. This separation of powers is an accident of English history. In most other countries the functions of the FA and the principal league have been subsumed in a single governing body controlling the entire game. Similarly the governing bodies of US team sports, the baseball and football commissioners, Major League Baseball (MLB), the National Football League (NFL), the National Basketball Association (NBA) and the National Hockey League (NHL), have all combined the functions of rule-making and co-ordination of competitive fixtures.

In any other business, if an industry body set the number and location of producers, allocated resources between them, set prices and redistributed revenue between producers it would without question be deemed illegal. Many sports organizations have carried out all of these functions at one time or another, and the competition authorities have been forced to recognize the unique nature of sports and allow leagues to carry out their functions as co-ordinators. The first involvement of the competition authorities arose in the US when in 1922 the Supreme Court held that baseball was exempt from the Sherman Act because it did not represent 'interstate commerce', a pre-requisite for the federal competition law to apply. This decision, which has been widely criticized since on the basis of fact, has never been overturned. Although cases have been brought against teams and Major League Baseball as a whole, the courts have argued that because of the sport's special status as the American national game, it is up to Congress to pass a law to amend the past ruling of the Supreme Court. This state of affairs has effectively licensed the baseball authorities to act in ways which go beyond the simple needs of co-ordination, since they face no effective restraint from the law.

The most obvious ways in which baseball has restricted competition is through the movement and contracting of players, and the original case on which the Supreme Court ruled concerned the attempt of a rival league to offer contracts to players from Major League Baseball. Major League Baseball has also controlled the location of baseball franchises in order to help maximize the revenues from the game and sold television rights on behalf of all the clubs. By selling rights collectively the baseball franchise owners have been able to extract a higher price for their television rights than they could have achieved through individual negotiation. While other US sports have not enjoyed the full exemptions granted to baseball, the competition authorities have still tended to look favourably on restrictive agreements. In particular the 1961 Sports Broadcasting Act exempted the collective selling of TV rights for sports leagues.

Perhaps the most compelling reason for the continuing restraint of the US competition authorities has been not merely that co-ordination is required to sustain the league, but the further argument that the league must redistribute income in order to maintain competitive balance. Some American sports leagues have engaged in substantial revenue sharing, which they argued is necessary to ensure a balanced and therefore attractive competition. This argument is analysed in more detail below in both the US and English contexts. The American example illustrates the fine line the competition authorities must tread. Given the special nature of the product it is almost impossible not to treat sports leagues differently from other industries. However, once exemptions are granted there is the danger that privileges will be abused.

In England there was no general competition law during the first century of football's existence, which might have led one to expect that English football would develop in a highly cartelized form. In reality, it developed in a highly fragmented pattern. As football grew, vested interests in the clubs, in the FA, in the Football League and elsewhere were already entrenched so that co-ordination opportunities were limited. Compared to the US, English football is much less closely regulated and structured. As we have seen in Chapter 3, the major co-ordinating restrictions were related to the players and were eliminated either by the courts or by the threat of court action in the early 1960s. Although William McGregor was a keen advocate of revenue sharing by the clubs, it was limited to £12 per match in the original rules of the Football League.

Traditionally the football authorities have shown little interest in maintaining a competitive balance and have done little to promote it actively. Competitive balance was always used as an argument to maintain the maximum wage and the retain-and-transfer system.[2] However, once these restrictions disappeared, while there continued to be a limited degree of revenue sharing, nothing was done to find new ways to maintain competitive balance. Without a strong central authority, each club lobbied to keep its financial independence and resisted collusive arrangements. Clubs resisted precisely those forms of agreement which would have helped to improve their profitability. The explanation of this apparent paradox is the prisoner's dilemma. While each club had an incentive to co-operate in order to improve the outcome for all, each club privately had an incentive to opt out of any agreement and pursue its own interests. The prisoner's dilemma encapsulates the inherent instability of cartels.

From the Football League to the Premier League

At its foundation the Football League was definitely the junior partner to the Football Association. The FA did not eagerly embrace the professional game, and many of its members saw the Football League as a somewhat disreputable collection of businessmen. The imposition of a maximum dividend by the FA in 1896 was clearly intended to restrain the pursuit of profit. In the last years of the nineteenth century the FA tried to impose its own transfer system on the League and enforced the maximum wage in 1900. However, after some wranglings the FA finally agreed in 1904 to relinquish financial control of the game, standing back from the restrictive arrangements placed on players' transfers and wages. In many ways the FA preferred to stand above the marketplace and the League was quite happy to accept the respectability that the FA's patronage gave it.

All the original Football League clubs came from the north, mostly from Lancashire, where professional football had taken root first. Arsenal was the first club from the south to join the Football League in 1893 and this act prompted its professional rivals Millwall to form the Southern League. Until the First World War the Southern League was a competitor to the Football League, if not for spectators then for players. Mutual recognition of player registrations was not achieved until 1910, finally closing off the limited labour market flexibility for players which had existed until that date.[3] However, many Southern League clubs wished to join the more prestigious Football League and during this period teams such as Tottenham, Chelsea and Fulham did so. Proposals for a National League collapsed in 1907 and 1909 over disagreements on terms. After the First World War a weakened Southern League sued for admission to the Football League and was finally admitted in 1920 as the Third Division. The creation of a Third Division North in the following year completed the league structure, which survived more or less unchanged until 1992.

In the US, where leagues contain many fewer teams and the competitors are much more dispersed, rival leagues are created from time to time in direct competition with the major ones. Since its formation in 1920, the National Football League has seen seven rival leagues set up to compete against it, the first being the American Football League in 1926, only six years after its own foundation.[4] The most recent challenge came in 1998.

Turner Network Television and NBC Sports, both television companies, announced that they are to set up a rival league to the NFL beginning in 1999. This decision was a response by the TV stations to losing their rights to broadcast the NFL. To rival the NFL the new league will need to create teams in each of the major geographic markets. With thirty teams covering the most attractive city locations the NFL is well placed to contest the market, but given the number of US cities without a franchise team any entrant stands a fighting chance. The key to the success or failure of the league will be its ability to attract the best players from the NFL. This will require the new league to finance a huge wage bill, and as we have seen in the previous chapters, competition for playing talent can have a severe impact on profitability.

The English Football League was much less susceptible to competition from leagues with newly created teams than its American counterparts. Once the Southern League had been absorbed the League established a more or less complete national coverage. Furthermore the divisional system with relegation and promotion enabled the League to sustain many more teams. It may also be that a greater commitment to maintaining traditions would have undermined any attempt to create a new competition. From 1922 until 1992 no significant changes occurred in the structure of league football. The creation of the Premier League represented a restructuring of the existing competitions rather than a new form of competition. Its main purpose appears to have been to settle old scores between the FA and the Football League and to allow the larger clubs to receive a bigger share of TV revenue.

With all its power the Football League did little to promote cohesion among the member clubs. Perhaps because profits were not supposed to be an objective of a football club, there was no focus for promoting collusive arrangements. The League maintained the restrictions on wages and transfers which helped to maintain competitive balance. As we saw in Chapter 5, there was much greater equality of income and equality in the distribution of playing talent during the 1950s when the restrictions on players remained. Once they were abolished the distribution of wealth between the divisions grew more unequal. During this period the League found itself powerless to make changes.

One reason for the paralysis of the Football League was its arcane voting structure. The day-to-day operations of the League were managed by a secretary reporting to a management committee of around ten, but changes to the rules had to be agreed by voting members. All First and Second Division clubs were members with a single vote, while those in the Third and Fourth Divisions were associate members with eight votes in total. These eight votes were cast as a block, backing whatever proposal a simple majority of the associate members individually voted for. Any rule change required a two-thirds majority. The practical consequence of this system was that associate members could veto any rule change if they could enlist the support of only six full members.

By the 1970s a divergence of interests between the big clubs and the lower divisions had become apparent to all. The bigger clubs sought to retain as much income for themselves as possible, to look for new methods of obtaining revenue, and in particular to maximize the commercial potential of football. The smaller clubs resisted changes which they perceived would widen the gulf between the divisions, and where possible demanded a share of whatever income the biggest clubs could attract. The medium-sized clubs, hopeful that they might one day grow, fearful that tomorrow they might shrink, tried to maintain a kind of balance.

The recession of the early 1980s exacerbated the tensions and the newspapers were filled with talk of a breakaway Super League. In 1982 the PFA decided at its AGM that if a Super League were created they would press for complete freedom of contract.[5] To many people talk of a Super League was just a threat used by the bigger clubs in order to obtain concessions from the rest. The growing militancy of the big clubs won a victory with the abolition of gate revenue sharing in 1983. In 1985 they let it be known to the newspapers that they were drawing up plans for a Super League to start in 1986. In the end a compromise agreement was brokered by Gordon Taylor, the secretary of the PFA, which left the league intact but gave an increased share of television revenues (50 per cent) to the First Division clubs. However, this agreement merely papered over the cracks. In 1985 the television contract was worth only £3m: a 50 per cent share divided between twenty-two clubs amounted to a mere £70,000 each, about 5 per cent of an average First Division wage bill. If Robert Maxwell was right and TV rights were really worth £90m, then a 50 per cent share would be worth £2m each, more than the wage bill! Since almost all televised league matches were First Division matches, why not go for the whole £90m?

Several factors held back the Super League advocates in 1985. The clubs were still reluctant to view themselves as profit-making institutions and were unsure that the financial gains expected were significant enough to take on all the risk and uncertainty that would accompany the break-up of the League. Rumoured changes were strongly opposed by the PFA, which threatened to strike if any changes adversely affected their members, and few clubs wanted a confrontation with the PFA. Moreover, while the national side might have been underperforming, few could argue that the Football League was not strong, if not the strongest in the world. For various reasons most of these constraints evaporated in the late 1980s.

Over time the big clubs were becoming increasingly commercially minded, more financially oriented and more self-confident with it. By 1990 Manchester United was preparing its stock market flotation and thus could claim that it needed to keep prospective shareholders happy. The arrival of pay television and the anticipation of pay-per-view had led everyone to realize that for once Robert Maxwell had understated his case. The enforced exile from Europe and the ascendancy of the Italian Serie A had led to grave misgivings about the quality of the English game.

At this point the FA raised its standard for change. Perpetually antagonistic to the Football League, the FA seized an opportunity to put one over on its old rival. In June 1991 the FA produced 'The Blueprint for the Future of Football',[6] a huge document full of detailed proposals containing a single bombshell: a plan to create 'The FA Premier League' consisting of the twenty-two clubs from the old First Division. Why create a new league when it was to be run on basically the same lines as the old First Division? It was planned to reduce the number of teams to twenty to alleviate fixture congestion, but this was hardly a revolutionary move. The new league would be simpler to administrate, but this would have little effect on the day-to-day affairs of the clubs. Promotion and relegation between the Premier League and the new Football League First Division would be retained. The only substantial issue which could be identified as a change was the control of television money. Instead of the Football League negotiating rights and splitting the proceeds among ninety-two clubs, the Premier League would negotiate its own deal and keep all the money.

The story behind the creation of the Premier League illustrates the instability of cartels. Even without the interference of competition authorities, cartels can break down if the interests of the members diverge sufficiently. However, usually the breakdown of a cartel helps the consumer by creating competition. In this case, the hierarchy of football was already sufficiently well established that the rump Football League could not pose a serious competitive threat to the members of the Premier League.

Competitive balance, attendance and revenue

Several arrangements used in US sports leagues, such as revenue sharing and salary caps, which would have been deemed illegal in other industries, have been defended using the competitive balance argument. The value of competitive balance derives from the notion that the sports supporter, both the match attendee and the television viewer, values outcome uncertainty. Three types of outcome uncertainty can be identified: match outcome uncertainty, seasonal outcome uncertainty and the absence of long-run domination.

Match outcome uncertainty concerns the result of a single match. Thus, when two equally matched teams meet, all other things being equal, you would expect the crowd to be bigger than when a strong team plays a weak team because interest is stimulated by match uncertainty. Seasonal outcome uncertainty surrounds championship and relegation issues within a season. All else being equal, the more teams in contention for the championship (and for relegation), the more attractive league matches become. Absence of long-run domination is where there is uncertainty at the beginning of the season as to who will win the championship. If one club has dominated over many seasons then this uncertainty will be low and it is expected that fewer people will be interested in the championship, thus decreasing attendances and television audiences.

Obviously, outcome uncertainty is only one of many factors that affect attendance, including, among other things, quality of the teams and stadium, price of entrance and travel, and availability and price of other leisure activities. An appendix to this chapter looks at the evidence linking outcome uncertainty and attendance and revenue. The general proposition that a league with outcome uncertainty, that has several strong teams competing for honours, is much more attractive than a league dominated by a few sides is generally accepted.

The way to maintain outcome uncertainty is to have a competitive balance in the league. Thus a league with equally matched teams will produce both match and seasonal outcome uncertainty and avoid long-run domination by any one club. This illustrates the tension in the league structure. It is in every club's interest to win the league, and win it every year. This will meet their objective of maximizing both performance and revenue. But every club wants the league to be competitively balanced in order to create an attractive competition. Thus there is a natural tension between the objectives of individual clubs and those of league administrators representing the combined interests of the clubs.

Table 7.1 shows the English champions in the fifty-two seasons since the Second World War. By far the most successful club has been Liverpool with fourteen wins, followed by Manchester United with nine wins and Arsenal with six. There are seven clubs who have won the championship on only one occasion.

Table 7.2 compares championship winners in the English and Scottish top divisions in the fifty-two seasons since the Second World War. Although the Scottish top division was for the majority of the period smaller than the English one, the difference in concentration of winners is quite striking. In Scotland there were only seven different winners and 77 per cent of the championships were shared between the two Glasgow clubs. In England sixteen different clubs won the

Table 7.1
Championship
winners 1946–7
to 1997–8

Club	Championship wins
Liverpool	14
Manchester United	9
Arsenal	6
Everton	4
Leeds	3
Wolverhampton	3
Derby	2
Portsmouth	2
Tottenham	2
Aston Villa	1
Blackburn	1
Burnley	1
Chelsea	1
Ipswich	1
Manchester City	1
Nottingham Forest	1

championship and although Liverpool and Manchester United dominated, they accounted for only 44 per cent of the championship wins. Scotland's top division has been characterized by long successive periods of domination, with both Glasgow clubs having won the title for nine consecutive years (Rangers 1988–89 to 1996–97 and Celtic 1965–66 to 1973–74). This kind of domination is unheard-of in England with the longest consecutive run being by Liverpool, who won the championship for three consecutive seasons from 1981–2. Thus the Scottish league has suffered long periods of domination by one club and the outcome-uncertainty theory would suggest that this will have had a negative impact on interest and attendances at Scottish games.

One way to represent long-run domination (Table 7.2) graphically is by means of a Lorenz Curve (or cumulative distribution), which is traditionally used to depict income distribution within a country. Figure 7.1 plots the cumulative

Table 7.2
English and
Scottish
champions
1946–7 to
1997–8

	England	Scotland
No. of different winners	16	8
Top three clubs (% championships)	Liverpool (27%) Manchester United (17%) Arsenal (12%)	Rangers (44%) Celtic (33%) Aberdeen (8%)

Winners and Losers / 258

percentage of championship wins along the vertical axis and the cumulative percentage of teams along the horizontal axis. The team with the most championship wins is plotted first, then the second most successful team and so on. Thus using Table 7.1, we can see that one club (Liverpool) has won fourteen championships, i.e. 4.5 per cent of clubs (one out of twenty-two) have won 31 per cent of championships (fourteen out of fifty-two). This is the first point plotted.[7] Now Manchester United, the second most successful club, is included and thus two clubs have won twenty-three championships, i.e. 9 per cent of clubs won 44 per cent of championships. This is the second point plotted. This process is then continued for all clubs. The straight 45 degree line represents the equal competitive balance, that is each team in the league wins an equal number of championships. The further to the left the bulge of the Lorenz Curve the more concentrated the championship wins and the worse the competitive balance of the league.

Figure 7.1 plots the Lorenz Curves for five European football leagues, including England and Scotland. England's curve is closest to the 45 degree line and thus exhibits the least concentration of championships in clubs. England is followed by Scotland, Italy, Spain and the Netherlands, which displays the greatest concentration. Over the period England's

Figure 7.1
Postwar
European
League Lorenz
curves

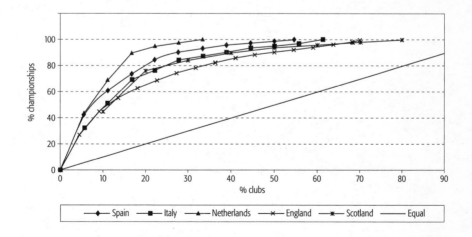

sixteen different champions compares favourably with Italy's twelve, Spain's nine, Scotland's eight and the Netherlands' six. In each country apart from Italy, two clubs have dominated the championships. In England Liverpool and Manchester United (45 per cent championships) are dominant, in Scotland Rangers and Celtic (76 per cent), in Spain Real Madrid and Barcelona (61 per cent) and in the Netherlands Ajax and PSV (68 per cent). In Italy three clubs, Juventus, AC Milan and Inter Milan (69 per cent), dominate all other clubs. Figure 7.1a zooms in on the most interesting part of Figure 7.1.

The Lorenz Curve measure is a good indicator of long-run domination but is not a perfect measure of competitive balance. It is possible for a league competition to be extremely close and exciting each year while still having a dominant champion. Conversely it is also possible that many different clubs could win the league but each championship race itself was not very close and thus not very exciting. For example, Manchester United could win three successive championships but only by a small margin from several competitors and this would be represented by the Lorenz Curve in exactly the same way as three consecutive wins by Real Madrid with no close contenders.

Figure 7.1a
Postwar
European
League Lorenz
curves (detail)

A more reflective measure of this seasonal outcome uncer-

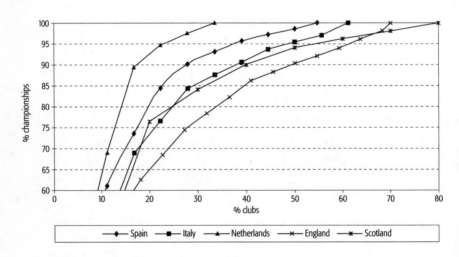

tainty is standard deviation, which measures the difference between each club's end-of-season points total and the average points total.[8] In other words, standard deviation measures the dispersion of clubs' points total in each season. In a competitively balanced league you would expect clubs' points total to be closer to the average than in an unbalanced league. The closer together the clubs' final points total, the lower the standard deviation and the better the competitive balance.

A standard deviation was calculated for each division in each season and then these standard deviations were averaged for each decade. That is for each decade there are ten single standard deviations reflecting the closeness of the final points total in each season. Figure 7.2 plots the average of these ten standard deviations for each decade since the end of the Second World War. Over time there has been an increasing level of standard deviation, suggesting a decrease in the competitive balance. In each of the divisions the standard deviation in the most recent decade is bigger than that in the decade immediately after the war, and this trend is particularly noticeable in the top division. Given the increasing concentration of wealth that has occurred in football the fall in the competitive balance is not surprising. In the last decade this trend has been reversed in the top, Second and Fourth

Figure 7.2
Competitive
balance in
English football

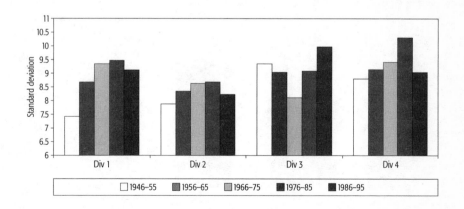

Divisions. However, this improvement in competitive balance should be treated with caution. The ten-year average is heavily influenced by the late 1980s, and the upward trend in standard deviation (i.e. downward trend in competitive balance) has resumed in the mid-1990s.

Figure 7.3 compares the standard deviation in the English top division with those of the top divisions in the Netherlands, Spain and Italy. Italy and Spain have lower standard deviations than England, suggesting a higher competitive balance. Indeed Italy displays the opposite trend to England in that it has a decreasing level of standard deviation. The Netherlands and Spain show a similar long-term upward trend to England.

The message coming from the standard deviation measures is different from that of the Lorenz Curves shown earlier. Under this standard deviation measure England, while more competitively balanced than the Netherlands, is less so than Spain and Italy. Allied with the Lorenz Curve analysis this suggests that although England has comparatively more champions than the main European leagues, its championship races are less close.

One explanation for this could be that though England has a pool of clubs with similar ability who are all capable of winning the championship, there is a large gap between these

Figure 7.3
Competitive balance in European football

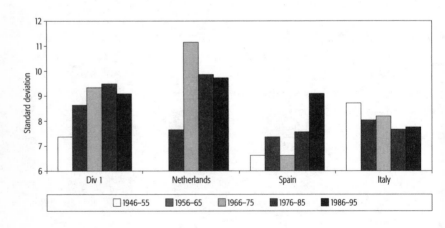

and the remaining clubs in the League. This interpretation does concur with current English experience; at the beginning of each season there is only a small number of clubs who can realistically be expected to win the League. Indeed recently, Steve Coppell, ex-manager of Crystal Palace, has talked about two Premier Leagues, one consisting of the clubs fighting for the championship and the other made up of those fighting to avoid relegation. In Italy and Spain although there are fewer eventual champions the gap between the champions and the rest of the league seems to be smaller than in England.

Maintaining competitive balance

The main threat to the competitive balance of the League is the unequal earning power of the member clubs. The two fundamental relationships explained in Chapter 5 show how expenditure leads to success on the pitch and success on the pitch increases revenue. However, it is hard to imagine Wimbledon getting bigger crowds than Manchester United even if Wimbledon's playing performance was far outstripping Manchester United's. Reputation was identified as one of the key reasons why Manchester United would achieve bigger revenues, but there are others. A club can be considered to have a core level of support which is independent of how well it is currently doing, and this core level of support is an important determinant of the revenue-earning potential of each club. The core level of support is related to several factors, most notably geography (i.e. catchment population and number of other clubs in the area) and history. The size of a club's catchment area can be an important determinant of attendances, although in this era of modern transport and with club supporters living all over the country this is perhaps becoming less important. The tradition of supporting a football club is often passed on through the generations, and therefore a key determinant of core support is the past performance and length of league membership that each club has. In a study of football attendances it has been shown that the earlier a club joined the Football League the higher its expected attendance.[9]

As a result of the uneven level of core support, the natural share of income between clubs will be uneven, and thus the competitive balance will be uneven as the richer clubs will be able to afford the most talented players. Figure 7.4 illustrates this point by showing the different amounts of revenue that the Premier League clubs earned in 1996–7. Manchester United, the biggest revenue generator, earned almost ten times as much as the smallest, Southampton. Everton, a middle-earning club, collected revenue double Southampton's but four times smaller than Manchester United's.

The most common way of addressing this imbalance is by cross subsidization. If there is a more balanced distribution of financial resources, then it is also possible to achieve a more balanced distribution of playing talent and hence a more evenly matched competition. The use of cross subsidy and its impact on English football is discussed in the following section. However, cross subsidy has not been the only means by which English football has attempted to maintain the competitive balance. Until 1961 the maximum wage and retain-and-transfer rules prevented players from earning a market rate for their services, and this stopped the richer clubs from turning their economic might into playing might. As we shall

Figure 7.4
Premier League clubs' revenue 1996–7

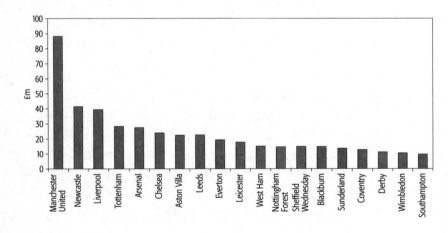

see, US sports take a much more interventionist approach to maintaining competitive balance than English Leagues.

Cross subsidization in English football: gate revenues
In the past revenue sharing has been applied to gate receipts. Between 1920 and 1983 20 per cent of net home gate was paid to the visiting side. The 20 per cent was based on the minimum entrance fee fixed for each club and deductions were made for costs of staging the fixture. What this arrangement created was a subsidy from clubs with big home gates to those with smaller ones. However, because of the small percentage allocated, the resultant cross subsidy did not make up a large proportion of clubs' turnover.

This can be illustrated by looking at the 1978–9 season and Birmingham City. Birmingham City was in Division 1 and had an average home attendance of 20,164, the nineteenth highest in the League, and less than half of Manchester United's, which averaged 46,430. Thus Birmingham City would be one of the biggest beneficiaries of the revenue sharing arrangement. If there was no revenue-sharing rule then the club would keep revenue from its own home crowd only, which totalled 423,444 (21 × 20,164). However, with the sharing rule Birmingham City kept 20 per cent of its away attendance, which in 1978–9 totalled 583,244. Thus it kept revenue from 455,404 spectators (423,444 × 0.8) + (583,244 × 0.2). Under the revenue sharing rule, Birmingham City kept revenue from an extra 31,960 spectators (455,404 – 423,444). At average entrance prices at the time of around £1.35 this resulted in a gain of £43,146. In that season the club's total revenue was £863,000, of which 72 per cent (i.e. £622,000) was gate receipts. The revenue-sharing agreement accounted for 7 per cent of its attendance revenue but only 5 per cent of its total revenue. Thus, despite Birmingham City being one of the clubs most likely to benefit from the cross-subsidy rule, the impact on its wage-spending ability was small and ultimately so was the impact on competitive balance. Indeed Birmingham

City spent £598,000 on wages in the 1978–9 season, dwarfing the additional revenue it received because of cross subsidization.

Today 100 per cent of revenue is kept by the home Premier League club. Cup competitions are different, and the revenue sharing arrangements are given in Table 7.3. The 'pool' is an amount of money collected by the organizer that is redistributed to all entrants of the competition. Thus as well as gate revenue sharing between the participants of cup games (vital for one-off knock-out ties) there is limited redistribution via the pool arrangements, which is independent of cup performance.

Cross subsidization in English football: television
While cross subsidization through the sharing of gate receipts ended in 1983, the sharing of television revenues has become increasingly important as this source of income has grown. English football clubs co-operate in selling their league television rights. Prior to the formation of the Premier League in 1992–3, television rights were sold by the Football League for all four divisions. Despite the fact that the television coverage focused on the top division, from the first deal in 1967 until 1986 each of the ninety-two clubs in the League received an equal share of revenue. In 1986 this changed with the First

Table 7.3 Gate receipts revenue sharing[10] (percentages)

	Home club	Away club	Pool	Association	Other
Premier League	100	0	0	0	0
FA Cup[1]	45	45	10	0	0
Semi-final[2]	30	30	10	25	5[3]
Final	32.5	32.5	10	25	0
League Cup	45	45	10	0	0
Champions' League	100	0	0	0	0
Final	40	40	0	10	10[4]
UEFA Cup	96	0	4	0	0
Final	45	45	0	10	0
Cup Winners' Cup	96	0	4	0	0
Final	40	40	0	10	10[4]

1 Different rates apply for replays
2 FA Cup semi-final revenue is pooled, i.e. in effect each club gets 15% of total receipts from the two games
3 Local FA groups
4 Host football associations

Division receiving 50 per cent, the Second Division 25 per cent and the Third and Fourth Divisions 12.5 per cent each. Within each division the revenue was shared equally between clubs.

After the break-up of the original league structure, the Premier League sold its own television rights and the Football League those for its three divisions. The distribution of Premier League television revenue for 1997–8 is shown in Table 7.4. In that season £136.5m was distributed between clubs; 45 per cent of this total was shared equally between those clubs currently in the League and 5 per cent was distributed between the recently relegated clubs. An award of £162,500 for the bottom club and an additional £165,000 for each place above the bottom made up 25 per cent of the total. A facility fee of around £250,000 for each time the club was

Table 7.4 Premier League 1997–8 domestic television payments	£s	Appearances BSkyB	BBC	Facility fee	Merit award	Equal shares	Total
	Arsenal	12	14	3,423,726	3,250,000	3,040,278	9,714,019
	Aston Villa	5	5	1,403,175	2,275,000	3,040,278	6,718,465
	Barnsley	3	5	898,011	325,000	3,040,278	4,263,313
	Blackburn	6	9	1,767,969	2,437,000	3,040,278	7,245,762
	Bolton	5	5	1,403,175	487,500	3,040,278	4,930,976
	Chelsea	9	9	2,525,715	2,762,500	3,040,278	8,328,506
	Coventry	5	3	1,347,069	1,625,000	3,040,278	6,012,361
	Crystal Palace	4	5	1,150,593	162,500	3,040,278	4,353,396
	Derby	5	5	1,403,175	1,950,000	3,040,278	6,393,467
	Everton	6	10	1,796,022	650,000	3,040,278	5,486,327
	Leeds	7	4	1,880,286	2,600,000	3,040,278	7,520,573
	Leicester	4	4	1,122,540	1,787,500	3,040,278	5,950,332
	Liverpool	10	10	2,806,350	2,925,000	3,040,278	8,771,641
	Manchester United	12	13	3,395,673	3,087,500	3,040,278	9,523,466
	Newcastle	6	9	1,767,969	1,300,000	3,040,278	6,108,269
	Sheffield Wednesday	3	2	813,852	812,500	3,040,278	4,666,648
	Southampton	4	5	1,150,593	1,482,500	3,040,278	5,673,388
	Tottenham	5	14	1,655,652	1,137,500	3,040,278	5,833,458
	West Ham	5	2	1,319,016	2,112,500	3,040,278	6,471,804
	Wimbledon	4	5	1,150,593	975,000	3,040,278	5,165,891
	Manchester City					1,488,888	1,488,888
	Middlesbrough					1,488,888	1,488,888
	Nottingham Forest					1,488,888	1,488,888
	QPR					1,488,888	1,488,888
	Sunderland					1,488,888	1,488,888
	Total			34,145,000	34,181,154	68,250,000	136,576,154

Source: Premier League

shown on Sky and £28,000 for each BBC *Match of the Day* appearance accounted for the remaining 25 per cent. The biggest earning club were the champions Arsenal, who collected £9.7m, just over 7 per cent of the total, and the smallest earner was Barnsley with £4.2m, around 3 per cent of the total.

The current sharing arrangement mean that clubs compete for television revenue. That is, the more successful a club the greater the merit award it will receive plus the more times it is likely to appear on television, collecting a larger share of appearance fees. However, the sharing arrangements are also a form of cross subsidy: each team is guaranteed at least three live games, plus a significant amount of income is received independently of performance and the number of television appearances.

American sports and the competitive balance

American sports take a much more interventionist line to maintain the competitive balance in their sports, with cross subsidization playing a greater role. Most notably in the National Football League (NFL, the dominant American football league) 40 per cent of gate receipts go to the visiting team and national television revenues (which make up approximately 70 per cent of average income) are shared equally between all teams. Often merchandising revenue is also split equally between clubs.[11]

In addition to the cross subsidization there are several restrictions on the free movement of players and on salaries. In 1880 the reserve option clause was introduced into baseball as a means of controlling player salaries. It was adopted by all other American sports leagues and continued until around 1975, when players won practical free agency. The reserve clause or option in effect bound a player for his entire playing career to the owner of the contract and depressed the salaries that players could expect, not allowing them to earn their appropriate market rate. Leagues claimed that the reserve clause prevented the richest clubs acquiring all the talent and thus helped maintain a competitive balance.[12]

Although the reserve clause option does not continue today, there are salary caps operating in both basketball and the NFL. The National Basketball Association (NBA) was the first to introduce a salary cap arrangement. In return for a fixed percentage of league revenues the players agreed to a salary cap. Under the agreement the league agrees to set aside a fixed percentage of total league revenues for player salaries and bonuses. Each club is then required to spend a minimum amount on salaries but must not spend more than a maximum amount. This measure prevents the wealthiest clubs from obtaining all the best players, dominating the league and reducing competitive balance.[13]

Another mechanism used in US sports to assist competitive balance is the rookie draft. In this system the team that comes bottom of the league has first choice in obtaining the up-and-coming talent from the feeder leagues. It was first introduced in the 1936 season by the NFL in response to a bidding war between the Philadelphia Eagles and Brooklyn Dodgers over Stan Koska, a star player of his day. Major League Baseball introduced its rookie draft in 1965 and the NHL followed a few years later.

Major League Baseball holds its draft every year in June. The thirty Major League clubs take turns in selecting players in reverse order of their win–loss ratio at the close of the previous season. Each club makes a selection in each round and the draft concludes after the fiftieth round is complete. Players are eligible for the draft only if they are resident in the US and have never signed a Major League or Minor League contract before. The majority of draft picks come from universities, for example the top draft pick in baseball in 1998 was Pat Burrell from the University of Miami, who was chosen by Philadelphia in the first round as they had the worst win–loss record of the previous season.

Football and the competition authorities

Recently across Europe competition authorities have been increasingly focused on sports leagues and in particular football. Although the unique nature of the league in sports has not directly been challenged, an increasing focus has been placed on transfer regulations and television contracts. Competition authorities generally accept the view that members of professional sports leagues are not completely independent economic competitors and depend upon co-operation of some degree for economic survival. However, the acceptable extent of this co-operation is being challenged. In particular, the authorities are concerned that co-ordination may be used to restrict competition in ways that limit players' freedom of contract or raise the prices that consumers pay to watch a given match.

The Bosman case and its impact on transfer regulations show that some of the older restrictions (e.g. retain-and-transfer) that the English Football League used to employ would not be acceptable today. Indeed the European authorities would scrutinize carefully some of the interventionist measures adopted by the United States, for example salary caps and the rookie draft.

The current preoccupation of European competition authorities is the football leagues' television contracts. In 1997 there were ongoing cases in the UK, Netherlands and Germany. In the UK the Office of Fair Trading (OFT) referred the television deal between the Premier League and BSkyB to the Restrictive Practices Court. In the Netherlands Feyenoord attempted to negotiate its own TV contract following the collective sale of rights by the Dutch Football Association (KNVB) to a pay TV channel called Sport 7. Feyenoord's case was upheld in court and the Dutch Minister for Economic Affairs wrote to KNVB stating that collective selling of rights was in breach of competition law. In November 1997 the German Supreme Court ruled that the German Football Association (DFB) did not have the right to sell broadcast rights to UEFA Cup matches on behalf of the clubs involved and that the latter were entitled to market the rights themselves. As a result the DFB persuaded the government to pass a law in 1998 exempting football from competition law.

In the UK the OFT has argued that the Premier League is acting as a cartel and that each club should sell the rights to its own home games individually. Cartels (agreements between producers to set a common price or otherwise restrict the market) increase profits for producers compared to what they could earn in a fully competitive market. Because restrictions adversely affect the interests of consumers cartels are generally considered to be against the public interest. Competition authorities have argued that this logic applies to the collective selling of broadcast rights. If instead of collective selling there were to be competition in the supply of football program-ming, charges to broadcasters would be lower. As a result the cost of subscribing to pay TV might also be expected to fall.

While restrictive agreements such as collective selling are generally prohibited under UK law, the Premier League has argued that collective selling is acceptable because it promotes the good of the game as a whole and is not simply a vehicle for making profits, and that the abolition of collective selling would be against the public interest because it would decrease the revenue going into the game. The Premier League claims that the revenue received from BSkyB has been put to good uses, improving the quality of the game by attracting and retaining top international stars, assisting the poorer clubs, improving stadiums and supporting the sport at the grass roots level. At the time of writing[14] the case was due to be decided by the Restrictive Practices Court in the spring of 1999.

In addition to the authorities attacking the joint selling of television rights, there are certain restrictions as to whom the football authorities can sell their television rights to. The Independent Television Commission oversees the televising of 'listed events', which because of their importance to the nation the government believes should be seen by the biggest audience possible. In 1998 the Department for Culture, Media and Sport determined that there should be two lists. The A list, whose events cannot be shown live exclusively by pay television and must be available live to terrestrial broadcasters on fair and reasonable terms. The B list events can be shown live exclusively on pay television as long as terrestrial television has access on fair and reasonable terms to delayed coverage or edited highlights.

The effect of listing an event is to reduce the competition for the rights. In the case of A listed events, pay TV services are effectively excluded from the market, and this tends to depress the value of the television rights considerably. The impact on football clubs is currently limited because it is mainly international events such as the FIFA World Cup and UEFA European Championships that have been listed. The only domestic game currently included in the list is the FA Cup Final (the Scottish FA Cup Final in Scotland).

Co-operation, cross subsidy and the future

As a result of the current approach taken by European com-petition authorities and the new UK competition legislation, methods used to increase competitive balance in the United States (such as the rookie draft) are unlikely to be an option in the UK. However, there are several outside forces that will affect co-operation in the English game and in particular the structure of the Premier League.

As discussed in Chapter 2, it is likely that developments in the broadcasting market will drive changes in the price of football's television rights. The next major development on the broadcasting horizon is the advent of digital television, which will increase the capacity of the cable and satellite networks from tens to hundreds of channels. With a maximum of ten games being played at any given time, it would require only ten channels to show all 380 Premier

League games over the season. Although no deal has currently been struck, discussions between the Premier League and BSkyB have already taken place surrounding the introduction of pay-per-view television. In December 1998 the Football League announced that it would sanction the broadcast of pilot matches on pay-per-view in early 1999. It is now not seen as a question of whether but more a question of when pay-per-view will be widely introduced.

The introduction of pay-per-view may have profound implications for the value of live TV rights for football and for the process by which such rights are sold. Throughout all the changes seen in the sale of football rights, one factor that has remained constant has been that they have been sold collectively by the League on behalf of the clubs. In addition to the threat from the Restrictive Practices Court, with digital broadcasting and greater plurality of broadcasters there is a chance this situation will change, resulting in individual clubs selling their rights in competition with one another.

The interests of the individual clubs and their attractiveness to television audiences differ widely. Once technology presents clubs with an option to go it alone, it will not be easy for the League to broker a collective deal that satisfies all. As Table 7.5 shows, some clubs attract many more viewers than others. The table gives total viewers for each club, the number of games televised and the average audience for the 1997–8 season.[15] A club's attractiveness is indicated by the number of times it was shown as well as the audience it received. Manchester United were shown twelve times, averaging nearly 1.5 million viewers each game. This contrasts sharply with Barnsley, who were shown only three times (the agreed minimum) and averaged just over 781,000. The biggest game of the season was Arsenal vs. Manchester United, which gained 2.9 million viewers, over five times the audience for the Crystal Palace–Wimbledon game (518,000). This sort of disparity in attractiveness to television audiences in pay-per-view creates significant differences in earning potential.

Table 7.5 Sky viewers 1997–8	Total Viewers (m)	Games televised	Average viewers (m)
Manchester United	17,766	12	1,481
Arsenal	16,493	12	1,374
Liverpool	14,108	10	1,411
Chelsea	9,578	9	1,064
Newcastle	7,863	6	1,311
Aston Villa	6,979	5	1,396
Everton	6,939	6	1,157
Blackburn	6,481	6	1,080
Leeds	5,791	7	827
Tottenham	5,217	5	1,043
Southampton	4,577	4	1,144
Derby	4,430	5	886
Coventry	4,229	5	846
West Ham	4,073	5	815
Bolton	3,956	5	791
Crystal Palace	3,722	4	931
Leicester	3,196	4	799
Wimbledon	3,098	4	775
Sheffield Wednesday	2,877	3	959
Barnsley	2,343	3	781

Source: Analysis of BARB data

Some evidence of the potential value of pay-per-view comes from the US, where the pay-per-view business is now ten years old. To date, pay-per-view revenues have been relatively insignificant when compared to subscription revenues. In 1995, for example, US pay-per-view revenues reached $590m compared to total revenues for the video rental industry of $9bn. There has been limited experience to date of pay-per-view in Britain. However, the pay-per-view services have been achieving buy rates of around 30 per cent (30 per cent of customers buying at least one pay-per-view event per month), which compares favourably with a US average of 3–4 per cent. The extent to which these early figures can be generalized to provide a guide to likely pay-per-view take-up over the longer term is open to debate.

Pay-per-view take-up was disappointing in Italy during its first season (1997–8). In 1997 only a small number of subscribers had been signed up. Fifty thousand agreed to pay just under £200 each per season for home and away games or £120 for away games only, yielding a total revenue of about

£8m (or about 5 per cent of the total value of Italian TV rights). Furthermore the main beneficiaries have been the big clubs, Juventus, Inter Milan and AC Milan, which between them account for more than 60 per cent of subscriptions.[16]

The implications of the developments in broadcasting for the value of TV football rights will depend in part on the manner in which pay-per-view services are introduced. Initial pay-per-view services in Europe (e.g. football in Italy) are being offered by the existing subscription service provider on an incremental basis, i.e. on top of the basic subscription package. This is because in each case the pay-per-view rights have been vested with the incumbent pay broadcaster. An alternative introduction strategy would be to offer pay-per-view as a stand-alone service with access not contingent on the take-up of a basic subscription package.

The introduction of pay-per-view, and the variance in clubs' potential income, will increase the incentive for the top clubs to do deals themselves independently of the League and thus end the cross subsidization of smaller clubs. Manchester United has already launched its own television channel to show highlights of previous games and magazine programmes. United has also commissioned studies on how much it could expect to earn with pay-per-view and in 1998 appointed broadcaster Greg Dyke, formerly in charge of ITV's football broadcasting (and the man responsible for bringing Roland Rat to the nation), to its board.

As well as selling their own rights top clubs will want to maximize the number of big games they play, thereby maximizing their pay-per-view revenue. It is likely that there will be pressure to increase the number of times major European clubs meet, and as a consequence of this there will be a reduction in the number of domestic games. There seems to be a growing acceptance that the much-discussed European Super League will be formed.

There are many who believe that pay-per-view will concentrate income in the hands of the top clubs, increasing further the gap between the big clubs and the rest. If this turned out to be true it would create further pressures for a restructuring of the Premier League. Given a relatively efficient market for players, increased concentration of wealth would lead to an increased concentration of talent and lower outcome uncertainty. Pay-per-view might strengthen the top clubs and increase their incentive to look to Europe for opposition.

Pay-per-view offers the Premier League a very clear challenge. Just as disputes over TV broke up the Football League, it may be that the Premier League will lose influence as clubs go it alone and sell their own rights. There is likely to be pressure from the big clubs for a smaller Premier League in order to schedule more games with major European sides in front of a Europe-wide pay-per-view audience. Some estimates put total pay television revenue at over £2.5bn by 2005.[17] The new co-operation will most likely be between European clubs, where a new competitive balance between the élite teams can be established. As yet the precise structure under which pay-per-view might be sold in the UK is unclear. What is clear is that clubs will have to consider the impact of any change in the distribution of income on the overall attractiveness of the league competitions in which they participate.

Appendix: Outcome uncertainty in the economic literature

Table 7.6 sets out the most important papers on the subject along with the exact form of outcome uncertainty tested, the variable(s) constructed, the data used and the conclusions reached.[18] All these studies employ regression analysis, which is described in Chapter 5. They develop a measure of outcome uncertainty and test to see if this affects attendances.

Four studies specifically focus on match uncertainty. Hart *et al.* (1975), Peel and Thomas (1988) and Kuypers (1996) look at English football, while Jones and Ferguson (1988) concentrate on the National Hockey League (based in the United States and Canada). Hart *et al.* study four English league clubs for two seasons in the late 1960s. They estimate an equation for each club separately and proxy outcome uncertainty by the logged difference in league positions. Their results show mixed support for the outcome uncertainty hypothesis. Jones and Ferguson in their study of the 1977–8 National Hockey League season set up a dummy variable equal to one if the match involves two teams from the top three or two teams from the bottom three league positions. This dummy is intended to reflect close games. Jones and Ferguson find no support for the outcome uncertainty hypothesis. Both these proxies for outcome uncertainty are rather crude. They do not take into account many important factors such as home advantage, injuries or star player absence – all of which can influence the expected outcome of the game without being reflected in league position.

An improvement on these measures was the use by Peel and Thomas (1988) of betting odds to reflect outcome uncertainty. If the odds were calculated efficiently, then all available information prior to the game should have been taken into account. However, Peel and Thomas used the probability of a home victory as the proxy for outcome uncertainty. This is incorrect because at both high and low probabilities of a home win, outcome uncertainty is low. Thus by using home probability they are really testing how supporters value expected success of the home team. Kuypers (1996) corrected this misuse but found that match uncertainty as proxied by the spread of odds for each game did not impact on either attendances or live television audiences.

More attention has been focused on testing seasonal outcome uncertainty, and there is a greater amount of evidence to support this hypothesis than there is in defence of the match outcome uncertainty hypothesis. Noll (1974) found weak support for a seasonal outcome uncertainty effect on attendances in his study of ice hockey and baseball. In the baseball study Noll used a dummy variable which indicated whether or not the championship race was close in a particular year. However, this dummy could not reflect how close the race was as it did not take account of either the number of teams in contention or the length of time that the race was close.

Borland (1987), in his study of Australian rules football, experimented with four different measures of seasonal uncertainty, but found support for only one and this was in only

Table 7.6
Outcome Uncertainty in the Literature

Authors	Testing	Variable	Data	Result
Noll (1974)	Seasonal	Whether team in contention for playoff	Ice hockey	Weak support
		Whether championship race close	Baseball	Weak support
Hart *et al.* (1975)	Match	Log difference in league positions	Four English football clubs 1969–70 to 1970–71	Mixed
Jennett (1984)	Seasonal	Championship/relegation significance of each game	Scottish League football 1975–81	Strong support
Borland (1987)	Seasonal	Difference in games won between first and last	Victorian Football League (Australian rules) 1950–86	Weak support
		Sum of coefficients of variation of game won		
		Average number of games behind the leader		
		Number of teams in contention		
Cairns (1987)	Seasonal	Dummy of contention in championship	Four Scottish football clubs 1969–70 to 1979–80	Strong support
Jones and Ferguson (1988)	Match	Dummy for top-of-the-table and bottom-of-the-table matches	NHL season 1977–8	No support
Whitney (1988)	Seasonal	Average expected probability of winning	Baseball 1970–84	Weak support
Peel and Thomas (1988)	Match	Betting odds (probability of home win)	1981–2 English football league matches	Probability of home win significant
Kuypers (1996)	Match	Betting odds (difference in maximum and minimum)	1993–4 individual English Premier League matches	No support
	Seasonal	New measure based on points and games left		Support
Baimbridge *et al.* (1996)	Seasonal	Dummy when both teams in top (bottom) four positions	1993–4 individual English Premier League matches	No support

Winners and Losers / 278

one specification of the model. The four proxies he used were: the difference in games won between the first and last team; the sum of the coefficients of variation in games won; the average number of games behind the leader; and the number of teams in contention.

Several studies look at the championship significance of single games. Jennett (1984) calculates the reciprocal of the number of matches required to win the championship prior to each match. He finds this measure significant but utilizes information not available to the spectator when he makes his decision to watch a game or not, namely the number of points required to win the championship. Cairns (1987) also finds that his championship significance variable is significant. He improves on Jennett by assuming that people compare teams' performance with each other and not against an unknowable championship winning total. However, in doing this, Jennett relies on arbitrary assumptions regarding the anticipated success rates of clubs. Whitney (1988) develops a variable of the average expected probability of winning the championship. Whitney includes both this variable and its square in his estimation but finds only weak support for the outcome uncertainty hypothesis. Baimbridge *et al.* (1996) test for seasonal uncertainty using rather crude dummy measures for when the two teams in a match are both in the top four league places or both in the bottom four league places. These measures take no account of the impact of seasonal uncertainty on games which include a championship contender and a non-championship contender. Unsurprisingly, using a measure similar to Jones and Ferguson's (1988) test of match outcome uncertainty, Baimbridge does not find any support for seasonal uncertainty. Kuypers (1996) develops a new measure of seasonal uncertainty using a championship and relegation significance variable which is just the product of the number of games left in the season and the number of points behind (above) the leader (relegation zone). Thus this measure both takes account of the impact of seasonal uncertainty on games involving only one team in the championship race and does not require any arbitrary assumptions as do Jennett and Cairns. The results provide support for the championship importance variable affecting both match attendance and live television audiences.

Absence of long-run domination has been tested explicitly only once. Borland (1987) found that there was no relation between long-run domination and lower attendances.

Why Manchester United makes money
Historically there has been no systematic relationship between the profit of football clubs and their
performance on the pitch. In fact, the reported
pre-tax profits of most clubs have averaged
around zero for the last fifty years. Even over
relatively short periods there are few instances of
clubs sustaining a significant level of profitability.
The exception to this story is Manchester United.
Since the stock market flotation in 1991 profits
and playing success have grown together, and the
profits have been significant. Why should this be?

Manchester United has a drawing power
which is second to none. Since the Busby era the
club has consistently attracted more revenue for a
given league position than any other club in
England. In fact, the drawing power of
Manchester United is barely affected by its league
position. For example, between 1972 and 1991
the club's average league position was 7.9 in the
ten seasons with the lowest attendance figures,
while in the ten years with the highest attendance
figures the average league position was 8.5. Thus
Manchester United had slightly better attendance
figures when its playing performance in the league
was worse! Manchester United is clearly different
from most clubs, for whom playing performance
has a more predictable effect. Put simply,
measured by the responsiveness of league attendance to league position, Manchester United has
exceptionally loyal fans.

As well as having the biggest gates, Manchester United also benefits from the fact that its
fans are among the least sensitive to changes in
admission prices. Sensitivity to prices (the own-
price elasticity of demand for league matches) can

be estimated from past attendance and revenue data, and for the average football club has a value of about –0.4.[1] This means that for an average club a 10 per cent increase in prices is likely to lead to a 4 per cent fall in demand for tickets. This indicates, as one might expect, that the demand for football as a spectator sport is relatively insensitive to price. However, the demand elasticity for Manchester United fans is estimated to be around –0.2, a significantly smaller figure than for most other clubs. For Manchester United this represents a significant competitive advantage. Put crudely, if all clubs raised their ticket prices by the same amount, total income for football clubs would rise, but the income of Manchester United would rise by more than the income of an average club.

Thus three factors combined are the basis of the club's ability to make profits: the biggest fan base, fans who remain loyal regardless of league position and fans who are relatively insensitive to changes in ticket prices. However, these factors are not enough. Manchester United did not make large profits in the 1970s and 1980s, because success on the pitch continued to elude it. It could rely on its fan base to generate enough money to buy the most expensive players in the market. As Table 6.5 in Chapter 6 illustrated, during the years of Liverpool dominance, Manchester United regularly outspent Liverpool in terms of the team wage bill as well as spending heavily in the transfer market. However, it failed to achieve success on the pitch, largely due to the exceptional nature of Liverpool during this period. Liverpool's 'architecture' overcame Manchester United's millions (themselves a product of that club's reputation). As failure persisted, the club spent more and more on players and so profits were limited.

Once Manchester United started winning trophies in the 1990s the benefits of the league's largest fan base started to be realized in the form of financial profit. Thanks to an exceptional level of performance on the pitch it was no longer necessary for Manchester United to invest all of its revenues in team building. Manchester United did not have to spend more money than everybody else, because the established core of its squad was strong enough to dominate league competition. The club continued to trade players in the 1990s, but the net financial outlay was small.

Viewed over a thirty-year period, Manchester United's average wage expenditure has yielded an average performance which lies just about on the regression line. In other words, on average it achieved a level performance in line with what one might have expected. But in fact the club has gone through two distinct phases. For most of the thirty years the performance was well below expectations, while in the 1990s it has been well above. It would be unfair to the management of the club to put this latter period of success down to good luck (any more than it would be reasonable to attribute its relative failure in the earlier period to bad luck). But it can reasonably be said that given the enormous amount of money spent over thirty years, it was inevitable at some point that an extremely successful team would be produced.

In the 1990s Manchester United has enjoyed the fruits of simultaneously possessing the strongest support in the land and an exceptional team. The combination of having an exceptional squad and being the most popular club is rare. For the majority of clubs spending money on league performance, there is never an opportunity to sit back and take profits for fear that the club starts to slide back down the league, lose support, lose revenue and fall into financial difficulties. Competition ensures that there are no economic profits to be made.

The most successful club on the pitch must in the long run be the club with the best team, either because it has the best players or because it possesses some special 'architecture'. If the club with the biggest income is not the most successful measured in terms of playing performance, competition will drive up the wages paid at both clubs. In a world where players have freedom of contract the most successful club can only hang on to the best players if it offers to pay the highest wages or if the best players prefer to play for the club because it offers them the opportunity to achieve more than they could elsewhere. This was essentially the position that Liverpool was in during its most successful years when Manchester United competed to buy the best players. Thus Liverpool was not in a position to make a significant profit because its finances were stretched by having to pay the players a sufficient amount to prevent them defecting to Manchester United.[2] Given the deeper purse at Manchester United, this meant paying out almost all the revenue in wages.

A team in Liverpool's situation (dominant on the pitch but relatively weak in terms of revenue-generating capacity) would have found it hard to produce significant profits. It might have tried to cash in on its success by selling players. Since Liverpool's distinctive capability lay in raising the perform-ance of players well above what they might have been expected to achieve elsewhere, the prices that other clubs would have paid might not have reflected their worth to Liverpool. Furthermore, long-term performance would have suffered, and a decline might have been accelerated if it became widely known that the club was pursuing such a cynical policy. After all, part of the attraction of Liverpool to footballers was its commitment to winning. The alternative strategy, which Liverpool actually pursued, was to hold on to its players and enjoy the fruits of success on the pitch. This comes down to a choice between success on the pitch (maximizing league performance) and maximizing profit. Liverpool in its heyday chose the former rather than the latter, and indeed, historically clubs have always valued playing performance above profits; few clubs would sell their best players without external financial pressure.

When the best team is the one with the greatest drawing power the situation is rather different. Once Manchester United was in possession of the best side in the league, there was no need to go on bidding for all the best footballers, and its own players were unlikely to want to move away to other English teams, who could neither pay more nor offer a better playing environment. This is not to say that the club's spending on players diminished. In each year spending on player wages increased, but having established a winning team, spending on transfers was much less substantial than that of its major rivals. Table 8.1 illustrates the point. Manchester United had the highest wage expenditure over the period 1991–7, but the smallest net spending on transfers. For the established clubs (Manchester United, Liverpool, Arsenal, Tottenham, Leeds, Everton and Aston Villa) wages were a fairly accurate predictor of average league position. For Newcastle and Blackburn, both buying their way up the league, the effect of wage spending is slightly less clear when averaged over only seven years. Both these clubs achieved higher league positions by buying better players who had to be paid more money. What the table illustrates is that the transfer spending of the top clubs bears almost no relation to league position. As clubs have chased Manchester United, they have spent dramatic sums on players. Newcastle, Blackburn and Liverpool have between them spent over £100m net on transfer fees, with only one Premier League Championship between them to show for it.

Clubs that have refused to join the scramble to match United, notably Tottenham under Alan Sugar, have simply failed to be in contention for the championship. Had Arsenal

Table 8.1
Average position and expenditures for the biggest Premier League teams 1991–7

Club	Average league position	Total wages bill(£m)	Net transfer spending (£m)	Total Player spending (£9m)
Manchester United	2	78.7	6.2	84.9
Liverpool	5	75.4	41.2	116.6
Newcastle	16	64.7	43.9	108.6
Arsenal	6	63.3	17.5	80.9
Tottenham	10	58.6	10.2	68.8
Blackburn	13	53.9	28.2	82.0
Leeds	8	53.1	28.6	81.7
Everton	12	50.1	28.9	79.0
Aston Villa	9	45.2	18.6	63.8

Note: Money converted to 1997 prices

The Future of the Football Industry / 285

not begun to invest heavily under Arsène Wenger the same might have happened to them.

Part of Manchester United's success has been its youth policy, which has yielded a number of top stars. In the early 1990s this helped to hold down the financial burden of buying in the transfer market. Manchester United actually spent more on transfers in the first three full years of Alex Ferguson's reign (£7.8m net from 1987–8 to 1989–90) than it did in the following six seasons (£5.4m from 1990–91 to 1996–7). This is without allowing for the effects of inflation – and in football terms you could have bought a lot more talent in the 1980s with £7.8m than you could in the 1990s. It is often said that Manchester United's youth policy has been responsible for a large part of the club's recent success. However, this argument is not entirely convincing.

Firstly, most big clubs develop a high share of their own players. Between 1978 and 1997 out of our sample of forty league clubs Arsenal, Luton and Tottenham had the highest shares of home-grown players (63 per cent, 61 per cent and 58 per cent respectively), more than Manchester United, whose share over the same period averaged 56 per cent. Secondly, United under Ferguson has not fielded a greater share of home-grown talent than it did in earlier years. Over the years, relative to most clubs, Manchester United has been a significant producer of home-grown talent. Thus in the years of relative underperformance (1978 to 1986) 59 per cent of a Manchester United squad was home grown, while since 1988 the average has been only 53 per cent. Furthermore, in the years United started to win again the average share was only around 50 per cent, and it is only since 1995 that the proportion has started to climb again. When one considers the architects of the early successes – Robson, Cantona, Ince, Pallister, Schmeichel, Bruce, Irwin – none was home grown. The only home-grown players to appear consistently in the club's first Premier League Championship victory were Mark Hughes (of pre-Ferguson vintage) and Ryan Giggs. Ferguson brought winning ways to Manchester United by buying talent, not by growing it.

Thirdly, home-grown talent is by no means a guarantor of success. Liverpool has traditionally been one of the lesser developers of home-grown talent, winning eight league championships with only 36 per cent of its own players over the 1978–97 period. Twenty-six out of our sample of forty clubs produced more home-grown talent. The point was made in Chapter 5: the relationship between playing success and the proportion of home-grown talent in the team, after allowing for wages, is not statistically significant.

Youth policies are widely touted in football as a better route to success, but the evidence suggests that it is no better and no worse, no cheaper and no dearer than the route of outside acquisition. The reason for this is straightforward: in both cases what matters is the ability to identify talent and nurture it within the team. A youth policy which fails to identify the most talented youngsters or fails to integrate them into the team is no better, and in the long run no cheaper than a strategy which depends on buying recognized players. Youth policies are expensive and speculative. They are expensive because they require investment in training and human resource management. They are speculative because youngsters may fail to develop as hoped, and even if they do they may quit to play for another club.

In recent years Manchester United's spending on players (salaries and transfers) has generally been limited to the maximum capacity to spend of its nearest rivals. Between 1991 and 1997 Liverpool spent £117m on players, Newcastle £109m and Blackburn £82m. Each of these clubs was spending up to the limit of its financial capacities, which ultimately depended on the strength of its support. Manchester United has yet stronger support, and the difference between the spending power of its rivals and the club's own revenues, after allowing for other operating costs and investment in stadium redevelopment, is approximately the size of the profit that the club generates. Even if Manchester United had spent as much as these clubs, it would still be generating a substantial profit given that it has a much larger annual income. The explanation of Manchester United's profitability is simple: they are the most successful team and the best supported club in the country.

In the future Manchester United will face increasing competition from its nearest rivals. While the club is endowed with a competitive advantage in terms of the strength of its reputation and support, the club has also been at the forefront of exploiting these advantages financially. Manchester United may be the strongest football 'brand' in the UK, but others such as Arsenal, Liverpool and Newcastle are also strong and can be developed to create more income, to buy more players, to put more pressure on the club's performance on the pitch. This process has already begun. However, Manchester United may be able to maintain an edge over its rivals by branching out into new, international markets. Already the club has a strong following in Europe and the Far East. Developing into these markets may be combined with entering new competitions such as a European Super League. The club's rivals in international competition, both for revenue and playing success, are already more likely to be Juventus and Barcelona than Manchester City or Bolton.

Profits through competition

By August 1998 there were ten quoted football clubs in the Premier League, eight in the First Division, two in the Second and one in the Third. Manchester United was by far the most valuable, with a market capitalization[3] in mid-1998 of £411m, while Newcastle and Chelsea were each valued at over £100m; Tottenham and Aston Villa were both valued at over £50m. Clubs such as Arsenal and Liverpool would be valued in the same range if they were to seek a stock market listing. Smaller Premier League and First Division clubs such as Southampton, Nottingham Forest and Sunderland were valued at less than £50m, while the company which owned Second Division Millwall were valued at only £4m. Most of these valuations were significantly lower than they would have been two years ago. Between 1995 and the beginning of 1997 the Nomura Index of Football Clubs, which is an indicator of market values, rose more than fourfold. In the first half of 1997 the index fell by about one-third as investors started to be a little more cautious about football clubs as investments. The 1998 Deloitte & Touche Survey of Club Accounts lists twenty football clubs quoted in the UK with a combined market capitalization of £1,054m on 30 June, compared to a combined peak valuation of £1,899m.

Yet relative to their reported profitability, these market valuations still seem very high. Of the seventeen clubs in Table 8.2 only four managed to produce a net profit over the three most recent years for which data was available and of these Sunderland and Chelsea produced a combined surplus of less than £1m. Manchester United is far and away the most profitable of the clubs, generating £63m of profit over the three

Table 8.2 Market valuation of football clubs and historic profits performance

	Market value (£m) (June 1998)	Peak market value (£m)	Division 1998–9	Cumulative pre–tax profit 1995–7 (£m)
Manchester United	411	475	Premier	63
Tottenham	67	138	Premier	10.6
Sunderland	32	62	First	0.6
Chelsea Village	113	244	Premier	0.1
Preston North End	9	11	Second	−0.1
Aston Villa	56	126	Premier	−0.3
West Bromwich Albion	9	20	First	−0.5
Charlton Athletic	17	22	Premier	−0.8
Birmingham City	17	29	First	−1.6
Burnden Leisure (Bolton)	20	68	First	−4
Sheffield United	14	36	First	−4.2
Southampton Leisure	19	41	Premier	−4.3
Loftus Road (QPR)	7	43	First	−5.5
Millwall Holdings	5	17	Second	−6.4
Nottingham Forest	23	36	Premier	−12.6
Caspian Group (Leeds)	48	130	Premier	−19.2
Newcastle United	107	201	Premier	−23.5

Pre-tax profits relate to the football clubs' companies in existence at the time. In some cases the company which now owns the football club may differ from these earlier companies.
Source for market valuations: Deloitte & Touche

The Future of the Football Industry / 289

years. However, this profit was less than the combined losses of all the other clubs. If past performance were any guide to market valuations, most football clubs would be worth a lot less.

In reality stock market valuations are based on beliefs about the future. The lesson to learn from the combination of big losses in the past and high stock market valuations today is that the stock market is expecting big changes in the way football clubs operate (including big changes in their profitability). The stock market interest in football clubs has been based on two things: the success of Manchester United and the huge injection of TV rights money into the game. Implicit is the assumption that in the future other clubs can become like Manchester United and that television money will mean profits for all in the future.

Yet each of these propositions is hard to sustain. Manchester United can generate profits because its rivals cannot match its spending on players and achieve a similar level of league performance. But these rivals, including the clubs listed on the stock market, do not presently possess any kind of distinctive capability which can enable them to outperform Manchester United on the pitch with a lower level of investment. New money brought into the game by television will not be siphoned off to pay dividends as long as clubs compete for the top honours. If individual clubs choose not to compete they will find themselves abandoned by their supporters and hence will sink into the lower leagues. TV money is like all the other money which has been brought into the game in the last fifty years. Ultimately it will be recycled into the purchase of players. As the suppliers of the resource which is scarce and in demand, the players will be the beneficiaries.

To see what happens when a club tries to opt out of the competitive struggle it is useful to consider the history of Tottenham Hotspur under the control of Alan Sugar. A man not previously known for his interest in soccer, he acquired the club in 1991 after it had fallen into debt. Tottenham had been the first major club to float on the stock market as far back as 1983, and it was widely cited as a classic example of how football clubs could not make money. The motivation for Sugar's involvement has often been questioned. At the time it was clear that BSkyB was targeting the acquisition of football broadcast rights to expand the take-up of its satellite services and Sugar's trading company Amstrad was the main UK manufacturer of satellite dishes used by BSkyB subscribers. Sugar himself has declared that he has always been a Tottenham fan, although he also said, 'I have not invested in a football club, I have invested in a company that owns one.'[4]

Alan Sugar has often criticized the economic structure of football. When Newcastle bought Alan Shearer for £15m he said, 'Maybe I've lost the plot somewhere . . . I've slapped myself around the face a couple of times but I still can't believe it.'[5] Talking about Newcastle expenditure in general he said, 'Newcastle have spent £43m. I don't care whether you win every cup going, you'll never recoup that amount.' Explaining why he would not do this at Tottenham just to bring success to the fans he said, 'I look at some of our fans as children. They're always asking their dad for new toys and you have to explain you can't afford them. I'm hoping our fans will grow up with me and understand that my medicine is good medicine.'

He also outlined his vision of building a successful club: 'We could easily go out and spend £7 million on Carlos Kickaball but it occurs to me that I would rather spend £5 million on a school. A proper school. A state-run school that teaches the three Rs but is also a football academy for youth players. I have a vision of that school having an 80-acre site with twelve playing fields. The most important thing is security of ownership of the students because you can invest a lot of time, effort, money and teaching in a young player and he can just clear off. We've got to reform that situation.'[6]

Alan Sugar clearly believes that the way that most clubs are currently run is not commercially viable, and what he intends for Tottenham is that it should be commercially viable. However, so far it is not entirely obvious that he has succeeded in this intention. Sugar inherited debts of around £11m, which were instantly relieved by the sale of Paul Gascoigne to Lazio for £5.5m. Since then the club has been among the lowest spenders of the big clubs and among the least successful. Since 1991 the club has averaged a mid-table position in the League (between tenth and eleventh), compared to an average of sixth in the previous six years. This difference is the difference between being in contention for league honours and winning a place in Europe, compared to worrying only about continued survival in the Premier League. Tottenham has not played in a European competition since 1992 (following their 1991 FA Cup victory). While in the 1980s Tottenham was one of the established 'big five' together with Liverpool, Manchester United, Everton and Arsenal, its status could not today be considered much greater than that of Newcastle, Blackburn or Chelsea. Worst of all for the die-hard Tottenham fan, the club is consistently second best to its arch-rival Arsenal, which has won the league title twice over this period.

Ominously, there are signs that support is beginning to suffer. Between 1991 and 1998 average Premier League attendances grew by 29 per cent. At Tottenham the average league gate was 5 per cent lower in 1998 (29,153) than it was in 1991 (30,632). Since 1991 the average gate has been 28,686, peaking in 1997 at 31,067. In every other year average attendance was lower than in 1991. All the club's major rivals enjoyed an increase in average attendances over the same period. The 1997–8 season almost led to disaster for the club. From early in the season it languished in the relegation zone and at the end of November the manager Gerry Francis resigned with the club in sixteenth place. Loss of Premier League status would have led to a significant loss of income (one estimate put the figure at £4m: over 10 per cent of annual revenue[7]). Faced with this threat Sugar finally sanctioned the return of Jürgen Klinsmann, who had played for the club in the 1994–5 season, on a reputed wage of £40,000 a week. Together with the acquisition of Nicola Berti and Mousa Saib the club increased its transfer spending and its wage bill. First half-year financial results announced in March 1998 showed no increase in profits, despite the significant increase in television revenue, with the extra money being ploughed into avoiding relegation. While this short-term expedient succeeded, the image of the club has suffered. The fans are disgruntled, investors must be concerned that profits can be dissipated so easily when performance declines, and as the 1998–9 season approached it was rumoured that even players were reluctant to move to the club given its problems.

Not all of Tottenham's difficulties can be laid at the feet of Alan Sugar. Over the period he has faced continued problems associated with the role of Terry Venables in the club and his sacking, despite being largely vindicated in the courts. Attendance figures need to be interpreted with caution given the reconstruction at most Premier League grounds, including Tottenham. And, like all ailing clubs, Tottenham can point to a significant and recurring injury list. But Sugar's stated wish to develop a club youth policy to grow its own talent rather than buying in the market looks like wishful thinking given the experience of most clubs pursuing such policies. Many fans believe that the club has suffered because of the chairman's demand that it should make a profit. In fact it achieved a cumulative pre-tax profit of £13.7m over the period 1991–7 (i.e. an average of about £2m per year), compared to £5.5m at Arsenal and £5.7m at Aston Villa. Tottenham's profits are neither phenomenally large (they are dwarfed by Manchester United's) nor are they large in relation to a business with a market capitalization of £67m.

Most 'blue chip' companies, considered to be reliable investments, ensure that they pay a dividend annually, in general aiming to raise the dividend every year or at least to avoid cutting it. Above all, companies try to avoid not paying out anything at all in a particular year. However, if a business is not generating profits, the directors may have little choice. In fact, Tottenham has already had to 'pass' its dividend once during Sugar's reign and in total very little has been paid out to shareholders. Put another way, if Alan Sugar is living off the club's accumulated reputation and taking the opportunity to make a quick profit, this profit is not very big. Tottenham would have to be much more profitable than it currently is (or have a much lower market price for its shares) to be viewed by the stock market as a reliable investment. Up until now, investors in Tottenham have tended to see it simply as a gamble, rather like a lottery ticket, with a low probability of ever paying off.

To earn larger profits than it does currently without spending more on players, Spurs would have to be much more attractive to fans than it is at present. It is hard to imagine support for Spurs growing in its current situation, when clubs such as Newcastle and Blackburn have been prepared to sustain enormous losses (£33m and £40m respectively over six years). Under today's competitive conditions, the club will either sink down the leagues by failing to spend on players or move into financial loss by struggling to compete on the pitch. Given the present structure of competition between English clubs, the Alan Sugar strategy does not appear sustainable.

In the two years following the wane of football club stock market flotations, football club share prices fell. Investors originally enthused about the potential profits from merchandizing and broadcasting became disillusioned. Just as it was beginning to seem as if the whole idea had been a financial disaster, up popped BSkyB with a £624m offer for Manchester United and share prices soared. Newspapers speculated about the reasons for the bid. Some argued that Rupert Murdoch, 40 per cent owner of BSkyB and generally considered to be the man who controls the company, was building a network of sports franchises that already included the LA Dodgers in baseball, the New York Knicks in basketball and a host of other sporting interests. Others said that the bid was driven by the likelihood that clubs will market their broadcast rights individually in the future, either because they are obliged to do so by the Restrictive Practices Court or because of the development of pay-per-view. Whatever the reason, investors began to speculate that other media companies would be interested in buying other clubs, causing share prices to rise. In December 1998 the cable TV and telecommunications company NTL acquired 6 per cent of Newcastle United PLC with an option to acquire a controlling interest should the BSkyB bid for Manchester United be approved. Some commentators also pointed out that if media companies were going to make money out of such investments, they would need to consider a fundamental restructuring of the competitive process.

Profits through co-operation

Judged by historic and current profits performance, the price tags currently attached to football clubs do not look sensible. In 1996 the top English clubs were valued more highly than top US football and baseball franchises, all of which face much less competition and have much larger audiences and drawing power than English football clubs. However, the price of an asset is not based on past performance or even current performance, rather it is based on an evaluation of the financial performance of that asset in the future. Investors will demand that football clubs pursue a profitable path of development. If the current directors of football clubs fail to do this the clubs will be taken over by new owners who will put in place directors more committed to a profit-making strategy.

Many profit-maximizing activities in a football club need not conflict with the objective of playing success: ticket prices or sponsorship deals which generate maximum income would be equally attractive to an owner pursuing either objective. Much of the City's enthusiasm was based on the potential income from broadcasting and other sponsorship deals, which have dramatically increased the income available to all clubs. Given that the annual value of Premier and Football League broadcast rights has risen from around £2m per season in the early 1980s to over £190m paid in the 1997–8 season, it is not hard to imagine that some of this income might feed through to profits some day. This is without considering the extra revenue which might accrue from pay-per-view and increased competition for sporting rights from digital broadcasters with hundreds of channels to fill. Furthermore, enthusiasm has been fuelled by the thought that traditionally football clubs have been poorly marketed, making limited attempts to sell extra services at games (food, drink and merchandise) and little effort to enhance sponsorship. It is only necessary to compare the kind of playing environment created at football and baseball matches in the US, and the amount of revenue that teams derive from these activities, to realize that English football clubs are capable of more. The requirements of the Taylor Report, forcing clubs to spend money on upgrading their facilities, might be viewed as an opportunity rather than a threat, an opportunity to create the kind of environment which might attract a broader spectrum of society, including wealthier supporters willing to spend money.

But income is no guarantee of profit. The Premier League has generated little more in profit for its members than the old Football League, largely because a large fraction of additional money generated from the first BSkyB contract has been spent on purchasing players. The first BSkyB contract, which covered the five seasons from 1992–3 to 1996–7, together with the contract for edited highlights on the BBC, was worth around £245m. The net transfer spending of Premier League clubs combined was approximately £240m over the five seasons.[8] This is even before accounting for the huge increase in wages which went with this expenditure. And even though clubs such as Blackburn and Newcastle outspent the rest by some margin, almost all clubs were net transfer spenders over the period.

Until the 1990s there were few serious studies of football which suggested that the directors and owners of clubs were interested in much more than playing success. The very fact that clubs were mostly unprofitable made it clear that whatever their intentions few were getting rich from investing in football. It is now widely believed that most football club owners are in it only for the money, particularly now that the stock market valuation of these assets is so high. In defence of owners it might be pointed out that there are few examples of individuals trying to sell out,[9] but the cynical response is that this is only because the owners believe that market values have not yet reached a peak. Yet if money is the only object, then why are clubs unable to retain the new money coming into the game as profit rather than seeing it diverted into the pockets of players and, currently, foreign football clubs? Alan Sugar would clearly point to the Newcastles and Blackburns of this world, whose owners appear to have invested in playing success to the point where they cannot reasonably expect to obtain an adequate financial return, and where any other club trying to compete with them is being drawn down the same route. Perhaps, among all the profit maximizers, there are still some owners out there maximizing playing success, and these owners are creating a competitive environment in which no one else can prosper either.[10]

One way or another, investors will look for a way to stop this process. Firms in highly competitive environments typically search for mechanism to limit the damage that it does to their profitability. Wealthy owners interested in playing success are never likely to disappear entirely from the game, so the rest of the clubs will need to try to find some way to live with them and still make money. Those looking for a way to achieve this end will look to the United States for a model of how to run their affairs, and two mechanisms employed there for controlling excesses in the game are already widely discussed: salary caps and closed leagues.

Salary caps

Before 1961 football wages were kept down by the maximum wage and this enabled clubs to remain financially solvent and pay dividends, even when clubs were not explicitly pursuing profits. Such a scheme would now almost certainly be ruled an illegal restraint on trade under British law. In the United States both the National Football League (NFL) and National Basketball Association (NBA) have negotiated a salary cap in order to hold down salaries. The basketball payroll cap was introduced in 1984 and permitted teams to spend no more than 53 per cent of their designated revenues on players; in football the payroll cap was introduced in 1994 and set at 64 per cent. Of the twenty clubs in the Premier League in 1996–7, only two had a payroll in excess of 64 per cent, while half had a payroll in excess of 53 per cent (see Table 8.3). However, if we include transfer fees to obtain a measure of total player spending then three-quarters of the teams in the Premier League would have exceeded the limits adopted in basketball or American football.

The US payroll caps are not illegal because they constitute

Table 8.3 Wages as a percentage of revenues for Premier League clubs 1996–7

Club	Revenue (£000)	Wages (£000)	Share of wages	Total player spending (£m)	Share of total player spending
Manchester United	88	23	26%	22	25%
Newcastle	41	17	43%	16	39%
Blackburn	14	14	100%	6	41%
Tottenham	28	12	43%	14	49%
Sunderland	13	6	43%	7	49%
Liverpool	39	15	38%	23	58%
Derby	11	4	40%	7	67%
Arsenal	27	15	56%	19	69%
Chelsea	24	15	63%	17	71%
Wimbledon	10	6	58%	8	76%
Leicester	17	9	51%	14	79%
Sheffield Wednesday	14	8	53%	12	83%
Middlesbrough	23	11	50%	20	87%
Everton	19	11	58%	16	87%
Aston Villa	22	10	46%	19	88%
West Ham	15	8	54%	15	98%
Southampton	9	5	52%	10	104%
Leeds	22	12	57%	24	111%
Nottingham Forest	14	8	56%	17	117%
Coventry	12	8	68%	17	141%

a freely negotiated collective bargaining agreement between the players' union and the leagues, represented by their governing body. In the UK this would mean the Professional Footballers' Association (PFA) negotiating directly with the Premier League, sanctioned by the clubs. In the US the players' unions have perceived it to be in their interest to negotiate these deals for a variety of reasons. Many members fear that unfettered rivalry will cause smaller teams to be driven out of the market, so reducing employment. Payroll caps have also been negotiated with minimum salary clauses so that as a result only the stars with the highest earning potential would be likely to oppose a cap. Under US collective bargaining laws, if a majority of the union backs an agreement, the minority has to accept the consequences. Payroll caps are not designed primarily as a means to increase profits but rather as a mechanism to preserve competitive balance. If, however, they have the effect of limiting the expenditure of clubs without imposing as great a reduction in revenue, then it is clear that they would be welcomed by investors.

Despite their apparent attractiveness, the effectiveness of salary caps has been widely questioned. The greatest problem with the salary cap is that the teams with greater revenue-generating capacity have an incentive to break the cap and teams with lesser drawing power wish to underspend it. Like the prisoner's dilemma, individual owners have an incentive to cheat on an agreement which is good for them, but only if they all stick to it. In practice, they all end up cheating on it. The league organizers try to monitor closely the spending of big teams, and impose minimum spending limits which can often threaten the viability of the smaller clubs. Spending caps cause great debates about exactly which items of expenditure should be included in designated revenues. For example, income from car parking or executive boxes has been excluded from calculations of the cap. However, in the end it is unlikely that a team committed to making illicit payments to players can be caught in the act. In the US everyone knows that big teams violate the cap, but there is never adequate evidence to constitute judicial proof. Recognizing these problems, salary caps have been introduced not with fixed limits but with a 'luxury tax' on spending over a certain limit, which can then be redistributed among the poorer clubs. Almost the only attraction of the luxury tax is that it reduces the incentive to cheat slightly, since exceeding the cap is legal, if costly.

If it were possible to design an enforceable salary cap, could it be applied to English football? A salary cap has already been introduced in Rugby League following the re-structuring of the game and the injection of £87m over five years by Rupert Murdoch's News Corporation. Indeed, it may well have been News Corporation that pushed the idea of the salary cap (Fox also belongs to Murdoch and broadcasts NFL matches among others). The cap is fixed at 50 per cent of pro-jected income that does not include sponsorship income and is based on assumed level of attendance over a season. While the cap was agreed by the clubs as part of the restructuring, there have already been complaints from the larger clubs such as Wigan that are finding it difficult to comply.[11]

Would a salary cap be workable in football? The first problem would be to get the clubs to agree, and it is obvious that the big clubs would reject it, largely because of the demands of European football. An England-only salary cap would put English teams in Europe at a considerable dis-advantage to foreign rivals. Yet an English salary cap without the participation of the top clubs would defeat the object of making competition more evenly balanced. A European-wide salary cap is a rather improbable proposition. If hundreds of European clubs were able to sit down together and agree spending limits, it would be the most remarkable show of solidarity in the history of football, and, judging by history, it must be unlikely that they could. A further problem would be the likely opposition of the players. Given the sport's financial weakness, Rugby League players have been willing to accept the cap as a means of securing their careers in the game. Football is completely different, it is the dominant televised sport in Europe and as such can generate enormous income. Even if a particular club or league were to fall into financial difficulties, most professional players would expect to be able to find employment elsewhere. This is particularly true of the top stars whose talents are in greatest demand. The final resort of the discontented footballer would be the courts, and these might prove the greatest obstacle to a salary cap system in Europe. Collective bargaining agreements in Europe are not protected from competition law. Since a salary cap is also likely to be viewed as a mechanism for increasing profitability (by reducing average spending on players) it is quite possible that such an agreement would be blocked by the European courts.

A closed (Super) League

Talk to anyone closely involved with the financing of the big clubs and they will tell you that a European Super League is inevitable. The clubs themselves have been talking about it for years. Going back to 1988, almost every year there is a rumour that a Super League is about to be formed. Often this has a lot to do with the distribution of TV income from the European club competitions run by UEFA. By threatening to form a breakaway Super League the clubs can pressure UEFA into giving them a bigger share of the income. However, this is more or less what the top clubs did in the 1980s to the Football League, and they did end up forming a breakaway league. In July 1998 Media Partners, a company controlled by Silvio Berlusconi, who owns AC Milan, put forward proposals for a European Super League. They offered the sixteen 'founder' clubs they approached a minimum of £20m per year in broadcast income, compared to the average of around £4m currently paid to participants in the Champions' League.[12] Faced with this threat, UEFA hurriedly brought forward proposals to extend the Champions' League and increase the minimum payments to participatory clubs. For the time being the clubs have accepted UEFA's proposals, but this is unlikely to be the end of the process.

Everyone agrees that a European Super League is inevitable, and some say that the transformation of the European Cup into the Champions' League already represents a Super League, at least in embryo. The reason for wanting to create such a competition is clear. The big clubs such as Manchester United, Liverpool, Arsenal, Newcastle, Aston Villa, Chelsea and one or two others do not want to play football against those whom they do not perceive as credible rivals. These are the clubs that have smaller gates and weaker finances, teams such as Wimbledon, Southampton, Coventry, Leicester and so on. Matches against these sides are not as attractive as those against their bigger rivals because they are not as balanced competitively and because fans are not attracted by the quality of the opposing team (and frequently their style of play). Even if they occasionally lose to these clubs, over a season there is a gulf in performance, a gulf which has been growing larger as the distribution of revenues has become more uneven. Even when a team like Tottenham do badly, the club is able to buy its way out of trouble.

Instead of playing league matches against the smaller clubs, the big clubs want to play the big European teams more frequently. Manchester United would rather play more matches against sides such as Juventus, Barcelona, Ajax and Borussia Dortmund, and to play them on a league rather than a cup basis. These games would be more attractive to spectators and enable the club to raise prices or invest in new capacity to attract larger attendances. But above all they would also make for more attractive TV and sponsorship rights. In the past it was match attendance which dictated the finances of football clubs; increasingly it is the estimated TV audience that advertisers are prepared to pay for. This has already happened in American football. NFL clubs obtain around 70 per cent of their income from broadcasting, compared to only 20 per cent for Premier League teams in 1996–7.[13]

The problem with the idea of a Super League is establishing exactly how it would work in practice. A conventional European League of twenty or so clubs could only operate on a European-wide basis with two or three teams even from the strongest national leagues. The problem for a club like Manchester United would be that, while it wants to play the top foreign sides, it does not want to give up popular fixtures against teams such as Chelsea, Newcastle and Blackburn. If these are not in the select few, then the only way to retain the fixtures is to compete in two leagues at once. Both Media Partners and UEFA favour this approach. While it is possible to compete in cup and league at the same time, the regularity of league competition is likely to make competing in two simultaneously problematic. It is difficult to envisage a national and an international league co-existing on the basis of equality.

One of the most durable of league rules is that clubs must always field their strongest team. Problems sometimes arise when a club is facing an important cup final and still has league fixtures, but such problems are by their nature not frequent. In a two-league system the problem could arise every week for many clubs. A Super League would be the most highly valued competition and therefore teams would be willing to sacrifice success in the national league. National leagues would become devalued to the point where the Super League teams would see little point in their continued participation. If the authorities tried to maintain the existing rule that participants in a Super League must qualify on the basis of national league performance the big clubs would ultimately choose to break away.

A Super League would also be difficult to administer because of the potential for conflicts of interest. UEFA would find it hard to run a Super League without being accused of favouring its own competition above the national leagues which it also supervises. The competition authorities might well challenge it in the courts for abusing a dominant position as a regulator. If the Super League were run by a new governing body (e.g. Media Partners, the company that proposed a Super League in 1998), it is difficult to see how disputes would be resolved. When two governing bodies claim jurisdiction over the same competitors the result is usually chaos. Leagues are unlikely to function well, and be popular with the public, when their participants are constantly in dispute.

An alternative solution would be to create a Super League with two or three divisions which could accommodate the top fifty European clubs, all of which might be capable of sustaining top-flight competition. However, the lesser clubs in this hierarchy might be less enthusiastic than the top ones. For example, Aston Villa is a top club in England, but might only rank as a second or even third division club in Europe. Attendance in a third division Super League might be no better, or possibly even worse, than in a domestic league. Furthermore, appearing in the third division of a Super League might actually damage the image and reputation of a top national team.

A European Super League would probably require a radical approach in order to work. A natural model to adopt would be that used for American football in the US. There a league of thirty teams is divided into two 'conferences', each consisting of three divisions. In the 'regular season' teams first play sixteen games, competing against each team in their own division and against selected sides from other divisions. The choice of opponents from other conferences is made on the basis of playing performance in past seasons, ensuring that the top teams regularly face each other and giving an advantage in the competition to the weaker ones (to promote competitive balance). Divisional champions and runners-up then progress through a system of 'post-season' play-offs to championships first for their own conference, and ultimately to the Superbowl final between the champions of each conference. Translated into a European environment, six or so divisions of ten or so teams could be created from the existing national leagues (e.g. Italy, Spain, Germany and Eastern Europe, Benelux and France, England and Scotland), and teams from these divisions could compete for divisional titles in a season of forty or so games, followed by play-offs leading to a European Club Cup Final. The main advantage of this structure would be to preserve the large number of valuable domestic games for each club, while significantly expanding the scope of European competition.

The important feature of a Super League is that it must create more 'event' games.[14] Event games are those which will hold a special resonance for all viewers, on the terraces or on TV. Local derbies and games between old rivals fall into this category, but also games against the top teams of the moment. It has been argued in the past that football lacks enough of these games, and has too many non-event matches. To a club like Manchester United a match against Liverpool is an event while a match against Coventry is a non-event. A Super League modelled on the NFL would maximize the capacity for event games by combining local rivalries with international competition.

Whatever structure is eventually adopted, a Super League is likely to generate more income for those clubs that participate. In particular TV contract income is likely to grow yet further, especially with potential for targeting consumers with pay-per-view systems. Bigger games might also make it possible to attract larger crowds to individual games. Far from finding TV a substitute for match attendance, the experience of the NFL suggests that live attendance can increase at the same time as broadcast revenues. As long as the event is attractive, people will be interested in seeing it live as well as on TV. But would increased income enable the clubs to make a profit? At the moment it appears that a significant fraction of all extra income is passed on to the players (Alan Sugar has dubbed this 'the prune juice effect').

If it were open to teams being promoted from junior national leagues, then the effect of the Super League would be little different from that of the Premier League: more money but no profits. The openness of the Premier League (like all European football leagues) helps to foster intense competition, by encouraging aspiring clubs to bid for players and so drive up salaries. A closed Super League which refused to admit new teams would limit the competitive threat. Tottenham's experience in 1997–8 illustrates the point. The club was forced to spend money on players because the financial loss from relegation would have been even greater. Had there been no threat of relegation, it is plausible to suppose that Alan Sugar would simply have written off the season and hoped for fewer injuries in the following year. Many of the major clubs see the Super League as a means to cut off the threat of relegation.

With a closed Super League, rump national leagues would remain. Because they would be deprived of actual competition with the big clubs, and fans could not even hold out the hope of promotion one day, these leagues would probably decline further in significance, possibly turning to amateur status. This would be likely to help reduce the wage bill of the remaining clubs because it would affect the bargaining process. If instead of the present ninety-two there were only ten or so major professional employers of football talent in England, the outside opportunities which currently enhance the bargaining power of players ('If you are not prepared to pay my salary someone else will') would be significantly eroded. As a result salary levels might be held down. The most exceptional talents would still receive very high wages (and a Super League might well bring them to a level match- ing that of baseball players in the US), but the increase in revenues could easily outstrip the increase in player salaries. A closed league would not eliminate competition altogether, but it would limit the competition for player talent sufficiently to enable a club such as Tottenham to pursue a profit-making strategy credibly. With the threat of relegation, the only credible policy under the current regime is for Tottenham to spend money trying to remain in the Premier League, a policy which will undermine the profit-making strategy. In a closed league Tottenham might remain rooted to the foot of it if it refused to invest in players, but would retain most of its attractive fixtures and would therefore be able to generate a profit.

Baseball, football, basketball and ice hockey are all run on a closed league basis with around thirty franchises (Major League Soccer is also being developed on similar lines). Most teams benefit from having very limited direct competition in their locality, guaranteeing strong local support and sellouts at most games. However, this does not mean that there are no other teams around. Minor League Baseball consists of junior teams which act as feeders for the major teams. College Football supplies young talent to the NFL teams. This hierarchical structure breaks down direct competition while ensuring the proper development of talent. Major teams support the minor teams financially, and face no competitive threat to their position. The only threat of competition is from a completely new league establishing itself as a rival. Such leagues have been feasible in the US since there are so many large cities and so few teams. A European Super League would have to be somewhat larger than thirty teams to discourage that kind of new entry, but it is hard to imagine a credible rival league if the Super League embraced the top sixty clubs.

Closed leagues in the US have enabled several franchise owners to amass considerable fortunes. While the profitability of these franchises is controversial,[15] they are frequently traded, often among professional investors, for large sums. It is clear why owners of clubs, particularly the big clubs, would want to create a closed league. It also seems clear that in the end whatever the big club owners want, they will get, simply because they are the owners. If they are private investors motivated by profit, they will seek out arrangements which are likely to enhance those profits. At the same time, the club owners must offer something that people want and will pay for, namely an attractive and exciting competition. Would a closed Super League be as good as, say, the Premier League?

It has been argued that it would not precisely because the clubs will face no real competitive threat. If Alan Sugar really was prepared to let his team languish at the bottom of the league, and others followed suit, the quality might not be that high. A recent study of basketball suggested that the annual value of Michael Jordan to teams other than the Chicago Bulls, measured in terms of gate and TV income caused by his appearances, was \$53m.[16] It is not hard to see how the incentive to invest in talent might be blunted and that lesser teams might free-ride on the talent of the bigger ones. If this threat is real, then one should expect that US team sports are not very competitive, since the major leagues are all closed. In fact, league competition in the US seems just as intense as it does here. One reason may be that governing bodies are empowered to take action against any club owner who is not trying to win, and the ultimate threat is that the franchise can be withdrawn, leaving the owner with an expensive payroll but nobody to play against. Furthermore, if the league itself does not promote intense competition on the pitch, it will face new entry by a rival league, as has occurred many times in the US, particularly in American football. A further incentive in American football and basketball is provided through the salary cap system, which specifies a *minimum* level of expenditure, as well as a maximum.

For the good of the game
A closed league would be a complete break with English and European tradition. Clubs would come to resemble franchises sold by the league authorities, as they are in the US. In time, with only ten Super League franchises in the UK these clubs might consider moving city in order to get a better stadium deal, as regularly occurs in the US. Wimbledon has already considered moving to Dublin, and with its international

marketing reach, one might reasonably ask exactly what it is that ties Manchester United to Manchester (especially when a majority of Mancunians are said to support the rival club Manchester City[17]). If football is organized for profit, investors will quickly learn to think the unthinkable. When the Brooklyn Dodgers baseball team moved from its historic venue of Ebbets Field in New York to Los Angeles in 1958 the American public was aghast. Now such moves are commonplace. It is reasonable to expect that a world of football clubs run for profit will look different from a world of football clubs run for playing success alone. If the root problem for a football club trying to make money is too much competition, profit-oriented clubs will seek to reform the structure of competition. The kinds of reforms that would look most attractive to a profit-oriented owner would amount to running European football along the lines of US sports leagues.

If a Super League does come about, the names of the teams in it might change, but the two fundamental relationships described in this book would still operate. However, the creators of a Super League might attempt to adopt some of the redistribution mechanisms found in the US as well as creating a closed league. A Super League might be accompanied by a salary cap system or some devices for increased revenue sharing. The fundamental relationships – wage expenditure generates league position, league position creates revenue – have become accentuated over time as English football has become more and more of a naked free market. In the US there is a much greater emphasis on redis- tribution in order to dampen the effect of spending power and therefore to create a more balanced competition. This tends to weaken the effect of both the fundamental relationships. In that sense at least competition in the future may look more like competition in the 1950s described in Chapter 5.

Is any of this a good thing? The answer depends on who you ask. There is no objective measure of whether football is any better or worse today than it was fifty years or a hundred years ago, nor is there any unambiguous indicator as to whether football today is as healthy as it might be under ideal circumstances. What we hear are a lot of conflicting opinions expressed by individuals, usually with a vested interest in a particular point of view.

The vested interests in football might be divided into a number of groups. Firstly, there are the legal owners of the football clubs, the shareholders, who have the right, directly or indirectly, to determine the policies of each club. Secondly, there are the employees, primarily the players, who earn their living from football. Thirdly there are the fans who watch the games. Finally, there are the suppliers of related products which contribute to the consumption of football by spectators, from the sellers of hot-dogs at the grounds to the TV companies broadcasting football matches. Among these suppliers one might also include sponsors and advertisers who contribute funds in exchange for the benefit they derive from associating their name with football.

In addition there are the governing authorities of the game. The Football Association represents the interests of all its affiliated members, namely, all registered football clubs in the country, but takes to itself a broader responsibility for the government and development of football as a whole. In this it is frequently supported or overruled by the national government, since the national game is viewed by politicians as a legitimate area of political involvement. The major clubs which have been the subject of this book are also governed by their league organizations, currently the FA Premier League Ltd and the Football League Ltd.

From its foundation football relied on an unwritten social contract between the administrators of the game and the vested interests of fans. Club directors controlled the game in an authoritarian fashion, without consultation and without much interest in the wishes of anybody else. However, the primary concern of the directors was the pursuit of playing success, and financial interests were secondary. More or less, the role of directors was to ensure the club did not go bankrupt, releasing the maximum possible funding for investment in the success of the team. This is not to say that the directors were purely altruistic in their actions, nor that all played to the rules of the game. Those who followed convention received their payoff via the social status of controlling a successful club. Some found ways to make money in spite of the accepted codes of behaviour, but by and large the unwritten contract was honoured.

The contract was first broken by the players. Unwilling to subordinate their own interests to what their supposed betters told them was the good of the game, they used the law to destroy the structure built up by the founding fathers of football. Freedom of contract, which was the ultimate aim and achievement of the players and their union, has brought the original structure of the Football League to breaking point. This is not a question of blaming the players for anything (particularly given the manifest injustice of the old system of player remuneration and registration), but of identifying where the process of change began. What could work under the old social contract has been slowly undermined by the market for players. The growing inequality between clubs has been the major symptom of these changes, and the break-up of the Football League and the creation of the Premier League have been the first significant breaks with the Victorian structure of football.

The commercialization of football business has been the second major shift brought about by the strain of competition for players. While clubs have always been commercial entities, this aspect of their activities has been significantly underplayed compared, say, to their American counterparts. The search for cash has focused directors more and more on ways to make money. There are many who believe that football clubs have become profit maximizers and that in so doing they have abandoned the traditions of the game and damaged it irreparably.

A striking rejection of all that has changed in football is provided in a recent book by Ed Horton,[18] who presents a fan's perspective on the 1990s. He argues that everything that has happened has been bad for football. The pursuit of profit has led to commercial exploitation of the game with no improvement in the service provided. Higher ticket prices have kept poorer fans away, more income in the game has simply exacerbated the inequality between clubs and so created a less balanced competition. TV exposure has reduced the attractiveness of football while stock market flotations have brought little extra money into the game.

In another book David Conn[19] argues that football has been turned into a business to the detriment of its traditions, its 'history, magic, soul'. He argues that left to the market football will inevitably be 'consolidated' and 'three or four or five clubs will dominate English football'. Pay-per-view and a European Super League will be introduced against the wishes of the fans. Both Horton and Conn see the supporters as the victims of the changes which occurred in the 1990s, and there is some evidence that these views reflect the opinion of a significant proportion of football fans. In the 1995 Carling FA Premier League Fan Survey only 53 per cent of fans attending matches who were also subscribers to BSkyB thought the FA Premier League had been good for the sport as a whole. The survey estimated that only about 40 per cent of supporters are subscribers, and given that these are most likely to be exposed to positive comment about the game, it is likely that a majority of fans overall is not enthusiastic about the changes that have occurred. This is hardly surprising when football clubs have paid so much attention to maximizing their income by exploiting the willingness to pay of supporters, but it is not only higher prices which upset the fans, it is also a sense of a loss of traditions.

Commercialization, however, inevitably means change. Changes are being introduced to attract money, but they are also forcing the clubs to balance the interests of the 'club' with the need to provide a return for the financial backers. When all the clubs were small businesses a local entrepreneur could fund a successful club more or less out of petty cash. Freedom of contract for players made that kind of management approach impossible, and the increased demand for funding has introduced professional investors. Unless clubs start to earn significantly better financial returns than they have in the past, pressures will begin to emerge from financial backers to restructure the leagues, and changes along American lines must be quite likely.

The changes to the game will undoubtedly affect the existing fans, and in many cases adversely. The current Premier League accounts for less than half of all professional football match attendances. Supporters at clubs left out of a closed Super League would undoubtedly suffer from reduced opportunities for competition. It is widely believed that football clubs would actually prefer to drive out the traditional football supporter and replace them with a wealthier kind of fan. Again one need only look to the US to see the difference in the atmosphere at matches and income bracket of the typical spectator, and to consider the difference in revenue generating potential to see what the ambitions of the top clubs might be.

Historically the owners of clubs refrained voluntarily from the naked commercial exploitation of the game, so that football in the 1980s looked little different from the way it was in the 1880s. This kind of football clearly appealed to some groups in society but not others. The game is now being changed in such a way as to appeal to other groups, leaving traditional supporters dissatisfied. Above all, football is being adapted to the needs of the much larger and lucrative TV audience rather than the needs of those who attend live matches. However, commercial exploitation can only be successful if the fans receive something that they want at prices they are willing to pay. The idea that commercial exploitation will 'kill the game' is highly improbable if only because the clubs themselves have an enormous incentive to foster the game. That they will foster those aspects of the game that are commercially valuable and ignore those parts that are not is also obvious, but looking at the US, it would be extremely difficult to argue convincingly that the popularity of sports has diminished as commercial exploitation increased.

Some claim that if the traditional supporters are driven out by high prices then their better-heeled replacements will prove more inclined to watch football on TV rather than turning out to support the club. Were this to happen the clubs would cut ticket prices in order to attract fans as unpaid extras in the production of TV spectaculars. It is possible to imagine that one day entry might be free, and clubs rely only on TV money for income. However, this would only happen if enough fans thought TV was a better option than going to a match. With attendances increasing significantly over the last decade, there is little sign of this happening yet.

The social structure of attendance at football has been changing for some years now. Low-income fans are being driven away and wealthier middle-income fans are being attracted to the game. Taken as an interest group, the traditional supporter is losing out from the changes in football. Their views are not well represented, but nor is it at all clear that the established football fans either can or should hold any ownership rights over the structure and selling of football, any more than customers in any other form of retailing have any right to dictate the way in which products are sold. Writers such as Horton and Conn avoid this issue by arguing that football is something more than a leisure product, presenting it as a cultural artefact, beyond the market-place. Football is the national game, part of our national heritage, and therefore there is a wider social context. The problem is finding a way to give this aspect of the game a legitimate voice.

Football's own governing bodies have done little to address this issue, and this has left a vacuum filled recently by the government. In 1997 the newly elected Labour government set up a football task force whose remit was 'to investigate and recommend new measures to deal with the public's concerns on issues such as racism, ticket prices, access for the disabled and the increasing commercialism in the game . . . encourage merchandising policies that reflect the needs of supporters as well as commercial considerations; reconcile the potential conflict between the legitimate needs of shareholders, players and supporters where clubs are floated on the Stock Exchange'.[20]

As long as football clubs are private commercial entities operating without public subsidies it is hard to see how such investigations can force the clubs to act in any particular way. Government might intervene to provide incentives or penalties for certain types of behaviour on the part of clubs. In September 1998 the task force, which is chaired by David Mellor, a former Conservative minister and keen football fan, began investigating the commercial activities of the clubs. Leaks in the press suggested that the task force would recommend the establishment of a regulator to oversee the pricing policies of clubs in relation to ground admission, replica kits and other merchandising. This idea has the strong support of Tony Banks, the current Minister for Sports.

Regulators have been introduced into many areas of economic activity in the UK in recent years. Following privatization of the telecom, electricity, water and gas industries and the railway network, regulators were created to oversee prices and protect consumer interests. Regulators have also been appointed in areas such as financial services.

The problem with regulation is that it seldom pleases anyone. Companies feel it is too intrusive, while consumers often fail to see any benefit. For example, since the privatization of the water industry there has been considerable public dissatisfaction with both the price and the quality of services delivered, despite the activities of a regulator (Ian Byatt) who is considered both highly active and highly effective.

The job of being a football regulator is likely to be an unenviable one. As with the manager of the England team, every success will be attributed to someone else, every failure will be taken as an indicator of incompetence.

Regulation is particularly difficult in any business subject to rapid change. Where firms are experimenting with new ways of operating, excessive regulation may discourage valuable innovators and tend to reward the inactive. Of course, many of those who advocate regulation want to prevent change and to return to a golden era that lies somewhere in the past. However, if regulation came to be seen as an obstacle to any change, its popularity would rapidly decline.

Ultimately it is likely that the government will regard regulation as an option of last resort. While it may view with concern the developments on the football industry, there is likely to be little enthusiasm for taking responsibility for its future development. From a government's point of view, it is always convenient to have someone else to blame, such as the market, when things go wrong.

But even if the government is likely to leave football in the market, private commercial entities are not entirely free to act in any way they see fit. The operation of football clubs is constrained by the competition laws of the UK and increasingly by those of the Treaty of Rome.[21]

As we have seen, the law has affected the conduct of the game since its beginning, and the flurry of competition law cases relating to broadcasting which began in 1997 illustrates that the regulatory authorities are unlikely to stand by as the structure of football changes. At the time of writing, the Premier League was scheduled to appear in the Restrictive Practices Court in January 1999 to defend the collective selling of TV rights (rather than by individual negotiations on the part of each club). This case arose as a result of a challenge from the Office of Fair Trading, which argued that the collective selling amounted to a cartel that operated against the public interest. Similar cases have recently been brought before the German and Dutch competition courts.

In all of them the actions of football clubs have been questioned on the grounds that they have represented a restriction of fair and open competition. The underlying philosophy behind the laws is that the operation of an open competitive market will ensure that the right goods and services are supplied to consumers at minimum feasible prices. Football, and all sporting leagues, sit uneasily in the context of competition law, since they operate in ways which are both highly co-operative and extremely competitive, but to the extent that football clubs have the incentive to use their co-operative structures to collude against the public interest, then perhaps the ultimate protection of the fan will be, as it was for the players, competition law.

As Media Partners and UEFA struggled to win the support of the top clubs for their respective versions of a Super League, it became clear that each side needed above all the support of the European Commissioner for Competition Policy, Karel Van Miert. He in turn has made it clear in public pronouncements that sports such as football are an essential part of European culture and that Brussels will seek to influence its development. It is also clear that the national competition laws of member states and the competition articles of the Treaty of Rome give governments and Brussels significant powers to intervene if the operations of leagues are structured in such a way as to exploit consumers unfairly.

At the beginning of this book it was argued that football clubs faced a dilemma reconciling the pursuit of profit with the pursuit of playing performance on the field. The analysis of the way in which Manchester United makes money suggested that this will be very difficult for other clubs to imitate. Alternative ways of generating profits based on distinctive capabilities are by their nature scarce. Throughout this book it has been argued that football conforms almost to an economic ideal of a highly competitive market where economic profits or rents are driven down to zero and all the rewards from the activity go to the suppliers of the scarce factors which are in high demand: the players. Football clubs are not monopolies; while some may enjoy the loyal support of some fans, there are reasonably close substitutes for each club. However, it is natural that football clubs, facing this competitive environment, will look for some way out which might enhance their long-term profitability, and almost inevitably they will try to limit competition. As clubs pursue a long-term search for profitability they will develop new ideas to enhance revenues and cut costs. A closed Super League is one possibility, but undoubtedly others will be suggested. Each of these reforms will be scrutinized by the competition authorities and resisted if they are found to represent a deliberate restriction of competition to the detriment of consumers' interests. For good or ill, it is likely that the future structure of football competition will be the outcome of a negotiating process between the clubs and the competition authorities.

Notes

❶ 1. Sugden, J. and Tomlinson, A. (1998), *Fifa and the Contest for World Football*, Polity Press, Cambridge, p. 1.

2. Before the advent of public-school football there existed an activity known as football which was highly disreputable. Little is known about how this game was played, the main references to it appearing in laws forbidding it or court cases describing its terrible consequences. By the end of the eighteenth century the game was dying out. The public-school system, which has exerted an enormous influence on British culture, revived it. 'Much of the success and much of the failure of modern England can be attributed to the Public Schools' (Trevelyan, G. M. (1942), *English Social History: A Survey of Six Centuries*, Longmans Green & Co., London). Surely one of its greatest contributions has been the formalization of the *game* of football.

3. Although perhaps the words of F. J. Wall imply a somewhat less altruistic motive. Writing in 1905, the then secretary of the FA wrote of its founders: 'The London business men took a wider view of the situation than did the others; ... the eleven London club representatives who gathered at the old hostelry in Great Queen Street forthwith claimed for themselves a

position which, subject to their being able to maintain it, was bound ultimately to make them the controlling body for the whole sport.' In Leatherdale, C. (ed.) (1997), *The Book of Football*, Desert Island Books, Westcliff-on-Sea, Essex, p. 51.

4. In 1871 there were fifty clubs registered to the FA, of which fifteen entered the Cup, in 1881 there were 128 and by 1905 there were 10,000 (Wall, in Leatherdale, op. cit.).

5. 'Football fever spread among the working-class population of the Midlands and the North. The over-mastering desire to win their games led certain northern clubs to look about for the most skilful players anywhere to be found; the big "gates" which resulted from the great popularity of the game enabled them to offer such players monetary inducements to join them' (Wall, in Leatherdale, op. cit.). Note the condescending tone; such grandees looked back nostalgically to the game's amateur roots and 'Corinthian' principles.

6. Vamplew, W. (1988), *Pay Up and Play the Game: Professional Sport in Britain, 1875–1914*, Cambridge University Press, Cambridge, p. 190.

7. By the 1990s the figure had risen to around 42,000.

8. Somewhere between the extremes lies a fairly large group of semi-

professional clubs, which can attract as many as a thousand spectators for an individual match and hold out the hope of some day breaking into the football league and turning fully professional. Clubs such as Wimbledon are a good example: they were in the Southern League until 1977, when they were elected to the Fourth Division. Within ten years they reached the First Division, where they have remained ever since. They are the role model for every aspiring semi-professional club. At the other end of the scale, Darwen, reputedly the first professional club and a member of the Second Division between 1893 and 1899, still survive today with crowds running into the low hundreds.

9. William McGregor, founder of the Football League, was involved in the management of Aston Villa before it became a limited company. 'George Kynoch and I were responsible for the lease of the Aston Villa ground. Someone had to be responsible for these things because Aston Villa was not then a limited liability company. In fact, people howled when I proposed it should be formed into one; but then people will howl at anything which is novel. It is all very well to howl, but when you are responsible for a lease, and when you get a handful of bills which have to be met, and no gate money is coming in, then you want something more practical than howling.' In Leatherdale, op. cit., p. 171.

10. Vamplew, op. cit., p. 295.

11. See e.g. Mason, T. (1980), *Association Football and English Society 1863–1915*, Harvester Press, Sussex; Tischler, S. (1981), *Footballers and Businessmen: The Origins of Professional Soccer in England*, Holmes and Meier, New York; and Korr, C.

(1986), *West Ham United*, Duckworth, London for an analysis of the structure of shareholdings in the clubs.

12. William McGregor, in Leatherdale, op. cit.

13. Between 1888 and 1914, 38 per cent of directors were 'industrialist-merchants', 13 per cent in alcohol or tobacco, 30 per cent professionals and only 4 per cent 'gentlemen' (Tischler, op. cit.). The growing significance of the first of these is illustrated by Birmingham City's appointment of Alfred Jones as director in the 1880s, 'a manufacturer of scales who was asked to balance the club's accounts' (Matthews, T. (1989), *Birmingham City: A Complete Record 1875–1989*, Breedon Books, Derby).

14. See Sanderson, F. (1966), 'Psychology', in *Science and Soccer*, edited by T. Reilly, E. & F. N. Spon, London, for an analysis of psychology in football and the development of motivation.

15. This is the forerunner of today's National League, still the dominant baseball league in the US. See Seymour, H. (1960), *Baseball: The Early Years*, Oxford University Press Inc., New York for a description of its early history.

16. Fort, R. and Quirk, J. (1995), 'Cross-Subsidisation, Incentives and Outcomes in Professional Team Sports Leagues', *Journal of Economic Literature*, Vol. XXXIII, September, pp. 1265–99.

17. Hardaker, A. (1977), *Hardaker of the League*, Pelham Books, London, p. 66.

18. Quoted in 1974 Commission on Industrial Relations Report, paragraph 30.

19. On Sugar's acquisition of Tottenham Hotspur PLC, Fynn, A. and Guest, L. (1994), *Out of Time:*

Why football isn't working, Simon and Schuster, London, p. 226.

20. By contrast, sports researchers in the US are almost unanimous in assuming that baseball, American football, hockey and basketball club owners are profit maximizers (e.g. Fort and Quirk, op. cit.)

21. E.g. Sloane, P. J. (1971), 'The Economics of Professional Football: The Football Club as a Utility Maximizer', *Scottish Journal of Political Economy*, 17, 2, pp. 121–46: 'the football club is seen to differ from the normal business enterprise. The profit goal would appear to exert a smaller influence on behaviour in the former case and the use of the profit maximising assumption has led to predicted results which do not appear to hold in practice'; Dabscheck, B. (1975). 'Sporting Equality: Labour Market versus Product Market Control', *Journal of Industrial Relations*, 17, 2, pp. 174–90; Arnold, A. J. and Webb, B. (1986), 'Aston Villa and Wolverhampton Wanderers 1971/72 to 1981/82: A Study of Finance Policies in the Football Industry', *Managerial Finance*, 12, 1, pp. 11–19: 'Firms in the football industry do not pursue overt financial objectives but are still subject to financial discipline'; Carmichael, F. and Thomas, D. (1993), 'Bargaining in the Transfer Market: Theory and Evidence', *Applied Economics*, No. 25, pp. 1467–76: 'Football League clubs aim to maximise utility through the maximisation of playing success as manifested in the number of games won and/or competitions won subject to a financial viability or minimum security constraint'; Szymanski, S. and Smith, R. (1997), 'The English football industry: profit, performance and industrial structure', *International Review of Applied Economics*, 11, 1, pp. 135–53; Dobson, S. and Gerrard, W. (1997), 'Testing for Rent Sharing in Football Transfer Fees: Evidence from the English Football League', Leeds University Business School Discussion Paper E97/03; Kuypers, T. J. (1996), 'The Beautiful Game? An Econometric Study of Why People Watch English Football', *Discussion Papers in Economics, University College London*, 96–101. For a full discussion on the objectives of football clubs see Cairns, J. A., Jennett, N. and Sloane, P. J. (1986), 'The Economics of Professional Team Sports: A Survey of Theory and Evidence', *Journal of Economic Studies*, 13, pp. 3–80.

22. For example, the paid-up share capital of Wolverhampton Wanderers in 1982 was £9,000, implying a maximum allowable dividend of £1,350, for a business which at that date had net assets of £423,000 (Arnold and Webb, op. cit., p. 14).

23. See e.g. Plender, J. (1996), *Stake in the Future*, Brealey Publishing, London.

24. The clubs included are Arsenal, Aston Villa, Barnsley, Birmingham, Blackburn, Bolton, Brentford, Bristol Rovers, Burnley, Bury, Cambridge, Coventy, Derby, Everton, Huddersfield, Hull, Leeds, Leicester, Liverpool, Luton, Manchester United, Mansfield, Newcastle, Oldham, Peterborough, Plymouth, Preston, Reading, Rotherham, Scunthorpe, Sheffield United, Sheffield Wednesday, Shrewsbury, Southampton, Southend, Swindon, Tottenham, West Bromwich, West Ham and Wrexham. The sample is representative of the entire League. Thus, the population average league position is 46 (given ninety-two clubs in the Football League) while for the sample the average position achieved

over the period 1978 to 1996 ranged from a minimum of 40 to a maximum of 36 (mean 38). There is thus a slight bias towards the higher-ranking clubs.

25. Correlation means a tendency for two different factors to move together in some way. Positive correlation means that when one factor moves in one direction then the other factor moves in the same direction, negative correlation means a tendency to move in the opposite direction.

26. Crick, M. and Smith, D. (1989), *Manchester United: Betrayal of a Legend*, Pelham Books, London, pp. 234–5. Atkinson bought nineteen players between 1982–3 and 1986. He sold four (Gidman, Beardsley, Brazil and Graham), Ferguson sold two (Barnes and Higgins) in his first season, 1986–7, three in his second (Stapleton, T. Gibson and Sivebaek), five in his third (Davenport, Olsen, O'Brien, Turner and Strachan) and two in his fourth (McGrath and C. Gibson). J. Hanrahan never played English league football and Remi Moses's career ended at the beginning of the Ferguson era. Thus the only player to survive under Ferguson for any length of time was the club captain, Bryan Robson.

27. Ferguson has paid a lot of attention to developing a youth policy for growing talent in-house, but at this time the only significant home-grown player to come through was Ryan Giggs.

28. Crick and Smith, op. cit., p. 197.

29. Ibid., p. 198.

30. United were actually 3-2 down in extra-time. Had United lost, it seems unlikely that Ferguson would have survived another season.

31. King, J. and Kelly, J. (1997), *The Cult of the Manager*, Virgin Books, London.

❷ 1. For example, say average club revenue was £1,000 in 1990 and £1,500 in 1995, an increase of 50 per cent (1500/ 1000–1). However, say that between 1990 and 1995 the inflation rate was 3 per cent p.a., a combined increase over five years of 16 per cent. Thus if revenue had just increased with inflation, then the revenue in 1995 would be £1,160. Therefore the real revenue increase over the period, i.e. the increase in revenue not due to inflation, was 1500/1160–1=29 per cent.

2. Based on a sample of around thirty-five clubs, although in some years the sample was slightly less.

3. Arnold, A. J. (1988), *A Game That Would Pay: A Business History of Professional Football in Bradford*, Duckworth, London.

4. The 1946-7 season is represented in charts as 1947.

5. 1949–1981: Bird, op. cit., average minimum price; 1981: Football Trust, op. cit., average price. Series were grafted together as average price and average minimum price were not significantly different when the two series were concurrent.

6. For growth in attendance see Rollin, J. (1997), *Rothmans Football Yearbook*, Headline Book Publishing, London; for Consumers Expenditure see Office for National Statistics (1997), *Economic Trends Annual Supplement*, HMSO, London. For admission prices see Bird, P. J. W. N. (1982), 'The Demand for League Football', *Applied Economics*, No. 14, pp. 637–49; and Football Trust (1995), *Digest of Football Statistics 1992/93*, University of Leicester.

7. Walvin, J. (1994), *The People's Game: The History of Football Revisited*, Mainstream Publishing, Edinburgh and London.

8. 1950 figures, Office of National Statistics.

9. The price elasticity of demand is the percentage change in demand in response to a 1 per cent change in price. Thus a price elasticity of -0.5 means that a 1 per cent increase (decrease) in price will lead to a ½ per cent fall (increase) in demand. If the price elasticity is between 0 and -1 demand is said to be inelastic, and if the elasticity is less than -1 it is said to be elastic. Demand for football is generally thought to be price inelastic.

10. One of the more recent studies, Dobson, S. M. and Goddard, J. A. (1995), 'The Demand for Professional League Football in England and Wales, 1925–1992', *Journal of the Royal Statistical Society*, Series D, Vol. 44, pp. 259–77, reports an estimate of -0.078 for data covering the period 1925 to 1992. This suggests that demand is extremely unresponsive to changes in price. Szymanski, S. and Smith, R. (1997), 'The English football industry: profit, performance and industrial structure', *International Review of Applied Economics*, 11, 1, pp. 135–53, using data from 1974 to 1989, report an estimate of -0.38. Other estimates include Bird, op. cit.: -0.2 and Simmons, R. (1996), 'The Demand for English League Football: A Club Level Analysis', *Applied Economics*, Vol. 28, pp. 139–55: -0.4.

11. *Social Trends* (1990), Central Statistical Office, HMSO, London.

12. Murray, W. J. (1994), *Football: A History of the World Game*, Ashgate Publishing Co., Vermont, USA.

13. Sir Norman Chester Centre For Football Research, Leicester University.

14. Murray, op. cit.

15. Sheffield Wednesday, their engineers Eastwood & Co. and South Yorkshire Police have accepted liability.

16. Pickering, D. (1995), *The Cassell Soccer Companion: History Facts Anecdotes*, Cassell, London.

17. Charlton v Bristol Rovers in the FA Cup.

18. In 1960 the League , together with ITV, tried to introduce live matches on Saturday evenings. Most of the clubs resisted and refused to allow cameras into their grounds. In the end only the second half of a match between Blackpool and Bolton was broadcast, after which the plans were shelved (Inglis, S. (1988), *League Football and the men who made it*, Willow Books, London, p. 228).

19. Prior to 1992–3 known as Division 1.

20. Quoted in Taylor, R. and Ward. A. (1996), *Kicking & Screaming: An Oral History of Football in England*, Robson Books, London.

21. Sam Chisholm, quoted in the *Daily Telegraph*, 13 February 1997.

22. ITV were also willing to let the BBC have a highlights package but the BBC were unwilling to do this deal.

23. Quoted in the *Independent*, 14 October 1996.

24. Analysis of BARB data.

25. See Kuypers, T. J. (1996), 'The Beautiful Game? An Econometric Study of Why People Watch English Football', *Discussion Papers in Economics, University College London*, 96–01, and Simmons, op. cit.

26. Taylor and Ward, op. cit.

27. See e.g. Inglis, op. cit., p. 263.

28. 'The Hottest Investment around', *International Fund Investment*, April 1997.

29. Walvin, op. cit. However, some deals were not permitted. In August 1980 Coventry announced a deal with Talbot, a car manufacturer, which would pay £250,000 for the club to be known as 'Coventry-Talbot'. The FA

vetoed the deal (*Rothmans Football Yearbook* 1981–2).

30. Liverpool has been sponsored by Carlsberg for several seasons.

31. *Guardian*, 25 June 1997.

32. Football League (1983), *Report of the Committee of Inquiry into Structure and Finance* (Chairman Sir Norman Chester), Lytham St Anne's.

33. PEP (1966), 'English Professional Football', *Planning*, Vol. XL, No. 496.

34. Football League, op. cit.

3

1. To estimate the average first-team salary it was first assumed that the average salary for all other employees was in line with the national average of around £20,000. The number of first-team players was estimated from the *Rothman's Football Yearbook* (forty in the Premier League, thirty in Division 1, twenty-five in Division 2 and twenty in Division 3). Given that the sample groups contain ten, nine, twenty, nineteen and ten clubs, it is possible to derive the estimates.

2. Football League (1983), *Report of the Committee of Inquiry into Structure and Finance* (Chairman Sir Norman Chester), Lytham St Anne's, p. 20.

3. *Business Age*, July 1998.

4. *Daily Telegraph*, 15 January 1998.

5. *Daily Telegraph*, 16 January 1998.

6. *Daily Telegraph*, 25 March 1998.

7. *Daily Telegraph*, 27 January 1998.

8. £67,000 a week. *Daily Telegraph*, 13 February 1998.

9. Most of the figures are estimates. In the case of the largest earners actual earnings are seldom disclosed. Figures for individual professions are averages taken from published salary surveys. Even figures which are public knowledge, such as the Prime Minister's salary, do not give a full picture because of various extra subsidies and fringe benefits associated with the job.

10. Includes all sources of income. *Daily Telegraph*, 7 December 1996.

11. *Electronic Telegraph*, 1 July 1998.

12. Assuming one film made per year and no other income sources. Sylvester Stallone, Arnold Schwarzenegger, Tom Cruise and Mel Gibson are said to command $20m per film, Tom Hanks $15m and Robin Williams about $14m. The highest paid woman star is Demi Moore, worth around $13m per film. British star Emma Thompson is worth $3m per film. *Daily Telegraph*, 8 April 1996 and 1 March 1997.

13. Contract with Chicago Bulls only. *Daily Telegraph*, 22 July 1996.

14. Salary only. *Daily Telegraph*, 7 December 1996.

15. Noel Gallagher of Oasis is estimated to have earned £7.5m in 1995, while Liam, his younger brother, earned £1m. George Michael earned £10m. Twenty British rock stars were estimated to earn over £1m. *Daily Telegraph*, 16 July 1997.

16. *Daily Telegraph*, 18 July 1997.

17. Salary only. *Financial Times*, 14 November 1997.

18. *Daily Telegraph*, 19 February 1996.

19. *Daily Telegraph*, 18 July 1997.

20. *Daily Telegraph*, 22 October 1996.

21. *Daily Telegraph*, 9 March 1998.

22. Salary only. *Daily Telegraph*, 28 January 1997.

23. Salary only. Ibid.

24. Head of Capital Markets for a financial market business, £145,000 per year; chief foreign exchange dealer, £80,850; corporate finance director, £112,500; investment analyst, £61,937 (Day Associates, 1997).

25. Incomes Data Services, 1997.

26. Manchester University.

27. *Daily Telegraph*, 17 September 1997.

28. *Daily Telegraph*, 7 February 1997.

29. *Daily Telegraph*, 17 September 1997.

30. Incomes Data Services, 1997.

31. It was reported that Luton demanded £300,000 compensation from Sheffield Wednesday following the move of David Pleat to that club, and this sum was said to equal four years' salary.

32. Small company: turnover up to £25m; medium company: £25m–£200m turnover; large company: turnover over £200m. Incomes Data Services, 1997.

33. *Daily Telegraph*, 16 July 1997.

34. Ibid.

35. Ibid.

36. Ibid.

37. *Daily Telegraph*, 31 January 1996.

38. Minimum, Association of University Teachers of England Scale.

39. *Daily Telegraph*, 1 December 1996.

40. New Earnings Survey, HMSO.

41. *Daily Telegraph*, 16 December 1996.

42. Mason, T. (1980), *Association Football and English Society 1863–1915*, Harvester Press, Sussex, p. 70.

43. Vamplew, W. (1988), *Pay Up and Play the Game: Professional Sport in Britain, 1875–1914*, Cambridge University Press, Cambridge.

44. Tischler, S. (1981), *Footballers and Businessmen: The Origins of Professional Soccer in England*, Holmes and Meier, New York, p. 63.

45. Quoted in ibid.

46. C. E. Sutcliffe, a League official, club director and journalist, quoted in ibid., p. 64.

47. Babe Ruth earned $80,000 in 1930, at a time when £1=$4.86. Dixie was undoubtedly impressed by this differential, and had in 1928 considered moving to the US, having been offered the princely sum of £25 per week to play in a fledgling US league.

48. Mason, T. (1994), 'The Bogota Affair' in Bale, J. and Maguire, J. (eds) (1994), *The Global Sports Arena: Athletic Migration in an Interdependent World*; Frank Cass, London.

49. Hardaker, A. (1997), *Hardaker of the League*, Pelham Books, London, pp. 95ff.

50. A not altogether foolish rule. In the late 1950s and early 1960s players would often insure their £4 win bonus by taking out a fixed odds bet against themselves.

51. Professional agents now have to be registered with the FA, but such respectability is a relatively recent phenomenon. Originally players might use an adviser, such as their accountant or a lawyer. However, the large sums of money involved attracted agents from show business and the point has now been reached where an agent can specialize entirely in managing the affairs of football players.

52. See Fynn, A. and Guest, L. (1994), *Out of Time: Why football isn't working*, Simon and Schuster, London, Chapter 10 for a full discussion of this point.

53. Trenton Potteries 1928. See Scherer, F. M. and Ross, D. (1990), *Industrial Market Structure and Economic Performance*, Houghton Mifflin, Boston for a discussion of this and related cases.

54. The reason for this was a Supreme Court judgment of 1922 which held that baseball was not subject to Federal Antitrust laws on the dubious grounds that it did not involve interstate

commerce. This judgment has been roundly criticized by legal opinion in the US, including subsequent Supreme Court judgments, but the Supreme Court has insisted that rectifying the situation is a matter for Congress, which in turn has chosen not to legislate. To this day this exemption has permitted sports teams to act in ways which would be deemed illegal in other businesses. However, free agency in baseball was achieved by the players' union in 1975.

55. Mason, T. (1980), op. cit., p. 133 fn 141.

56. Bennett, A. (1912, reprinted 1990), *The Matador of the Five Towns*, Alan Sutton Publishing Ltd, Gloucester.

57. Bowler, D. (1996), *Shanks: The Authorised Biography of Bill Shankly*, Orion Books, London, pp. 111ff.

58. In Leatherdale, C. (1997), *The Book of Football*, Desert Island Books, Westcliff-on-Sea, Essex, p. 162.

59. Speight, A. and Thomas, D (1997), 'Arbitrator Decision-Making in the Transfer Market: An Empirical Analysis', *Scottish Journal of Political Economy*, 44, 2, pp. 198–215.

60. And a case brought over a domestic transfer might be expected to yield the same conclusion.

61. The fact that most individuals prefer to avoid risk is the reason that insurance companies exist. In a way long-term employment contracts are like insurance policies too, insuring the player against risks such as loss of form, injury and so on.

62. In effect, part of the value of a player which could be captured by the club has been surrendered to the player, so that on average players are better off and clubs are worse off.

63. This provides each player with a lump sum at age thirty-five based on years of service multiplied by average earnings, equivalent to 3 or 4 per cent of total earnings. It has operated in this form since 1982.

64. In addition to these there were 28 movers whose fee was unknown, 4 going to the FLAC, 105 free transfers, 23 on monthly contract, 70 non-contract, 85 on trial, giving a total of 549 moves.

65. Chester, N. (1968), *Report of the Committee on Football*, HMSO, London, Table 11, p. 78.

66. Of course, some large clubs will have a positive net income and some small ones will have a positive net expenditure, but the greater proportion fit into the two other categories.

67. Frank, R. H. and Cook, P. J. (1995), *The Winner-Take-All Society*, Free Press, New York.

4 1. This chapter gives a very brief overview of business strategy that is intended to provide a framework for thinking about business issues in relation to football. Business strategy is a huge subject in its own right and what is presented here is at best a partial view. There is much disagreement in the field about how to understand business behaviour and performance; the approach adopted here follows the lines that were developed at the London Business School's Centre for Business Strategy in the early 1990s. During that time a group of economists, including the first author, tried to apply the standard techniques of economic analysis to the study of firm behaviour. Much of this work was synthesized by Kay, J. (1995), *Foundations of Corporate Success*, Oxford University Press, Oxford. For a brief survey of approaches to business strategy see Clutterbuck, D. and Crainer, S. (1990),

Makers of Management, Macmillan, London.

2. In the first year after flotation six directors resigned, including Douglas Hall and Freddy Shepherd, who resigned following the public outrage after they were secretly taped mocking the fans and players and making several other unsavoury comments. Between them they controlled 64 per cent of the company's shares and they decided to reinstate themselves in July 1998. On the pitch the club did little better, struggling to avoid relegation in the League and losing the FA Cup Final. In December 1998 NTL launched a bid to takeover the ailing company.

3. Although each club would claim to have some supporters in each other's countries, and perhaps elsewhere in the world, in practice the scale of their rivalry is limited.

4. The classic reference for industry analysis is Porter, M. E. (1980), *Competitive Strategy: Techniques for Analyzing Industries and Competitors*, Free Press, New York.

5. For many years the dominant approach to analysing industries was known as the Structure, Conduct, Performance Paradigm, which essentially argued that industry conditions (supply and demand) determined industry conduct (the intensity of competition) and therefore determined performance (profitability). The approach has been less popular in recent years for its apparent failure to capture feedback effects (i.e. from performance to conduct and from conduct to structure). For a fuller explanation of this approach see Scherer, F. M. and Ross, D. (1990), *Industrial Market Structure and Economic Performance*, Houghton Mifflin, Boston.

6. For example, patent protection is established by government legislation so as to influence the outcome of competition in innovative industries such as pharmaceuticals. Governments passed laws specifically to encourage the development of valuable medicines, and these laws have influenced structure and conduct. Teece, D. J. (1986), 'Profiting from technological innovation: Implications for integration, collaboration, licensing and public policy', *Research Policy*, 15, pp. 285–305 provides an analysis of the relationship between innovation and public policy.

7. On a further seventeen occasions clubs have won two championships with only a one-year gap. However, on only four occasions have clubs won two championships with a two-year gap.

8. Note that it is assumed here that winning championships, rather than profitability, is a measure of success. However, the issue here is not the objective of the clubs, merely to illustrate the point that there is a large variation in the performance of clubs, a fact which is likely to be true for any other indicator of performance.

9. At least this was the claim of the authorities responsible for the reforms: see e.g. The Football Association (1991), *The Blueprint for the Future of Football*, Lancaster Gate, produced by the FA and proposing the foundation of the Premier League.

10. Becker, G. S. (1962), 'Irrational Behavior and Economic Theory', *Journal of Political Economy*, 70, pp. 1–13, pointed out that even if consumers allocated their budgets completely at random, it would still be the case that higher prices would lead to a fall in demand, merely as a consequence of the fact that consumers' budgets are limited.

11. This famous quotation comes from Schumpter, J. A. (1943), *Capitalism, Socialism and Democracy*, Unwin, New York.

12. A dominant position means the possession of monopoly or near-monopoly power.

13. While the common complaint against monopoly is unfairness, economists have tended to argue that monopoly is inefficient, because the monopolist may charge a price which may exclude some consumers from the market even though their willingness to pay exceeds the (marginal) cost of production. This, however, assumes that the monopolist is unable to price-discriminate effectively.

14. E.g. Utterback, J. M. (1994), *Mastering the Dynamics of Innovation*, Harvard Business School Press, Boston.

15. Although there have been some notable exceptions, not least Thomas Edison, whose electric light bulb business turned into General Electric, which remains one of the dominant forces in the light bulb (and electric power) industry today.

16. This minimum may look relatively large in accounting terms, but given the amount invested in achieving that profit the return may in reality be negligible.

17. One of the most difficult issues associated with the measurement of company performance is determining exactly the costs and revenues associated with any given activity. The treatment of capital costs which relate to long-term investment in production poses some problems. These issues are however tangential to the current book. The treatment of capital costs is discussed at some length in Kay, J. (1993), *Foundations of Corporate Success*, Oxford University Press, Oxford, Chapter 13.

18. Competition may in a sense be good for the industry. For example, if competition leads to a greater degree of innovation then the long-term prospects for the industry may be enhanced. At the national level, economists have long argued that a competitive domestic economy is more likely to be successful internationally. However, this seldom discourages domestic firms from arguing for protection from foreign competition, which, it is usually argued, is 'unfair'.

19. There is a long tradition in economics which argues that monopoly, cartels and monopolistic practices are inefficient and that on this basis these practices should be outlawed. However, while the economic viewpoint has some influence, the notion of fairness associated with the legal tradition has been much more influential in the thinking of legislators (see e.g. Whish, R. (1993), *Competition Law*, Butterworth, London).

20. The discussion in this section is based on a technique for analysing decision-making problems known as Game Theory. Game Theory has been influential in fields such as political science and biology, but has been applied most thoroughly in economics. For an entertaining introduction see Dixit, A. and Nalebuff, B. (1991), *Thinking Strategically: The Competitive Edge in Business, Politics and Everyday Life*, W. W. Norton, New York.

5 1. Most of the clubs which did not report a figure were in financial difficulties, in which case they are not necessarily required to file a complete annual report. 'Abbreviated' accounts need not include wage and salary data.

2. Positions are measured continuously from one to ninety-two, so that in

1996–7 twentieth was bottom of the Premier League, twenty-first was first place in the First Division and so on.

3. The R^2 is in fact the proportion of the total *squared* variation in league position, rather than the simple sum of variations, which is explained by wage expenditure. Because the residual for any observation can be either positive or negative, the total unexplained variation would appear much smaller if we simply summed the residuals since a large fraction of them would cancel. By squaring both the total variation and the explained variation we get a better indication of the explanatory power of wage expenditure.

4. A third reason why markets sometimes fail to operate efficiently is that there are effects of the transactions which take place in the market that are not included in the market price. The classic example is pollution. Typically when we buy petrol the price we pay does not allow for the costs we impose on others through our contribution to poor air quality and the associated medical problems. Thus transactions may occur at prices which are profitable and efficient if considered from the point of view of the buyer and the seller alone but the transactions are undesirable from the point of view of society as a whole. The effects not captured in the market transaction are called 'externalities'. Leagues have often argued that transactions between clubs and players must be restricted for the wider good of the game. These arguments will be considered in more detail in Chapter 7.

5. A problem arises if performance is affected by factors which are known but not quantifiable. However, most influences, however difficult to measure, can usually be quantified in one way or another. It is rare to be able to identify a known influence which is not susceptible of *any* quantification.

6. In the earlier regression wage expenditure was used to explain variation in league position; to the extent that transfer expenditure follows the same path as wage expenditure, it adds nothing further to the explanation of variation in league position.

7. To be precise, instead of using wages relative to the average, averaged over twenty years, transfer spending relative to the average, averaged over twenty years, was used.

8. The data in the table refers to the forty clubs excluding Derby County.

9. This data was collected by Michael Crick for an earlier study (Szymanski, S. (1997), 'Discrimination in the English Football Leagues: A Market Test', Imperial College Management School Working Paper) and has not been updated.

10. Furthermore, the correlation between current transfer spending and performance in future years is always lower than with the current year's performance (although only slightly).

11. The figures have been adjusted for price inflation, although this does not entirely capture the effect of above-average growth in the spending of football clubs. As a consequence the figures tend to give more weight to more recent years.

12. The statistical test for this, known as Wu-Hausman test, indicates that causality flows in a particular direction.

13. See Szymanski, op. cit. for fuller treatment of racial discrimination in football.

14. This phenomenon is known as 'regression towards the mean' and was first noted by the nineteenth-century biologist and statistician Sir Francis Galton. He noted that the sons of

fathers who deviated by x inches from the mean height of all fathers themselves deviated by less than x inches from the mean height of all sons. If this were not the case, the variance of height in the population would increase continuously, and height of sons with tall fathers would over time rise without limit. As a statistician Galton measured this effect using the statistical technique known as regression described above in relation to figures 1, 2 and 3. This is somewhat confusing, since 'regression towards the mean' is not the same as 'regression' used in the more general sense in this chapter.

6 1. Currently ten clubs treat the player's registration (without which he cannot play professional football in England) as an asset.
2. Herbert Chapman and Kenny Dalglish are the only two other managers in English football ever to have won the League Championship with more than one club.
3. Before 1982 Nottingham Forest was legally a club, not a limited company, and therefore did not have to file annual accounts at Companies House.
4. These and similar comments can be found in books about Clough such as Murphy, P. (1993), *His Way: The Brian Clough Story*, Robson Books, London; Rogan, J. (1989), *The Football Managers*, Queen Anne Press, London; and King, J. and Kelly, J. (1997), *The Cult of the Manager*, Virgin Books, London.
5. Clough, B. (1994), *The Autobiography*, Partridge Press, London, p. 186.
6. Bowler, D. (1996), *Shanks: The Authorised Biography of Bill Shankly*, Orion Books, London, p. 182.
7. Shankly was manager for twenty-five years; Busby, twenty-seven years; Clough, twenty-eight years.
8. Such comparisons must be treated cautiously because of the wage inflation over the period.
9. Bowler, op. cit., pp. 276 and 316.
10. *Management Week*, 14 December 1990.
11. Dalglish, K. (1996), *Dalglish: My Autobiography*, Hodder & Stoughton, p. 143.

7 1. Smith, Adam (1776, 1933 edn), *An Inquiry into the Nature and Causes of the Wealth of Nations*, Dent, London.
2. For example, in 1951 an arbitration committee established by the government investigated the grievances of the Players' Union, which called for an abolition of the maximum wage and an end to the transfer system. The League argued that 'One cardinal principle was that of equality among the clubs. Every club should have the chance of fielding a team of the highest quality, and spectators everywhere should have a chance of seeing first-class football (Ministry of Labour (1952), Report of the Committee of Investigation appointed by the Ministry of Labour and National Service to inquire into a difference in the Football Industry, b.o. 36–207, HMSO, London). The Committee sided with the League and upheld the existing system.
3. Without mutual recognition, players could be 'poached' by clubs in different leagues. Poaching did not mean breaking legal contracts but moving clubs once a contract had expired.
4. See Leifer, E. (1995), *Making the Majors*, Harvard University Press, Boston for more details.
5. Harding, J. (1991), *For the Good of the Game: The Official History of the*

Professional Footballers' Association,
Robson Books, London.

6. FA (1991), *The Blueprint for the Future of Football*, Lancaster Gate.

7. It is assumed that a total of twenty-two clubs could win the championship, although this is an approximation. The League had fewer than twenty-two clubs in it for several seasons due to restructuring, and relegation and promotion of clubs make the number of potential winners larger than league size when looking at several seasons.

8. Standard deviation is defined as

$$\sqrt{\frac{n\sum x^2 - (\sum x)^2}{n\,(n\text{-}1)}}$$

where n= number of clubs and league and x=points total.

9. See Dobson, S. M. and Goddard, J. P. (1995), 'The Demand for Professional League Football in England and Wales, 1925–1992', *Journal of the Royal Statistical Society*, forthcoming.

10. Julian Easthope, Union Bank of Switzerland, Football and Finance, IPC Conferences, April 1997.

11. Sheehan, R. (1996), *Keeping Score: The Economics of Big Time Sports*, Diamond Communications, South Bend, Indiana, provides an interesting study of the breakdown of income in American team sports.

12. As well as helping the profitability of the clubs' owners. The claim that talent would not become concentrated at the big clubs under this system has been consistently challenged by US economists (see e.g. Quirk, J. and Fort, R. (1992), *Pay Dirt: The Business of Professional Team Sports*, Princeton University Press, New Jersey). They argue that talent will always move to whichever market values it most highly. Thus reserve clauses simply change the distribution of income, without

changing the distribution of sporting outcomes.

13. However, in its execution this cap did have some unusual exemptions which limited its effectiveness. See Fort, R. and Quirk, J. (1995), 'Cross-Subsidisation, Incentives and Outcomes in Professional Team Sports Leagues', *Journal of Economic Literature*, Vol. XXXIII, September, pp. 1265–99.

14 August 1998.

15. These figures underestimate the differences in pay-per-view subscriptions that might be expected. Viewers for each match are allocated to both participating clubs. Thus Wimbledon's figures will benefit if they play Manchester United. If a game was watched by one million viewers then one million was allocated to both clubs.

16. *New Media Markets*, 22 January 1997.

17. Shurmer, M. (1997), 'Future Demand for Pay-TV in the UK', *Telecommunications Policy*, Vol. 21, No. 7, pp. 611–18.

18. Full details of all academic publications mentioned in this Appendix are given in the Bibliography on page 334.

8 1. Measurement of demand elasticities varies according to different studies. The figures mentioned here are based on Szymanski, S. and Smith, R. (1997), 'The English football industry: profit, performance and industrial structure', *International Review of Applied Economics*, 11, 1, pp. 135–53, and similar estimates have been reported in other studies.

2. This barrier was further enforced by a traditional animosity which ensured that the two clubs never traded players. From a financial point of view this

barrier to trading may have helped to prevent a damaging bidding war.

3. This is the combined value of all the company shares (valued at the current market price).

4. Quoted in Tomas, J. (1996), *Soccer Czars*, Mainstream, Edinburgh, p. 21. When he bought the club he was said to know little of the club's history. One story told by Terry Venables is that when the Double was mentioned he said, 'Double, what Double?' (In 1961 Tottenham won the First Division championship and the FA Cup.)

5. *Daily Telegraph*, 11 October 1996.

6. *Daily Telegraph*, 9 April 1996.

7. *Daily Telegraph*, 16 January 1998.

8. 1997, £50m, 1996, £105.6m, 1995, £38.4m, 1994, £25.1m, 1993, £22.8m.

9. Martin Edwards at Manchester United was noted for trying to sell out during the 1980s, although he failed twice, once to Robert Maxwell and once to Michael Knighton.

10. Vrooman, J. (1995), 'A general theory of professional sports leagues', *Southern Economic Journal*, 61, 4, pp. 971–90 develops a theory of sports leagues which implies that owners interested primarily in playing success will ultimately drive profit-maximizing owners out of business.

11. *Daily Telegraph*, 19 March 1988.

12. In that season Manchester United reached the quarter-finals and received £5.2m while Newcastle went out at the group stage and received £2.8m. The winners, Real Madrid, received £8.2m

(TV Sports Markets newsletter, 17 July 1998).

13. For Premier League see Deloitte & Touche (1998), 'England's Premier Clubs'; for NFL see Sheehan, R. (1996), *Keeping Score: The Economics of Big Time Sports*, Diamond Communications, South Bend Indiana.

14. The idea of event games is usually associated with Alex Fynn; see for example Fynn, A. and Guest, L. (1994), *Out of Time: Why football isn't working*, Simon and Schuster, London.

15. Clubs do not provide the accounting data that can be found in English football. See e.g. Noll, R. (1985), 'The Economic Viability of Professional Baseball', Report to the Major League Baseball Players' Association for an analysis of baseball club profitability.

16. Hausman, J. and Leonard, G. (1997), 'Superstars in the National Basketball Association: Economic Value and Policy', *Journal of Labor Economics*, 15, 4, pp. 586–624.

17. This claim is disputed.

18. Horton, E. (1997), *Moving the Goalposts: Football's Exploitation*, Mainstream, Edinburgh.

19. Conn, D. (1997), *The Football Business: Fair Game in the '90s?*, Mainstream, Edinburgh.

20. Department of Culture, Media and Sport press release issued 30 July 1997.

21. UK competition law is currently being rewritten to bring it into line with the Treaty of Rome.

Bibliography

Business Strategy

Becker, G. S. (1962), 'Irrational Behavior and Economic Theory', *Journal of Political Economy*, 70, pp. 1–13.

— (1976), *The Economic Approach to Human Behavior*, University of Chicago Press, Chicago.

Chandler, A. D. (1962), *Strategy and Structure: Chapters in the History of the American Industrial Enterprise*, MIT Press, Boston.

Clutterbuck, D. and Crainer, S. (1990), *Makers of Management*, Macmillan, London.

Dixit, A. and Nalebuff, B. (1991), *Thinking Strategically: The Competitive Edge in Business, Politics and Everyday Life*, W. W. Norton, New York.

Frank, R. H. and Cook, P. J. (1995), *The Winner-Take-All Society*, Free Press, New York.

Greene, William H. (1993), *Econometric Analysis*, Macmillan Publishing Co., New York.

Kay, J. (1993), *Foundations of Corporate Success*, Oxford University Press, Oxford.

Plender, J. (1996), *Stake in the Future*, Brealy Publishing, London.

Porter, M. E. (1980), *Competitive Strategy: Techniques for Analyzing Industries and Competitors*, Free Press, New York.

Scherer, F. M. and Ross, D. (1990), *Industrial Market Structure and Economic Performance*, Houghton Mifflin, Boston.

Schumpeter, J. A. (1943), *Capitalism, Socialism and Democracy*, Unwin, New York.

Smith, Adam (1776, 1933 edn), *An Inquiry into the Nature and Causes of the Wealth of Nations*, Dent, London.

Teece, D. J. (1986), 'Profiting from technological innovation: Implications for integration, collaboration, licensing and public policy', *Research Policy*, 15, pp. 285–305.

Utterback, J. M. (1994), *Mastering the Dynamics of Innovation*, Harvard Business School Press, Boston.

Whish, R. (1993), *Competition Law*, Butterworths, London.

Football and Sport

Journal Articles and Research Reports

Arnold, A. J. and Beneviste, I. (1987), 'Wealth and Poverty in the English Football League', *Accounting and Business Research*, 17, pp. 195–203.

— (1988), 'Cross Subsidisation and Competition Policy in English Professional Football', *Journal of Industrial Affairs*, Vol. 15, pp. 2–14.

Arnold, A. J. and Webb, B. 'Aston Villa and Wolverhampton Wanderers 1971/72 to

1981/82: A Study of Finance Policies in the Football Industry', *Managerial Finance*, 12, 1, 11–19.

Atkinson, S., Stanley, L. and Tschirhart, J. (1988), 'Revenue Sharing as an incentive agency problem', *Rand Journal of Economics*, Vol. 19, No. 1, pp. 27–43.

Baimbridge, M., Cameron, S. and Dawson, P. (1996), 'Satellite Television and the Demand for Football: A Whole New Ball Game?', *Scottish Journal of Political Economy*, Vol. 43, No. 3, August, pp. 317–33.

Bird, P. J. W. N. (1982), 'The Demand for League Football', *Applied Economics*, No. 14, pp. 637–49.

Borland, J. (1987), 'The Demand for Australian Rules Football', *The Economic Record*, September, pp. 221–30.

Brown, R. and Jewell, R. (1994), 'Is there customer discrimination in college basketball – the premium fans pay for white players', *Social Science Quarterly*, 75, 2, pp. 401–13.

Cairns, J. A. (1987), 'Evaluating Changes in League Structure: The Organisation of the Scottish Football League', *Applied Economics*, 19(2), pp. 259–75.

— (1988), 'Outcome uncertainty and the demand for football', *University of Aberdeen Department of Economics Discussion Paper*, 88–02.

— (1990), 'The Demand for Team Sports', *British Review of Economic Issues*, 12, 28, pp. 1–20.

Cairns, J.A., Jennett, N. and Sloane, P.J. (1986), 'The Economics of Professional Team Sports: A Survey of Theory and Evidence', *Journal of Economic Studies*, 13, pp. 3–80.

Carmichael, F., Forrest, D. and Simmons, R. (1996), 'The Soccer Transfer Market: who gets transferred and for how much?', mimeograph, University of Salford.

Carmichael, F. and Thomas, D. (1993), 'Bargaining in the Transfer Market: Theory and Evidence', *Applied Economics*, No. 25, pp. 1467–76.

Chester, N. (1968), *Report of the Committee on Football*, HMSO, London.

Commission on Industrial Relations Report (1974), 'Professional Football', Report No. 87, HMSO, London.

Corry, D., Williamson, P. and Moore, S. (1993), 'A Game Without Vision', Institute for Public Policy Research Pamphlet.

Dabscheck, B. (1975), 'Sporting Equality: Labour Market versus Product Market Control', *Journal of Industrial Relations*, 17, 2, pp. 174–90.

dell'Osso, F. and Szymanski, S. (1991), 'Who Are the Champions?', *Business Strategy Review*, 2, 2, pp. 113–30.

Dobson, S. and Gerrard, W. (1997), 'Testing for Rent Sharing in Football Transfer Fees: Evidence from the English Football League', Leeds University Business School Discussion Paper, E97/03.

Dobson, S. M. and Goddard, J. A. (1995), 'The Demand for Professional League Football in England and Wales, 1925–1992', *Journal of the Royal Statistical Society*, forthcoming.

Economist (1992), The Sports Business Survey, 25 July.

Football Association (1991), 'The Blueprint for the Future of Football', Lancaster Gate.

Football League (1983), *Report of the Committee of Inquiry into Structure and Finance* (Chairman Sir Norman Chester), Lytham St Anne's.

Football Trust (1995), *Digest of Football Statistics 1992/93*, University of Leicester.

Fort, R. and Quirk, J. (1995), 'Cross-Subsidisation, Incentives and Outcomes in Professional Team Sports Leagues', *Journal of Economic Literature*, Vol. XXXIII, September, pp. 1265–99.

Gartner, M. and Pommerehne, W. (1978), 'Der Fussballzuschauer – ein Homo Oeconomicus?', *Jahrbuch für Sozial Wissenschaft*, 29, pp. 88–107.

Hart, R. A., Hutton, J. and Sharrot, T. (1975), 'A Statistical Analysis of Association Football Attendances', *Applied Statistics*, 24, No. 1, pp. 17–27.

Hausman, J. and Leonard, G. (1997), 'Superstars in the National Basketball Association: Economic Value and Policy', *Journal of Labor Economics*, 15, 4, pp. 586–624.

HMSO (1990), *The Hillsborough Stadium Disaster, Inquiry by Lord Justice Taylor, Final Report*, Cm 962, HMSO.

Hynds, M. and Smith, I. (1994), 'The Demand for Test Match Cricket', *Applied Economic Letters*, 1, pp. 103–6.

Janssens, P. and Kesenne, S. (1987), 'Belgian soccer attendances', *Tijdschrift voor Economie en Management*, 32, pp. 305–15.

Jennett, N. (1984), 'Attendances, Uncertainty of Outcome and Policy in the Scottish Football League', *Scottish Journal of Political Economy*, Vol. 31, No. 2, pp. 176–98.

Jennett, N. and Sloane, P. J. (1985), 'The future of League football: a critique of the report of the Chester Committee of Enquiry', *Leisure Studies*, 4, pp. 39–56.

Jones, J. C. H. and Ferguson, D. G. (1988), 'Location and Survival in the National Hockey League', *The Journal of Industrial Economics*, Vol. XXXVI, No. 4, pp. 443–557.

Kahn, L. (1991), 'Discrimination in professional sports: A survey of the literature', *Industrial and Labour Relations Review*, 44, 3, pp. 395–418.

Kuypers, T. J. (1996), 'The Beautiful Game? An Econometric Study of Why People Watch English Football', *Discussion Papers in Economics, University College London*, 96–101.

— (1997), 'Football on the box', *New Economy*, Vol. 4, No. 4.

— (1997), PhD thesis, University College London.

Longley, N. (1995), 'Salary discrimination in the National Hockey League', *Canadian Public Policy*, 21, 4, pp. 413–22.

Ministry of Labour (1952), Report of the Committee of Investigation appointed by the Ministry of Labour and National Service to inquire into a difference in the Football Industry, S.O. 36–207, HMSO, London.

Noll, R. (1985), 'The Economic Viability of Professional Baseball', Report to the Major League Baseball Players' Association.

Peel, D. and Thomas, D. (1988), 'Outcome Uncertainty and the Demand for Football: An Analysis of Match Attendances in the English Football League', *Scottish Journal of Political Economy*, 35(3), pp. 242–9.

— (1996), 'Attendance Demand: an investigation of repeat fixtures', *Applied Economics Letters*, 3, pp. 391–4.

PEP (1966), 'English Professional Football', *Planning*, Vol. XLII, No. 496.

Purdy, D., Leonard, W. and Eitzen, D. (1994), 'A re-examination of salary discrimination in major league baseball by race ethnicity', *Sociology of Sport Journal*, 11, 1, pp. 60–69.

Reilly, B. and Witt, R. (1995), 'English League Transfer prices: is there a racial dimension?', *Applied Economics Letters*, 2, pp. 220–22.

Rivett, Patrick (1975), 'The structure of League Football', *Operational Research Quarterly*, 26, pp. 801–12.

Ruddock, L. (1979), 'The Market for Professional Footballers: An Economic Analysis', *Economics*, 15, pp. 70–72.

Shurmer, M. (1997), 'Future Demand for Pay-TV in the UK', *Telecommunication Policy*, Vol. 21, No. 7, pp. 611–18.

Simmons, R. (1996), 'The Demand for English League Football: A Club Level Analysis', *Applied Economics*, Vol. 28, pp. 139–55.

Sloane, P. J. (1969), 'The Labour Market in Professional Football', *British Journal of Industrial Relations*, 7, 2, pp. 181–99.

— (1971), 'The Economics of Professional Football: The Football Club as a Utility Maximizer', *Scottish Journal of Political Economy*, 17, 2, pp. 121–46.

Smart, R. A. and Goddard, J. A. (1991), 'The determinants of standing and seated football attendances: evidence from three Scottish League clubs', *Quarterly Economic Commentary*, 16, pp. 61–4.

Speight, A. and Thomas, D. (1997), 'Arbitrator Decision-Making in the Transfer Market: An Empirical Analysis', *Scottish Journal of Political Economy*, 44, 2, pp. 198–215.

Szymanski, S. (1996), 'Gazza and Greenbury: Similarities and Differences', *Hume Papers on Public Policy*, 3, 4, pp. 39–58.

— (1997), 'Discrimination in the English Football Leagues: A Market Test', Imperial College Management School Working Paper.

Szymanski, S. and Smith, R. (1997), 'The English football industry: profit, performance and industrial structure', *International Review of Applied Economics*, 11, 1, pp. 135–53.

Vrooman, J. (1995), 'A general theory of professional sports leagues', *Southern Economic Journal*, 61, 4, pp. 971–90.

Walker, B. (1986), 'The Demand for Professional League Football and the Success of Football League Teams: Some City Size Effects', *Urban Studies*, 23, pp. 209–20.

Whitney, J. (1988), 'Winning games versus winning championships: the economics of fan interest and team performance', *Economic Inquiry*, 26, October, pp. 703–24.

— (1993), 'Bidding till bankrupt: destructive competition in professional team sports', *Economic Inquiry*, 31, January, pp. 100–115.

Williams, J. (1994a), 'Lick my boots: racism in English football', Sir Norman Chester Centre for Football Research, Leicester University.

— (1994b), 'The Carling Fan Survey: a national survey of F A Premier League club fans', Sir Norman Chester Centre for Football Research, Leicester University.

Books

Andreff, W. and Nys, J-F. (1986), *Economie du Sport*, Presses Universitaires de France, Paris.

Arnold, A. J. (1988), *A Game That Would Pay: A Business History of Professional Football in Bradford*, Duckworth, London.

Bale, J. and Maguire, J. (1994), *The Global Sports Arena: Athletic Talent Migration in an Interdependent World*, Frank Cass, London.

Bennett, A. (1912), *The Matador of the Five Towns*, Alan Sutton Publishing Ltd, Gloucester.

Bourg, J-F. and Gouguet, J-J. (1998), *Analyse économique du sport*, Presses Universitaires de France, Paris.

Bowler, D. (1996), *Shanks: The Authorised Biography of Bill Shankly*, Orion Books, London.

Brown, H. (ed.) (1970), *The Football League Book*, Arthur Baker, London.

Busby, M. (1973), *Soccer At The Top*, Sphere, London.

Clough, B. (1994), *The Autobiography*, Partridge Press, London.

Conn, D. (1997), *The Football Business: Fair Game in the '90s?*, Mainstream, Edinburgh.

Crick, M. and Smith, D. (1989), *Manchester United: Betrayal of a Legend*, Pelham Books, London.

Delaney, T. (1963), *A Century of Soccer*, The Football Association.

Delbourg, P. and Heimermann, B. (1998), *Football et Littérature*, Stock, Paris.

Fynn, A. and Guest, L. (1994), *Out of Time: Why football isn't working*, Simon and Schuster, London.

Green, G. (1954), *Soccer, the world game*, The Sportsman's Book Club, London.

Guttman, A. (1994), *Games & Empires: Modern Sports and Cultural Imperialism*, Columbia, New York.

Hagstrom, R. (1998), *The Nascar Way: The Business that drives the Sport*, Wiley, New York.

Hardaker, A. (1977), *Hardaker of the League*, Pelham Books, London.

Harding, J. (1991), *For the Good of the Game: The Official History of the Professional Footballers' Association*, Robson Books, London.

Heimermann, B., Constant, C. and Hubac, T. (1998), *l'ABCdaire du Football*, Flammarion, Paris.

Hopcraft, A. (1968), *The Football Man*, Simon and Schuster, London.

Horrie, C. and Clarke, S. (1994), *Fuzzy Monsters: Fear and Loathing at the BBC*, Mandarin Books, London.

Horton, E. (1997), *Moving the Goalposts: Football's Exploitation*, Mainstream, Edinburgh.

Hugman, B. (1992), *Football League Players' Records*, Tony Williams Publications, Taunton.

Husting, A. (1998), *L'Union Européenne et le Sport*, Juris-Service, Lyon.

Inglis, S. (1988), *League Football and the men who made it*, Willow Books, London.

— (1996), *Football Grounds of Britain*, Collins Willow, London.

Kelly, S. (1995), *Back Page Football: A century of newspaper coverage*, Queen Anne Press, Harpenden.

King, J. and Kelly, J. (1997), *The Cult of the Manager*, Virgin Books, London.

Klatell, D. and Marcus, N. (1996), *Inside Big Time Sports*, MasterMedia Ltd, New York.

Korr, C. (1986), *West Ham United*, Duckworth, London.

Kuper, S. (1994), *Football Against the Enemy*, Phoenix, London.

Lambert, C. (1995), *The Boss*, Cassell, London.

Leatherdale, C. (ed.) (1997), *The Book of Football*, Desert Island Books, Westcliff-on-Sea, Essex.

Leifer, E. (1995), *Making the Majors*, Harvard University Press, Boston.

Mason, T. (1980), *Association Football and English Society 1863–1915*, Harvester Press, Sussex.

— (1995), *Passion of the People: Football in South America*, Verso, London.

Mason, T. 'The Bogotá Affair' in Bale, J. and Maguire, J. (eds) (1994), *The Global Sports Arena: Athletic Migration in an Interdependent World*, Frank Cass, London.

Matthews, T. (1989), *Birmingham City: A Complete Record 1875–1989*, Breedon Books, Derby.

Murphy, P. (1993), *His Way: The Brian Clough Story*, Robson Books, London.

Murray, W. J. (1994), *Football: A History of the World Game*, Ashgate Publishing Co., Vermont.

Pickering, D. (1995), *The Cassell Soccer Companion: History Facts Anecdotes*, Cassell, London.

Pringle, A. and Fissler, N. (1996), *Where are they now?*, Two Heads Publishing, London.

Quirk, J. and Fort, R. (1992), *Pay Dirt: The Business of Professional Team Sports*, Princeton University Press, New Jersey.

Robinson, M. (ed.) (1997), *Football League Tables 1888–1997*, Soccer Books, Cleethorpes.

Robson, B. (1992), *Glory Glory Man United: My Years at Old Trafford*, Collins Willow, London.

Rogan, J. (1989), *The Football Managers*, Queen Anne Press, London.

Rollin, J. (ed.) (various years), *Rothmans Football Yearbook*, Headline Book Publishing, London.

Rose, D. (1996), *The Ultimate Football League Table*, Douglas Rose, London.

Sanderson, F. (1996), 'Psychology' in *Science & Soccer*, edited by T. Reilly, E & FN Spon, London.

Seymour, H. (1960), *Baseball: The Early Years*, Oxford University Press Inc, New York.

Sharpe, I. (1952), *40 Years in Football*, Hutchinson, London.

Sheehan, R. (1996), *Keeping Score: The Economics of Big Time Sports*, Diamond Communications, South Bend, Indiana.

Sparling, R. (1926), *The Romance of the Wednesday 1867–1926*, Desert Island Books, Westcliff-on-Sea, Essex.

Sugden, J. and Tomlinson, A. (1998), *Fifa and the Contest for World Football*, Polity Press, Cambridge.

Tabner, B. (1992), *Through the Turnstiles*, Yore Publishing, Harefield, Herts.

Taylor, R. and Ward, A. (1996), *Kicking and Screaming: An Oral History of Football in England*, Robson Books, London.

Tischler, S. (1981), *Footballers and Businessmen: The Origins of Professional Soccer in England*, Holmes and Meier, New York.

Tomas, J. (1996), *Soccer Czars*, Mainstream, Edinburgh.

Trevelyan, G. M. (1942), *English Social History: A Survey of Six Centuries*, Longmans Green & Co., London.

Vamplew, W. (1988), *Pay Up and Play the Game: Professional Sport in Britain, 1875–1914*, Cambridge University Press, Cambridge.

Wall, F. J. in Leatherdale, C. (ed.) (1977), *The Book of Football*, Desert Island Books, Westcliff-on-Sea, Essex.

Walvin, J. (1994), *The People's Game: The History of Football Revisited*, Mainstream Publishing, Edinburgh and London.

Wenner, L. (1989), *Media, Sports, and Society*, Sage Publications, London.

Williams, J. and Wagg, S. (1991), *British Football and Social Change: Getting into Europe*, Leicester University Press, Leicester.

Zimbalist, A. (1992), *Baseball and Billions*, Basic Books, New York.

Financial Reports
Touche Ross (1992, 1993, 1994), Survey of Football Club Accounts
Deloitte & Touche (1995, 1996, 1997, 1998), Annual Review of Football Finance

Arsenal Bond Prospectus 1992
Hammers Bond Prospectus 1991
Manchester United Placing Prospectus 1991
WBA Share Issue Document 1996

Data Appendix

The main financial data and league performance data used in the book is listed below. The financial data was collected from club accounts filed at Companies House. In the 1990s Deloitte & Touche have published a more comprehensive data set in its Annual Review of Football Finances. Here we have only reported those forty clubs which have formed the basis of our own statistical analysis. These forty were the clubs that provided a more or less complete financial record. Other clubs reported their accounts in such a way (e.g. by not reporting wage spending) that their usefulness for this study was limited. Some clubs have tended not to include transfer fee data in their accounts. In many cases clubs used to combine wages and transfer fees as a single figure, although nowadays this practice is rare.

Data for all clubs is available on microfiche from Companies House since around 1974. For earlier years it is necessary to inspect the archive records, which was done for almost all clubs. No complete record was found for any club going back to the First World War, but those records that could be found are included. In addition, a small number of pre-First World War accounts are included.

Club	Year	League position	Division	Revenue (£)	Wages (£)	Net transfers (£)	Pre-tax profits (£)
Arsenal	1948	1	1	142,890	47,914		21,445
	1949	5	1	162,136	32,215		59,126
	1950	6	1	161,953	37,055		44,688
	1951	5	1	151,834	33,521	6,550	42,273
	1952	3	1	179,177	35,212	11,775	62,129
	1953	1	1	164,268	40,173	3,450	31,715
	1954	12	1	170,040	39,786	−10,845	49,822
	1955	9	1	159,064	37,534	36,660	14,436
	1956	5	1	148,072	39,566	20,050	6,390
	1957	5	1	151,853	33,424	−3,500	39,011
	1958	12	1	179,442	42,853	5,800	17,106
	1959	3	1	211,011	46,217	57,244	1,079
	1960	13	1	190,633	47,871	−3,000	32,267
	1961	11	1	196,480	45,425	18,584	12,812
	1962	10	1	203,375	61,252	−3,640	16,074
	1963	7	1	207,221	71,429	33,900	19,568
	1964	8	1	255,717	89,105	45,075	40,552
	1965	13	1	258,939	87,810	−12,745	27,457
	1966	14	1	260,263	78,910	−64,750	79,206
	1967	7	1	299,091	91,472	82,500	−100,269
	1968	9	1	363,886	114,547	51,980	5,487
	1969	4	1	450,933	123,058	−11,354	−8,926
	1970	12	1	501,481	129,045	10,561	67,434
	1971	1	1	653,063	174,549	−139,952	16,394
	1972	5	1	682,585	139,899	119,214	60,669
	1973	2	1	733,360	399,373	86,376	106,277
	1974	10	1	544,000	365,000	−80,000	3,000
	1975	16	1	597,000	415,000	−47,000	20,000
	1976	17	1	690,000	471,000	−70,000	23,000
	1977	8	1	925,000	520,000	220,000	−155,000
	1978	5	1	1,477,000	690,000	59,000	187,000
	1979	7	1	1,619,000	891,000	306,000	−174,000
	1980	4	1	2,628,000	1289000	657,000	393,000
	1981	3	1	2,076,000	1,176,000	787,000	488,000
	1982	5	1	2,236,000	· 1,373,000	343,000	41,000
	1983	10	1	2,412,000	1,233,000	−171,000	468,000
	1984	6	1	2,546,000	1,409,000	1,263,000	−838,000
	1985	7	1	2,690,000	1,582,000	715,000	−485,000
	1986	7	1	2,769,000	1,711,000	−160,000	44,000
	1987	4	1	4,618,000	1,999,000	12,000	951,000
	1988	6	1	5,439,000	1,952,000	588,000	867,000
	1989	1	1	6,550,000	2,331,000	−191,000	1,649,000
	1990	4	1	7,648,000	2,793,000	1,696,900	815,000
	1991	1	1	11,295,000	4,529,000	−332,000	749,000
	1992	4	1	13,739,000	6,061,000	1,393,000	−165,000
	1993	10	1	15,342,000	6,923,000	379,000	2,483,000
	1994	4	1	21,471,000	7,742,004	889,588	5,630,355
	1995	12	1	23,936,000	8,901,000	4,904,000	1,941,000
	1996	5	1	20,975,000	10,062,000	6,155,000	−3,611,000
	1997	3	1	27,158,000	15,279,000	3,476,000	−1,575,000
Aston Villa	1908	2	1	11,457	5,719		443
	1911	2	1	16,141	4,324		5,924
	1912	6	1	12,946	5,538		1,579

Winners and Losers / 340

Club	Year	League position	Division	Revenue (£)	Wages (£)	Net transfers (£)	Pre-tax profits (£)
Aston Villa (cont'd)	1913	2	1	20,408	7,719		5,617
	1914	2	1	20,167	6,726		6,777
	1922	5	1	40,499	13,348		5,792
	1923	6	1	31,442	9,227		2,008
	1924	6	1	38,224	14,578		3,353
	1925	15	1	34,667	14,786		3,343
	1926	6	1	38,474	13,828		11,972
	1927	10	1	37,814	22,924		687
	1928	8	1	60,963	14,447		8,805
	1929	3	1	64,034	20,323		12,504
	1947	8	1	117,971	34,162		20,288
	1948	6	1	132,380	37,429		26,055
	1949	10	1	150,026	79,346		-1,401
	1950	12	1	131,754	45,220		15,392
	1951	15	1	128,268	57,695		-13,178
	1952	6	1	121,331	31,212		19,345
	1953	11	1	137,343	32,912	18,300	-309
	1954	13	1	114,289	33,245	12,420	-3,587
	1955	6	1	124,189	35,490	-10,230	16,251
	1956	20	1	158,373	35,967	40,900	-42,581
	1957	10	1	147,317	36,994	-77	678
	1958	14	1	134,980	43,991	-10,170	12,786
	1959	21	1	158,350	49,675	12,725	-4,688
	1960	1	2	177,979	53,456	20,435	-15,806
	1961	9	1	209,909	56,922	21,410	19,651
	1962	7	1	295,313	59,835	22,549	106,202
	1963	15	1	207,813	67,935	18,025	-12,081
	1964	19	1	188,527	67,082	12,000	-51,202
	1965	16	1	187,957	71,398	15,375	-14,829
	1966	16	1	181,272	74,314	21,225	-13,406
	1967	21	1	148,696	68,254	-56,350	78,689
	1968	16	2	150,720	81,937	68,173	76,070
	1969	18	2	198,256	84,420	75,296	-67,508
	1970	21	2	262,335	110,431	211,267	-175,136
	1971	4	3	344,848	122,569	6,770	77,506
	1972	1	3	383,808	161,578	167,153	-91,085
	1973	3	2	383,141	146,265	63,858	-31,963
	1974	14	2	362,000	167,000	-130,000	123,000
	1975	2	2	545,000	255,000	129,000	-95,000
	1976	16	1	847,000	262,000	299,000	-135,000
	1977	4	1	1,274,000	412,000	28,000	280,000
	1978	8	1	1,477,000	398,000	434,000	-420,000
	1979	8	1	1,608,000	575,000	32,000	-183,000
	1980	7	1	1,705,000	848,000	1,052,000	372,000
	1981	1	1	2,084,000	1,026,000	450,000	247,000
	1982	11	1	2,631,000	987,000	43,000	243,000
	1983	6	1	2,266,000	1,203,000	450,000	-504,000
	1984	10	1	2,218,000	1,125,000	-48,000	312,000
	1985	10	1	1,965,000	1,182,000	-242,000	254,000
	1986	16	1	2,114,000	1,057,000	478,000	-200,000
	1987	22	1	2,080,000	1,183,000	178,000	-93,000
	1988	2	2	2,661,000	1,715,000	55,000	-176,000
	1989	17	1	4,568,000	1,609,000	23,000	1,124,000

Data Appendix / 341

Club	Year	League position	Division	Revenue (£)	Wages (£)	Net transfers (£)	Pre-tax profits (£)
Aston Villa (cont'd)	1990	2	1	5,881,000	2,609,000	629,000	1,051,000
	1991	17	1	7,208,000	2,457,000	910,000	1,530,000
	1992	7	1	7,463,000	4,411,000	-2,876,000	3,542,000
	1993	2	1	10,175,000	4,498,000	3,197,000	-191,000
	1994	10	1	13,014,000	6,248,000	2,311,000	1,118,000
	1995	18	1	13,001,000	7,139,000	-668,000	3,717,000
	1996	4	1	18,865,000	7,717,000	5,851,000	-65,000
	1997	5	1	22,079,000	10,070,000	9,336,000	-3,926,000
Barnsley	1908	16	2	4,162	1,985	-1,051	788
	1910	9	2	10,320	2,792	-18	4,943
	1932	21	2	8,288	5,605	-45	-844
	1933	8	3	9,305	4,808	-3,350	-31
	1950	13	2	44,050	20,907	-1,770	-3,409
	1951	4	2	45,644	21,220	-6,035	4,487
	1953	22	2	41,955	20,500	-12,805	1,388
	1954	2	3	37,616	19,246	-15,194	5,129
	1955	1	3	33,496	19,504	360	-6,846
	1956	18	2	33,114	21,674	-1,520	-2,265
	1957	19	2	36,084	20,020	-1,615	-1,489
	1958	14	2	45,414	24,627	2,670	-3,296
	1959	22	2	50,614	25,556	-15,400	5,167
	1960	17	3	44,528	19,890	-15,365	-6,569
	1961	8	3	47,297	25,359	2,075	-6,503
	1962	19	3	52,115	27,512	-23,791	2,357
	1963	18	3	55,730	30,819	3,575	-7,629
	1964	20	3	57,337	33,857	-9,400	1,087
	1965	24	3	56,788	33,667	-18,515	-7,697
	1966	16	4	59,436	33,393	-19,325	-2,436
	1967	16	4	64,184	33,369	4,980	-11,693
	1968	2	4	71,948	41,323	1,420	2,444
	1969	10	3	86,537	46,393	12,725	486
	1970	7	3	85,707	51,802	-675	-1,477
	1971	12	3	98,542	59,062	-21,875	2,290
	1972	22	3	100,588	64,087	-17,000	3,889
	1973	14	4	98,282	68,565	-2,500	-32,997
	1974	13	4	59,000	58,000	-13,000	0
	1975	15	4	57,000	60,000	-7,000	-2,000
	1976	12	4	86,000	71,000	-4,000	-4,000
	1977	6	4	220,000	96,000	-104,000	0
	1978	7	4	113,000	132,000	14,000	12,000
	1979	4	4	263,000	199,000	104,000	15,000
	1980	11	3	325,000	282,000	238,000	-195,000
	1981	2	3	467,000	398,000	124,000	-243,000
	1982	6	2	613,000	530,000	23,000	-144,000
	1983	10	2	532,000	517,000	34,000	-175,000
	1984	14	2	445,000	435,000	-5,000	-94,000
	1985	11	2	402,000	479,000	-74,000	-125,000
	1986	12	2	343,000	470,000	-60,000	-170,000
	1987	11	2	443,000	480,000	-356,000	0
	1988	14	2	673,000	584,000	-50,000	-50,000
	1989	7	2	1,077,000	607,000	18,000	40,000
	1990	19	2	1,407,000	784,000	-424,000	540,000
	1991	8	2	2,065,000	976,000	-507,000	756,000

Club	Year	League position	Division	Revenue (£)	Wages (£)	Net transfers (£)	Pre-tax profits (£)
Barnsley (cont'd)	1992	16	2	1,596,000	1,183,000	−319,000	58,000
	1993	13	2	1,961,000	1,297,000	−192,000	266,000
	1994	18	2	1,772,153	1,497,610	45,000	−352,490
	1995	6	2	2,040,000	1,360,000	10,000	109,000
	1996	10	2	2,296,000	1,684,000	−391,000	185,000
	1997	2	2	3,658,000	2,613,000	−273,000	346,000
Birmingham City	1929	15	1	34,769	22,664		−7,781
	1930	11	1	28,165	16,539		1,412
	1931	19	1	36,353	20,916		2,146
	1933	13	1	25,748	14,624		−696
	1936	12	1	30,415	11,278		5,075
	1937	11	1	29,460	15,511		−2,237
	1938	18	1	39,336	15,397		−11,348
	1947	3	2	58,804	33,169		4,626
	1948	1	2	66,943	31,360		9,440
	1949	17	1	73,707	39,237		8,708
	1950	22	1	58,131	26,600		11,239
	1951	15	2	58,131	31,991		548
	1952	3	2	53,995	33,741		−1,579
	1953	6	2	50,145	21,187		9,497
	1954	7	2	47,186	28,371		1,329
	1955	1	2	64,868	44,032		−11,454
	1956	6	1	92,081	42,081		13,388
	1957	12	1	95,188	45,483		9,648
	1958	13	1	107,128	65,135	.	−9,895
	1959	9	1	102,833	62,154		363
	1960	19	1	101,232	63,687		−4,300
	1961	19	1	126,742	85,843		−8,355
	1962	17	1	111,372	51,725		15,392
	1963	20	1	106,941	63,435		6,817
	1964	20	1	140,411	110,372		−48,520
	1965	22	1	96,676	51,942		8,331
	1966	10	2	78,640	119,718		−85,363
	1967	10	2	141,831	130,762		−34,542
	1968	4	2	195,654	49,453		−4,263
	1969	7	2	186,924	173,313		−49,951
	1970	18	2	167,936	89,248		9,000
	1971	9	2	194,327	180,304		−65,231
	1972	2	2	299,944	419,030		−205,565
	1973	10	1	379,220	255,048		−5,566
	1974	19	1	424,000	281,000	0	1,000
	1975	17	1	478,000	293,000	0	17,000
	1976	19	1	564,000	336,000	120,000	−121,000
	1977	13	1	678,000	359,000	62,000	−16,000
	1978	11	1	803,000	478,000	45,000	59,000
	1979	21	1	863,000	598,000	−646,000	703,000
	1980	3	2	892,000	717,000	684,000	−222,000
	1981	13	1	1,044,000	832,000	141,000	−165,000
	1982	16	1	1,067,000	1,184,000	50,000	−459,000
	1983	17	1	1,079,000	915,000	−221,000	−203,000
	1984	20	1	1,159,000	933,000	−39,000	−93,000
	1985	2	2	1,006,000	1,011,000	−361,000	−400,000
	1986	21	1	873,000	760,000	−112,000	−258,000

Data Appendix / 343

Club	Year	League position	Division	Revenue (£)	Wages (£)	Net transfers (£)	Pre-tax profits (£)
Birmingham City	1987	19	2	714,000	573,000	-532,000	-222,000
(cont'd)	1988	19	2	830,000	633,000	-199,000	-68,000
	1989	23	2	841,000	820,000	-350,000	-310,000
	1990	7	3	1,076,000	798,000	305,000	-357,000
	1991	12	3	1,567,000	1,137,000	-406,000	167,000
	1992	2	3	2,012,000	1,423,000	465,000	-778,000
	1993	19	2	3,120,000	1,715,000	905,000	-798,000
	1994	22	2	3,763,132	2,666,097	642,368	-1,131,157
	1995	1	3	6,942,000	3,626,000	1,279,000	256,000
	1996	15	2	7,337,000	4,792,000	-391,000	185,000
	1997	10	2	7,622,000	4,900,000	-209,000	1,125,000
Blackburn Rovers	1929	7	1	38,732	17,730		6,048
	1930	6	1	39,231	20,895		-4,969
	1931	10	1	25,277	14,357		-2,978
	1933	15	1	18,770	9,301		-2,003
	1934	8	1	18,880	8,124		1,376
	1935	15	1	33,452	23,596		-12,428
	1936	22	1	23,313	13,737		-2,579
	1937	12	2	17,099	7,330		1,203
	1938	16	2	23,625	12,109	3,233	-5,256
	1939	1	2	29,155	12,651	2,357	7,075
	1948	21	1	52,642	18,930	13,220	4,071
	1949	14	2	47,461	23,613	6,900	-2,228
	1950	16	2	56,578	23,876	-9,275	10,713
	1951	6	2	62,436	24,897	9,988	-13,469
	1952	14	2	64,691	27,825	17,575	-3,316
	1953	9	2	52,505	27,087	-900	4,413
	1954	3	2	59,388	26,000	1,088	11,959
	1955	6	2	64,709	28,294	-3,075	8,829
	1956	4	2	57,322	27,697	-1,175	3,383
	1957	4	2	70,792	29,603	11,825	-16,907
	1958	2	2	79,577	35,059	19,000	1,300
	1959	10	1	111,345	41,958	-4,750	31,091
	1960	17	1	123,836	45,144	-1,940	27,137
	1961	8	1	91,900	48,442	-3,925	10,272
	1962	16	1	98,125	49,823	-14,450	11,870
	1963	11	1	64,828	51,650	-3,400	-12,119
	1964	7	1	95,307	53,911	-2,850	8,442
	1965	10	1	106,166	53,263	-31,950	17,127
	1966	22	1	104,753	58,921	8,600	-18,337
	1967	4	2	106,978	66,661	-19,920	-7,316
	1968	8	2	163,736	67,954	53,395	-84,990
	1969	19	2	162,259	74,709	-71,837	26,364
	1970	8	2	165,612	79,713	38,690	78,186
	1971	21	2	77,391	79,059	15,945	-51,178
	1972	10	3	155,588	87,939	-77,746	34,959
	1973	3	3	98,883	104,217	59,469	-111,135
	1974	13	3	100,000	105,000	-100,000	47,000
	1975	1	3	142,000	110,000	69,000	-110,000
	1976	15	2	195,000	161,000	-2,000	-61,000
	1977	12	2	234,000	173,000	-2,000	-46,000
	1978	5	2	290,000	187,000	-94,000	111,000
	1979	22	2	279,000	223,000	-141,000	108,000

Club	Year	League position	Division	Revenue (£)	Wages (£)	Net transfers (£)	Pre-tax profits (£)
Blackburn Rovers	1980	2	3	373,000	376,000	−81,000	−82,000
(cont'd)	1981	4	2	590,000	525,000	−194,000	8,000
	1982	10	2	462,000	455,000	−44,000	−264,000
	1983	11	2	537,000	401,000	9,000	−12,000
	1984	6	2	607,000	407,000	−10,000	48,000
	1985	5	2	653,000	446,000	14,000	106,000
	1986	19	2	521,000	457,000	−30,000	−78,000
	1987	12	2	702,000	556,000	0	−6,000
	1988	5	2	919,000	682,000	−145,000	185,000
	1989	5	2	1,230,000	857,000	−277,000	347,000
	1990	5	2	1,161,000	1,084,000	−390,000	106,000
	1991	19	2	1,339,000	1,798,000	709,000	−440,000
	1992	6	2	2,067,000	3,746,000	6,839,000	−7,929,000
	1993	4	1	6,305,000	5,168,000	6,248,000	−6,366,000
	1994	2	1	7,825,365	6,034,733	7,292,000	−8,208,805
	1995	1	1	14,068,000	9,212,000	4,559,000	−3,954,000
	1996	7	1	16,325,000	10,844,000	8,170,000	−9,056,000
	1997	13	1	14,302,000	14,337,000	−8,533,000	8,093,000
Blackpool	1928	19	2	26,400	9,590	9,075	−7,664
	1930	1	2	23,546	8,851	2,245	2,616
	1931	20	1	29,294	11,930	8,724	−1,863
	1932	20	1	27,130	11,043	6,612	392
	1933	22	1	26,632	11,718	1,245	3,850
	1934	11	2	39,015	10,644	17,340	−15,124
	1935	4	2	26,034	10,776	2,752	−1,819
	1936	10	2	32,605	10,551	−11,760	11,406
	1937	2	2	30,008	11,102	7,833	−2,107
	1938	12	1	37,971	13,122	12,895	−4,517
	1939	15	1	38,045	13,514	11,433	−7,947
Bolton Wanderers	1930	15	1	37,676	14,093	5,523	2,059
	1948	17	1		18,720	13,404	5,614
	1949	14	1	73,651	21,976	11,619	6,273
	1950	16	1	73,583	22,937	23,979	−2,374
	1951	8	1	69,646	25,590	11,879	2,829
	1952	5	1	89,312	26,570	26,449	−6,434
	1953	14	1	75,400	30,292	793	7,598
	1954	5	1	98,934	29,723	−3,984	21,999
	1955	18	1	76,913	29,756	1,065	−2,047
	1956	8	1	81,376	30,227	−844	−4,912
	1957	9	1	80,464	30,685	−11,910	4,561
	1958	15	1	123,664	47,723	−6,313	5,593
	1959	4	1	102,582	40,862	131	12,213
	1960	6	1	90,298	40,986	1,215	4,185
	1961	18	1	103,644	43,835	11,826	−7,240
	1962	11	1	97,733	46,657	−16,669	4,341
	1963	18	1	98,194	52,821	−7,569	−7,352
	1964	21	1	109,615	56,223	14,991	−27,935
	1965	3	2	101,449	60,867	−2,455	−27,990
	1966	9	2	97,614	56,270	−1,012	−22,493
	1967	9	2	110,184	61,022	−30,776	7,484
	1968	12	2	130,414	67,098	19,158	49,066
	1969	17	2	123,407	72,326	−15,728	−27,606
	1970	16	2	127,005	78,054	−11,251	−28,290

Data Appendix / 345

Club	Year	League position	Division	Revenue (£)	Wages (£)	Net transfers (£)	Pre-tax profits (£)
Bolton Wanderers	1971	22	2	161,079	86,716	−75,270	25,809
(cont'd)	1972	7	3	161,345	110,718	−2,017	−51,640
	1973	1	3	176,304	107,382	−3,279	11,627
	1974	11	2	215,000	123,000	19,000	−27,000
	1975	10	2	191,000	146,000	−60,000	5,000
	1976	4	2	347,000	176,000	−6,000	24,000
	1977	4	2	467,000	233,000	−4,000	−13,000
	1978	1	2	562,000	352,000	149,000	−219,000
	1979	17	1	813,000	431,000	742,000	−675,000
	1980	22	1	803,000	617,000	−424,000	142,000
	1981	18	2	527,000	661,000	105,000	−653,000
	1982	19	2	665,000	687,000	−251,000	−310,000
	1983	22	2	680,000	562,000	−2,000	320,000
	1984	10	3	548,000	480,000	16,000	−366,000
	1985	17	3	588,000	408,000	−97,000	−233,000
	1986	18	3	728,000	465,000	33,000	−359,000
	1987	21	3	704,000	483,000	−12,000	−401,000
	1988	2	4	746,000	587,000	38,000	−610,000
	1989	10	3	1,048,000	592,000	50,000	319,000
	1990	6	3	1,264,000	642,000	111,000	−315,000
	1991	4	3	1,687,000	871,000	287,000	432,000
	1992	13	3	1,892,000	981,000	96,000	−717,000
	1993	2	3	2,629,000	1,254,000	160,000	−434,000
	1994	14	2	4,917,000	1,832,706	329,681	−129,539
	1995	3	2	5,488,000	2,647,000	851,000	−536,000
	1996	20	1	6,742,000	3,312,000	−553,000	−164,000
	1997	1	2	7,653,000	6,159,000	1,587,000	−3,293,000
Bradford City	1909	18	1	13,005	5,945	2,545	2,560
	1910	7	1	11,195	4,780	1,425	1,535
	1911	5	1	15,235	4,680	1,100	6,100
	1912	11	1	12,425	6,460	100	1,320
	1913	13	1	9,210	6,980	−2,835	−1,625
	1914	9	1	10,680	6,985	−960	−580
	1915	10	1	8,955	5,925	2,675	−1,060
Bradford Park Avenue	1912	11	1	7,810	4,580	3,115	1,150
	1913	13	1	6,925	4,410	−820	405
	1914	2	1	9,505	4,485	1,150	2,210
	1915	9	1	7,550	4,835	3,080	375
Brentford	1930	18	2	18,815	10,076	−1,025	1,827
	1947	21	1	62,132	17,515	910	8,260
	1948	15	2	69,522	20,155	200	3,070
	1949	18	2	84,628	29,806	−8,013	4,395
	1950	9	2	54,646	24,731	2,125	−3,001
	1951	9	2	53,929	27,658	−10,950	1,059
	1952	10	2	62,422	28,605	3,200	−3,830
	1953	17	2	61,811	25,192	−13,350	11,746
	1954	21	2	43,740	25,329	−1,862	−2,266
	1955	11	3	53,855	22,819	−16,600	12,221
	1956	6	3	40,858	23,446	1,600	−3,750
	1957	8	3	40,371	21,634	2,400	−4,897
	1958	2	3	45,805	25,944	−900	5,481
	1959	3	3	51,322	27,789	5,450	612
	1960	6	3	47,291	29,295	1,140	−3,758

Club	Year	League position	Division	Revenue (£)	Wages (£)	Net transfers (£)	Pre-tax profits (£)
Brentford (cont'd)	1961	17	3	53,352	27,131	−14,450	7,645
	1962	23	3	58,724	24,815	19,200	−11,125
	1963	1	4	86,626	33,065	35,300	−35,316
	1964	16	3	92,542	41,182	29,265	−26,576
	1965	5	3	101,138	48,372	29,150	−30,408
	1966	23	3	76,230	44,406	9,750	−16,557
	1967	9	4	65,495	45,710	250	−9,218
	1968	14	4	59,215	32,702	−3,607	10,499
	1969	11	4	62,305	34,254	3,288	6,670
	1970	5	4	64,935	40,470	3,275	2,500
	1971	14	4	75,743	37,739	3,101	13,815
	1972	3	4	109,149	51,790	−608	22,711
	1973	22	3	105,316	55,280	4,312	15,819
	1974	19	4	91,000	58,000	−19,000	−2,000
	1975	8	4	104,000	64,000	10,000	−11,000
	1976	18	4	138,000	72,000	24,000	−1,000
	1977	15	4	131,000	83,000	−4,000	6,000
	1978	4	4	232,000	125,000	−12,000	75,000
	1979	10	3	242,000	178,000	50,000	−45,000
	1980	19	3	317,000	241,000	−4,000	−17,000
	1981	9	3	375,000	292,000	30,000	−68,000
	1982	8	3	420,000	363,000	103,000	−248,000
	1983	9	3	511,000	356,000	36,000	−132,000
	1984	20	3	577,000	419,000	1,000	−89,000
	1985	13	3	652,000	477,000	66,000	−293,000
	1986	10	3	955,000	481,000	−43,000	−6,000
	1987	11	3	1,569,000	452,000	75,000	270,000
	1988	11	3	1,021,000	475,000	23,000	38,000
	1989	7	3	1,105,000	589,000	−157,000	135,000
	1990	13	3	834,000	546,000	292,000	−351,000
	1991	6	3	1,047,000	760,000	35,000	−44,000
	1992	1	3	1,231,000	945,000	165,000	47,000
	1993	22	2	1,838,000	1,286,000	8,000	60,000
	1994	16	3	1,202,681	1,115,600	−694,400	137,774
	1995	2	3	1,379,000	1,037,000	144,000	−396,000
	1996	15	3	1,301,000	976,000	−358,000	114,000
	1997	4	3	1,921,000	1,016,000	−531,000	960,000
Bristol City	1910	16	1	6,964	4,067	−50	−78
Bristol Rovers	1931	15	3	11,534	7,067	−456	−594
	1933	9	3	16,542	7,446	−3,084	3,369
	1934	7	3	15,312	8,336	1,496	−577
	1935	8	3	14,048	8,364	450	−119
	1936	17	3	15,031	8,393	−697	−741
	1937	15	3	14,643	8,768	555	−589
	1938	15	3	15,283	7,950	1,804	−3,746
	1939	2	3	12,283	7,223	−150	−1,170
	1948	20	3	26,769	13,329		3,285
	1949	5	3	43,897	15,284		−567
	1950	9	3	43,377	14,398	850	1,783
	1951	6	3	61,202	22,187	−3,500	629
	1952	7	3	58,748	24,474	425	−1,120
	1953	1	3	75,025	27,494	2,446	−401
	1954	9	2	78,595	29,136	−900	7,017

Data Appendix / 347

Club	Year	League position	Division	Revenue (£)	Wages (£)	Net transfers (£)	Pre-tax profits (£)
Bristol Rovers (cont'd)	1955	9	2	80,513	29,504	−400	5,737
	1956	6	2	86,447	31,168		6,462
	1957	9	2	80,478	35,981	−1,875	2,297
	1958	10	2	80,681	39,051		1,270
	1959	6	2	79,592	35,424	−6,000	3,815
	1960	9	2	84,341	40,738	−1,300	1,445
	1961	17	2	76,864	39,178	2,750	−5,830
	1962	21	2	78,925	42,571	−9,620	−85
	1963	19	3	78,062	46,342	16,500	−41,435
	1964	12	3	73,885	40,762		−8,849
	1965	6	3	93,891	51,169	−4,500	−3,898
	1966	16	3	82,362	47,846	−400	−25,726
	1967	5	3	87,861	44,376	−8,000	232
	1968	15	3		51,487	−8,175	−2,608
	1969	16	3	90,292	38,550	−31,143	16,886
	1970	3	3	110,123	42,311	15,275	−17,277
	1971	6	3	121,879	58,493	−38,932	3,917
	1972	6	3	115,112	56,889	20,161	−8,024
	1973	5	3	190,338	77,031	−27,909	8,531
	1974	2	3	216,000	86,000	18,000	−35,000
	1975	19	2	189,000	95,000	−27,000	−17,000
	1976	18	2	210,000	105,000	0	−24,000
	1977	15	2	195,000	106,000	−34,000	6,000
	1978	18	2	410,000	119,000	−15,000	−5,000
	1979	16	2	313,000	149,000	−153,000	72,000
	1980	19	2	371,000	234,000	28,000	−308,000
	1981	22	2	638,000	319,000	96,000	−383,000
	1982	15	3	406,000	447,000	−111,000	−434,000
	1983	7	3	502,000	331,000	−122,000	−98,000
	1984	5	3	457,000	341,000	−92,000	−185,000
	1985	6	3	551,000	372,000	−125,000	−42,000
	1986	16	3	345,000	352,000	−140,000	−198,000
	1987	19	3	296,000	254,000	−57,000	2,000
	1988	7	3	417,000	279,000	−114,000	10,000
	1989	5	3	646,000	334,000	−57,000	46,000
	1990	1	3	1,137,000	636,000	−1,388,000	1,284,000
	1991	13	2	1,142,000	631,000	−55,000	155,000
	1992	11	2	1,335,000	1,107,000	−268,000	70,000
	1993	24	2	1,534,000	1,353,000	867,000	−1,219,000
	1994	8	3	1,400,851	1,311,240	−809,750	75,943
	1995	4	3	1,537,000	1,347,000	71,000	−774,000
	1996	10	3	1,397,000	1,170,000	−868,000	288,000
	1997	17	3	1,374,000	1,546,000	−1,041,000	3,000
Burnley	1926	20	1	21,863	9,160	35	3,537
	1927	5	1	24,758	11,100	4,163	291
	1928	18	1	20,857	12,006	1	14
	1930	21	1	21,543	12,102	−2,620	1,213
	1931	8	2	16,640	9,137	−199	−2,056
	1932	19	2	17,676	7,581	−7,447	3,413
	1933	19	2	16,521	7,797	1,940	−3,443
	1934	13	2	14,349	9,047	819	−857
	1935	12	2	17,637	8,901	2,651	−531
	1936	15	2	16,679	8,620	−3,917	3,007

Winners and Losers / 348

Club	Year	League position	Division	Revenue (£)	Wages (£)	Net transfers (£)	Pre-tax profits (£)
Burnley (cont'd)	1937	13	2	25,091	10,510	−7,237	8,554
	1947	2	2	53,977	13,987	−1,800	17,916
	1948	3	1	65,944	19,799	175	18,815
	1949	15	1	59,296	18,434	−975	15,098
	1950	10	1	71,134	20,732	−5,250	19,882
	1951	10	1	94,930	21,370	−32,975	18,398
	1952	14	1	83,404	22,646	18,760	−3,688
	1953	6	1	69,361	22,831	6,067	2,240
	1954	7	1	86,808	26,484	−9,700	12,622
	1955	10	1	68,835	27,931	4,050	−3,119
	1956	7	1	87,468	27,361	−19,000	8,512
	1957	7	1	79,326	30,844	−11,350	3,223
	1958	6	1	86,408	32,379	−9,550	5,091
	1959	7	1	97,397	36,835	−12,250	9,381
	1960	1	1	136,345	41,936	−28,970	13,654
	1961	4	1	146,099	64,718	−16,175	9,570
	1962	2	1	169,529	77,532	−26,479	23,775
	1963	3	1	186,420	99,057	−55,425	20,960
	1964	9	1	134,508	81,317	−24,900	3,991
	1965	12	1	152,190	79,836	−64,075	33,024
	1966	3	1	145,215	100,675	−43,120	1,966
	1967	14	1	175,663	116,242	−28,750	−1,543
	1968	14	1	173,783	123,263	−26,408	1,548
	1969	14	1	271,221	160,478	−120,858	42,389
	1970	14	1	266,467	172,902	−60,921	−46,069
	1971	21	1	265,558	172,770	−95,786	−27,137
	1972	7	2	256,603	171,375	−125,131	6,664
	1973	1	2	350,529	231,078	−173,781	−1,269
	1974	6	1	256,000	237,000	−918,000	−224,000
	1975	10	1	289,000	276,000	−259,000	−50,000
	1976	21	1	391,000	314,000	−116,000	−78,000
	1977	16	2	333,000	343,000	−224,000	−147,000
	1978	11	2	326,000	329,000	−27,000	−157,000
	1979	13	2	484,000	422,000	−23,000	−152,000
	1980	21	2	442,000	449,000	−287,000	0
	1981	8	3	377,000	444,000	0	−342,000
	1982	1	3	424,000	496,000	23,000	−182,000
	1983	21	2	742,000	487,000	87,000	−28,000
	1984	12	3	553,000	561,000	−4,000	324,000
	1985	21	3	513,000	519,000	1,000	344,000
	1986	14	4	418,000	436,000	−2,000	192,000
	1987	22	4	490,000	347,000	105,000	101,000
	1988	9	4	781,000	882,000	−55,000	135,000
	1989	16	4	779,000	492,000	−61,000	−2,000
	1990	16	4	1,001,000	520,000	−165,000	−174,000
	1991	6	4	1,355,000	685,000	94,000	19,000
	1992	1	4	1,923,000	808,000	159,000	240,000
	1993	13	3	2,417,000	989,000	342,000	226,000
	1994	6	3	2,967,083	1,249,256	688,000	119,915
	1995	22	2	3,441,000	1,341,000	1,011,000	−298,000
	1996	17	3	2,351,000	1,314,000	−398,000	563,000
	1997	9	3	3,701,000	1,675,000	884,000	−789,000
Bury	1908	7	1	8,669	4,135	550	1,095

Club	Year	League position	Division	Revenue (£)	Wages (£)	Net transfers (£)	Pre-tax profits (£)
Bury (cont'd)	1947	17	2	31,637	10,579	−240	1,545
	1948	20	2	38,287	14,405	1,020	385
	1949	12	2	51,039	15,450	−13,750	10,149
	1950	18	2	55,219	15,515	−14,600	7,879
	1951	20	2	51,885	16,647	10,285	−14,291
	1952	17	2	43,069	15,872	1,960	−4,022
	1953	20	2	45,982	15,675	−4,750	−1,536
	1954	17	2	52,847	20,290	−840	−2,325
	1955	13	2	44,318	19,605	3,325	−5,070
	1956	15	2	40,399	18,277	−3,385	753
	1957	21	2	42,275	18,283	1,725	−7,550
	1958	4	3	47,723	22,566	1,000	−2,178
	1959	10	3	54,259	24,715	−7,423	4,831
	1960	7	3	71,774	25,366	19,875	−23,585
	1961	1	3	81,825	22,910	−32,600	34,856
	1962	18	2	69,372	26,005	14,830	−5,429
	1963	8	2	71,174	30,338	10,957	−7,335
	1964	18	2	77,549	31,892	−30,695	13,325
	1965	16	2	68,749	46,177	−17,730	5,969
	1966	19	2	74,910	46,520	−18,783	4,564
	1967	22	2	110,770	54,552	32,139	−41,222
	1968	2	3	113,873	71,638	−34,500	20,630
	1969	21	2	86,529	62,613	−54,818	39,726
	1970	19	3	90,616	68,433	5,914	−47,443
	1971	22	3	93,103	65,354	−38,765	−558
	1972	9	4	83,400	64,734	−10,153	−20,804
	1973	12	4	69,883	62,574	−19,972	3,931
	1974	4	4	85,000	61,000	17,000	12,000
	1975	14	3	117,000	85,000	−20,000	12,000
	1976	13	3	150,000	104,000	0	−30,000
	1977	7	3	147,000	116,000	−33,000	13,000
	1978	15	3	201,000	132,000	−64,000	42,000
	1979	19	3	186,000	154,000	−40,000	−1,000
	1980	21	3	289,000	264,000	−72,000	21,000
	1981	12	4	225,000	292,000	−99,000	−40,000
	1982	9	4	262,000	290,000	−168,000	65,000
	1983	5	4	286,000	265,000	1,000	−89,000
	1984	15	4	219,000	261,000	−93,000	−40,000
	1985	4	4	320,000	305,000	−1,000	−116,000
	1986	20	3	343,000	332,000	−62,000	−93,000
	1987	16	3	364,000	391,000	−11,000	−174,000
	1988	13	3	412,000	417,000	−2,000	187,000
	1989	13	3	397,000	459,000	−72,000	−147,000
	1990	5	3	802,000	648,500	−80,000	−404,000
	1991	7	3	1,207,000	838,000	430,000	−661,000
	1992	21	3	1,404,000	716,000	0	147,000
	1993	7	4	1,178,000	534,000	10,000	123,000
	1994	13	4	1,348,350	663,419	−72,835	−70,785
	1995	4	4	1,326,000	840,000	187,000	−331,000
	1996	3	4	1,095,000	1,084,000	122,000	−922,000
	1997	1	3	1,889,000	1,348,000	533,000	−851,000
Cambridge	1974	21	3	131,000	86,000	0	−15,000
	1975	6	4	113,000	78,000	−5,000	−29,000

Club	Year	League position	Division	Revenue (£)	Wages (£)	Net transfers (£)	Pre-tax profits (£)
Cambridge (cont'd)	1976	13	4	135,000	83,000	2,000	−18,000
	1977	1	4	187,000	112,000	4,000	−7,000
	1978	2	3	253,000	139,000	18,000	−15,000
	1979	12	2	414,000	173,000	47,000	54,000
	1980	8	2	473,000	261,000	−147,000	177,000
	1981	13	2	528,000	255,000	78,000	−45,000
	1982	14	2	394,000	275,000	70,000	−199,000
	1983	12	2	456,000	294,000	−3,000	−57,000
	1984	22	2	459,000	294,000	−101,000	36,000
	1985	24	3	351,600	322,000	−26,000	1,000
	1986	22	4	402,000	338,000	−36,000	−1,000
	1987	11	4	547,000	325,000	−24,000	2,000
	1988	14	4	448,000	351,000	33,000	43,000
	1989	8	4	515,000	377,000	−62,000	−98,000
	1990	6	4	873,000	419,000	58,000	−76,000
	1991	1	3	1,072,000	753,000	111,000	−343,000
	1992	5	2	1,601,000	1011,000	288,000	−494,000
	1993	23	2	3,083,000	1259,000	−1,142,000	557,000
	1994	10	3	1,841,807	1121,586	−776,732	84,877
	1995	20	3	937,000	884,000	−439,000	15,000
	1996	16	4	591,000	807,000	−734,000	166,000
	1997	10	4	784,000	842,000	−380,000	−107,000
Chelsea	1930	2	2	37,731	18,701		1,939
	1931	12	1	58,410	37,130		−3,430
	1932	12	1	47,797	20,937		3,754
	1933	18	1	44,036	20,639		−2,970
	1934	19	1	43,692	25,668		92
Coventry	1929	11	3	16,593	8,578	565	1,278
	1930	6	3	15,797	8,712	760	−628
	1932	12	3	15,631	7,500	1,425	485
	1933	6	3	14,532	9,647	325	509
	1934	2	3	17,236	7,978	2,050	1,110
	1935	3	3	16,674	8,589	955	1,238
	1936	1	3	28,367	12,966	6,305	3,462
	1937	8	2	29,560	14,257	3,670	4,705
	1938	4	2	29,833	15,903	−1,620	6,586
	1939	4	2	17,843	10,418	2,215	1,977
	1947	8	2	48,632	19,203	15,850	−7,330
	1948	10	2	49,499	23,358	2,360	9,402
	1949	16	2	64,260	24,999	22,666	−13,643
	1950	12	2	66,661	25,614	26,250	−7,196
	1951	7	2	62,249	26,353	−11,180	19,988
	1952	21	2	53,985	26,409	−7,000	14,182
	1953	6	3	37,849	25,050	−2,950	−386
	1955	9	3	43,110	37,992	−6,200	−2,756
	1956	8	3	40,416	26,074	3,190	−1,921
	1957	16	3	55,661	28,486	−14,820	6,563
	1958	19	3	54,711	26,438	−9,205	9,462
	1959	2	4	58,025	33,304	7,550	−4,215
	1960	4	3	64,852	33,928	9,910	−3,810
	1961	15	3	57,850	32,223	8,950	−8,512
	1962	14	3	63,863	38,250	−2,750	−10,761
	1963	4	3	84,080	44,639	28,150	−2,252

Club	Year	League position	Division	Revenue (£)	Wages (£)	Net transfers (£)	Pre-tax profits (£)
Coventry (cont'd)	1964	1	3	126,858	59,828	4,875	14,715
	1965	10	2	160,308	84,213	40,400	9,158
	1966	3	2	164,652	93,824	−23,650	3,023
	1967	1	2	184,359	119,069	29,955	−4,923
	1968	20	1	274,535	167,435	178,940	13,106
	1969	20	1	229,183	139,467	−144	45,157
	1970	6	1	268,439	162,025	17,339	−2,633
	1971	10	1	320,318	183,939	12,260	7,727
	1972	18	1	290,596	223,794	26,149	−64,481
	1973	19	1	365,233	233,775	24,333	−9,223
	1974	16	1	406,000	258,000	116,000	−26,000
	1975	14	1	337,000	270,000	−63,000	11,000
	1976	14	1	446,000	300,000	−133,000	159,000
	1977	19	1	536,000	325,000	6,000	96,000
	1978	7	1	736,000	423,000	109,000	−21,000
	1979	10	1	746,000	540,000	100,000	−52,000
	1980	15	1	832,000	667,000	−557,000	297,000
	1981	16	1	1,272,000	894,000	−1,175,000	331,000
	1982	14	1	1,340,000	1,089,000	−385,000	−161,000
	1983	19	1	1,129,000	921,000	−388,000	−133,000
	1984	19	1	1,239,000	928,000	−273,000	−125,000
	1985	18	1	1,315,000	883,000	241,000	−442,000
	1986	17	1	1,191,000	992,000	36,000	−1,309,000
	1987	10	1	2,339,000	1,128,000	117,000	375,000
	1988	10	1	2,315,000	1,325,000	1,053,000	−627,000
	1989	7	1	2,341,000	1,550,000	−734,000	770,000
	1990	12	1	3,433,000	1,886,000	500,000	−382,000
	1991	16	1	3,605,000	2,653,000	27,000	−745,000
	1992	19	1	3,443,000	3,175,000	−20,000	−1,668,000
	1993	15	1	4,592,000	2,989,000	−96,000	−364,000
	1994	11	1	5,177,413	3,595,933	787,077	−1,337,080
	1995	16	1	7,189,000	4,065,000	1,149,000	−618,000
	1996	16	1	8,965,000	5,783,000	7,802,000	−8,545,000
	1997	17	1	12,265,000	8,396,000	8,859,000	−10,451,000
Crystal Palace	1922	14	2	27,680	9,993	2,682	−1,633
	1923	16	2	20,001	9,088	702	−1,110
	1924	15	2	20,543	7,799	212	−4
	1925	21	2	25,047	7,916	260	3,543
	1926	13	3	28,329	8,285	1,420	3,321
	1927	6	3	22,337	7,707	564	1,327
	1928	5	3	21,364	8,136	−337	451
	1929	2	3	23,118	10,003	4,956	2,391
	1930	9	3	18,249	8,800	1,744	863
	1931	2	3	20,605	9,456	666	3,612
	1932	4	3	20,062	8,948	1,355	2,598
	1933	5	3	17,099	9,887	302	−2,389
	1934	12	3	21,222	9,026	5,208	−4,070
	1935	5	3	18,706	9,533	1,277	−1,721
	1936	6	3	19,954	9,517	4,155	−3,052
	1937	14	3	19,117	8,638	3,728	−2,993
	1938	7	3	21,583	9,262	4,874	−2,050
	1939	2	3	20,929	9,965	3,504	−1,828
Derby	1907	19	1	5,434	3,339	294	−632

Club	Year	League position	Division	Revenue (£)	Wages (£)	Net transfers (£)	Pre-tax profits (£)
Derby (cont'd)	1908	6	2	5,657	3,511	861	−874
	1909	5	2	7,094	3,776	−642	778
	1910	4	2	6,659	3,728	1,166	−729
	1911	6	2	7,600	3,929	175	−2
	1912	1	2	9,084	4,031	352	−122
	1913	7	1	8,712	4,366	728	−750
	1914	20	1	9,740	3,982	1,151	−2,043
	1915	1	2	6,812	3,838	−2,687	501
	1947	14	1	42,230	19,487	−10,625	303
	1948	4	1	73,983	29,683	−10,390	1,983
	1949	3	1	86,682	28,317	16,590	1,025
	1950	11	1	83,713	30,366	11,410	253
	1951	11	1	77,141	28,185	−5,700	7,892
	1952	17	1	79,234	27,684	−10,524	11,906
	1953	22	1	76,463	31,260	−9,205	4,179
	1954	18	2	68,563	27,268	3,680	−14,366
	1955	22	2	76,452	21,848	22,835	−29,311
	1956	2	3	58,158	21,376	5,840	−3,852
	1957	1	3	57,196	19,386	7,320	4,200
	1958	16	2	72,807	24,015	3,850	7,544
	1959	7	2	81,666	32,466	8,550	−9,572
	1960	18	2	71,546	30,067	4,815	−6,904
	1961	12	2	64,981	30,689	−25	−2,161
	1962	16	2	74,519	33,715	1,000	1,408
	1963	18	2	74,992	34,242	23,050	−26,527
	1964	13	2	75,166	35,408	5,950	−3,033
	1965	9	2	85,336	39,945	7,700	−2,292
	1966	8	2	91,566	43,872	−2,000	9,875
	1967	17	2	130,659	41,631	34,000	−15,341
	1968	18	2	172,728	51,445	61,100	−1,980
	1969	1	2	194,732	111,800	75,232	−52,517
	1970	4	1	314,981	136,642	104,592	−43,323
	1971	9	1	345,386	129,330	170,390	−74,481
	1972	1	1	462,506	233,190	23,995	27,033
	1973	7	1	657,691	223,921	105,721	203,860
	1974	3	1	485,454	244,235	310,009	−4,357
	1975	1	1	562,486	292,879	52,783	−49,320
	1976	4	1	855,335	334,351	243,418	−1,129
	1977	15	1	1,297,979	nr	173,732	38,679
	1978	12	1	1,580,000	nr	469,000	−352,000
	1979	19	1	1,921,000	nr	−82,000	218,000
	1980	20	1	1,875,000	nr	830,000	−963,000
	1981	6	2	1,871,000	605,000	−513,000	127,000
	1982	16	2	1,299,000	551,000	−229,000	−124,000
	1983	13	2	861,000	566,000	155,000	−364,000
	1984	20	2	961,000	527,000	146,000	−196,000
	1985	7	3	923,000	479,000	178,000	−303,000
	1986	3	3	1,378,000	751,000	324,000	−275,000
	1987	1	2	1,714,000	911,000	399,000	−350,000
	1988	15	1	2,621,000	1,107,000	824,000	−361,000
	1989	5	1	2,912,000	1,551,000	1,317,000	−1,122,000
	1990	16	1	3,431,000	2,029,000	−502,000	520,000
	1991	20	1	3,760,000	2,475,000	1,026,000	249,000

Data Appendix / 353

Club	Year	League position	Division	Revenue (£)	Wages (£)	Net transfers (£)	Pre-tax profits (£)
Derby (cont'd)	1992	3	2	2,852,000	2,620,000	3,427,000	2,177,000
	1993	8	2	4,183,000	3,115,000	−650,000	−1,167,000
	1994	6	2	3,620,000	3,453,000	−114,000	−2,953,000
	1995	9	2	3,329,000	3,351,000	−1,200,000	11,000
	1996	2	2	4,516,000	4,256,000	−1,797,000	−2,038,000
	1997	12	1	10,738,000	4,256,000	2,892,000	−3,549,000
Everton	1926	11	1	46,392	9,882		9,064
	1927	20	1	55,424	27,690		−3,122
	1929	18	1	52,510	12,872		9,406
	1930	22	1	52,531	35,574		−12,560
	1931	1	2	50,950	10,658		9,755
	1932	1	1	59,305	13,457		10,166
	1933	11	1	59,718	16,435		2,172
	1934	14	1	45,577	16,435		−2,401
	1935	8	1	61,899	10,949		5,353
	1936	16	1	47,141	20,407		−8,813
	1937	17	1	55,367	15,352		3,332
	1938	14	1	52,648	15,552		−828
	1939	1	1	67,987	12,206		10,121
	1948	14	1	77,236	17,137	3,241	25,780
	1949	18	1	80,495	22,554	24,050	−2,351
	1950	18	1	77,512	23,651	1,600	11,472
	1951	22	1	86,070	30,826	12,635	−9,967
	1952	7	2	78,769	25,424	−4,000	8,655
	1953	16	2	72,859	27,654	−469	−2,926
	1954	2	2	151,561	24,742	−12,550	21,374
	1955	11	1	152,909	25,628	−550	14,982
	1956	15	1	164,369	24,594	−14,575	7,593
	1957	15	1	151,472	26,465	965	−20,401
	1958	16	1	182,100	24,474	−13,450	35,122
	1959	16	1	188,122	27,033	35,350	−16,712
	1960	16	1	214,121	31,358	84,160	−49,504
	1961	5	1	215,549	28,159	53,300	25,054
	1962	4	1	265,123	44,336	40,470	12,651
	1963	1	1	313,165	67,054	84,970	19,659
	1964	3	1	309,133	79,418	51,725	15,912
	1965	4	1	267,594	76,687	33,925	13,331
	1966	11	1	313,304	71,895	−32,000	22,773
	1967	6	1	398,291	103,750	178,250	−44,952
	1968	5	1	386,782	108,231	−78,250	25,541
	1969	3	1	463,052	102,177	−38,000	56,967
	1970	1	1	399,455	149,162	80,000	30,611
	1971	14	1	555,440	177,687	129,000	25,562
	1972	15	1	494,587	226,368	87,820	13,396
	1973	17	1	490,443	250,682	91,600	−21,755
	1974	7	1	499,000	287,000	−24,000	29,000
	1975	4	1	628,000	343,000	57,000	8,000
	1976	11	1	659,000	386,000	50,000	−49,000
	1977	9	1	1,097,000	543,000	359,000	−114,000
	1978	3	1	1,291,000	679,000	292,000	0
	1979	4	1	1,631,000	796,000	382,000	3,000
	1980	19	1	1,904,000	965,000	624,000	31,000
	1981	15	1	1,885,000	1,140,000	343,000	64,000

Club	Year	League position	Division	Revenue (£)	Wages (£)	Net transfers (£)	Pre-tax profits (£)
Everton (cont'd)	1982	8	1	1,722,000	1,193,000	89,000	-100,000
	1983	7	1	2,186,000	1,187,000	-200,000	92,000
	1984	7	1	2,959,000	1,344,000	907,000	-503,000
	1985	1	1	4,693,000	1,709,000	657,000	720,000
	1986	2	1	4,152,000	1,931,000	714,000	13,000
	1987	1	1	4,316,000	2,263,000	-6,000	454,000
	1988	4	1	5,108,000	2,240,000	-868,000	1,594,000
	1989	8	1	5,799,000	3,161,000	2,200,000	-1,847,000
	1990	6	1	5,929,000	3,209,000	498,000	-217,000
	1991	9	1	7,057,000	3,973,000	1,743,000	-1,179,000
	1992	12	1	6,813,000	4,970,000	1,091,000	-2,124,000
	1993	13	1	7,994,000	4,519,000	-707,000	957,000
	1994	17	1	8,858,407	5,176,211	1,228,212	-450,626
	1995	15	1	13,546,000	7,431,000	10,377,000	-9,373,000
	1996	6	1	17,004,000	10,065,000	8,403,000	-7,962,000
	1997	15	1	18,882,000	10,933,000	5,549,000	-2,890,000
Exeter	1922	21	3	14,991	7,712	-3,745	1,136
	1923	20	3	13,059	7,160	632	-2,257
	1924	16	3	13,231	7,704	50	-2,199
	1925	7	3	11,880	7,223	0	-278
	1926	20	3	11,594	6,943	-1,050	13
	1927	12	3	14,575	7,935	-1,775	567
	1928	8	3	14,555	8,553	100	-226
	1929	21	3	12,532	7,268	500	-1,221
	1930	16	3	13,667	7,550	802	921
	1931	13	3	15,768	7,876	-855	1,556
	1932	7	3	12,889	7,522	578	-2,365
	1933	2	3	13,941	7,391	-100	-1,680
	1934	9	3	12,372	7,201	-300	-1,806
	1935	11	3	11,480	7,004	-125	-2,620
	1936	22	3	12,275	6,859	-695	-3,322
	1937	21	3	12,759	7,137	-250	-1,780
	1938	17	3	12,490	7,218	-1,850	-1,410
Fulham	1930	7	3	22,323	12,797	275	-2,770
	1931	9	3	19,117	11,634	175	-4,340
	1932	1	3	23,718	12,149	3,325	-1,845
	1938	8	2	21,847	14,586	-750	-37
Grimsby	1930	18	1	26,337	8,116	1,630	2,612
	1931	13	1	33,743	8,583	-4,848	9,964
	1932	21	1	30,700	9,188	885	-93
	1933	12	2	19,790	8,235	355	-3,922
	1934	1	2	19,613	7,764	-670	671
	1935	5	1	23,685	10,002	728	244
	1936	17	1	28,883	10,079	-480	-2,894
	1937	12	1	29,507	8,894	-4,920	5,960
	1938	20	1	25,489	10,316	1,883	-3,574
	1939	10	1	38,267	9,413	-5,654	6,748
Huddersfield	1974	10	3	117,000	144,000	-66,000	-44,000
	1975	24	3	145,000	139,000	-54,000	-20,000
	1976	5	4	183,000	133,000	-43,000	1,000
	1977	9	4	214,000	139,000	9,000	33,000
	1978	11	4	219,000	149,000	-22,000	35,000
	1979	9	4	221,000	183,000	-8,000	79,000

Data Appendix / 355

Club	Year	League position	Division	Revenue (£)	Wages (£)	Net transfers (£)	Pre-tax profits (£)
Huddersfield (cont'd)	1980	1	4	386,000	269,000	−31,000	39,000
	1981	4	3	655,000	345,000	168,000	129,000
	1982	17	3	362,000	395,000	−32,000	131,000
	1983	3	3	532,000	450,000	−130,000	8,000
	1984	12	2	681,000	466,000	−115,000	30,000
	1985	13	2	523,000	472,000	−223,000	−34,000
	1986	16	2	497,000	538,000	−65,000	74,000
	1987	17	2	600,000	557,000	34,000	−215,000
	1988	23	2	683,000	707,000	−487,000	220,000
	1989	14	3	636,000	680,000	41,000	−372,000
	1990	8	3	808,000	709,000	−85,000	−163,000
	1991	11	3	739,000	810,000	−70,000	−437,000
	1992	3	3	1,240,000	1,070,000	−15,000	−365,000
	1993	15	3	1,269,000	1,139,000	−295,000	−9,000
	1994	11	3	2,406,773	1,111,290	−227,722	373,001
	1995	5	3	3,264,000	1,606,000	457,000	−300,000
	1996	8	2	3,430,000	1,870,000	748,000	−513,000
	1997	20	2	3,745,000	2,251,000	405,000	−166,000
Hull City	1947	11	3	53,191	18,835	−2,165	6,656
	1948	5	3	65,947	20,531	12,260	−2,897
	1949	1	3	107,004	23,762	15,825	20,086
	1950	7	2	123,793	31,205	23,200	7,384
	1951	10	2	124,259	29,021	5,801	11,924
	1952	18	2	117,309	37,106	−9,694	15,679
	1953	18	2	93,795	33,293	2,650	−5,037
	1954	15	2	105,223	32,093	−9,528	9,305
	1955	19	2	75,183	29,634	−225	−1,894
	1956	22	2	68,603	29,362	4,800	−12,587
	1957	8	3	42,206	16,290	2,125	−3,524
	1958	5	3	58,961	29,676	−350	−6,794
	1959	2	3	64,402	31,060	−8,420	2,366
	1960	21	2	74,593	34,382	9,050	−14,289
	1961	11	3	62,432	31,858	−2,750	41
	1962	10	3	56,030	26,099	3,450	−6,068
	1963	10	3	62,446	31,562	150	−4,138
	1964	8	3	129,620	41,074	36,100	−58,951
	1965	4	3	237,203	53,760	130,000	−150,581
	1966	1	3	190,223	63,360	−8,000	30,218
	1967	12	2	219,025	74,964	−1,000	52,082
	1968	17	2	177,073	79,536	8,000	4,260
	1969	11	2	144,148	72,627	−3,000	−6,415
	1970	13	2	175,514	75,736	−16,500	30,032
	1971	5	2	354,522	100,828	104,504	−53,942
	1972	12	2	336,725	107,861	−46,207	53,958
	1973	13	2	227,545	110,001	−5,528	−15,381
	1974	9	2	210,000	106,000	66,000	−70,000
	1975	8	2	195,000	120,000	−13,000	−9,000
	1976	14	2	226,000	134,000	−79,000	43,000
	1977	14	2	245,000	215,000	33,000	−134,000
	1978	22	2	325,000	240,000	31,000	−89,000
	1979	8	3	153,000	276,000	−173,000	66,000
	1980	20	3	185,000	269,000	−14,000	−146,000
	1981	24	3	111,000	261,000	−95,000	−308,000

Club	Year	League position	Division	Revenue (£)	Wages (£)	Net transfers (£)	Pre-tax profits (£)
Hull City (cont'd)	1982	8	4	134,000	301,000	0	−355,000
	1983	2	4	345,000	308,000	−31,000	10,000
	1984	4	3	474,000	254,000	−5,000	41,000
	1985	3	3	582,000	390,000	−37,000	92,000
	1986	6	2	534,000	451,000	194,000	7,000
	1987	14	2	624,000	445,000	−19,000	107,000
	1988	15	2	799,000	589,000	77,000	−30,000
	1989	21	2	864,000	739,000	−167,000	−14,000
	1990	14	2	800,000	821,000	45,000	482,000
	1991	24	2	1,021,000	1,338,000	−116,000	−756,000
	1992	14	3	744,000	1,032,000	−920,000	110,000
	1993	20	3	1,091,000	753,000	−200,000	1,000
	1994	9	3	1,067,796	868,451	−30,000	−250,436
	1995	8	3	1,095,000	861,000	−100,000	−176,000
	1996	24	3	941,000	1,036,000	−865,000	204,000
	1997	17	4	799,000	1,091,000	−350,000	−570,000
Leeds	1974	1	1	724,000	420,000	−9,000	50,000
	1975	9	1	1,247,000	629,000	234,000	−158,000
	1976	5	1	919,000	432,000	4,000	53,000
	1977	10	1	949,000	393,000	103,000	1,000
	1978	9	1	1,149,000	503,000	−40,000	291,000
	1979	5	1	1,139,000	718,000	672,000	−865,000
	1980	11	1	1,218,000	797,000	−293,000	30,000
	1981	9	1	1,076,000	941,000	−62,000	−433,000
	1982	20	1	1,090,000	907,000	1,010,000	−1,554,000
	1983	8	2	1,016,000	701,000	−321,000	−8,000
	1984	10	2	928,000	726,000	47,000	−261,000
	1985	7	2	905,000	686,000	37,000	−169,000
	1986	14	2	784,000	693,000	221,000	−522,000
	1987	4	2	1,365,000	852,000	98,000	12,000
	1988	7	2	1,580,000	1,034,000	317,000	−192,000
	1989	10	2	1,751,000	1,785,000	1,387,000	−1,948,000
	1990	1	2	3,727,000	3,143,000	1,848,000	−3,078,000
	1991	4	1	7,379,000	3,882,000	3,655,000	−2,500,000
	1992	1	1	8,569,000	4,489,000	306,000	508,000
	1993	17	1	13,324,000	5,253,000	2,583,000	510,000
	1994	5	1	13,866,904	6,399,933	−451,521	2,819,233
	1995	5	1	14,753,000	7,579,000	3,269,000	−2,427,000
	1996	13	1	18,751,000	10,071,000	6,198,000	−7,073,000
	1997	11	1	21,785,000	12,312,000	11,778,000	−9,689,000
Leicester	1974	9	1	446,000	153,000	−35,000	4,000
	1975	18	1	414,000	156,000	−150,000	109,000
	1976	7	1	558,000	306,000	174,000	−193,000
	1977	11	1	615,000	313,000	285,000	366,000
	1978	22	1	622,000	379,000	−369,000	−176,000
	1979	17	2	509,000	470,000	−71,000	38,000
	1980	1	2	793,000	561,000	160,000	160,000
	1981	21	1	1,118,000	652,000	299,000	−319,000
	1982	8	2	1,010,000	754,000	−75,000	−261,000
	1983	3	2	1,669,000	706,000	29,000	431,000
	1984	15	1	1,464,000	776,000	−15,000	146,000
	1985	15	1	1,543,000	735,000	−955,000	−833,000
	1986	19	1	1,344,000	830,000	344,000	543,000

Data Appendix / 357

Club	Year	League position	Division	Revenue (£)	Wages (£)	Net transfers (£)	Pre-tax profits (£)
Leicester (cont'd)	1987	20	1	1,585,000	955,000	−451,000	147,000
	1988	13	2	1,426,000	968,000	−324,000	−235,000
	1989	15	2	1,831,000	1,119,000	−28,000	−359,000
	1990	13	2	2,033,000	1,272,000	−800,000	286,000
	1991	22	2	2,584,000	1,638,000	−57,000	−759,000
	1992	4	2	6,331,000	1,858,000	−812,000	804,000
	1993	6	2	5,007,000	2,414,000	871,000	−729,000
	1994	4	2	6,232,646	3,132,157	2,267,498	−2,165,627
	1995	21	1	9,697,000	4,241,000	−1,417,000	2,464,000
	1996	5	2	9,272,000	5,449,000	980,000	−1,548,000
	1997	9	1	17,320,000	8,914,000	4,709,000	−3,594,000
Lincoln	1926	15	3	11,330	6,158	−880	981
	1927	11	3	11,610	7,478	900	−2,583
	1928	2	3	10,833	6,276	−500	1,920
	1929	6	3	10,704	6,799	−835	459
	1930	5	3	10,281	6,397	−125	−674
	1931	2	3	11,833	6,810	−1,140	1,137
	1932	1	3	14,474	7,347	−1,635	1,376
	1933	18	2	16,918	8,781	3,162	−2,560
	1934	22	2	14,751	8,543	−60	−1,898
	1935	4	3	10,786	6,968	−2,075	−1,086
	1936	4	3	9,965	6,454	−100	−2,442
	1937	2	3	12,158	6,053	−1,870	802
	1938	7	3	11,891	7,060	330	−197
	1939	17	3	12,611	7,169	−1,920	−1,891
Liverpool	1930	12	1	34,144	11,315		8,495
	1931	9	1	29,812	11,071		2,723
	1932	10	1	30,983	14,380		2,595
	1933	14	1	27,385	13,490		−1,284
	1934	18	1	39,217	23,651		−4,203
	1935	7	1	30,075	8,933		6,627
	1936	19	1	33,041	17,654		−1,993
	1937	18	1	26,667	8,888		2,259
	1938	11	1	41,188	23,261		−5,359
	1939	11	1	45,641	11,194		12,824
	1947	1	1	69,994	26,177		17,208
	1948	11	1		19,064		20,891
	1949	12	1	92,965	18,893		41,965
	1950	8	1	96,479	22,512		34,522
	1951	9	1	72,408	23,549		2,710
	1952	11	1		24,026	6,386	11,800
	1953	17	1	82,052	23,734	6,715	11,365
	1954	22	1	75,885	23,090	35,370	−12,925
	1955	11	2	93,969	22,777	−449	9,025
	1956	3	2	81,947	26,284	8,055	8,500
	1957	3	2	83,924	23,799	16,540	−4,366
	1958	4	2	115,476	27,380	9,275	14,126
	1959	4	2	105,488	29,952	−2,175	10,069
	1960	3	2	106,888	31,660	13,590	4,991
	1961	3	2	138,041	29,634	45,330	35,230
	1962	1	2	162,177	35,595	38,950	13,417
	1963	8	1	178,116	43,556	−220	12,755
	1964	1	1	231,845	59,219	4,600	73,283

Club	Year	League position	Division	Revenue (£)	Wages (£)	Net transfers (£)	Pre-tax profits (£)
Liverpool (cont'd)	1965	7	1	274,759	77,574	4,200	52,461
	1966	1	1	407,566	101,383	1,500	148,212
	1967	5	1	332,221	83,629	112,500	15,425
	1968	3	1	377,964	93,558	108,227	85,213
	1969	2	1	713,226	84,,950	35,804	46,152
	1970	5	1	416,891	101,789	56,717	
	1971	5	1	557,902	122,715	38,458	67,380
	1972	3	1	626,914	209,322	72,222	102,581
	1973	1	1	771,690	286,639	107,065	123,932
	1974	2	1	915,000	366,000	62,000	105,000
	1975	2	1	907,000	347,000	103,000	94,000
	1976	1	1	1,174,000	488,000	64,000	105,000
	1977	1	1	1,618,000	576,000	206,000	115,000
	1978	2	1	2,329,000	766,000	327,000	259,000
	1979	1	1	2,365,000	690,000	491,000	154,000
	1980	1	1	2,741,000	1,000,000	513,000	−84,000
	1981	5	1	3,342,000	1,230,000	721,000	29,000
	1982	1	1	3,653,000	1,557,000	559,000	−189,000
	1983	1	1	2,691,000	1,375,000	576,000	90,000
	1984	1	1	3,190,000	1,436,000	1,203,000	160,000
	1985	2	1	3,896,000	1,974,000	490,000	819,000
	1986	1	1	3,579,000	2,198,000	167,000	35,000
	1987	2	1	4,001,000	2,259,000	1,893,000	−470,000
	1988	1	1	4,104,000	2,924,000	−833,000	445,000
	1989	2	1	4,769,000	2,796,000	1,812,000	145,000
	1990	1	1	6,748,000	3,917,000	1,138,000	1,384,000
	1991	2	1	9,382,000	6,156,000	2,242,000	−783,000
	1992	6	1	14,844,000	8,300,000	3,630,000	−153,000
	1993	6	1	17,496,000	7,663,000	3,882,000	1,607,000
	1994	8	1	17,284,000	9,789,000	2,635,000	716,000
	1995	4	1	19,878,000	10,384,000	6,723,000	−2,753,000
	1996	3	1	27,396,000	13,234,000	12,328,000	−4,882,000
	1997	4	1	39,153,000	15,030,000	7,520,000	7,579,000
Luton	1930	13	3	12,382	8,224	711	−1,394
	1931	7	3	11,131	8,115	−265	−116
	1947	13	2	41,450	13,342	11,853	1,186
	1948	13	2	60,193	20,688	−10,063	8,432
	1949	10	2	50,950	21,690	5,483	3,589
	1950	17	2	46,975	24,505	−4,138	5,452
	1951	19	2	63,728	26,723	22,967	−16,886
	1952	8	2	82,304	25,338	−29,743	22,110
	1953	3	2	51,027	24,483	5,348	−2,926
	1954	6	2	54,232	29,208	−5,971	3,039
	1955	2	2	60,005	30,897	−10,275	3,919
	1956	10	1	70,252	29,376	2,300	6,227
	1957	16	1	69,897	29,890	9,425	4,403
	1958	8	1	85,726	33,656	−10,540	22,003
	1959	17	1	112,992	40,994	−8,198	40,049
	1960	22	1	89,161	45,485	18,571	−12,680
	1961	13	2	79,007	45,713	−13,175	6,090
	1962	13	2	69,045	43,086	4,114	−1,983
	1963	22	2	80,899	44,175	12,350	−18,219
	1964	18	3	74,130	44,020	−18,107	9,888

Data Appendix / 359

Club	Year	League position	Division	Revenue (£)	Wages (£)	Net transfers (£)	Pre-tax profits (£)
Luton (cont'd)	1965	21	3	82,770	45,630	14,591	-17,420
	1966	6	4	81,337	45,660	-10,388	11,884
	1967	17	4	64,408	39,551	-2,163	-8,595
	1968	1	4	97,107	53,970	60,876	-51,270
	1969	3	3	136,975	89,698	-36,712	36,782
	1970	2	3	134,104	107,334	119,250	-173,116
	1971	6	2	181,885	103,179	-169,500	4,165
	1972	13	2	158,278	103,748	-33,518	-37,860
	1973	12	2	205,257	129,760	97,038	-37,860
	1974	2	2	251,000	186,000	119,000	119,000
	1975	20	1	383,000	223,000	-62,000	-62,000
	1976	7	2	321,000	233,000	-120,000	-120,000
	1977	6	2	333,000	213,000	-118,000	-34,000
	1978	13	2	451,000	233,000	40,000	95,000
	1979	18	2	305,000	279,000	-326,000	8,000
	1980	6	2	703,000	488,000	426,000	-72,000
	1981	5	2	682,000	492,000	-151,000	-200,000
	1982	1	2	681,000	627,000	-259,000	-124,000
	1983	18	1	1,648,000	761,000	318,000	-481,000
	1984	16	1	2,124,000	759,000	-700,000	501,000
	1985	13	1	1,656,000	1,049,000	868,000	-1,415,000
	1986	9	1	2,188,000	1,050,000	-522,000	-103,000
	1987	7	1	2,257,000	1,146,000	134,000	869,000
	1988	9	1	3,859,000	1,881,000	701,000	327,000
	1989	16	1	4,844,000	2,292,000	503,000	682,000
	1990	17	1	4,399,000	2,313,000	-647,000	-1,031,000
	1991	18	1	4,620,000	2,903,000	-1,328,000	-254,000
	1992	20	1	6,971,000	2,809,000	-2,796,000	776,000
	1993	20	2	3,922,000	1,897,000	-388,000	-341,000
	1994	20	2	4,962,699	2,002,874		785,687
	1995	16	2	2,928,000	2,086,000	-1,583,000	354,000
	1996	24	2	3,004,000	2,591,000	-46,000	-2,064,000
	1997	3	3	2,955,000	2,842,000	-1,753,000	-113,000
Manchester City	1909	19	1	12,038	6,098	1,576	-1,614
Manchester United	1950	4	1	106,413	27,345	-39,966	35,604
	1951	2	1	89,636	28,819	-9,314	22,677
	1952	1	1	89,950	30,661	2,995	16,330
	1953	8	1	87,079	32,319	15,409	1,734
	1954	4	1	99,948	34,257	-20,315	19,104
	1955	5	1	87,625	36,395	-3,128	6,559
	1956	1	1	115,675	39,024	-16,950	1,463
	1957	1	1	156,445	43,694	-4,200	39,784
	1958	9	1	261,013	44,218	45,550	97,957
	1959	2	1	178,312	56,557	18,675	26,051
	1960	7	1	183,218	56,460	10,933	29,744
	1961	7	1	171,789	61,830	-10,175	15,251
	1962	15	1	187,178	76,891	-16,425	19,531
	1963	19	1	271,181	92,088	89,750	-51,429
	1964	2	1	259,777	104,578	10,120	44,877
	1965	1	1	354,950	131,216	-49,300	89,155
	1966	4	1	365,723	129,530	-19,504	101,199
	1967	1	1	398,305	185,877	-12,000	90,771
	1968	2	1	492,171	194,056		107,104

Club	Year	League position	Division	Revenue (£)	Wages (£)	Net transfers (£)	Pre-tax profits (£)
Manchester United	1969	11	1	569,418	204,028	78,063	112,490
(cont'd)	1970	8	1	527,118	230,180	45,356	65,419
	1971	8	1	526,221	248,503	−18,930	91,860
	1972	8	1	532,308	342,027	306,805	−322,989
	1973	18	1	600,424	289,052	449,403	−408,920
	1974	21	1	678,000	328,000	101,000	−1,000
	1975	1	2	890,000	354,000	6,000	165,000
	1976	3	1	1,465,000	439,000	47,000	303,000
	1977	6	1	2,028,000	522,000	−72,000	565,000
	1978	10	1	1,776,000	630,000	301,000	−132,000
	1979	9	1	2,419,000	702,000	564,000	99,000
	1980	2	1	2,471,000	849,000	360,000	210,000
	1981	8	1	2,857,000	1,092,000	739,000	−352,000
	1982	3	1	3,350,000	1,503,000	2,135,000	−2,282,000
	1983	3	1	3,662,000	1,554,000	−252,000	636,000
	1984	4	1	5,226,000	1,941,000	−724,000	1,731,000
	1985	4	1	6,738,000	2,806,000	249,000	280,000
	1986	4	1	6,677,000	2,576,000	1,496,000	−824,000
	1987	11	1	6,718,000	2,666,000	−802,000	878,000
	1988	2	1	7,585,000	2,543,000	2,496,000	−1,296,000
	1989	11	1	9,556,000	3,012,000	19,000	−1,707,000
	1990	14	1	11,592,000	3,909,000	5,157,000	−2,728,000
	1991	6	1	17,816,000	5,214,000	801,000	5,306,000
	1992	2	1	12,193,000	5,291,000	2,625,000	80,000
	1993	1	1	14,064,000	6,182,000	3,986,000	−145,000
	1994	1	1	20,852,000	9,002,000	675,000	2,881,000
	1995	2	1	60,622,000	13,020,000	−3,733,000	20,014,000
	1996	1	1	53,316,000	13,275,000	1,300,000	15,399,000
	1997	1	1	87,939,000	22,552,000	−293,000	27,577,000
Mansfield	1974	17	4	65,000	6,200	−23,000	−13,000
	1975	1	4	122,000	93,000	14,000	−44,000
	1976	11	3	157,000	107,000	−63,000	73,000
	1977	1	3	205,000	135,000	33,000	32,000
	1978	21	2	272,000	170,000	31,000	−2,000
	1979	18	3	220,000	218,000	−218,000	129,000
	1980	23	3	329,000	250,000	103,000	−150,000
	1981	7	4	204,000	279,000	−160,000	23,000
	1982	20	4	210,000	239,000	49,000	−202,000
	1983	10	4	217,000	246,000	13,000	−164,000
	1984	19	4	274,000	256,000	12,000	−131,000
	1985	14	4	430,000	404,000	15,000	−217,000
	1986	3	4	297,000	362,900	14,000	−266,000
	1987	10	3	502,000	355,000	−4,000	−111,000
	1988	18	3	408,000	391,000	−63,000	−215,000
	1989	15	3	421,000	515,000	−633,000	181,000
	1990	15	3	366,608	522,437		−709,486
	1991	24	3	957,421	683,331		143,982
	1992	3	4	998,534	763,426		−454,957
	1993	22	3	502,300	328,475		1,727,357
	1994	12	4	1,109,315	519,061		167,166
	1995	6	4	1,346,000	622,000	−179,000	196,000
	1996	19	4	1,078,000	669,000		−107,000
	1997	11	4	985,000	691,000		−182,000

Club	Year	League position	Division	Revenue (£)	Wages (£)	Net transfers (£)	Pre-tax profits (£)
Middlesbrough	1930	16	1	36,792	11,162	14,030	−7,228
	1931	7	1	26,224	9,558	−1,637	4,145
	1932	18	1	24,102	10,070	1,685	−837
	1933	17	1	29,786	10,551	9,364	−9,781
	1934	16	1	24,611	9,191	−2,201	3,666
Millwall	1922	12	3	27,958	11,259	533	−2,199
	1923	7	3	28,281	8,879	958	57
	1924	3	3	24,489	7,642	5,742	606
	1925	5	3	33,876	9,177	822	4,925
	1926	3	3	33,854	8,830	1,132	8
	1927	3	3	30,915	9,285	90	4,335
	1928	1	3	36,179	9,601	374	4,145
	1929	14	2	37,678	10,168	1,843	4,847
	1930	14	2	26,193	12,151	7,650	1,700
	1931	14	2	26,223	10,590	2,760	−4,720
	1932	9	2	26,223	8,623	652	2,329
	1933	7	2	25,460	9,030	245	1,203
	1934	21	2	30,119	9,666	3,570	−5,255
	1935	12	3	22,114	7,921	1,410	−2,635
	1936	12	3	18,631	6,859	−90	871
	1937	8	3	43,735	13,752		7,453
	1938	1	3	45,181	19,705		2,589
	1939	13	2	48,832	17,726		7,811
Newcastle	1933	5	1	31,974	12,604		2,728
	1934	21	1	36,756	19,956		−4,647
	1948	2	2	116,373	37,783		24,744
	1949	4	1	122,612	14,715		49,765
	1950	5	1	101,984	30,667		10,073
	1951	4	1	116,612	40,341		7,098
	1952	8	1	129,928	15,019		42,638
	1953	16	1	153,035	85,970		−38,619
	1954	15	1	117,494	59,804		1,099
	1955	8	1	123,788	46,627		7,092
	1956	11	1	102,297	33,916		2,767
	1957	17	1	98,485	31,031		3,367
	1958	19	1	119,103	24,301		42,591
	1959	11	1	129,278	50,633		14,386
	1960	8	1	126,274	50,302		6,183
	1961	21	1	145,257	84,001		−5,748
	1962	11	2	132,471	71,223		14,660
	1963	7	2	133,924	73,165		4,257
	1964	8	2	195,729	132,513		−52,034
	1965	1	2	158,552	50,405		46,464
	1966	15	1	190,623	88,318		23,640
	1967	20	1	195,376	116,971		4,091
	1968	10	1	240,000	85,598		32,528
	1969	9	1	258,023	116,657		−51,968
	1970	7	1	248,398	113,470		14,590
	1971	12	1	240,348	132,551		−60,728
	1972	11	1	279,377	150,635		12,504
	1973	9	1	343,730	167,180		65,390
	1974	15	1	491,900	216,000	291,000	−53,000
	1975	15	1	488,000	263,000	109,000	−69,000

Winners and Losers / 362

Club	Year	League position	Division	Revenue (£)	Wages (£)	Net transfers (£)	Pre-tax profits (£)
Newcastle (cont'd)	1976	15	1	711,000	384,000	4,000	205,000
	1977	5	1	569,000	340,000	−194,000	−12,000
	1978	21	1	605,000	442,000	−69,000	−57,000
	1979	8	2	601,000	519,000	−17,000	−317,000
	1980	9	2	881,000	605,000	−292,000	56,000
	1981	11	2	839,000	657,000	486,000	−877,000
	1982	9	2	888,000	556,000	−85,000	−167,000
	1983	5	2	2,106,000	994,000	217,000	−31,000
	1984	3	2	2,266,000	737,000	480,000	−252,000
	1985	14	1	2,635,000	740,000	339,000	590,000
	1986	11	1	2,412,000	1,013,000	−319,000	650,000
	1987	17	1	2,705,000	1,129,000	733,000	−263,000
	1988	8	1	2,644,000	1,414,000	−449,000	83,000
	1989	20	1	3,656,000	2,647,000	−1,175,000	7,000
	1990	3	2	4,119,000	2,604,000	49,000	−1,312,000
	1991	11	2	4,418,000	2,754,000	669,000	−2,541,000
	1992	20	2	5,293,000	3,375,000	406,000	−2,208,000
	1993	1	2	8,743,900	4,662,000	2,599,000	−374,000
	1994	3	1	17,004,000	6,575,000		3,766,000
	1995	6	1	24,723,000	7,105,000	12,143,000	−8,159,000
	1996	2	1	28,970,000	19,746,000	27,596,000	−23,604,000
	1997	2	1	41,134,000	17,487,000	−1,436,000	8,302,000
Northampton	1924	8	3	15,772	7,853	260	−983
	1925	9	3	13,025	7,071	−50	−916
	1927	18	3	12,837	7,117	−1,229	−790
	1928	2	3	17,362	8,380	1,100	21
	1929	3	3	18,044	9,070	310	1,145
	1930	4	3	15,104	8,423	525	−105
	1931	6	3	14,085	8,435	435	−1,849
	1932	14	3	15,525	8,577	1,504	−3,034
	1933	8	3	13,414	7,513	−250	−640
	1934	13	3	15,676	7,510	−1,545	2,118
	1935	7	3	13,748	7,433	−1,185	−437
	1936	15	3	15,492	7,006	340	−762
	1937	7	3	17,055	7,865	2,464	−225
	1938	9	3	18,473	8,804	−3,027	1,463
	1939	17	3	17,413	9,196	2,236	−4,635
Norwich	1929	17	3	11,697	7,136	200	−205
	1930	8	3	15,364	8,123	1,695	−1,134
	1931	21	3	14,934	8,175	1,962	−2,228
	1932	10	3	16,562	7,793	−697	2,413
	1933	3	3	15,316	8,521	1,051	−900
	1934	1	3	18,089	9,517	1,067	444
	1935	14	2	25,086	9,665	−3,760	4,593
	1936	11	2	24,631	9,882	6,091	−1,793
Oldham	1950	11	3	32,752	12,848	4,200	1,767
	1951	15	3	29,998	15,034	15,400	−13,301
	1952	4	3	40,004	15,631	9,000	2,728
	1954	22	2	46,570	20,071	4,000	1,320
	1955	10	3	33,450	19,800	−4,505	−5,220
	1956	20	3	24,374	16,296	−1,700	−5,503
	1958	15	3	33,580	18,487	2,160	−2,671
	1959	21	4	29,404	18,370	−3,750	−2,876

Data Appendix / 363

Club	Year	League position	Division	Revenue (£)	Wages (£)	Net transfers (£)	Pre-tax profits (£)
Oldham (cont'd)	1961	12	4	53,563	24,702	14,975	313
	1962	11	4	67,653	30,768	13,125	3,725
	1963	2	4	67,884	36,630	12,485	169
	1964	9	3	64,192	37,877	5,275	3,788
	1965	20	3	72,550	42,113	9,850	−9,039
	1966	20	3	47,484	48,264	51,325	−53,999
	1967	10	3	76,300	60,418	51,100	−48,789
	1968	16	3	54,370	57,883	−22,210	452
	1969	24	3	43,022	51,176	−24,350	16,369
	1970	19	4	41,512	54,739		−1,799
	1971	3	4	72,740	66,700	5,850	2,868
	1972	11	3	77,828	72,262	3,455	−710
	1973	4	3	89,217	79,113	−30,138	29,154
	1974	1	3	227,000	63,000	−2,000	−34,000
	1975	18	2	200,000	121,000	12,000	−2,000
	1976	17	2	219,000	131,000	−10,000	13,000
	1977	13	2	274,000	184,000	−1,000	−29,000
	1978	8	2	319,000	213,000	2,000	−33,000
	1979	14	2	380,000	231,000	−125,000	102,000
	1980	11	2	486,000	333,000	20,000	−79,000
	1981	15	2	481,000	380,000	−99,000	−97,000
	1982	11	2	454,000	267,000	0	−196,000
	1983	7	2	465,000	384,000	−100,000	−88,000
	1984	19	2	497,000	377,000	−273,000	116,000
	1985	14	2	510,000	388,000	−215,000	68,000
	1986	8	2	449,000	486,000	−263,000	−43,000
	1987	3	2	828,000	537,000	52,000	−178,000
	1988	10	2	1,106,000	687,000	−502,000	344,000
	1989	16	2	1,215,000	623,000	92,000	−158,000
	1990	8	2	3,327,000	1,003,000	382,000	581,000
	1991	1	2	2,970,000	1,739,000	−39,000	112,000
	1992	17	1	3,978,000	2,868,000	−7,000	−535,000
	1993	19	1	4,719,000	2,458,000	719,000	−290,000
	1994	21	1	5,763,771	3,088,367	−8,750	704,967
	1995	14	2	4,023,000	2,739,000	−412,000	−147,000
	1996	18	2	3,270,000	2,573,000	−1,211,000	309,000
	1997	23	2	3,098,000	2,779,000	−1,514,000	381,000
Orient	1930	12	3	18,628	9,087		−2,772
	1934	11	3	15,133	8,685		−95
	1935	14	3	16,728	9,373		−2,572
	1937	12	3	12,398	7,466		−1,103
Peterborough	1974	1	4	138,000	93,000	25,000	−32,000
	1975	7	3	146,000	114,000	22,000	−25,000
	1976	10	3	169,000	128,000	24,000	−9,000
	1977	16	3	144,000	114,000	−23,000	23,000
	1978	4	3	178,000	154,000	−20,000	18,000
	1979	21	3	193,000	185,000	−8,000	−5,000
	1980	8	4	192,000	223,000	−38,000	−57,000
	1981	5	4	259,000	270,000	3,000	−51,000
	1982	5	4	264,000	263,000	−82,000	22,000
	1983	9	4	235,000	224,000	−32,000	−44,000
	1984	7	4	274,000	228,000	2,150	−40,000
	1985	11	4	319,000	233,000	3,735	−50,000

Club	Year	League position	Division	Revenue (£)	Wages (£)	Net transfers (£)	Pre-tax profits (£)
Peterborough (cont'd)	1986	17	4	327,000	237,000	10,000	−58,000
	1987	10	4	381,000	267,000	−35,000	−35,000
	1988	6	4	333,000	324,000	41,000	−195,000
	1989	17	4	518,000	480,000	−13,000	−273,000
	1990	9	4	933,063	635,661		−298,798
	1991	4	4	1,508,301	897,227		79,637
	1992	6	3	1,598,665	1,033,882		−100,141
	1993	10	2	2,942,533	841,881		887,622
	1994	24	2	2,946,774	974,389		634,149
	1995	15	3	2,080,000	1,236,000	120,000	−210,000
	1996	19	3	2,669,000	1,277,000	0	−746,000
	1997	21	3	3,452,000	1,973,000		−139,000
Plymouth	1922	2	3	20,859	13,061	768	−338
	1923	2	3	17,006	10,837	118	−983
	1924	2	3	18,644	12,280	−6,275	1,805
	1926	2	3	22,169	11,158	5,210	3,631
	1927	2	3	16,856	11,453	241	−2,654
	1928	3	3	14,696	10,171	−305	−1,671
	1929	4	3	14,514	9,570	200	216
	1931	18	2	23,457	14,354		2,384
	1932	4	2	25,621	13,052		3,537
	1934	10	2	22,742	14,497		−2,656
	1935	8	2	20,059	12,611		−1,650
	1936	7	2	22,863	10,942	4,776	−446
	1937	5	2	25,777	11,596	6,374	369
	1938	13	2	26,766	13,394	5,293	−4,161
	1939	15	2	21,086	13,866	−2,700	1,485
	1947	19	2	40,831	17,579	4,800	−2,677
	1948	17	2	51,794	23,490	12,407	−9,844
	1949	20	2	47,911	21,432	1,250	6,637
	1950	21	2	71,558	24,522	24,512	−16,229
	1951	4	3	51,131	24,538	−7,950	5,948
	1952	1	3	53,531	24,695	−1,700	6,276
	1953	4	2	63,023	31,051	1,426	−385
	1954	19	2	60,922	28,075	1,975	−6,858
	1955	20	2	50,990	25,149	75	306
	1956	21	2	57,493	27,338	2,635	−6,128
	1957	18	3	44,891	21,448	1,025	−4,459
	1958	3	3	74,425	30,018	6,615	10,870
	1959	1	3	101,830	29,501	20,675	14,009
	1960	19	2	91,076	37,476	18,250	7,641
	1961	11	2	102,405	33,271	−5,138	20,341
	1962	5	2	83,206	38,198	3,550	6,308
	1963	12	2	115,055	36,538	−3,738	16,152
	1964	20	2	121,552	44,808	24,725	−27,866
	1965	15	2	156,874	53,522		−29,680
	1966	18	2	145,889	48,139	−33,967	30,147
	1967	16	2	154,823	65,761	−46,450	21,977
	1968	22	2	60,535	63,316	38,520	−45,223
	1969	5	3	59,219	51,380	11,900	446
	1970	17	3	53,701	52,873	−26,650	24,358
	1971	15	3	60,478	53,824	16,750	−24,767
	1972	8	3	139,783	60,130	15,600	4,321

Data Appendix / 365

Club	Year	League position	Division	Revenue (£)	Wages (£)	Net transfers (£)	Pre-tax profits (£)
Plymouth (cont'd)	1973	8	3	181,556	77,331	56,700	−15,223
	1974	17	3	213,000	105,000	−22,000	3,000
	1975	2	3	274,000	155,000	−33,000	−1,000
	1976	16	2	376,000	176,000	3,000	−6,000
	1977	21	2	377,000	212,000	−74,000	−2,000
	1978	19	3	659,000	215,000	−37,000	32,000
	1979	15	3	796,000	271,000	−121,000	132,000
	1980	15	3	505,000	296,000	−187,000	97,000
	1981	7	3	573,000	339,000	−29,000	−66,000
	1982	10	3	554,000	368,000	155,000	−353,000
	1983	8	3	545,000	319,000	−60,000	−34,000
	1984	19	3	1,256,000	332,000	56,000	76,000
	1985	15	3	974,000	373,000	5,000	−81,000
	1986	2	3	1,324,000	490,000	−25,000	107,000
	1987	7	2	1,767,000	485,000	171,000	195,000
	1988	16	2	1,587,000	569,000	72,000	31,000
	1989	18	2	1,657,000	633,000	−115,000	127,000
	1990	16	2	1,740,000	879,000	181,000	−325,000
	1991	18	2	2,331,000	962,000	−145,000	−98,000
	1992	22	2	1,967,000	1,319,000	541,000	−1,475,000
	1993	14	3	2,579,000	1,335,000	−290,000	−202,000
	1994	3	3	3,231,160	1,293,456	−467,290	433,690
	1995	21	3	1,852,000	1,007,000	170,000	−546,000
	1996	4	4	2,371,000	1,489,000	−473,000	143,000
	1997	19	3	2,297,000	1,301,000	−532,000	483,000
Portsmouth	1930	13	1	31,394	10,541		5,830
	1934	10	1	37,894	9,714	2,366	10,592
	1935	14	1	38,809	9,086	−7,449	14,961
	1936	10	1	34,990	10,460	10,624	−5,166
	1937	9	1	30,502	10,846	980	3,617
	1938	19	1	39,873	10,615	13,840	−6,289
	1939	17	1	43,972	10,810	4,075	9,075
Preston	1909	10	1	8,866	4,919	670	−179
	1910	12	1	8,953	4,854	385	−749
	1911	14	1	8,322	4,812	−285	398
	1912	19	1	7,932	4,870	710	−352
	1913	1	2	7,938	4,391	−536	641
	1914	19	1	7,546	4,581	280	−1,697
	1915	2	2	12,008	4,528	1336	1,676
	1948	7	1	58,637	18,344	13,425	12,792
	1949	21	1	72,041	22,465	17,650	13,405
	1950	6	2	63,146	22,670	21,800	−2,910
	1951	1	2	65,168	25,898	18,200	1,562
	1952	7	1	74,796	27,841	9,660	15,899
	1953	2	1	94,394	31,273	−13,520	40,604
	1954	11	1	83,585	34,180	17,450	2,489
	1956	19	1	83,388	31,537	19,900	−9,406
	1957	3	1	68,568	34,506	6,000	3,927
	1958	2	1	85,333	45,122	−3,550	10,737
	1959	12	1	101,517	49,760	−13,000	15,063
	1960	9	1	102,095	51,016	−4,434	12,014
	1961	22	1	89,041	46,957	−17,025	9,946
	1962	10	2	78,298	43,892	9,991	−9,943

Club	Year	League position	Division	Revenue (£)	Wages (£)	Net transfers (£)	Pre-tax profits (£)
Preston (cont'd)	1963	17	2	88,923	44,144	20,555	−30,363
	1964	3	2	100,549	59,417	520	12,932
	1965	12	2	94,605	62,785	3,210	−16,942
	1966	17	2	102,749	63,588	−2,688	12,460
	1967	13	2	128,968	67,565	−34,975	25,539
	1968	20	2	165,629	79,064	43,321	−53,523
	1969	14	2	142,311	86,967	12,128	−18,920
	1970	22	2	145,792	87,961	−15,283	13,697
	1971	1	3	183,983	108,482	−50,073	28,146
	1972	18	2	167,462	127,382	42,515	−72,602
	1973	19	2	207,223	111,974	−71,787	3,892
	1974	21	2	145,000	125,000	47,000	−139,000
	1975	9	3	162,000	128,000	−122,000	43,000
	1976	8	3	158,000	166,000	−131,000	8,000
	1977	6	3	198,000	172,000	−105,000	31,000
	1978	3	3	289,000	191,000	−3,000	−1,000
	1979	7	2	497,000	274,000	106,000	63,000
	1980	10	2	354,000	335,000	−496,000	311,000
	1981	20	2	433,000	396,000	63,000	−355,000
	1982	14	3	530,000	481,000	−294,000	−73,000
	1983	16	3	649,000	350,000	20,000	−151,000
	1984	16	3	407,000	299,000	12,000	−105,000
	1985	23	3	443,000	303,000	−31,000	−64,000
	1986	23	4	391,000	262,000	−11,000	−64,000
	1987	2	4	765,000	337,000	−9,000	115,000
	1988	15	3	1,007,000	456,000	−60,000	−1,000
	1989	6	3	836,000	547,000	−73,000	18,000
	1990	19	3	898,000	635,000	−73,000	−254,000
	1991	17	3	991,000	815,000	−53,000	212,000
	1992	17	3	1,436,000	810,000	−370,000	165,000
	1993	21	3	1,385,000	761,000	−297,500	165,000
	1994	5	4	1,676,234	1,108,065	25,000	27,986
	1995	5	4	1,860,000	1,186,000	−27,000	−254,000
	1996	1	4	2,876,000	1,388,000	4,000	62,000
	1997	15	3	3,847,000	2,145,000	−392,000	113,000
Queen's Park Rangers	1923	11	3	12,769	8,242	−250	−1,292
	1925	19	3	13,860	9,512	500	−1,973
	1926	22	3	20,431	8,611	2,100	−3,692
	1929	6	3	17,338	9,840	900	1,431
	1930	3	3	19,361	9,934	−2,836	3,355
	1931	8	3	17,293	9,885	350	−4,561
Reading	1947	9	3	29,602	11,270	−2380	7,854
	1948	10	3	40,335	15,752	15,350	−8,805
	1949	2	3	46,856	18,045	−305	7,887
	1950	10	3	48,299	22,167	−2,250	−952
	1951	3	3	54,447	24,495	3,250	−4,625
	1952	2	3	50,139	23,099	−705	6,922
	1953	11	3	47,397	23,170	−6100	−666
	1954	8	3	47,053	24,873	−11,300	2,779
	1955	18	3	49,386	24,462	−8,500	−3,859
	1956	17	3	43,954	23,876	−9,300	−4,358
	1957	13	3	40,971	21,908	2,000	−6,910
	1958	5	3	50,706	24,285	3,500	4,482

Club	Year	League position	Division	Revenue (£)	Wages (£)	Net transfers (£)	Pre-tax profits (£)
Reading (cont'd)	1959	6	3	68,562	28,403	−5,900	2,905
	1960	11	3	62,240	32,848	4,800	−14,018
	1961	18	3	50,805	31,630		−4,990
	1962	7	3	58,000	31,937	4,900	2,560
	1963	20	3	80,088	38,436	15,300	−18,952
	1964	6	3	70,343	41,190	4,436	−2,921
	1965	13	3	79,250	45,166	3,500	5,808
	1966	8	3	82,420	42,243	−1,813	8,070
	1967	4	3	99,418	46,683	16,046	3,490
	1968	5	3	113,966	47,770	25,569	−1,523
	1969	14	3	91,913	49,769	3,055	801
	1970	8	3	95,730	63,551	−23,611	17,898
	1971	21	3	128,943	56,805	19,005	−19,371
	1972	16	4	102,567	54,941	747	10,480
	1973	7	4	122,044	57,629	27,925	−7,999
	1974	6	4	137,000	75,000	24,000	−16,000
	1975	7	4	136,000	77,000	−24,000	19,000
	1976	3	4	204,000	106,000	15,000	−3,000
	1977	21	3	218,000	110,000	3,000	9,000
	1978	8	4	222,000	118,000	28,000	−25,000
	1979	1	4	371,000	167,000	−8,000	7,000
	1980	6	3	249,000	221,000	−19,000	50,000
	1981	10	3	229,000	284,000	62,000	−72,000
	1982	12	3	440,000	290,000	−37,000	−8,000
	1983	21	3	420,000	295,000	−95,000	9,000
	1984	3	4	448,000	389,000	−104,000	63,000
	1985	9	3	490,000	340,000	−93,000	5,000
	1986	1	3	761,000	508,000	131,000	−161,000
	1987	13	2	1,016,000	525,000	−52,000	128,000
	1988	22	2	1,589,000	820,000	100,000	0
	1989	18	3	1,465,000	862,000	−330,000	1,000
	1990	10	3	997,000	890,000	91,000	−371,000
	1991	15	3	930,000	1,018,000	252,000	-828,000
	1992	12	3	1,090,000	1,103,000	−62,000	−381,000
	1993	8	3	1,732,000	1,285,000	−20,000	6,000
	1994	1	3	1,945,846	1,637,867	58,548	−252,137
	1995	2	2	2,999,000	1,981,000	369,000	−172,000
	1996	19	2	2,840,000	3,079,000	-1,303,000	209,000
	1997	18	2	3,311,000	3,035,000	−275,000	−539,000
Rotherham United	1974	15	4	65,000	64,000	−1,000	−56,000
	1975	3	4	76,000	66,000	−20,000	−32,000
	1976	16	3	109,000	75,000	29,000	−58,000
	1977	4	3	138,000	89,000	-10,000	−14,000
	1978	20	3	151,000	94,000	15,000	−49,000
	1979	17	3	201,000	147,000	12,000	-114,000
	1980	13	3	276,000	218,000	−32,000	−87,000
	1981	1	3	338,000	329,000	60,000	-488,000
	1982	7	2	588,000	290,000	285,000	−39,000
	1983	20	2	613,000	394,000	84,000	−138,000
	1984	18	3	617,000	472,000	-127,000	−142,000
	1985	12	3	611,000	451,000	−131,000	−117,000
	1986	14	3	546,900	402,000	−78,000	−175,000
	1987	14	3	558,000	484,000	−145,000	−250,000

Club	Year	League position	Division	Revenue (£)	Wages (£)	Net transfers (£)	Pre-tax profits (£)
Rotherham United	1988	20	3	308,000	328,000	-22,000	-80,000
(cont'd)	1989	1	4	474,000	382,000	-49,000	-103,000
	1990	9	3	802,000	520,000	39,000	-300,000
	1991	23	3	1,208,000	664,000	-218,000	-113,000
	1992	2	4	973,000	578,000	-138,000	-116,000
	1993	11	3	1,084,000	745,000	69,000	-214,000
	1994	15	3	1,014,089	797,755	-62,750	-293,768
	1995	17	3	828,000	906,000	40,000	-504,000
	1996	16	3	1,132,000	1,004,000	-116,000	-171,000
	1997	23	3	799,000	1,106,000	-212,000	-478,000
Scunthorpe	1974	18	4	85,000	67,000	7,000	-25,000
	1975	24	4	61,000	72,000	6,000	-41,000
	1976	19	4	83,000	78,000	6,000	-52,000
	1977	20	4	106,000	92,000	-18,000	-21,000
	1978	14	4	119,000	123,000	-51,000	-7,000
	1979	12	4	164,000	140,000	-105,000	-21,000
	1980	14	4	181,000	185,000	-7,000	-25,000
	1981	16	4	172,000	202,000	-1,000	-88,000
	1982	23	4	272,000	193,000	-21,000	-19,000
	1983	4	4	310,000	243,000	0	51,000
	1984	21	3	353,000	294,000	3,000	-140,000
	1985	9	4	465,000	280,000	18,000	-52,000
	1986	15	4	463,000	305,000	-68,000	-82,000
	1987	8	4	481,000	318,000	64,000	-222,000
	1988	3	4	697,000	373,000	5,000	6,000
	1989	4	4	867,000	418,000	75,000	-72,000
	1990	11	4	770,000	589,000	96,000	-242,000
	1991	8	4	873,000	729,000	-421,000	121,000
	1992	5	4	1,039,000	775,000	-47,000	-195,000
	1993	14	4	1,052,000	666,000	-33,000	-102,000
	1994	11	4	896,107	704,540	-185,500	-7,478
	1995	7	4	1,111,000	662,000	-63,000	10,000
	1996	12	4	959,000	688,000	-292,000	31,000
	1997	13	4	1,072,000	889,000	-188,000	-163,000
Sheffield United	1909	12	1	8,606	5,806	920	-1,912
	1929	11	1	32,288	11,951	8,533	-4,092
	1930	20	1	27,982	11,364	4,721	946
	1931	15	1	29,108	11,273	4,322	2,766
	1932	7	1	26,634	11,170	6,467	-976
	1933	10	1	19,509	10,564	397	-513
	1934	22	1	20,917	10,413	19	1,173
	1935	11	2	24,219	10,778	4,157	-9,662
	1936	3	2	32,658	10,708	139	18,587
	1937	7	2	28,266	11,082	-2,231	4,695
	1938	3	2	29,265	11,945	3,072	2,633
	1939	2	2	32,361	12,504	30,840	3,344
	1947	6	1	56,704	15,065	-9,076	21,365
	1948	12	1	58,950	17,357	3,077	9,626
	1949	22	1	68,038	19,950	2,527	11,968
	1950	3	2	69,988	20,790	-10,502	16,640
	1951	8	2	60,333	20,980	8,010	-7,125
	1952	11	2	72,428	21,960	11,405	4,593
	1953	1	2	69,496	22,554	3,967	7,730

Club	Year	League position	Division	Revenue (£)	Wages (£)	Net transfers (£)	Pre-tax profits (£)
Sheffield United (cont'd)	1954	20	1	78,307	21,797	15,250	7,413
	1955	13	1	61,101	25,944	−225	2,196
	1956	22	1	79,247	27,005	12,548	−10,786
	1957	7	2	76,066	27,667	−18,615	8,506
	1958	6	2	83,989	30,665	−16,757	8,296
	1959	3	2	94,855	37,399	15,860	−16,186
	1960	4	2	85,203	35,912	4,099	4,561
	1961	2	2	96,390	36,747	5,808	8,485
	1962	5	1	134,520	46,557	−19,336	28,693
	1963	10	1	124,072	53,038	−19,701	12,472
	1964	12	1	125,776	53,130	−28,763	10,357
	1965	19	1	116,494	53,593	−6,429	300
	1966	9	1	149,365	63,336	−39,276	16,852
	1967	10	1	142,996	63,547	−6,938	13,711
	1968	21	1	246,729	71,584	−94,121	104,451
	1969	9	2	203,336	80,161	46,218	−95,795
	1970	6	2	198,498	78,876	−59,079	32,271
	1971	2	2	258,078	114,377	49,657	−56,382
	1972	10	1	329,843	120,367	−7,849	91,809
	1973	14	1	322,813	138,519	68,484	5,935
	1974	13	1	282,000	157,000	146,000	−170,000
	1975	6	1	327,000	213,000	−36,000	−83,000
	1976	22	1	463,000	180,000	6,000	91,000
	1977	11	2	369,000	189,000	141,000	32,000
	1978	12	2	431,000	203,000	15,000	−60,000
	1979	20	2	524,000	311,000	204,000	411,000
	1980	12	3	663,000	347,000	−454,000	259,000
	1981	21	3	597,000	391,000	−215,000	−725,000
	1982	1	4	634,000	526,000	−293,000	−854,000
	1983	11	3	659,000	483,000	299,000	−691,000
	1984	3	3	940,000	456,000	−3,000	76,000
	1985	18	2	890,000	470,000	25,000	−129,000
	1986	7	2	920,000	576,000	−65,000	−290,000
	1987	9	2	914,000	561,000	−75,000	−204,000
	1988	21	2	984,000	564,000	−94,000	92,000
	1989	2	3	1,483,000	818,000	56,000	−61,000
	1990	2	2	2,473,000	1,375,000	646,000	−273,000
	1991	13	1	3,528,000	1,856,000	1,851,000	−1,543,000
	1992	9	1	4,265,000	2,419,000	371,000	−128,000
	1993	14	1	6,060,000	2,975,000	42,000	1,093,000
	1994	20	1	5,430,863	3,145,848	−1,504,350	509,033
	1995	8	2	4,325,000	3,145,000	128,000	−264,000
	1996	9	2	4,311,000	3,910,000	−174,000	−859,000
	1997	5	2	5,133,000	3,560,000	2,966,000	−3,054,000
Sheffield Wednesday	1907	13	1	10,347	5,262		1,018
	1913	3	1	14,471	4,652	−329	5,382
	1914	18	1	17,035	5,414		3,367
	1915	7	1	10,369	5,004		−1,564
	1928	14	1	31,098	14,112	7,546	−1,839
	1929	1	1	41,054	14,981	−6,672	10,821
	1930	1	1	38,092	16,669	12,230	1,614
	1931	3	1	25,398	14,834	2,775	94
	1932	3	1	27,659	14,286	−1,952	450

Club	Year	League position	Division	Revenue (£)	Wages (£)	Net transfers (£)	Pre-tax profits (£)
Sheffield Wednesday	1947	21	2	40,269	16,814	1,145	2,269
(cont'd)	1948	4	2	63,916	24,847	16,360	2,596
	1949	8	2	68,310	24,806	17,250	1,077
	1950	2	2	80,727	26,679	−7,420	10,591
	1951	21	1	94,294	30,599	38,575	−14,304
	1952	1	2	90,563	36,183	−4,992	8,025
	1953	18	1	95,462	34,854	4,100	7,321
	1954	19	1	91,082	36,602	8,300	5,635
	1955	22	1	78,781	33,938	19,550	−12,384
	1956	1	2	75,012	39,770	−5,600	1,015
	1957	14	1	81,117	37,830	600	7,292
	1958	22	1	82,476	44,508	2,150	2,639
	1959	1	2	117,259	53,665	−33,715	19,339
	1960	5	1.	124,505	57,320	−6,970	28,919
	1961	2	1	131,056	61,925	9,150	16,699
	1962	6	1	158,751	72,221	6,650	27,007
	1963	6	1	183,335	74,648	−49,749	35,051
	1964	6	1	125,053	80,265	8,325	−29,970
	1965	8	1	142,990	77,961	−7,725	3,401
	1966	17	1	166,006	89,060	49,250	−45,230
	1967	11	1	238,641	99,458	60,350	−30,963
	1968	19	1	233,444	110,179	−4,944	27,003
	1969	15	1	229,803	117,056	127,325	−116,388
	1970	22	1	372,234	115,765	−134,094	138,556
	1971	15	2	200,435	116,891	−34,177	−24,261
	1972	14	2	195,000	133,953	103,603	−165,252
	1973	10	2	290,349	177,511	−30,100	−47,544
	1974	19	2	212,000	183,000	7,000	−103,000
	1975	22	2	226,000	181,000	2,000	−87,000
	1976	20	3	256,000	189,000	13,000	−56,000
	1977	8	3	296,000	195,000	−5,000	53,000
	1978	14	3	383,000	200,000	−8,000	129,000
	1979	14	3	475,000	261,000	154,000	92,000
	1980	3	3	731,000	365,000	−148,000	450,000
	1981	10	2	945,000	388,000	151,000	225,000
	1982	4	2	911,000	529,000	193,000	−209,000
	1983	6	2	1,075,000	595,000	188,000	−176,000
	1984	2	2	1,587,000	839,000	−140,000	120,000
	1985 `	8	1	2,173,000	904,000	−118,000	499,000
	1986	5	1	1,950,000	1,182,000	−166,000	392,000
	1987	13	1	2,323,000	1,148,000	163,000	244,000
	1988	11	1	2,193,000	1,410,000	326,000	−449,000
	1989	15	1	2,336,000	1,731,100	−189,000	−57,000
	1990	18	1	2,791,000	2,240,000	1,024,000	−1,761,000
	1991	3	2	4,572,000	3,461,000	−567,000	168,000
	1992	3	1	7,516,000	3,672,000	2,615,000	−2,420,000
	1993	7	1	12,806,000	4,702,000	1,615,000	1,370,000
	1994	7	1	11,914,000	5,427,000	2,514,000	−199,000
	1995	13	1	10,995,000	5,660,000	−206,000	983,000
	1996	15	1	10,078,000	6,412,000	1,032,000	−2,254,000
	1997	7	1	14,335,000	7,571,000	4,355,000	−3,242,000
Shrewsbury	1974	22	3	52,000	60,000	−21,000	−59,000
	1975	2	4	70,000	79,000	3,000	−52,000

Club	Year	League position	Division	Revenue (£)	Wages (£)	Net transfers (£)	Pre-tax profits (£)
Shrewsbury (cont'd)	1976	9	3	118,000	88,000	12,000	−24,000
	1977	10	3	129,000	100,000	10,000	−29,000
	1978	11	3	132,000	120,000	−56,000	19,000
	1979	1	3	241,000	173,000	9,000	−4,000
	1980	13	2	341,000	263,000	110,000	−152,000
	1981	14	2	344,000	306,000	−9,000	−12,000
	1982	18	2	348,000	375,000	−55,000	−88,000
	1983	9	2	352,000	307,000	−108,000	59,000
	1984	8	2	370,000	304,000	−18,000	−17,000
	1985	8	2	392,000	350,000	−62,000	47,000
	1986	17	2	353,000	347,000	−68,000	−84,000
	1987	18	2	403,000	363,000	−36,000	−70,000
	1988	18	2	498,000	412,000	−11,000	−77,000
	1989	22	2	517,000	543,000	−192,000	−1,000
	1990	11	3	498,000	679,000	−312,000	−60,000
	1991	18	3	606,000	749,000	−100,000	−289,000
	1992	22	3	587,000	747,000	−260,000	−167,000
	1993	9	4	652,000	609,000	−13,000	−213,000
	1994	1	4	857,749	789,004	−313,615	181,886
	1995	18	3	827,000	740,000	−87,000	43,000
	1996	18	3	1,095,000	908,000	110,000	−237,000
	1997	22	3	869,000	837,000	−165,000	−7,000
Southampton	1922	1	3	21,994	11,641	−175	369
	1923	11	2	28,482	11,984	−1,200	717
	1924	5	2	25,245	11,589	−320	−3,078
	1925	7	2	22,034	13,072	−150	153
	1926	14	2	24,709	11,041	−5,300	5,601
	1927	13	2	23,369	9,922	−125	3,648
	1929	4	2	26,422	15,214	−100	1,174
	1930	7	2	25,341	13,091	−3,900	2,932
	1931	9	2	22,541	14,732	−600	1,198
	1932	14	2	23,561	13,422	−100	−2,300
	1933	12	2	21,926	10,876	−5,700	3,096
	1934	14	2	23,796	7,983	−4,259	5,360
	1935	19	2	17,604	8,254	231	−749
	1936	17	2	19,483	8,714	−1,020	932
	1937	19	2	23,789	8,774	3,069	−1,456
	1938	15	2	30,128	11,398	5,000	−1,646
	1939	18	2	26,389	11,553	490	38
	1947	14	2	41,032	22,935		1,596
	1948	3	2	64,188	39,174		10,088
	1949	3	2	76,057	45,705		15,569
	1950	4	2	66,845	40,923		9,114
	1951	12	2	78,717	26,857	8,750	3,086
	1952	13	2	73,140	33,575	−4,122	7,585
	1953	21	2	76,727	31,300	7,561	−9,519
	1954	6	3	47,023	27,785	395	−2,269
	1955	3	3	55,006	29,605	10,100	−10,701
	1956	14	3	39,245	24,032	−750	1,447
	1957	4	3	49,620	26,163	850	4,864
	1958	6	3	59,796	31,405	5,000	1,511
	1959	14	3	66,173	34,179	−9,275	9,061
	1960	1	3	85,138	38,602	16,150	−6,284

Club	Year	League position	Division	Revenue (£)	Wages (£)	Net transfers (£)	Pre-tax profits (£)
Southampton (cont'd)	1963	11	2	139,960	40,947	34,092	18,751
	1964	5	2	124,493	44,854	902	28,340
	1965	4	2	150,779	42,708	46,276	−14,094
	1966	2	2	158,202	55,960	25,034	20,120
	1967	19	1	224,071	67,692	106,096	−9,857
	1968	16	1	386,461	68,963	−33,807	102,228
	1969	7	1	226,284	77,655	−8,975	92,756
	1970	19	1	272,394	84,900	122,112	−38,034
	1971	7	1	263,207	95,314	−31,903	68,036
	1972	19	1	270,094	94,050	118,867	−42,421
	1973	13	1	329,884	104,480	−38,631	93,780
	1974	20	1	253,000	139,000	308,000	−220,000
	1975	13	2	178,000	167,000	28,000	1,000
	1976	6	2	479,000	220,000	2,000	132,000
	1977	9	2	520,000	246,000	210,000	21,000
	1978	2	2	916,000	311,000	−100,000	23,000
	1979	14	1	919,000	402,000	272,000	143,000
	1980	8	1	806,000	545,000	1,058,000	−954,000
	1981	6	1	1,800,000	689,000	−205,000	554,000
	1982	7	1	1,821,000	1,051,000	523,000	−168,000
	1983	12	1	1,665,000	1,034,000	230,000	46,000
	1984	2	1	1,168,000	936,000	26,000	287,000
	1985	5	1	1,720,000	1,234,000	−162,000	154,000
	1986	14	1	1,554,000	935,000	402,000	−364,000
	1987	12	1	1,644,000	972,000	168,000	−212,000
	1988	12	1	1,457,000	1,001,000	−455,000	390,000
	1989	13	1	1,805,000	1,102,000	1273,000	−1,343,000
	1990	7	1	4,502,000	1,765,000	−301,000	719,000
	1991	14	1	5,711,000	2,217,000	459,000	175,000
	1992	16	1	5,532,000	2,943,000	2138,000	−1,603,000
	1993	18	1	9,492,000	3,360,000	−1,004,000	1,548,000
	1994	18	1	7,239,686	3,939,584	1,117,000	−1,118,149
	1995	10	1	7,397,000	4,780,000	481,000	878,000
	1996	17	1	7,646,000	4,124,000	3,059,000	−1,519,000
	1997	16	1	9,238,000	4,776,000	4,875,000	−3,624,000
Southend	1974	12	3	84,000	65,000	−36,000	−51,000
	1975	18	3	102,000	82,000	−65,000	26,000
	1976	23	3	125,000	95,000	5,000	−32,000
	1977	10	4	118,000	105,000	−17,000	−46,000
	1978	2	4	169,000	138,000	−57,000	9,000
	1979	13	3	237,000	166,000	−82,000	79,000
	1980	22	3	253,000	197,000	−15,000	67,000
	1981	1	4	344,000	224,000	−9,000	−67,000
	1982	7	3	423,000	238,000	16,000	−80,000
	1983	15	3	495,000	236,000	−74,000	13,000
	1984	22	3	727,000	254,000	60,000	−387,000
	1985	20	4	390,000	251,000	−8,000	−172,000
	1986	9	4	445,000	259,000	11,000	−235,000
	1987	3	4	646,000	281,000	−56,000	−26,000
	1988	16	3	651,000	327,000	46,000	−76,000
	1989	21	3	662,000	336,000	−83,000	−30,000
	1990	3	4	962,000	687,000	−77,000	−99,000
	1991	2	3	1,319,000	895,000	160,000	−288,000

Data Appendix / 373

Club	Year	League position	Division	Revenue (£)	Wages (£)	Net transfers (£)	Pre-tax profits (£)
Southend (cont'd)	1992	12	2	2,102,000	1,326,000	−136,000	−95,000
	1993	18	2	4,449,000	1,672,000	−1,507,000	808,000
	1994	15	2	3,808,811	2,121,215	−1,395,000	−219,881
	1995	13	2	2,043,000	2,091,000	−2,404,000	936,000
	1996	14	2	2,449,000	2,488,000	39,000	−1,293,000
	1997	24	2	2,449,000	2,488,000	38,000	−1,293,000
Sunderland	1930	9	1	32,743	19,837		258
	1931	11	1	34,330	19,298		490
	1932	8	1	34,877	21,581		−5,452
	1933	12	1	26,819	11,165		2,272
	1934	6	1	26,656	9,620		3,842
	1935	2	1	34,276	13,482		3,634
	1936	1	1	37,567	15,062		1,608
	1937	8	1	50,634	21,185		3,993
	1938	8	1	53,120	15,824	−14,521	9,941
	1939	16	1	36,295	15,016	2,794	4,143
Swindon	1926	6	3	14,720	7,970		851
	1949	4	3	47,572	15,380	5,100	592
	1950	14	3	38,445	17,240	4,950	−257
	1951	17	3	39,880	18,722	550	−1,698
	1952	16	3	45,650	16,214	1,360	4,160
	1953	18	3	51,400	16,596	−2,675	1,181
	1954	20	3	43,211	16,792	1,350	−1,484
	1955	21	3	38,950	17,295	3,835	−6,264
	1956	24	3	40,771	15,391	3,085	−3,658
	1957	23	3	46,578	17,336	6,220	−12,093
	1958	4	3	54,860	25,689	6,507	−11,793
	1959	15	3	56,946	28,298	4,650	−11,194
	1960	16	3	68,964	27,445	−1,415	−13,693
	1961	16	3	66,300	28,371	−5,122	−1,373
	1962	9	3	67,151	29,455	540	−4,968
	1963	2	3	86,273	38,308	−1,300	6,095
	1964	14	2	178,128	51,915	−24,315	38,260
	1965	21	2	144,187	58,167	32,870	−25,361
	1966	7	3	176,898	49,147	−24,850	30,925
	1967	8	3	149,444	53,625	13,937	−1,602
	1968	9	3	157,268	58,419	14,001	2,349
	1969	2	3	170,370	81,304	49,564	−13,880
	1970	5	2	171,647	90,224	6,771	−12,097
	1971	12	2	131,398	95,757	16,550	−29,292
	1972	11	2	172,799	97,300	−18,900	−25,188
	1973	16	2	184,201	108,201	−46,800	−34,400
	1974	22	2	127,000	121,000	−22,000	−57,000
	1975	4	3	172,000	126,000	53,000	−99,000
	1976	19	3	191,000	134,000	−35,000	7,000
	1977	11	3	278,000	155,000	14,000	5,000
	1978	10	3	275,000	161,000	68,000	−29,000
	1979	5	3	353,000	251,000	63,000	4,000
	1980	10	3	628,000	349,000	118,000	−1,000
	1981	17	3	452,000	442,000	−190,000	62,000
	1982	22	3	380,000	479,000	−131,000	−94,000
	1983	8	4	445,000	296,000	−172,000	16,000
	1984	17	4	408,000	348,000	−18,000	−115,000

Club	Year	League position	Division	Revenue (£)	Wages (£)	Net transfers (£)	Pre-tax profits (£)
Swindon (cont'd)	1985	8	4	448,000	280,000	−50,000	−10,000
	1986	1	4	678,000	325,000	16,000	14,000
	1987	3	3	764,000	379,000	60,000	−102,000
	1988	12	2	1,218,000	457,000	140,000	34,000
	1989	6	2	1,282,000	632,000	92,000	−137,000
	1990	4	2	2,310,905	1,335,537	−193,940	−202,081
	1991	21	2	3,970,916	1,924,035	−1,687,250	514,599
	1992	8	2	2,520,672	2,235,424	−408,719	1,120,164
	1993	5	2	3,372,607	2,681,192	−455,250	−760,813
	1994	22	1	5,414,699	2,711,163	659,757	98,374
	1995	21	2	4,772,000	3,393,000	−1,834,000	1,204,000
	1996	1	3	4,441,000	3,236,000	859,000	−1,734,000
	1997	19	2	4,695,000	3,276,000	−449,000	−529,000
Tottenham	1909	2	2	13,597	4,510	3,083	4,073
	1910	15	1	20,055	5,090	3,097	5,945
	1911	15	1	17,093	5,593	2,374	3,493
	1912	12	1	16,767	5,275	1,421	3,593
	1913	17	1	16,362	5,401	5,080	333
	1914	17	1	20,551	5,906	2,664	5,087
	1922	2	1	53,389	16,007	−1,796	17,417
	1923	12	1	47,383	14,742	−3,100	10,453
	1924	15	1	35,407	14,291	4,556	−1,476
	1925	12	1	35,133	14,535	1,042	3,213
	1926	15	1	40,864	14,382	1,887	5,184
	1927	13	1	37,087	14,760	−1,209	5,476
	1928	21	1	38,919	15,030	746	4,133
	1929	10	2	37,262	16,158	5,043	−7,061
	1930	12	2	43,145	14,887	11,313	−10,023
	1931	3	2	41,933	15,604	6,264	−6,687
	1932	13	1	40,143	14,552	10,174	−7,151
	1933	2	2	40,604	14,111	3,952	8,954
	1934	3	2	52,144	15,289	2,017	15,839
	1935	22	2	53,952	15,714	7,880	8,776
	1936	5	2	46,953	15,114	11,180	2,320
	1937	10	2	46,783	16,625	8,587	−4,851
	1938	5	2	44,967	15,748	−2,116	7,412
	1939	8	2	51,755	16,654	3,092	3,309
	1947	6	2	67,882	17,708	4,476	8,923
	1948	8	2	88,454	18,388	−10,379	19,517
	1949	5	2	114,028	26,075	−13,957	44,776
	1950	1	2	135,464	30,341	3,245	37,025
	1951	1	1	163,120	40,832	9,285	24,631
	1952	2	1	166,321	48,195	−26,439	73,725
	1953	10	1	124,553	45,245	4,744	27,359
	1954	16	1	126,868	52,311	12,286	13,963
	1955	16	1	105,348	44,938	36,595	−17,868
	1956	18	1	110,317	40,674	52,964	−23,652
	1957	2	1	132,287	49,898	−4,323	44,159
	1958	3	1	158,727	55,250	6,189	39,531
	1959	18	1	155,137	62,680	29,524	5,636
	1960	3	1	185,834	61,717	34,148	23,070
	1961	1	1	266,224	63,626	−3,429	123,031
	1962	3	1	327,773	104,332	93,862	41,902

Club	Year	League position	Division	Revenue (£)	Wages (£)	Net transfers (£)	Pre-tax profits (£)
Tottenham (cont'd)	1963	2	1	328,849	107,721	−4,956	125,044
	1964	4	1	262,803	112,875	−159,278	−95,209
	1965	6	1	270,407	115,347	65,575	425
	1966	8	1	267,700	108,330	41,855	34,129
	1967	3	1	352,282	137,916		35,724
	1968	7	1	390,231	139,031	34,256	101,556
	1969	6	1	376,454	157,102	98,359	1,639
	1970	11	1	371,656	149,514	91,816	6,199
	1971	3	1	512,281	209,109	162,943	−12,041
	1972	6	1	660,688	229,692	4,628	233,831
	1973	8	1	817,131	289,284	127,791	303,614
	1974	11	1	654,000	285,000	49,000	36,000
	1975	19	1	545,000	325,000	239,000	−365,000
	1976	9	1	848,000	288,000	160,000	−5,000
	1977	22	1	797,000	328,000	89,000	29,000
	1978	3	2	1,232,000	398,000	−108,000	382,000
	1979	11	1	1,541,000	481,000	723,000	−270,000
	1980	14	1	2,019,000	770,000	974,000	−577,000
	1981	10	1	2,823,000	1,167,000	−18,000	461,000
	1982	4	1	3,872,000	1,553,000	83,000	189,000
	1983	4	1	3,566,000	1,593,000	617,000	−448,000
	1984	8	1	4,336,000	2,063,000	492,000	−146,000
	1985	3	1	5,273,000	2,480,000	34,000	282,000
	1986	10	1	3,342,000	2,672,000	68,000	−662,000
	1987	3	1	4,534,000	2,792,000	1,301,000	330,000
	1988	13	1	4,208,000	2,413,000	171,000	930,000
	1989	6	1	6,253,000	5,123,000	1,821,000	951,000
	1990	3	1	28,018,000	5,399,000	2,104,000	−1,006,000
	1991	10	1	18,713,000	5,259,000	−335,000	−1,781,000
	1992	15	1	19,308,000	5,372,000	1,475,000	3,057,000
	1993	8	1	25,265,000	6,248,000	1,910,000	3,361,000
	1994	15	1	15,061,000	6,207,000	748,000	−1,535,000
	1995	7	1	21,296,000	8,358,000	−578,000	157,000
	1996	8	1	27,394,000	11,453,000	4,908,000	2,912,000
	1997	10	1	27,874,000	12,057,000	1,528,000	7,573,000
West Bromwich Albion	1910	11	2	5,976	4,995	−146	−1,381
	1949	2	2	69,414	16,445		13,746
	1950	14	1	77,743	46,561		−1,354
	1951	16	1	63,438	27,862		2,186
	1952	13	1	74,562	31,601		4,417
	1953	4	1	79,632	32,865		6,266
	1954	2	1	101,385	39,146		11,767
	1955	17	1	81,341	44,646		1,464
	1956	13	1	74,827	34,895		7,119
	1957	11	1	72,647	32,693		1,963
	1958	4	1	126,034	56,269		13,359
	1959	5	1	115,722	38,002		16,737
	1960	4	1	103,623	33,329		10,683
	1961	10	1	99,893	55,196		929
	1962	9	1	102,952	51,287		9,560
	1963	14	1	91,953	44,532		5,352
	1964	10	1	99,811	58,663		257
	1965	14	1	99,459	53,359		5,371

Club	Year	League position	Division	Revenue (£)	Wages (£)	Net transfers (£)	Pre-tax profits (£)
West Bromwich Albion (cont'd)	1966	6	1	185,935	71,598		30,984
	1967	13	1	149,286	156,551		−27,447
	1968	8	1	248,031	149,762	5,900	497
	1969	10	1	258,892	137,587	69,650	−40,133
	1970	16	1	315,688	181,403	850	26,171
	1971	17	1	280,950	167,926	−24,167	2,475
	1972	16	1	280,495	189,737	21,588	70,850
	1973	22	1	328,736	192,700	90,476	104,184
	1974	8	2	250,000	207,000	0	−127,000
	1975	6	2	269,000	204,000	−220,000	80,000
	1976	3	2	244,000	240,000	63,000	−128,000
	1977	7	1	452,000	277,000	184,000	38,000
	1978	6	1	834,000	331,000	−170,000	153,000
	1979	3	1	1,228,000	503,000	815,000	−133,000
	1980	10	1	1,577,000	598,000	1,000	342,000
	1981	4	1	1,725,000	859,000	−235,000	31,000
	1982	17	1	1,566,000	932,000	−638,000	585,000
	1983	11	1	2,027,000	881,000	−630,000	285,000
	1984	17	1	1,348,000	940,000	−42,000	−125,000
	1985	12	1	1,470,000	886,000	−86,000	66,000
	1986	22	1	1,393,000	941,000	254,000	−405,000
	1987	15	2	1,434,000	982,000	−128,000	−456,000
	1988	20	2	846,000	925,000	−51,000	−456,000
	1989	9	2	1,017,000	998,000	−363,000	218,000
	1990	20	2	2,327,000	1,231,000	419,000	−260,000
	1991	23	2	2,223,000	1,317,000	107,000	−412,000
	1992	7	3	2,088,000	1,524,000	−557,000	−138,000
	1993	4	3	3,162,000	1,651,000	349,000	−255,000
	1994	21	2	4,431,220	1,924,854	492,000	−221,268
	1995	19	2	4,592,000	2,134,000	0	−489,000
	1996	16	2	6,073,000	3,095,000	938,000	−185,000
West Ham	1947	12	2	53,608	16,435	−1,650	13,029
	1948	6	2	57,757	25,198	9,450	4,937
	1949	7	2	58,422	23,548	10,025	6,633
	1950	19	2	51,515	30,826	7,150	2,145
	1951	13	2	51,266	31,438	−5,425	1,222
	1952	12	2	56,001	32,455	4,790	1,988
	1953	14	2	57,482	34,039	3,525	1,260
	1954	13	2	63,870	38,031	−5,115	2,388
	1955	8	2	60,676	39,293	−11,777	−2,380
	1956	16	2	62,929	37,486	−4,000	−5,032
	1957	8	2	59,933	35,847	−17,500	−9,716
	1958	1	2	88,735	46,053	6,450	1,456
	1959	6	1	107,089	48,576	14,300	12,922
	1960	14	1	117,087	50,982	−1,900	9,713
	1961	16	1	100,177	55,753	−10,712	8,879
	1962	8	1	113,970	68,189	30,900	3,658
	1963	12	1	127,123	70,307	−38,950	−461
	1964	14	1	164,683	83,872	−18,500	17,866
	1965	9	1	220,660	103,662	−2,000	49,014
	1966	12	1	213,637	111,825	−60,500	35,523
	1967	16	1	213,944	110,500	77,500	24,185
	1968	12	1	194,285	122,898	32,555	13,775

Data Appendix / 377

Club	Year	League position	Division	Revenue (£)	Wages (£)	Net transfers (£)	Pre-tax profits (£)
West Ham (cont'd)	1969	8	1	258,403	125,324	−23,250	52,675
	1970	17	1		133,195	−64,080	31,438
	1971	20	1	315,633	157,335	112,166	64,942
	1972	14	1	393,666	165,124	−63,960	106,795
	1973	6	1	397,557	180,781	700,041	90,848
	1974	18	1	399,000	226,000	109,000	−86,000
	1975	13	1	581,000	306,000	99,000	−22,000
	1976	18	1	885,000	400,000	47,000	174,000
	1977	17	1	643,000	399,000	13,000	−111,000
	1978	20	1	837,000	480,000	70,000	41,000
	1979	5	2	774,000	728,000	66,000	−100,000
	1980	7	2	1,612,000	554,000	536,000	−27,000
	1981	1	2	2,084,000	983,000	860,000	−252,000
	1982	9	1	2,011,000	1,014,000	1,074,000	−733,000
	1983	8	1	2,096,000	998,000	478,000	635,000
	1984	9	1	2,239,000	1,133,000	−266,000	−46,000
	1985	16	1	2,204,000	1,203,000	−27,000	420,000
	1986	3	1	2,340,000	1,352,000	136,000	139,000
	1987	15	1	3,087,000	1,486,000	507,000	137,000
	1988	16	1	2,554,000	1,754,000	746,000	−675,000
	1989	19	1	4,233,000	2,041,000	−1,447,000	1,623,000
	1990	7	2	5,304,000	2,934,000	1,123,000	−1,467,000
	1991	2	2	6,638,000	3,946,000	558,000	−1,064,000
	1992	22	1	7,768,000	3,646,000	−407,000	−2,046,000
	1993	2	2	6,571,000	3,764,000	520,000	174,000
	1994	13	1	9,461,000	3,801,000	633,000	1,155,000
	1995	14	1	10,075,000	5,484,000	3,117,000	−2,740,000
	1996	10	1	11,995,000	6,207,000	2,800,000	653,000
	1997	14	1	15,256,000	8,298,000	6,657,000	−5,495,000
Wrexham	1974	4	3	155,000	78,000	4,000	−15,000
	1975	13	3	104,000	86,000	−70,000	32,000
	1976	6	3	187,000	112,000	−106,000	69,000
	1977	5	3	312,900	144,000	78,000	−32,000
	1978	1	3	469,000	214,000	−58,000	126,000
	1979	15	2	653,000	261,000	19,000	−46,000
	1980	16	2	675,000	441,000	30,000	−79,000
	1981	16	2	824,000	500,000	81,000	−162,000
	1982	21	2	610,000	459,000	105,000	−183,000
	1983	22	3	380,000	377,000	−166,000	−97,000
	1984	20	4	288,000	198,000	−10,000	−24,000
	1985	15	4	229,000	200,000	11,000	−80,000
	1986	13	4	262,000	218,000	−18,000	−58,000
	1987	9	4	359,000	254,000	−13,000	−137,000
	1988	10	4	272,000	282,000	−98,000	−82,000
	1989	7	4	373,000	295,000	−156,000	37,000
	1990	21	4	664,000	434,000	−201,000	−106,000
	1991	24	4	734,000	481,000	0	−73,000
	1992	14	4	1,263,000	525,000	−454,000	347,000
	1993	2	4	1,243,000	681,000	−214,000	124,000
	1994	12	3	1,365,515	694,412	250,000	−722,000
	1995	13	3	1,571,000	858,000	0	154,000
	1996	8	3	1,056,000	979,000	0	−204,000
	1997	8	3	1,732,000	1,397,000		481,000

Winners and Losers / 378

Index

Figures in italics refer to Tables; those in bold indicate a club's financial data and league performance (Appendix).

transfers, *121, 176, 178, 210, 212*
wages, *121,* 159, *160, 164, 167, 178*
baseball, 47, *47,* 85, *85,* 100, 198, 248,
249, *294,* 306, 307, 309
basketball, 47, *47,* 48, 84, *85,* 294–5, 307,
308
Bassett, William, 89, 102
Bates, Ken, 242
Bateson, Mike, 108
BBC, 56, 58, 59, 60, 63, *64,* 68, 267, 268,
296
Beardsley, Peter, 106, 237
Beckham, David, 83, 84, *85*
behaviour, 15
Belle, Albert, *85*
Bennett, Arnold, 101
Bennett, Reuben, 238
Berlusconi, Silvio, 301
Berti, Nicola, 293
Best, George, 31, 49, 201, 224
betting odds, 277–8
'Big Five', 226, 292
Big Match (television programme), 56
Birmingham City, 18, **343–4**
and cross subsidization, 265
English international caps, *176*
English internationals, *176*
first-team players, *176*
flotation, 75
home-grown players, *176*
incorporation (1888), 5
league position, *160, 164, 167, 187, 189,
191, 199*
manager's tenure, *176, 176*
market value, *289*
peak market value, *289*
population, *199*
pre-tax profit, *289*
professional players, *176*
revenue, *187, 189, 191*
sponsorship, 70
transfers, *121, 126, 178, 212*
wages, *121, 160, 164, 167, 178,* 265,
266
well attended, 78
Birtles, Gary, 217
black players, *175,* 183, *184, 185*

Blackburn Rovers, 102, 107, 292, 303,
344–5
league position, *160, 164, 167, 187, 189,
191, 199, 285*
losses, 25, 294
manager's tenure, *176*
origins, 3
player expenditure, 35
population, *199*
and professionals, 88
revenue, *187, 189, 191, 264,* 267, *298*
spending on players (1991–7), 287
television viewers, *274*
total player spending, *298*
transfers, 106, *121, 126,* 157, *176, 177,
178, 210, 212, 285, 285,* 296
wages, *121,* 157, *160, 164, 167,* 177,
178, 285, 285, 298
Walker and, 17, 241–2
wins the league championship, *129,* 157,
258
Blackpool, 102, **345**
league position, *160, 187*
revenue, *187*
transfers, *122*
wages, *122, 160*
'blue-chip' companies, 293
Boca Juniors, 197
Bogotá affair, 92
Bolton Wanderers, 18, 102, **345–6**
English international caps, *176*
English internationals, *176*
first-team players, *176*
home-grown players, *176*
league position, 159, *160, 164,* 167–8,
167, 187, 189, 191, 199
manager's tenure, *176, 176*
population, *199*
professional players, *176*
revenue, *187, 189, 191,* 267
stadium, 39, 54, 70
television viewers, *274*
transfers, *121, 176, 178, 210, 212*
wages, *121,* 159, *160, 164, 167, 167,
178*
boot sponsorship, 71
Borland, J., 278–9, *278,* 280

and profits, 24–9, 35
   revenue and, 186–92, 224, *225*, *227*, 309
   wage expenditure and, 157–66, 172, 173,
      185, *185*, 192, 309
Leeds City, 93, 153
Leeds Sporting, *75*
Leeds United, **357**
   attendances, 49, *49*
   Clough and, 216–17, 220
   English international caps, *176*
   English internationals, *176*
   first-team players, *176*
   flotation, 18
   high wages, 35
   home-grown players, *176*
   Internet website, 65
   and the League Championship of 1972,
      209, 211
   league position, *160, 164, 187, 189, 199,*
      285
   losses, 25
   manager's tenure, *176*
   player expenditure, 35
   population, *199*
   professional players, *176*
   revenue, *187, 189, 264, 267, 298*
   in the Second Division, 52
   shirt sales, *71*
   sponsorship, *70*
   television viewers, *274*
   total player spending, *298*
   transfers, *121, 176, 178, 212, 285*
   wages, 35, *121, 160, 164, 178, 285, 285,*
      298
   wins the FA Cup, 220
   wins the Fairs Cup twice, 220
   wins the First Division Championship,
      216
   wins the league championship, *129,* 220,
      258
Leicester City, 18, 302, **357–8**
   English international caps, *176*
   English internationals, *176*
   first-team players, *176*
   flotation, *75*
   home-grown players, *176*
   league position, *160, 164, 187, 189, 199*

manager's tenure, *176*
population, *199*
professional players, *176*
revenue, *187, 189, 264, 267, 298*
television viewers, *274*
total player spending, *298*
transfers, *121, 176, 178, 212*
wages, *121, 160, 164, 178, 298*
leisure businesses, rival, 37
leisure industry, 1
leisurewear *see* sports/leisurewear
Lentini, Gianluigi, 106
Leyton Orient, **370**
   league position, *160, 187*
   revenue, *187*
   transfers, *122*
   wages, *122, 160*
licences, 197
limited companies
   football clubs as, 1, 15, 23, 159
   issue of shares, 72
   limited liability, 5, 6
   owned by shareholders, 5
   run by directors, 5
   Small Heath as the first (1888), 5, 6
limited liability, 5, 6
Lincoln City, **358**
   league position, *199*
   population, *199*
Lineker, Gary, 106, 213
Littlewoods Cup, 69
Littlewoods of Liverpool, 76
Live TV, *64, 70*
Liverpool, 23, 56, 124, 245, 292, 302, 305,
   358–9
   'architecture', 233–41, 242, 282
   attendances, 44, 229–30, *230*, 237
   the boot room, 238–41
   catering, 38
   clothing range, 39
   consistently successful on the pitch, 25,
      123, 164
   domination of league championships,
      260
   emerging power, 225
   English internationals, *176*
   English international caps, *176*

Napoli, 106
National Basketball Association (NBA), 47, 48, 248, 269, 298
National Dairy Council, 69
National Football League (NFL), 47–8, 47, 85, 248, 252, 268, 269, 298, 300, 302, 305, 307
National Front, 51
National Hockey League (NHL), 248, 269, 277
National League of Professional Baseball Clubs, 11
National League [proposed], 251–2
national markets, 105
Nationwide Building Society, 67, 70
NBC Sports, 252
Netherlands
  competition courts, 316
  football rivalry with Germany, 10
  Lorenz Curve, 259, 259, 260, 260
  television contracts, 270
New York Knicks, 294
Newcastle Brown Ale, 70
Newcastle United, 196, 245, 292, 302, 303, 362–3
  attendances, 42, 44, 78
  English international caps, 176
  English internationals, 176
  financial problems, 25, 123
  first-team players, 176
  flotation, 18, 75, 75, 123
  home-grown players, 176
  incorporated (1890), 5
  lack of major trophies, 123
  league position, 160, 164, 167, 187, 189, 191, 199, 285
  losses, 294
  management, 123, 176
  market value, 289
  NTL acquires shares, 295
  peak market value, 289
  population, 199
  pre-tax profit, 289
  professional players, 176
  revenue, 187, 189, 191, 264, 267, 298
  in the Second Division, 52
  shirt sales, 71

spending on players (1991–7), 287
sponsorship, 70
television viewers, 274
total player spending, 298
transfers, 107, 121, 176, 178, 212, 285, 285, 291, 296
turns professional (1889), 5
value, 288
wages, 121, 160, 164, 167, 177, 178, 285, 285, 298
wins the league championship, 129
News Corporation, 67, 300
News International, 61–2, 67
Newton Heath, 221
Nike, 39, 70, 71–2
Noll, R., 278, 278
Nomura Index of football club stock market prices, 29–30, 289
Northampton, 363
Norwich City, 363
  league position, 160, 187
  revenue, 187
  sponsorship, 70
  transfers, 121
  wages, 121, 160
Nottingham Forest, 18, 33, 215, 235
  Clough and, 204–5, 206, 211, 211, 217, 220
  compared with Derby County, 205, 206
  flotation, 75
  league position, 160, 187, 205, 206
  market value, 289
  peak market value, 289
  pre-tax profit, 289
  revenue, 187, 211–12, 213, 264, 267, 298
  sponsorship, 70
  total player spending, 298
  transfers, 102, 121, 211, 212, 217, 218
  value, 288–9
  wages, 121, 160, 211, 298
  wins the European Cup, 50, 205
  wins the league championship, 129, 202, 204, 205, 219, 258
  wins the Super Cup, 205